Barry Link

Andrew Rice has written about Africa for *The New York Times Magazine*, *The New Republic*, and *The Economist*. His article "The Book of Wilson," published in *The Paris Review*, received a Pushcart Prize. He spent several years in Uganda as a fellow of the Institute of Current World Affairs and now lives in Brooklyn.

THE TEETH MAY SMILE
BUT THE HEART DOES NOT FORGET

THE TEETH MAY SMILE BUT THE HEART DOES NOT FORGET

MURDER AND MEMORY IN UGANDA

ANDREW RICE

PICADOR

A METROPOLITAN BOOK • HENRY HOLT AND COMPANY • NEW YORK

www.picadorusa.com

Picador® is a U.S. registered trademark and is used by Henry Holt and Company under license from Pan Books Limited.

For information on Picador Reading Group Guides, please contact Picador. E-mail: readinggroupguides@picadorusa.com

Sections of this book have appeared, in different form, in the newsletter of the Institute of Current World Affairs and in *The New Republic*.

Designed by Kelly S. Too

The Library of Congress has cataloged the Henry Holt edition as follows:

Rice, Andrew, 1975–
    The teeth may smile but the heart does not forget : murder and memory in Uganda / Andrew Rice.—1st ed.
        p. cm.
    ISBN 978-0-8050-7965-4
    1. Laki, Eliphaz, d. 1972. 2. Laki, Duncan. 3. Extrajudicial executions—Uganda. 4. Gowon, Yusuf—Trials, litigation, etc. 5. Atrocities—Uganda. 6. Uganda—Politics and government—1971–1979. 7. Uganda—Politics and government—1979– 8. Amin, Idi, 1925–2003. I. Title.
    DT433.283.R5 2009
    967.6104'2—dc22

                                                                2008041984

Picador ISBN 978-0-312-42973-7

First published in the United States by Henry Holt and Company

10 9 8 7 6 5 4 3 2

To my grandfather, Edward Rice,
who passed down his wandering spirit,

and to my friend, Allan Begira Abainenamar,
who helped me to understand

CONTENTS

PART 1

Prologue: 1979   3
1. The Western Rift   7
2. The Key   22
3. UYO-010   39
4. The Big Man   51

PART 2

5. Decent Rest   57
6. The Brightest Star   66
7. A Serious Young Man   91
8. Singapore   103
9. A Shallow Grave   115
10. Exhumation   121

PART 3

11. The Prisoner   133
12. Among the Cannibals   143
13. The Lions   159
14. September 1972   175
15. Bad Omen   191
16. The Scars   208

PART 4

17. The Prosecution   227
18. Taking the Stand   242
19. The Defense   251
20. Judgment   266
21. Reprise   282
Epilogue: Ndeija   296

Notes   303
Acknowledgments   347
Index   351

THE TEETH MAY SMILE
BUT THE HEART DOES NOT FORGET

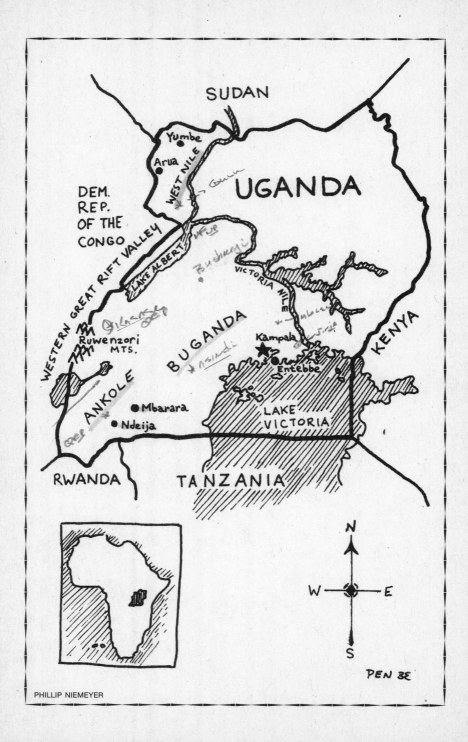

SUDAN

Yumbe

Arua

WEST NILE

DEM.
REP.
OF THE
CONGO

UGANDA

Gulu

LAKE ALBERT

Budongo

VICTORIA NILE

WESTERN GREAT RIFT VALLEY

Ruwenzori
MTS.

BUGANDA

Masindi

Kampala

Entebbe

Jinja

ANKOLE

Mbarara

Ndeija

LAKE
VICTORIA

KENYA

RWANDA

TANZANIA

N

W   E

S

PEN 3E

PHILLIP NIEMEYER

PART 1

PROLOGUE: 1979

Eliphaz Laki wasn't coming home. Duncan knew it. Everybody knew it. But hope was an obstinate emotion. It dug into Duncan like a tick, feeding off the doubts his rational mind couldn't quite extinguish. There were rumors, thirdhand tales told in hushed voices: His father was in hiding, in exile. He'd been sighted in Tanzania. A rebel army was forming there, across the river to the south. The stories didn't make sense to Duncan, though. He knew his father loved his family; he would have found a way to send word. Duncan heard other, darker, whispers, too. Some said Laki had been taken by soldiers and shot. But there was no body, and there'd been no burial, no inquest, no explanation. Eliphaz Laki had disappeared, and his son was left with hope—stubborn, secret, maddening hope.

The end was near; liberation was coming. The rebels said so, in their scratchy broadcasts from across the border. Duncan listened furtively on the family radio. A gentler government scarcely seemed conceivable to him. Duncan was sixteen years old. Soldiers had ruled Uganda for half his life. The General—even now, the name felt dangerous to utter—was hulking and powerful, a former boxing champion who boasted that he feared no one but God. He did not seem subject to mortal failures like defeat. But the rebels kept advancing. In his imagination, Duncan conjured a homecoming scene: his father, balding, lean and battle-weary in a soldier's fatigues, walking up the red-dirt road that ran through the village of Ndeija, past the longhorn cattle grazing in his fields, under the broad leaves of his banana trees, up to the door of his modest yellow farmhouse.

Duncan was a wiry, studious, inward young man. People said he was very much like his father. Eliphaz Laki had been someone worthy of emulation: a prominent civil servant, a regional administrator known as a *saza* chief. (*Saza* means "county.") Duncan had just finished his exams at boarding school, and the Christmas holidays had brought him home to the family farm, in the cool green hill country of western Uganda. He knew he might be staying for a while. Everywhere, cities and towns were emptying out in a mass reverse migration, as teachers and businessmen and civil servants abandoned their offices and returned to their ancestral lands. A farm was a good place to wait out a war. A new year was beginning, 1979, and a foreboding mood had settled over the country. Visitors to Ndeija brought news of fighting to the east.

On January 25 of that year, the eighth anniversary of the coup that had brought the military to power, the General addressed his troops at a parade in Kampala, the capital. The army's chief of staff, an officer named Yusuf Gowon, welcomed his commander to the podium. The General's rumbling voice piped out of radios in every town and village across the country. It was "God's wish," he said, that had made him a dictator.

> A person of my caliber—President Idi Amin Dada—is famous the world over. If you try to find out who is the most famous president in the world, look at books in numerous countries and nations and languages in Europe and everywhere else. You are bound to find my name there. Wherever you go and mention Uganda, they will respond by saying: "Amin"—and that in itself is a great thing.

Loud applause clattered over the radio. Then the General quieted his soldiers with a disclosure. The rebels had crossed the border. Even the villagers of Ndeija, gathered to listen from afar, could hear the uneasiness edging into Idi Amin's usual braggadocio.

> I wish to call on every soldier to be very courageous. . . . If we are invaded by an enemy we shall fight until we drive them out, until we completely clear them out. I have given this warning to you now. When I give the order to drive out the enemy we shall fight on the ground, in the sea and we shall fight in the air, until we have finished.

In the weeks that followed, the army failed to fight anywhere. Amin's soldiers, who'd once walked with such swagger, "looked haggard, harassed," a Ugandan novelist later wrote, "as if they had been fed on poisoned food for a month." They fell back and waited for the end to come. Ugandans were done with dying for Amin.

Amin was the one who had started this war, a few months before, by launching a plundering incursion across the border into Tanzania. The bullying general had expected little resistance from the Tanzanians, who were ruled by a civilian president, Julius Nyerere, whom Amin had publicly derided as a weakling with "grey hair and female traits." Uganda's neighbor, however, had responded to this provocation with an unexpectedly potent counterattack. Fighting alongside the Tanzanian army was a growing force of Ugandan rebels, who recognized Amin's tantalizing vulnerability. In mid-February 1979, the liberators' northward advance reached Mbarara, the western provincial capital, twenty-five miles from Ndeija. Those fleeing the battle told of a fearsome artillery barrage—three-quarters of the town's buildings were leveled or damaged—and of the jubilant scene when a detachment of Ugandan rebels marched in. Among the fighters were some prominent exiles from the area, friends of Duncan's father who had similarly disappeared. They had been given up for dead and resurrected as liberators.

One evening, Duncan and some friends were sitting around a fire near Ndeija's main road, heating long, fibrous blades of *omutete* grass, which popped when burned like natural firecrackers. A Land Rover pulled up, loaded with camouflage-clad Ugandan government troops. Ndeija was nestled in a strategic valley, along a river that ran between the two tallest hills in the county. The soldiers set up camp at the base of the far hill, near the pasture where the Laki children grazed cows. Many others soon joined them, on the retreat from Mbarara. They dug deep trenches and waited for the rebels and their Tanzanian allies.

Duncan's frightened mother moved the family away from the soldiers' encampment, to a small mud hut hidden amid the banana groves. But Duncan refused to abandon his father's house. He slept there, alone, as the battle drew near. The invaders were armed with Katyusha rockets. The missiles took flight with a high-pitched whine and landed with a percussive boom. Duncan felt the explosions grow closer. Then Amin's men were out of their trenches, running for the high ground. Some dropped their rifles as they fled through the Laki family's fields.

At daybreak, the liberators marched into Ndeija in boots caked with orangey mud, their Kalashnikovs slung jauntily over their shoulders.

They were Tanzanians, mostly, sober socialists from the south. The villagers greeted them with nervous hospitality. Everyone came out to watch them march through: women wearing headscarves and color-splashed wrap dresses; gray-bearded elders, leaning on intricately carved wooden walking sticks; boys and girls in their starchy school uniforms. But there were no cheers, no flowers, no celebrations. Fear didn't ease all at once. On their advance, the liberators had found written messages tacked to trees around wells and watering holes, begging them not to leave until Amin was finished off. The notes were always anonymous.

The newcomers weren't like Amin's men. They didn't rape or kill anyone in Ndeija, or loot the wooden grocery stalls along the main road. Even their Swahili was soft and lyrical, so different from the harsh dialect of the Ugandan soldiers. Duncan met their commander along the road. He was a well-spoken, polished Tanzanian officer. The commander wore a pair of field glasses on a strap around his neck, and when Duncan asked, he let the teenager look through them. Duncan held the binoculars to his eyes and surveyed the war. Along the main road, trucks and tanks were trundling in from Mbarara. Up in the hills, the liberating troops were advancing on the enemy. They marched in perfectly disciplined lines, like safari ants, Duncan thought.

Duncan was happy. He was free. But he didn't see the man he was looking for.

Other kids from Ndeija were running away to join the swelling liberation army. It seemed like they all wanted to fire one of those devastating Katyusha rockets. One of Duncan's friends, a boy whose brother had been killed by Amin's men, had joined up, saying that it was time to strike back. But Duncan wasn't interested in revenge. He wanted something else. He was going to the university; he was planning to study to be an attorney. Soldiers had taken his father away. Perhaps the law could bring him home.

1

THE WESTERN RIFT

Around 30 million years ago, for reasons no one really understands, Africa tore apart. The Arabian Peninsula broke away from the continent, forming the Red Sea. Tectonic plates heaved and volcanoes erupted. A deep trough, 3,500 miles long, opened up along Africa's eastern edge. It is known today as the Great Rift Valley. At its southern end, the rift follows the route of the Zambezi River, and then it splits in two around Lake Malawi. The eastern branch, site of the earliest human fossil finds, runs through Kenya and Ethiopia, up to the Middle East. The Western Rift reaches Congo, forming the long, narrow network of African Great Lakes along its route. Uganda, a country roughly the size of Oregon, rests between these two branches, as if in the crook of a tree.

All along the periphery of the Western Rift, there are reverberant echoes of the geologic tumult. Between Uganda's Lake Edward and Lake Albert, a snowcapped massif—a range called the Mountains of the Moon by ancient Greek cartographers, who knew of it only by rumor—spikes up nearly seventeen thousand feet. Even beyond the rift's immediate environs, the terrain undulates. Kampala, a day's drive eastward, is a city of gently rounded hills. According to the city's lore, there were originally seven, a number with classical resonance.

So far as history records, the first European to set foot in Kampala was the British explorer John Hanning Speke. Late in 1861, the year Charles Dickens published *Great Expectations* and the Confederacy shelled Fort Sumter, Speke's expedition arrived on the shores of Lake Victoria. The tall, abstentious former soldier had traveled to the unmapped heart of Africa to search for the source of that ancient and mighty river, the Nile. He found it in the land that subsequently came to be known as Uganda, after the name of its most populous tribe, the Baganda. Speke was astonished to discover that the Baganda possessed a sophisticated society, led by a *kabaka*, a monarch clad in robes of barkcloth who ruled from the summit of Kampala's central hill. He returned to Victorian London to describe the exotic kingdom to a fascinated public. Soon after, the first Protestant and Catholic missionaries arrived, and they quickly set about dividing the Baganda along sectarian lines, competing to win converts away from indigenous beliefs and Islam, which had arrived via trade routes a generation or so before. The Baganda soon fell into religious warfare, which Britain settled in customary fashion, subjugating all the belligerents with its superior firepower. After pacifying the region's most powerful people, the British turned their attention to other tribes, yoking dozens of disparate societies and cultures into one fictive agglomeration called the Protectorate of Uganda.

Colonization was complete by the end of the nineteenth century, and the British authorities divided Kampala's hills up according to faction, transforming the landscape into a living monument to their divide-and-rule strategy. The Ugandan Catholics constructed a splendid brick cathedral at the peak of one hill. The Anglicans built a rival cathedral upon another. The Muslims had their own hill, topped by a gold-domed mosque. The Indians, brought over from South Asia by the British as merchant middlemen, populated their hill with colonnaded shops.

After independence came, in 1962, Uganda convulsed along the regional, ethnic and religious fault lines that colonialism had created. The first head of state, a royal *kabaka*, was driven into exile by his prime minister, a commoner Anglican from the north. The prime minister, in turn, was overthrown in 1971 by a Muslim soldier, General Idi Amin. Amin was driven out eight years later by a Tanzanian-sponsored invasion, and after that five rulers followed in quick succession, each more repressive and incompetent than the next. Though even the best estimates are just educated guesses, it is believed that somewhere between 100,000 and 300,000 Ugandans were killed during Amin's regime, while an equal or greater number may have perished during the seven-year period of chaos and civil war that lasted from Amin's ouster until 1986.

In January 1986, a lanky young rebel named Yoweri Museveni marched into Kampala at the head of a motley army of peasants and rifle-toting children. By that time, the hilled city was desolated. The shops of the old Indian district were gutted and abandoned. Their owners had been kicked out by Amin, who had claimed that God commanded him to expel the alien merchant class in the name of creating "black millionaires." The city's churches, its banks and its elite university were all in ruins. Amin had murdered the university's vice chancellor, the governor of the central bank and even the Anglican archbishop. His successors, though less flagrant, had been hardly less cruel. Kampala's streets were still strewn with unburied corpses the day Museveni took the oath of office on the steps of Uganda's bullet-gouged parliament building. Wearing a simple private's uniform and spit-shined combat boots, resting his hand upon a Bible throughout his address, the new president spoke without notes, in a relaxed, unpretentious manner. "No one should think that what is happening today is a mere change of guard," he said.

> It is a fundamental change in the politics of our country. In Africa, we have seen so many changes that change, as such, is nothing short of mere turmoil. We have had one group getting rid of another one, only for it to turn out to be worse than the group it displaced. Please do not count us in that group of people: the National Resistance Movement is a clearheaded movement with clear objectives and a good membership.

As the new president talked with refreshing frankness about potholed roads ("Is it a bad road only for Muslims and not for Christians?") and puffed-up African leaders who jetted off to New York while their people walked barefoot, the crowd of thousands began to laugh, and when he called on them to set aside their old grudges, they felt the first tentative stirrings of renewal.

The rest of the world was skeptical, but Museveni worked hard to fulfill his promises. By the time I went to live there in 2002, on a fellowship from an American foundation, Uganda was known the world over as a rare African success story. Most of the country was at peace, though a couple of low-intensity rebellions flickered in the distant north. The economy was thriving, engorged by massive amounts of foreign aid. Museveni was hailed as one of a "new breed" of African presidents, a rebel leader who'd reputedly turned into a benevolent autocrat, wise, witty and tolerant of dissent. Living in Kampala, I watched the construction of gleaming skyscrapers and fancy shopping malls. The streets were clogged with late-model SUVs and the nightclubs teemed with students and boisterous young professionals. More than half the population was under the age of eighteen. A new generation was coming of age, one that had never known terror.

The era of Idi Amin had come to feel as distant as a long-passed plague. It wasn't as if Ugandans had forgotten Amin. How could they have? He was the most famous Ugandan who had ever lived. Over the years, the dictator had served as the protagonist of an acclaimed documentary (by Barbet Schroeder, with background music performed by Amin himself on the accordion), a famous Richard Pryor comedy sketch and even a blaxploitation flick. More than a quarter century after the dictator's fall, Forest Whitaker harnessed the propulsive power of Amin's personality in *The Last King of Scotland*, winning an Academy Award for his forceful portrayal. In that film, Whitaker opens his performance with a rousing speech to an adoring black throng, bellowing: "I am you!"

Most Ugandans didn't see Amin as representative of who they were, as individuals or as a nation, but they were just as fascinated by him as everyone else, even though they knew from experience that the dictator's cruelty was anything but cinematic. They had heard all the stories of his buffoonish antics: how he'd thumbed his nose at the world, declaring himself "Conqueror of the British Empire," embracing Palestinian terrorists, praising Hitler, taunting the powerful by telegram. (To Richard Nixon: I AM SURE THAT A WEAK LEADER WOULD HAVE RESIGNED OR EVEN COMMITTED SUICIDE AFTER BEING SUBJECTED TO SO MUCH HARASSMENT BECAUSE OF THE WATERGATE AFFAIR.) They knew the macabre—though flimsily substantiated—tales of Amin's depravity, how he'd supposedly dined on the flesh of his enemies and dismembered a cheating wife. They recognized that he was the very caricature of a brutish African dictator, and they realized that most of the world would never know anything of Uganda besides him.

So you could not say that Uganda suffered from amnesia. Yet there were strange silences and elisions. Kampala's street peddlers sold pirated DVDs of *The Last King of Scotland*, but there was no memorial to Amin's victims, no death camps to tour. There was no plaque on the High Court building in the center of Kampala to mark the spot where Amin's agents dragged the chief justice of the Supreme Court out of his chambers to be murdered. There was no national holiday to commemorate the anniversary of Amin's overthrow. There were no history exhibits at the musty national museum, which was filled with stuffed birds and chipped pots—or rather, there were history exhibits, but they came to an abrupt end with the 1960s. The era was hardly discussed in schools.

The truth was that Uganda was deeply ambivalent about memorializing the past, for reasons that were tied to the politics of the present. One of Yoweri Museveni's first official acts after his rebel army conquered Kampala in 1986 had been to create an investigatory body called the Uganda Commission of Inquiry into Violations of Human Rights. "What you need," Museveni had lectured his countrymen, "is to develop enough strength to enable you to sweep that kind of garbage to where it belongs: the dungheap of history." Trying Amin himself wasn't an option: The ousted dictator had long ago taken up residence in Saudi Arabia, where he was living in fattened exile. But Museveni promised his countrymen that they could begin to mend their nation just by speaking the truth.

Museveni appointed respected Supreme Court Justice Arthur H. Oder to chair the investigatory commission. Justice Oder was charged with creating a historical record of past atrocities and empowered to recommend prosecutions on the basis of the evidence he collected. In the first years of Museveni's rule, the judge and his committee members held emotional public hearings all over the country. Hundreds of people testified, in proceedings that were often broadcast live on national television and the radio.

By the time I got to Uganda, however, those hearings were only dimly remembered. The Oder Commission had run out of government funding in its second year, and after that the inquiry had lost momentum, sputtering along with the help of sporadic cash infusions from the Ford Foundation and the Danish government. The money problems had signified more than just the usual African bureaucratic breakdowns. The Oder Commission had fallen victim to a dramatic shift in the government's political priorities, a change in policy and tone. Justice had been set aside in favor of reconciliation.

For Museveni, it had been an unfortunate but necessary sacrifice, dictated by the difficult circumstances under which he seized power. Even though Museveni had conquered Kampala in 1986, large swaths of the country remained outside his control for years afterward. He faced a number of insurgencies, including one made up of former soldiers from Idi Amin's army. After Amin's fall, these soldiers had retreated back to their tribal homeland, a lawless border region in the northwest near Congo and Sudan, where they had formed several rebel armies led by some of Amin's top lieutenants. For years, the rebels had battled a series of unstable Ugandan regimes, and they had kept on fighting against Museveni. Eventually, the new president had decided to offer the rebels a deal: If they laid down their weapons and returned to their homes and farms, they would be granted amnesty.

For the most part, the bargain worked out for both sides. Museveni consolidated his power and, running as a peacemaker, won a legitimizing presidential election in 1996. Amin's men lived unmolested in the northwestern province of West Nile, their homeland, shielded by protective relatives and tribal bonds. But the amnesty process undermined the Oder Commission, which found that its questions were no longer appreciated. In 1995, nine long years after it was appointed, the commission finally produced several hundred pages of findings, along with fifteen volumes of hearing transcripts. A thousand copies were printed, but they were not distributed for years. I never met a Ugandan who had read Justice Oder's report, and most were unaware that it even existed.

One morning in 2002, I visited Arthur Oder in his cluttered chambers in the Supreme Court building. If anyone could explain Uganda's contradictory relationship with its past, I figured, it would be the man appointed to judge it. Oder, who was British-educated, was graying and portly, with an air of professorial dishevelment about him. I'd expected him to tout the commission's work, but when I asked about it, he was surprisingly downcast.

"It was a success to some extent," he told me. "It gave the people who were able to speak to us the opportunity to speak their minds. To tell their stories—what happened to them and their relatives. This is there for the record." Also, a permanent Human Rights Commission had grown out of the exercise. Yet, for all his efforts, Justice Oder believed he had failed in his larger mission. The lessons of Amin's era were being forgotten. "The failure to recognize what other people did in the past—that is ingrained here," he said. "We depend on oral history, which is very unfortunate."

At the Human Rights Commission's library, I had read Justice Oder's report, and it struck me as a lengthy refutation of his own opinion: thousands and thousands of pages of testimony recorded for posterity. Amin himself may have possessed some monstrous flair, but the nature of his terror, like all terror, was squalid and petty in the details. People were killed because they made a joke to the wrong person, or because they lent money to the wrong person, or because they presented the wrong person with a bar tab, or just because the wrong person happened to stop them at a roadblock, and happened to be drunk, and happened to like the car they were driving. People were killed for no reason at all. There were accounts of men who'd been buried alive, women who'd been sodomized with hot pokers, prisoners who'd been issued hammers by their guards and ordered to beat each other's brains out. Oder had even testified about his own near-death experience. One day in 1977, during a general roundup of his tribe, the secret police dropped by his law office. Oder was out at the time. Afterward, he hid at friends' houses, sleeping in a bat-ridden attic at one point, before someone figured out a way to smuggle him across the border to Kenya and exile.

Like most Ugandans, Justice Oder had lost his share of friends and family members during Amin's era and the civil wars that followed it. He felt strongly that those who perpetrated the killing should be held accountable. His commission forwarded evidence against roughly two hundred individuals to Uganda's chief criminal prosecutor. "Nobody bothered to follow up," a commission investigator told me. Only a few offenders, maybe a dozen, were convicted at trial, and these cases involved relatively minor charges.

"There is a dilemma," Justice Oder said. "You can pursue justice at the cost of perpetuating conflict. Or you can pursue peace by excusing some of the things that happened, although atrocities should never be condoned. But we," the judge went on, speaking for the commission, "expressed this dilemma and said that when it is weighed, when you put it on a scale and balance it, you see that there is a case for prosecuting the main culprits. To serve different purposes: one, to satisfy those who were wronged; two, to maybe be a deterrent for the future, so that people know that if they do such things they will not get away with it with impunity."

Museveni's government pondered this same dilemma and chose to ignore the commission's prosecution recommendations. And the Ugandan people seemed to have endorsed this decision. Public sentiment was complex—people were fatigued, people wanted the wars to end, people were wary of courtroom confrontations—but the decisive factor, according to Ugandans themselves, was a simple desire to forgive. Reconciliation is an integral concept in African culture. Tribes have elaborate traditional ceremonies meant to symbolically redress wrongs. More often than not, when I talked to a Ugandan who'd suffered under Amin's regime, he would tell me he knew who informed on him or killed his relatives. It was the farmer down the road, or a rival at work, or the brother-in-law he had never liked. "But we have reconciled," he would inevitably say.

I often heard it posited—by Ugandans, among others—that Africans are inured to tragedy because so many terrible things have befallen them, that justice and memorialization are First World luxuries. "People in Africa, they've got so many immediate problems," said one older acquaintance of mine, whose father had been killed in 1972. "They don't know why they should bother with someone who's been dead for a long time." But in reality, there was nothing economically or culturally intrinsic about Uganda's approach. In Rwanda, Uganda's neighbor to the west, the countryside is dotted with memorials to those killed in the 1994 genocide. A strange sort of necrotourism industry has developed at the sites of the worst atrocities. You can climb down into crypts and photograph stacks of skulls and bones. To be sure, those memorials are the product of the most unimpeachable of human sentiments. But they exist because remembrance serves the political interests of Rwanda's present rulers, who came to power by defeating the genocide's perpetrators in a civil war.

In Uganda, the politics were different. Since giving up rebellion, many of those who'd served Amin had entered politics as members of Museveni's ruling party. One of the dictator's top generals had rejoined the army and had been appointed a deputy prime minister, despite substantial evidence that he'd led a 1971 massacre. In the period after Amin's overthrow, and also during the initial years of Museveni's regime, a handful of Amin's henchmen had been tried and convicted for murder, including Kassim Obura, the head of a feared secret police unit; Brigadier Ali Fadhul, a former battalion commander; and Lieutenant Colonel Nasur Abdallah, a tyrannical former military governor of Kampala. But these cases were isolated exceptions, and since the peace agreements, Museveni had even attempted to reverse some sentences. For instance, he'd pardoned Lieutenant Colonel Abdallah in September 2001. When I visited the former Death Row inmate a year afterward, he maintained that it was not politics, but charity, that had saved his life.

"You don't believe the president can have mercy?" he asked, as he played with one of his grandchildren in the garden of his home, which stood next door to a mosque in a town north of Kampala. A thickset, garrulous man of fifty-nine, the lieutenant colonel showed me through his house where he displayed a wooden plaque given to him by a fellow prisoner at the time of his release. "Long Live His Excell Y.K. Museveni," it read, "who rescued U from the hot cave." Abdallah had become a vociferous campaigner for Museveni's ruling Movement Party. "Amin loved me so much," he said. "Museveni also loves me so much."

Since he'd become a free man, Abdallah had launched himself on a campaign, directed at both the president and the press, arguing that Museveni's next pardon should go to Amin himself. The exiled dictator, who was nearing eighty, had made it known that he wanted to return home from Saudi Arabia, and there were intermittent signals that the government might let him. In anticipation, Amin's family was building him a retirement home on a patch of ancestral land up north. Abdallah was just one of many well-known Ugandans, mostly Amin's tribesmen or fellow Muslims, who had taken up the cause of rehabilitating the dictator's reputation. Though it was difficult to gauge public opinion, the apologists appeared to be a minority, but they were vocal. The opinion sections and letters pages of Kampala's newspapers were full of factually twisted missives that extolled, in the words of one letter-writer, Amin's "result-oriented management."

"With time, Amin's image is getting cleaned in the memories of people," said a Ugandan politician, a former member of the underground. "He is becoming less and less of a monster." The apologists portrayed Amin as a jolly man, a good sport, who loved to box and play rugby and captained the presidential basketball team. (One of the many titles Amin awarded himself was "Uganda's Sportsman Number One.") He was a nationalist who had tweaked the country's former colonial masters and granted economic power to the people. This Amin was undone not by his own mistakes but by an international conspiracy involving the British, the Israelis, the CIA, various international corporations, Ugandan exiles and a few allied domestic malcontents. All that talk about Amin the killer, Amin the illiterate, Amin the cannibal—it had been concocted by a Western press bent on smearing an African leader who could stand on his own.

"It's just sickening," Oder said of the revisionism. "A lot of people were killed. People were slaughtered," he said. "That's the problem— history is what somebody in power sees now. Not what he *did*. Not what anyone else *did*."

These twin histories of Amin's regime—one that said he was devil and one that hailed him as a savior—ran like parallel threads through Uganda's fragile patchwork peace. If you pulled one frayed strand of truth, you never knew what might unravel. So Ugandans talked a great deal about this individual Idi Amin—the legend, the celebrity—and talked very little about what had actually happened in their country during the time he ruled. They could not come to terms with their history because even the most basic facts were still in dispute. Ugandans had simply set aside their arguments, for the time being, because silence was the price of peace.

Every so often, though, some artifact would surface, a reminder of dormant rifts. Once, I visited the palace of the present *kabaka*, the great-great-grandson of the ruler encountered by the explorer John Speke. A Cambridge-educated lawyer, the current *kabaka* grew up in exile and now plays a largely ceremonial role. His white-columned mansion is nonetheless larger and grander than the president's residence. It stands on Kampala's Mengo Hill, not far from the Supreme Court. There were no organized tours, but a stooped caretaker agreed to show the palace grounds in return for a few thousand shillings, or about five dollars. As we walked through the gardens, we came to a grassy path. In broken English, the caretaker asked if I would like to see where it led.

We descended a hill, through a field of yellow wildflowers, to a recessed concrete bunker. It was about as wide and long as a railroad car and overgrown with weeds. I suddenly remembered something I'd read: During Amin's time, when the royal family was in exile, the palace had been used as a military barracks. I carefully made my way inside the dank and muddy cavity. Along one wall was a line of cells. As my eyes adjusted to the dim light, I could see the walls were bullet-pocked and covered with graffiti. One faded message, written in the local tribal language, read: YOU HAVE KILLED ME!

This was the Uganda I came to know. The country appeared rehabilitated, but the past always lurked just a few steps down the garden path. I was intrigued by the ways Ugandans accommodated that past: what they chose to remember, what went unspoken. Their reconciled approach ran contrary to the remedies that the "international community"—the nebulous fraternity of foreign diplomats, United Nations agencies and humanitarian organizations that held so much sway over Africa—invariably prescribed to traumatized nations. We were supposed to be living in a new era of accountability, of truth commissions and an International Criminal Court, of justice that knows no borders and pays no heed to rank or station. We were supposed to believe that it is only by understanding the crimes of the past, and by bringing individuals to account for them—whether through shame or judgment before a court—that a damaged society can regain its sanity. The idea that an entire nation might decide to let its murderers go free, that it might suffer so much and commemorate it so little, upended everything I thought I knew about the human response to loss.

Perhaps Uganda was right, and the past was irrelevant; maybe justice was disruptive; maybe the living owed nothing to the dead and the disappeared. The stories of these lost Ugandans—of their aspirations and their betrayals—remained as irretrievable as their bones, decaying beneath the earth in unmarked tombs. Maybe it really was best to leave them undisturbed.

Then, one day in July 2002, I ran across a brief article in the Ugandan state newspaper, *The New Vision*. "The former chief of staff of the defunct Uganda Army under Idi Amin, Maj. Gen. Yusuf Gowon," it began, "was yesterday committed to the High Court to answer charges of murder." The article went on to describe how Gowon and two other retired soldiers, a sergeant and a private, had been arrested in connection with the disappearance of a *saza* chief some thirty years before.

A couple of days after reading the news item, I went down to the courthouse where Gowon's hearing had taken place. I convinced a prosecutor to let me take a look at the case file. In a handwritten affidavit, the victim's son, a lawyer, described how he'd discovered a solitary clue, setting off an improbable chain of events that no one—not the police, not the prosecutors and certainly not the defendants—could ever have anticipated. If convicted of murder, Gowon and his codefendants faced sentences of death by hanging.

No officer as high-ranking as Gowon, Amin's second-in-command, had ever been brought to justice. Of the countless murders Amin's regime countenanced, this one had been singled out for prosecution. Why was this one general being held accountable, and why was this one victim so important?

The two-lane highway that took me to Ndeija runs west out of Kampala, winding through banana plantations and terraced fields of beans and coffee, before flattening into the marshes that rim Lake Victoria. Along one swampy straightaway, where fishmongers waved glittering tilapia in the intense midmorning sun, there stood the rusted hulk of an old armored personnel carrier. Back in 2002, there were still a few of these inadvertent monuments along the roads of Uganda, corroded tanks that sat forlornly where they'd been abandoned by Amin's troops as they retreated in 1979. But even these remnants were gradually disappearing, being hauled away for scrap.

A little beyond the marshes, I crossed the invisible border separating two neighboring tribes: the Baganda, who occupied the central region around Kampala, and the Banyankole, the people of the west. The westerners spoke their own language and historically they'd had their own hereditary ruler. They still called the region by the name of this tribal kingdom, Ankole.

The highway passed through sonorous green eucalyptus groves and patches of sunlit grass. Stately longhorn cattle grazed along the roadside. It was August, the dry season, "the month," a western Ugandan novelist once wrote, "of dusty roads, of singed hills, brown valleys, of lean livestock and of abandoned, bare earthed fields." The rolling terrain was parched and dun-shaded. Along one stretch of savanna, a tremendous brushfire raged, and the road was swallowed by thick black smoke.

Past Mbarara, once the capital of Ankole's kings, the road reared up into the foothills of the Western Rift. Along the hazardous margins of the narrow highway, men pushed bicycles to market, teetering beneath aluminum milk pots. Every few miles, a trading center appeared. These hodgepodge settlements, with their half-finished brick storefronts and their chaotic taxi stands and their billboards advertising Omo Detergent and Nile Special Beer and Lifeguard Condoms, hummed with the hustling song of African life. Taxi touts called out from the windows of their swerving, beat-up minibuses; market women haggled over the price of cassava and charcoal; earsplitting loudspeakers disgorged the repentance cries of hoarse-voiced evangelists.

It had taken some time, but I had finally managed to track down the man named in the affidavit, Duncan Muhumuza Laki. It turned out that in the two years that had passed since he'd solved the murder of his father, Eliphaz, he'd relocated to the United States. But Duncan still visited his home country regularly, and now he was back on one of these trips, staying at the family farmhouse in Ndeija. He'd invited me out to visit.

The road west hewed close to the route of the Rwizi River, which runs across the valley floor and cuts through the center of Ndeija. When Eliphaz Laki was still a boy, the lowland between the hills was a papyrus-choked swamp, and when the waters rose they would make the valley impassable. As the seasonal rains began to fall, people would shout temporary good-byes to their neighbors across the way, a phrase that sounds, in their tribal language, like *in-day-shuh*. "Ndeija!" The village's name, bequeathed by the river, roughly means, "I'll come back."

The swamp was drained long ago, and today a steel bridge spans the river. When I reached Ndeija, I hung a right off the main road, at the wooden shacks where the local vendors were selling cascading bunches of big green bananas, which Ugandans steam to make a starchy mush called *matooke*, the national dish. I crossed the bridge and followed an unpaved path up to Duncan's farm. In Uganda, a man of substance must own land. His farm symbolically links him to the agricultural society from which he came, and it is the place where he will one day be buried. The hillsides around Ndeija were dotted with spacious new farmhouses, topped by shiny metal roofs, an indicator of rising wealth. The wars were over, people out west were prospering and they were no longer afraid to show it. Duncan's own sturdy brick residence had a bright green roof. It stood next to the smaller colonial-style farmhouse his father had built decades before.

Until recently, Duncan had been a lawyer in Kampala for the Uganda Revenue Authority, the country's tax collection agency. But just a few weeks short of his fortieth birthday, he had embarked on a new life in the northern suburbs of New Jersey. Both he and his wife, Cathy, a doctor, had attended graduate school in America, and Cathy now worked as a neonatal specialist at a hospital in Harrison. They were building a house in the Monmouth County town of Morganville, and Duncan was studying for the New York bar examination. His three kids were growing up American. When I walked up to his farmhouse in Ndeija and introduced myself to his oldest boy, Kagi, an eleven-year-old, he hardly looked up from his portable Pokemon video game.

Duncan came out the front door to greet me. He was a tall man, with an austere forehead, a fast-retreating hairline and a pair of soft mournful eyes. People always told him he looked a lot like his father. He walked with a slow, loping gait, and he had a soft-spoken, slightly slumped demeanor. Duncan led me around the side of the house, to a large stone that lay in the grass near a red-flowering bottlebrush tree. It was not a gravestone; no coffin was buried beneath it. It was something immeasurably sadder, a monument to a mystery, a life deprived of the finality of an end date. A plaque affixed to the stone read:

In Memory Of
Eliphaz Mbwaijana Laki

Lord Grant Us Decent Rest
And Disappearance No More

One universal of human culture is the desire to consecrate and send off the dead. In Uganda, popular devotion to Christianity and Islam coexists with a quiet but abiding belief in the power of ancestral spirits, intelligent forces that invisibly work their wills within the world of the living. "They were never seen, but their presence was felt," one early anthropologist wrote of these gods of tradition, "for the wind which blew amongst the trees and grass of the grazing-grounds showed the presence of ghosts of the [cattle herdsmen], while those of the peasants were heard rustling amongst the grain or in the plantain trees." Popular belief dictated that a man was to be buried on his own land, by the hands of his own family. One who was not so honored was liable to become an unsettled spirit, wandering unhappily, tormenting his living descendants.

Duncan did not believe in ghosts, yet he nevertheless felt haunted. "I found it hard to believe that he had died," he told me. His voice, low and lugubrious, conveyed the events surrounding his father's disappearance with an attorney's detachment, as if he were keeping his analytical distance. Duncan was not an angry man, despite everything. He told me he was a born-again Christian. He believed in forgiveness and a higher law.

"Call it denial, call it whatever you want," he went on. "I thought one day maybe he'd surface. Maybe he went someplace. Maybe he is one of these vagabonds by the roadside. I could not bring myself to the point where I could see him dead."

Deep in the unspoken corners of his heart, Duncan told me, he had secreted away the certainty, no matter how irrational, that somehow, somewhere, his father could be found. Even after it became evident that Eliphaz Laki would not, after so many years, come walking through the door of the family farmhouse, Duncan had never lost hope that he could discover what had happened to his father, recover some remnant of him, redeem him. For most of his life, a life that traced the arc of his nation's downfall and troubled rebirth, Duncan had looked for an answer. And finally, miraculously, he unearthed one.

That afternoon, Duncan took me to see the place where his search had led. As we drove through the deadened dry-season landscape, watching out for the herds of cattle that sometimes strayed into the road, he pointed out the homes and farms of other men who'd been murdered by Amin. "That one belonged to my uncle, Bananuka," Duncan said as we passed one. "He was taken and he was butchered. . . . Dismembered."

Eliphaz Laki LAKI FAMILY

The road twisted suddenly. "Slow down," Duncan said. "Right here." I turned off the paved highway, onto a narrow gravel path. Duncan directed me to a line of scrubby bushes, where we got out of the car. We followed a footpath into a deserted meadow. The terrain sloped downward into the middle distance, and then it rose abruptly to form a rounded ridgeline. Off to the north, we could see the rocky peaks of the higher mountains around Ibanda, about thirty miles away, the town where soldiers had picked up his father in September 1972. Eliphaz Laki had disappeared during the dry season, and the scene must have been largely unchanged. The savanna was dotted with thorny, flat-topped acacias. The wind hissed as it passed through the brown knee-high grass.

We hopped over a shallow depression in the ground. Duncan took me around the side of an enormous anthill, tall as a man, which was covered with purple flowers and brambles.

"They killed him here," Duncan said.

2

THE KEY

In the beginning, there was nothing but hope. That first night, atop the hills surrounding Mbarara—indeed, across all of Uganda—bonfires blazed in celebration of a new nation. The air was suffused with the smell of woodsmoke and the sound of jubilant drumming. Eliphaz Laki followed the dancing flames of a hundred handheld torches. It was October 1962, and Uganda was finally gaining its independence. Gripping the little hand of his ten-year-old daughter, Justine, Laki walked with a torchlight procession through dust-blown streets of the western provincial capital, to the town square for the midnight ceremonies commemorating the formal end of colonial rule.

It was the culmination of a long and nostalgic day. Over the course of seventy years, Britain had remade this impossibly green patch of Africa—this "fairytale" kingdom, as Winston Churchill had called it—in its own image. The first European explorers who'd come to Uganda had encountered a people who worshipped the spirits of their ancestors, who wore barkcloth and ivory, who paid obedience to tribal kings. Eliphaz Laki was a High Church Anglican, inevitably dressed in a smart gray suit and a representative of an elected government. Mingled with the joy of freedom on that day of feasting, thanksgiving prayers and toasts of banana beer was the wistfulness that marks any passage. Colonialism may have been a moral abomination, but Laki had known nothing else. His wife was about to give birth, though, and Laki knew this child of independence was promised a life he could scarcely imagine.

Laki was a politician of some importance: a chief. To foreigners, this word brought to mind the image of a spear-carrying warrior, but under the colonial administration chiefs were more like civil servants. Laki was part of a generation that had been trained in mission schools for self-rule. This recently minted elite was anglicized and contemptuous of any suggestion of African inferiority. Playing on Bantu language rules, which prefaced the name of every tribe with the prefix *Ba*, they were nicknamed the "Ba-men"—new men. Laki considered himself a public servant and a patriot. When he'd first been offered a chieftaincy by the colonial authorities, he'd written back, "I am ready to serve my country." And now, as of this night, Uganda really was his country.

In Africa, the colonial era had come to an end the way a skyscraper falls: with a series of shudders and a swift collapse. Independence—*uhuru*, as the Africans called it—had come to Sudan in 1956, and then to the Gold Coast, since renamed Ghana, and now it was cascading across the continent with a momentum no one could control. In the course of less than a decade, the British administrators in Uganda had gone from locking up nationalist rabble-rousers to preparing for an immediate exit. They had presided over the election of a Ugandan prime minister. He was a young, bow-tied politician from the north of the country named Apollo Milton Obote. Laki was a member of Obote's political party, the Uganda People's Congress. Its slogan—"Unity, Justice, Independence"—seemed to embody the idealism of those heady days.

At that very moment, at a parade ground in the capital, Kampala, Prime Minister Obote was addressing a crowd of tens of thousands of spectators, including the Duke and Duchess of Kent. As the hour for the handover approached, the prime minister's warbling voice rang out over Uganda's radio waves.

Countrymen and friends: At midnight tonight Uganda shall become independent. We shall have a Uganda flag, a national anthem and a coat of arms. These will be our symbols, but independence does not begin and end with the selection and raising of a flag, the singing of a national anthem, and the display of a coat of arms.

Our independence shall mean great responsibilities for all of us without exception. . . . I pray to God to give us and our country the will to safeguard our freedom and to serve our country in peace. I pray that He may give us reason and in reason we may seek and find, and may what I have said tonight bind us into the community of hope who shall

think and strive and toil in such patterns, that work of more noble
worth may yet be done.

All these and more: For God and My Country.

As the clock struck twelve in Mbarara, a police department honor guard
gathered at the base of the town flagstaff. The Union Jack was lowered,
and the Ugandan flag was raised in its place. The new standard was
striped red, black and yellow, and bore the image of the national bird, a
crested crane. The British flag was folded up and handed to the only
white man on hand, a departing colonial administrator. Laki's daughter
still remembers the saddened look on his face as he turned and walked
away, alone.

One month to the day after independence, on November 9, 1962,
Eliphaz Laki and his wife had their new child: a son, just as his father
had hoped. They named him Duncan.

Duncan was there the day his father disappeared. He was just nine
years old.

The date was September 22, 1972. Almost a decade had passed since
that night of independence. The year before, Milton Obote had been
ousted by General Amin's military coup. Obote was now in exile, and
Amin controlled the government.

It was a Friday, a school day. Duncan and his father were living
in the western town of Ibanda, where Eliphaz Laki was serving as the
local *saza* chief. Duncan rose early that morning, put on his school
uniform—khaki shorts, a white buttoned-up shirt—and came out for
breakfast. As always, his father was already up, sitting at the wooden
table in the dining room of the chief's official residence. Eliphaz Laki
was a tall, rawboned man in his fifties, with a high, furrowed forehead
and deep-set eyes. Duncan was in awe of him. Laki was a Big Man, as
they say in Africa. To his children, he just seemed big: a distant power,
stern and imposing.

In the tribal language of Ankole, the word for "king" literally means
"provider." In the old days, chiefs had been tribal elders who ruled like
feudal lords, and if the office no longer possessed quite the same grandeur,
it was still invested with a sense of paternal authority. Laki, whose background was in public health, had dug wells to bring safe drinking water
to the countryside. He'd built schools and roads. He'd paid for the local
people's hospital visits and schoolbooks, bicycles and shoes. He'd been

Duncan Laki outside the chief's house in Ibanda   ANDREW RICE

the first man from his village of Ndeija ever to buy a car, a Volkswagen Beetle. When Laki had brought it home, the villagers had rejoiced with pride. In the years before the overthrow of Obote, Laki had driven that Beetle all over the west's rough back roads, preaching the gospel of the Uganda People's Congress. Automobiles were still rare enough that the prominent men of Ankole were recognized simply by their license plates. Laki's was "UYO-010."

Duncan loved riding in the Volkswagen. To him, the car represented his father's place in the world. Laki favored little Duncan, whom he called "Shusha." When Laki was transferred to the chieftaincy of Ibanda, a distant, mountainous county a day's drive from Ndeija, he took Duncan and two younger brothers with him in the Beetle, while leaving his wife and most of their thirteen children back at the family farm. They were there, far from home, together.

Since the coup, Laki, like many other civil servants loyal to Obote, had managed to hold onto his job, though he had endured months of suspicion and mistreatment. He tried to keep his children from sensing his disquiet. On the morning of his disappearance, Laki went through his normal routine, leading the boys in morning prayers and feeding them their usual breakfast, a grayish porridge made from millet, along with bananas and milky tea. They turned on the BBC. The news that month was of Fischer and Spassky, Nixon and McGovern, and terror at the Munich Olympics. Duncan hurried to get ready before the BBC's string section struck up, signaling the top of the hour. His father insisted on punctuality.

As he left, Duncan asked his father for a shilling to buy ink. Laki fished in his pocket and gave his son the coin. In the years that followed, Duncan would often wonder, *Did I touch his hand?*

Duncan tried to stay out of the piercing September sun as he walked down the dirt road to school. Ibanda was situated near the foot of a craggy mountain. The town consisted of little more than his father's official residence—a handsome house with a long veranda and a peaked red roof—the county administration building across the street, a few churches, a school and a strip of whitewashed shops. The shelves were mostly bare these days. Duncan couldn't find any ink. So the shilling stayed in his pocket.

Duncan was worried. Like many precocious children, he was acutely attuned to adult anxieties. And anyone, even a nine-year-old, could tell something was desperately wrong in Uganda. One morning that week, on his walk to school, Duncan had seen a soldier pull to the side of the road in a civilian car. He'd heard a furious thumping sound from inside the car's trunk. When the soldier opened the trunk to shout some harsh words in Swahili, Duncan had stared into the pleading faces of two battered men.

The latest round of trouble had started the previous Sunday. Rebels allied to the exiled Obote, including a previously unknown militant named Yoweri Museveni, had attacked a nearby military barracks. But their operation had been a fiasco, and the national radio station had proclaimed another glorious victory for General Amin. On September 21, just the day before, an announcer had come on the air to read out a communiqué: "A military spokesman says the situation in the country is calm and there is no cause for panic at all."

There was no mystery about the identity of this anonymous "military spokesman." Everyone knew only one man spoke for Uganda's army. "A few dissidents who might have originated from the invading forces, which were routed, are being hunted seriously by members of the security forces and the public," the announcement continued. "The operation is already very effective."

The army had fanned out across the western countryside, rounding up anyone suspected of sympathizing with the rebels. Duncan didn't know it, but every day his father had learned that another old friend had gone missing, men who, like him, had served Milton Obote. Laki's uncle: gone. The godfather of his children: gone. His close friend, once the secretary general of the region, its highest elected official: gone. There was only so much Laki could do to shield his son from the horror creeping closer to their door. One day, the secretary general's three sons, the youngest just eighteen, were shot dead not far from Ibanda, and their bodies left to rot in the equatorial sun. Duncan heard the gunshots at school.

But the charade of normal childhood went on. Sitting in class that Friday morning, Duncan watched as his cousin James came running up to the schoolhouse, wearing a pained expression. James found the headmaster, a friend of Duncan's father. They talked briefly, in hushed tones. But no one said anything to Duncan. Class continued.

At midday, Duncan went home for lunch. As he climbed the steep driveway that ran up to the chief's residence, he saw another cousin, Francis, waiting outside. Francis worked as a handyman around the house. He met Duncan outside the door and delivered the news.

"Your father has been taken," he said.

Even at his age, Duncan knew the implications of the word *taken*. But somehow, he couldn't believe it had happened. He ran into the house looking for his father. He retrieved the unspent shilling from his pocket and left it on his father's bedside table. Then Duncan ran back outside. Where was the Volkswagen? He pulled open the door of the garage. It was empty.

As he looked into the vacant garage, Duncan's first instinct was to run. He dashed clear across town to his headmaster's house. Maybe he could explain. But the headmaster had no answers for the boy. The truth, which he couldn't tell Duncan, was that he was petrified. A friend of Laki's, and also a political opponent of Amin's, he had been hiding from the soldiers at night, sleeping outside in his fields, hoping to somehow survive the purge. What could he possibly say to his pupil?

So Duncan kept running. He found a minister, the pastor of the family's church. But he too lacked the words to dispel the boy's confusion or console his heart. He said a prayer and sent Duncan back home.

Duncan's mother arrived at the residence that afternoon. She had heard about the killings of other politicians, and had made the long trek from the family farm in Ndeija, hoping to warn her husband. But she'd gotten there too late. She sat in the living room, stunned. She had nothing to tell her children. She departed the next morning, taking Duncan's brothers with her back to the farm. Duncan still had a few months to go until the end of the school year, so he stayed behind with a distant cousin, who took him in and cared for him. Duncan went through those first months almost alone. The townspeople looked upon him with wary sympathy. Only a few weeks before, his father had been the most important man in Ibanda. Now his name was hardly mentioned. It was as if he'd vanished from the town's memory, too.

The whole Laki family was in disarray. No one had any idea what had happened to the missing chief, whether he was dead or imprisoned or had somehow managed to escape into exile, as others reportedly had. When Duncan's older sister Joyce heard about her father's disappearance, she rushed to Mbarara, to the office of a provincial administrator, to find out what he knew of Laki's whereabouts. The administrator pointed to a dark red stain on his floor. "Do you see that blood?" he asked her. He told Joyce it belonged to another civil servant who'd just been dragged off by the army. "I don't have much to tell you," the administrator said. "Just pray."

No one could help. Not the police: They'd been cowed into submission or were actively collaborating with the army. Not the law: The day before Laki had disappeared, intelligence agents had abducted the chief justice of Uganda's Supreme Court from his chambers in broad daylight. Not global outrage: Since the military coup the year before, Tanzanian president Julius Nyerere had called Idi Amin a "killer," the *New York Times* editorial page had inveighed against his "bizarre" behavior and President Richard Nixon, in a taped phone call, had snickered that he was a "prehistoric monster." But there was no serious thought of saving Uganda. It was the 1970s, the era of détente, when the rivalries of the Northern Hemisphere were fought by proxy in the Southern. Every day, it seemed, among the darker peoples of the lesser continents, some civil war flared, some tyrant emerged. Their cowering subjects, once tied together within European empires, were now bound by the common experience of terror.

Amin's exploits filled the world's newspapers in the 1970s. But all the attention was tinged with a kind of anthropological bemusement. "The Wild Man of Africa," *Time* magazine proclaimed, next to a cover picture of the saluting general. The British newspapers called him "Big Daddy"—a nickname Amin gleefully embraced—and retailed lurid, unsubstantiated tales of human heads stacked in a freezer, of human sacrifices and blood rituals. These only served to further distance Amin's very real atrocities from the realm of reasoned discourse, and, not for the first or last time, an African nation's misery was shrugged off as an unapproachable horror. The world turned the page, and Ugandans continued to die.

"What cannot be told," a human rights group that examined the situation in Uganda concluded in a 1974 report, "are the circumstances of the deaths of countless . . . anonymous victims, most of them ordinary citizens who have disappeared without attracting public attention. For these people, there were no investigations, no commissions of inquiry, no reports, and no help has been provided to their families."

One day shortly after his father's disappearance, Duncan's whole primary school class was summoned to Ibanda's modest police station. A contingent of soldiers was waiting for them there, armed with rifles and bayonets. An olive-uniformed police officer, a man from a faraway tribe, stepped forward and issued an order: "Bring the *saza* chief."

Duncan was startled. His father was the *saza* chief. But another man stepped forward, Eliphaz Laki's freshly appointed replacement. Under the new chief's supervision, the children's lesson proceeded. Three bound prisoners were brought forward—thieves, the schoolchildren were told. The prisoners were pushed facedown to the ground. Then the soldiers stabbed them repeatedly with their bayonets. After several long minutes of writhing and screaming, the prisoners were finally shot dead.

"This is a good example!" the policeman shouted to the class.

No one acted like what had happened was anything other than normal. In Amin's Uganda, public acts of brutality had become so much a part of everyday existence that they ceased to rouse outrage or disgust. Those who opposed Amin were routinely shot by firing squads in public squares. The point was made, even to little children. Duncan didn't dare utter a rebellious word.

Finally, at the Christmas holidays, Duncan rejoined his family at the farm. There, he felt safe. Full of a child's naive resolution, he confided to his brothers and sisters that he'd sworn to one day track down their father and his precious car. Duncan's mother shushed him. Anyone could be spying for Amin, she scolded—the farm help, the village men who idled over jugs of banana beer. It was no time for a boy's careless talk.

But Duncan could be heedless. He asked a friend who knew about such shady matters—the friend's brother was an intelligence operative—if it was possible to track down his father's missing Volkswagen. Duncan's friend asked around and, sure enough, found out that a military man was often seen driving the car in Mbarara. Duncan knew to end his inquiries there. But the family continued to hear rumors about the Volkswagen. It materialized every so often, like an apparition. Once, Duncan's brother Dennis glimpsed the Volkswagen near the Kampala taxi park, an area where many of Amin's tribesmen owned businesses. Another time, Duncan's sister Joyce was standing outside a hotel in Mbarara when the Beetle pulled up. The driver seemed to have made a halfhearted attempt to disguise the vehicle. Once white, it had been repainted a light shade of blue. But the license number was the same: UYO-010. Joyce watched as a soldier got out of the car and went inside the hotel restaurant. She waited for him to return, just to see what he looked like. But she never said a word to him.

In Amin's Uganda, all questions stopped at the barracks gate, and every citizen was required to glorify the dictatorship. In 1975, when Duncan was twelve, Kampala hosted the annual summit of the Organization of African Unity and Amin turned the gathering of heads of state into a lavish celebration of his regime. He promoted himself to field marshal and pressed thousands of schoolchildren, including Duncan, into service in an elaborate military drill. Before the summit began, Duncan was brought to practice the routine at the Kampala soccer stadium, where an enormous portrait of the dictator had been erected above the stands. As a band played and soldiers goose-stepped, the children stood in formation and held up open books, like little white pixels, spelling out messages that could be read from afar:

WE ARE HAPPY UNDER THE CARE OF MARSHAL AMIN

THE IMPERIALISTS ARE OUR ENEMIES

In fact, Amin was neither a communist or a capitalist; he deployed Cold War rhetoric for his own military benefit, like so many of his Third World counterparts. There were some forty successful military coups in Africa in the first two decades after independence. When the Organization of African Unity summit began, Amin met his counterparts at the airport in the company of a troupe of bare-breasted dancers and tribal drummers. It was like a monster's ball. There was Mobutu Sese Seko, the corrupt despot of Zaire, in his trademark leopard-skin cap. There was Jean-Bédel Bokassa, the murderous tyrant of the Central African Republic, in a dress tunic dripping with dozens of shiny medals. Amin himself had debuted a new sky-blue field marshal's uniform for the occasion.

The summit went on for weeks. Before it was over, one of the visiting generals, the dictator of Nigeria, was informed of his overthrow, and four others hastened home early to put down coups. But that hardly dampened the festivities. Duncan was a spectator at a motor rally through the streets of Kampala. Amin competed in his red Maserati. There was a nationally televised wedding between the polygamous president and his latest girlfriend, a dancer with a military jazz band. There was a party at Lake Victoria, featuring a mock attack on white supremacist South Africa, represented by an island offshore. When Amin's planes misfired, dropping their bombs harmlessly into the lake, he summarily fired the air force commander, who was subsequently liquidated.

The OAU summit, 1975, at the Kampala soccer stadium, under an enormous portrait of the dictator THE NEW VISION

In his most memorable stunt, Amin, wearing his army uniform and an Arab-style kaffiyeh, had a group of white expatriates carry him into a party on a litter. The whole country saw the spectacle pictured on the front page of the next day's issue of the official state newspaper. "The British explorers and colonialists . . . would ride in chariots pushed by Africans," a caption beneath the photograph read. "For the toil and sweat they did not reap anything much. Isn't the President setting up a chapter that balances history?"

Duncan observed the festivities quietly, stifling his resentment. His mother, his uncle and many others had cautioned him against talking about his family background. A Ugandan usually has at least three names, which can be used in interchangeable order: a Christian name, a given "African" name and a family name passed down by his father. During the years Amin ruled, he always went by Duncan L. Muhumuza. He never discussed what the *L* stood for. His father's name was hazardous.

· · ·

RADIO UGANDA, APRIL 6, 1979

I am Field Marshal Idi Amin Dada, C-in-C of the Uganda Armed Forces. I want to say this: I do not want people to be afraid. . . . I think the enemy has not yet come deep inside Uganda. You should not be afraid. . . . I think I cannot leave Kampala. . . . I have given you, the people of Uganda, all the wealth, all the businesses, all the factories, shops, buildings and motorcars. Now I have freed you from the work of being porters. You have become like Europeans. You have become like those people, the imperialists, who were leading us. And now you are leading yourselves. Now you want to bring shame upon yourselves, by permitting the imperialists to come and lead you? . . . Nothing whatsoever can defeat our children, men, women and old people. We are bound to defeat these enemies. We will fight. We have food, we have arms, we have equipment, we have military fighting spirit. . . . These people who are trying to seize this area will sit on fire. In no way can they survive.

Idi Amin's voice sounded desperate and scornful. Just a few days before, he'd vowed to "die in defense of his motherland." But now, secretly, he was making preparations to flee. A few days later, he flew out of Uganda on a military plane. Conflicting rumors said he was bound for Sudan,

Libya or Iraq. His abandoned soldiers, realizing the end had come, fled north across the Nile. The reversal was complete: They were now rebels and the invaders were rulers. An unfamiliar voice broke through the radio static, declaring that Kampala had fallen to the liberators. "From today," the announcement said, "the racist, fascist, and illegal regime of the dictator Idi Amin is no longer in power."

Finally, disastrously, the country rose up. The cry went out for "justice," which in 1979 meant collective reprisal. In Kampala, mobs set upon those who belonged to Amin's northern tribe, chanting the word *anyanya* (poison). They hung tires soaked in kerosene around the northerners' necks and set them alight. Out west, Christians turned on those who practiced Islam, Amin's religion. One day, riding his bike to school, Duncan passed a field of amputated ocher tree stumps, the remnants of what was once someone's banana plantation. Duncan asked a bystander what had befallen the farm. "That was Mohammed's home," the man replied.

Duncan, who was just out of high school, asked his mother if the time might be right to look for the Volkswagen. His mother forbade any such thoughts. Leave the past in the past, she told him, and stick to the plan: Makerere University and a law degree. Duncan obeyed his mother. Jane Laki was sick. As Amin's regime had failed, she had grown weaker and weaker. In early 1980, the family took her to a hospital in Kampala, which was overcrowded and out of everything and rife with rats. The doctors told them it was cervical cancer and there wasn't much they could do. Jane, just fifty years old, told her children she was thankful that God had at least allowed her to see the end of Idi Amin. On her deathbed, in the hospital, she asked her daughter to read a letter Eliphaz Laki had written her just before his disappearance. In it, in a way, he had said good-bye.

Until the end, Duncan's mother kept a spare ignition key to her husband's Volkswagen in one of her drawers. When she died, in May 1980, Duncan found it and kept it.

At the end of that year, there was an election to pick a president, concluding a transitional period marred by political instability. Milton Obote, the previous prime minister, returned from exile in Tanzania to make the race. A number of other candidates ran against him, including Yoweri Museveni, the former leader of an anti-Amin rebel group and a participant in the failed 1972 rebel attack on Mbarara. Duncan joined Museveni's party. Obote, who had once represented the optimism of independence, was now cynical and embittered. The politicians of

Duncan's father's generation, who expected family allegiance to Obote, explained their loyalty with a parable: If you're going to be torn apart by a hyena, they said, better it should be one from your own village, because then it won't scatter your bones. The young upstart Museveni replied, If you don't want to be eaten, don't vote for a hyena. That argument appealed to Duncan.

Obote won the presidency in an election full of fraud and abuse. After the vote, Museveni returned to the bush with a small band of guerrillas, declaring that Uganda had merely traded one dictator for another. The rebels of his National Resistance Movement hid out in a scrubby area north of Kampala known as the Luwero Triangle, where they steadily gathered strength and popular support.

Just as the civil war was beginning, Duncan entered Kampala's Makerere University to study law. Built by the British in the 1920s, Makerere had once been an estimable institution, but by the time Duncan arrived, in the early 1980s, the place was just another crumbling sector of an embattled city. In his shabby dorm room, Duncan fell asleep to the crackle of gunfire. No one left the campus at night, and even in the daytime walking in the streets could be an adventure. Once, at a roadblock, a group of soldiers stopped Duncan and stole his shoes.

Many Makerere students, frustrated with their political impotence, were putting down their books and picking up arms. Classmates of Duncan's were sneaking out of the city to join Museveni in the bush. Duncan's elder brother Dennis, for his part, enlisted to fight the rebels as an artilleryman in Obote's government army. The Laki family was dismayed, but Dennis told them he believed the military would continue to hold sway in Uganda for the foreseeable future, and it could only be reformed from within. Duncan resisted taking a side in the war. He didn't believe in guns.

In 1986, right around the time Duncan was finishing law school, Museveni captured Kampala, ending the worst part of the civil war. Duncan took the public service exam and secured a job in the Ministry of Lands. His office oversaw the region of Luwero, where the most intense fighting in the civil war had taken place. His brother Dennis, who had survived, had told him very little about what he'd seen as a government soldier. But now, the truth was becoming evident. Milton Obote had massacred civilians on a scale that dwarfed even Idi Amin's atrocities. After Museveni's men had finally marched into Kampala, the people of Luwero had exhumed the mass graves that seeded the countryside, stacking the bones of the dead along the highway that ran up from Kampala as a grim memorial.

Duncan went to live in Luwero to preside over the reopening of the Land Ministry's branch office, which had been closed during the war. Driving north into the marshes, he saw a group of local women sitting by the side of the road, in traditional dresses with their distinctive winglike shoulder pads, selling vegetables off blankets. Next to the peddlers, he saw stacks of round, bleached-white objects. At first, he thought they were cabbages, but then he realized they were skulls.

Eventually, the new government reburied the bones. It was time to move on.

In 1990, when Duncan was twenty-eight, he decided that the family should hold a memorial service for Eliphaz Laki. That December, a few days after Christmas, his father's friends and relatives gathered at the farm in Ndeija. They placed a simple stone in the ground near the house Laki had built for his family, the one that pled for "decent rest."

Yoweri Museveni attended the memorial service. His presence acknowledged a secret and personal debt. Over the years, Laki's children had come to realize that there was much their father had not revealed to them. He'd been involved in the clandestine resistance to Amin's dictatorship. He wasn't a victim, they now knew, but a martyr. He'd given his life so that a better future might prevail.

In his address to the memorial service, President Museveni praised Laki as a man of integrity and told those assembled, cryptically, that there were those who had chosen the other side. Someone had turned Laki over to Amin. This person—or people—remained hidden among them. The mourners listened silently. They already knew that Laki had been betrayed.

Laying the stone, Museveni said, would help to mend the wrong that had been done to Laki. By recognizing how he lived and why he died, the president said, the family had consecrated their father's sacrifice. Perhaps his soul really had found rest. Laki's children could only pray that it was true. The chief's body had never even been recovered.

Outwardly, like the country itself, Duncan appeared to be prosperous and at peace. But the people of his Banyankole tribe had a proverb: The teeth may smile, but the heart does not forget. Duncan could never keep the absence of finality from preying on his mind. In conversation,

The memorial stone at the Laki farm in Ndeija ANDREW RICE

others solemnly referred to his father as "the late Laki," but he could never bring himself to use those words or to speak about his father in anything but the present tense. His family, his government, his better judgment—all of them told Duncan that his father was dead, that seeking the truth was a dangerous indulgence. But something persisted, an inner determination to know.

Religion gave him some solace. Evangelical churches, many of them constructed out of simple reeds, had sprung up all over the country during the civil war years. Duncan joined a Pentecostal church in Kampala and became born-again, ending a period of spiritual drift. He met Cathy Kanyesigye, a medical student, and they married. In April 1991, they had their first child, a son.

Later that year, Duncan left Uganda. He'd won a scholarship to study commercial law at a school in Chicago. When he got off the plane at O'Hare International Airport, he was almost leveled by the sticky August heat. The weather in Uganda was never so unpleasant. Everything in America was disorienting. The cars drove on the wrong side of the road, the light switches worked the opposite way, and the natives spoke English with an indecipherable accent, which was all the more aggravating because they seemed to think *he* had an accent. Duncan's roommate, a black American from Maryland, helped him to adjust. He celebrated Thanksgiving and discovered the White Sox.

Eventually, Cathy joined him and continued her medical schooling. She and Duncan had two more children. They moved to New Jersey, where Cathy did her residency. For the rest of the decade, Duncan would live an expatriate's disjointed existence, shuttling between the United States, where his wife was pursuing her career as a doctor, and Uganda, where he had a law practice. Wherever he traveled, Duncan brought his father's spare Volkswagen key, keeping it on a chain in his dresser drawer. Every so often, he would take it out, just to look and wonder.

Duncan was learning more about the world, that he was not alone in his sorrow. The age of dictatorship seemed to be receding. In 1991, the year Duncan came to America, the Soviet Union ceased to exist. President Bush—the first President Bush—was talking of a "new world order." With the Cold War easing, the countries of the developing world were no longer such battlefields. Nations like Chile, Argentina and South Africa were casting aside their tyrannical regimes and setting up truth commissions. People were discovering the fates of their lost loved ones.

In 1999, Duncan went home to work as an attorney for the Uganda Revenue Authority, the country's tax agency. The job involved a lot of collections cases, chasing down tax cheats, and he ended up spending many days at the agency's central motor vehicle registry in Kampala. For assessment purposes, it had nearly a half-million vehicle records, dating back to colonial times. Sifting through all those license plate numbers, Duncan's mind kept returning to one: UYO-010.

One day, Duncan walked into the motor vehicle registry, cutting purposefully through the front room—past the sweaty men waving papers, past the slackjawed bureaucrats pounding stamps and staplers, past a laser-printed sign that read NO CORRUPTION WITH ME. A ceiling fan turned lazily overhead. Duncan negotiated a narrow warren of wood-paneled cubicles and descended a staircase into the registry's records room. Nothing in his manner betrayed the seriousness—the outright foolhardiness—of the thing he was about to do.

The registry was hardly a model of organization. Sheaves of documents were piled everywhere: haphazardly on desks, high on file cabinets, in boxes on a metal shelf that leaned precariously to the right. It would be a miracle, Duncan thought, if he found what he was looking for. He located the custodian of the oldest records. What were the chances, he asked, that a car's registration might still be around after three decades? The custodian said he could check. He requested the license plate number. On a slip of paper, Duncan wrote down "UYO-010," and left.

The next day, Duncan returned. Good news, the custodian told him. He'd found the file. Duncan fought to keep the sudden rush of emotions—joy, apprehension, disbelief—from registering on his face. The custodian handed him the folder. Duncan carefully opened it. The pages were limp and yellowed with age, tattered around the edges. UYO-010, they revealed, was a "toga white" Volkswagen Beetle, purchased in 1968 by one Eliphaz Laki, for the sum of 25,200 shillings, then the equivalent of about $3,500.

Another page. This one bore the date November 29, 1972. It was a document transferring ownership of the car. The paper bore the supposed signature of Eliphaz Laki—clearly forged—and another name, scrawled in a shaky, inexperienced hand. The car's new owner, the document said, was someone called Mohammed Anyule. Duncan, dazed, stared at the page. November 1972. Two months after his father vanished. Was this the man who killed Eliphaz Laki?

3

UYO-010

Mohammed Anyule was a northern name. That made sense. Amin was from the north and a Muslim. He had staffed the army and secret police with his kinsmen.

Duncan had the contents of the file folder photocopied and notarized and stuffed the papers into his briefcase. He hurried out of the car registry. His plan, such as it was, only went this far. He had a clue now, a name, but no idea what to do with it. Duncan needed advice. He went to see his uncle Yona.

Uncle Yona's full name was Yonasani Kanyomozi. He wasn't really a blood relation but he was as close to Duncan as any family member. Yona's own father had died when he was a boy and Eliphaz Laki, who'd met him by chance one day while on his official rounds, had helped to see to his upbringing, contributing to his education and even buying him his first pair of shoes. After Laki disappeared, his protégé had returned the favor, acting as a guardian and benefactor to the missing chief's children. Uncle Yona was a politician. He'd served in a half-dozen governments, through wars and purges and a stint in exile. He'd managed to live past sixty. He was a very canny man.

Uncle Yona kept an office along Kampala Road, in a tall building topped by a giant Bell Beer billboard. Duncan made his way there through the traffic-clogged streets of the revitalized capital. Out on the corners, newspaper hawkers waved muckraking tabloids. Uganda now had its own pop stars and talk shows and reality TV celebrities. The sounds of American R&B and Congolese *soukous* poured out of sidewalk bars and cafés. Everyone was talking into cell phones. Two years before, President Bill Clinton had visited Kampala, and he'd rhapsodized about an "African renaissance." Uganda's warring parties had finally settled their differences, but the truce was brittle, and Duncan now possessed information that could conceivably upset it.

Tall and dapper, with a thin mustache and square, distinguished chin, Uncle Yona welcomed Duncan into his wood-paneled office. Its windows looked out on the hills beyond the city center, which were dotted with new stucco mansions. Yona absorbed Duncan's news quietly. He took a close look at the photocopied documents. Then he locked them away in his office safe.

Uncle Yona's small eyes tended to dart around when he was thinking. He always looked like he was guarding something. Finally, he spoke, deliberately, measuring the effect of every word. "If you've found this," he told Duncan, "you have to follow it up." But the situation demanded . . . caution. There were political considerations.

Duncan understood. It was election season in Uganda. President Museveni was facing a spirited challenger, an army colonel who'd once been his personal physician. Two weeks earlier, Museveni had traveled to campaign in the town of Idi Amin's birth, in Uganda's far northwest. The president had been received by a delegation that included some of Amin's old generals, who'd come home from exile under Museveni's tolerant amnesty policies. "I am not a warmonger," the president told the campaign rally. "I will ask you people . . . to be my witness." The president said he only wanted peace—and their votes.

According to one of the documents he had discovered, Mohammed Anyule was from a town called Yumbe, not far from where Museveni had given his speech. So this Anyule might be found—if he'd returned from exile, if he was still alive. The question was whether any of the authorities would be willing to look for him. The amnesties offered to Amin's men were not absolute; they'd been pardoned for the act of rebellion, not the murders they'd committed during their time in power. But Museveni's government had made a tacit choice not to pursue old crimes. Uncle Yona told Duncan they could forget about turning to the police. Uganda's cops were overworked, incompetent and corrupt, and they knew that some cases weren't supposed to be solved.

There might be another way, Yona said. He had heard about a pair of private detectives.

· · ·

Duncan agonized for three months. It wasn't easy to move forward. Some of his siblings were implacably opposed. Respect their mother's dying wishes, they said: Don't make everyone revisit the anguish. "You are going to get into things," they warned Duncan. "No-go areas. Dead ends. Just let it go. Why scratch old wounds?"

But Duncan thought the world had changed. At the very moment he was making up his mind, the newspapers were full of news from far-away Belgrade. Black-clad Serbian commandos had just stormed the home of the retired strongman Slobodan Milošević, arresting him pending extradition to the Hague, where he was to stand trial for war crimes before a United Nations tribunal. A similar court, sitting in nearby Arusha, Tanzania, was prosecuting the perpetrators of the genocide in Rwanda. The world no longer saw such atrocities as crimes against individuals, tribes or even nations, but as offenses against all humanity. If it was now possible to seek justice in places like the Balkans or Rwanda, why not in Uganda, too? Finally, in April 2001, Duncan told his uncle he was ready to meet the private investigators.

The detective agency's offices were situated in the thicket of narrow streets surrounding the exhaust-choked earthen bowl of Kampala's taxi park. Along the brightly painted shopkeepers' walls, President Museveni, who'd just won a chaotic reelection, smiled benevolently from peeling campaign posters. Duncan found the right building, a concrete office bloc, and climbed the stairs to the third floor. Only one of the detectives was in, the junior partner, Brian Tibo. He was a diminutive young man, earnest and mild-mannered. He introduced himself with enthusiasm, telling Duncan he was new to the profession, having learned about it by reading many detective novels. To Duncan, the detective's experience was almost beside the point. The important thing was, Tibo was from Yumbe.

Duncan knew he couldn't find Mohammed Anyule himself. The north was like another country. "Uganda," that fanciful British creation, had never been much more than some lines on a map. There were more than fifty languages spoken in the country, derived from various linguistic families, and the tribal languages of the north were as different from Duncan's mother tongue as French is from Hungarian. English was Uganda's official national language, but hardly anyone spoke it up there. No one in the north would talk to someone from a western tribe, anyway. Those people protected their own. Only someone who knew the culture and the territory could locate the man he was looking for.

Duncan worried, however, about entrusting the case to a tribesman of the prime suspect, so he held back some information. He invented a complicated story to explain why he was searching for this very old Volkswagen. The detective could tell there was more to the case than a mere missing car, but he didn't probe too deeply. A client was a client. He told Duncan his firm was willing to search for anything and anyone for a price. He asked for two hundred thousand shillings, the equivalent of about one hundred dollars, to start.

The name Anyule sounded faintly familiar to Tibo from his days growing up in Yumbe. But he cautioned Duncan that he didn't know a great deal about the events of the early 1970s. "I was very young," he said. Most of his older male relatives had served in Amin's army, though. They might know who Mohammed Anyule was.

One morning soon afterward, Tibo traveled north aboard a rickety, careening bus. The road wound out of the green hills of the south, into the wide, treeless savannas of the heartland, over the roiling torrent of the Nile at Karuma Falls, and into the rocky terrain of his home region. It was late in the afternoon when the bus pulled into the provincial capital, Arua, a seedy smuggling town near the permeable borders with Congo and Sudan. Tibo decided to spend the night there. He paid a visit to an old soldier, his paternal uncle.

During the time the military ruled the country, his uncle had been a high-ranking official in the Agriculture Ministry. Now he worked as a night watchman. Tibo brought the old man a bag of sugar and some other foodstuffs. He accepted the gifts with famished appreciation and slaughtered a scrawny chicken in honor of his nephew's homecoming. They ate. Slowly, jocularly, Tibo steered the conversation toward the subject of the past. He was a young man, he said, in search of a wife, and he'd come to seek an elder's advice. He'd heard tales of the older generation's romantic prowess—it seemed as if every one of them had fathered dozens of children. (Polygamy is an accepted practice throughout Uganda.) "There are some famous men I very much want to meet," Tibo said. "I want to find out what the magic was."

"You—you, are still young," the old man said with an avuncular chuckle. "We had money. We were sleeping on money! Women liked that. *That* was the magic. When you are in the government, you can take anything." In those days, when Amin's tribesmen had all the enriching levers of power at their disposal, the envious had nicknamed them the *mafuta mingi*, a phrase that in Swahili means both "very fat," and "very slick."

Tibo then asked his uncle if he happened to know a fellow named Mohammed Anyule. "I know Hajji," the old man replied. Anyule had been a private in the army, a military driver. During the 1970s he'd made a hajj, or pilgrimage, to Mecca, which entitled him to the lifelong honorific. Only a wealthy man could afford such a trip.

"Hajji used to be a smart man," Tibo's uncle continued. "He had about six wives, and was known as a very good womanizer. He could come to your house and take your wife right away." Private Anyule had fled to exile after Amin's overthrow, like everyone else, but he'd since come home. As far as the old man knew, he'd settled back in Yumbe.

The next morning, Tibo took a minibus taxi back to his hometown. Along the road, women walked balancing huge sisal sacks on their heads. They wore wrap dresses, made of vibrant *kitenge* fabric imported from Congo, and long flowing headscarves. Yumbe was a rundown trading town. Out front of its bars, groups of young men lingered next to their bicycles, divvying up bags of khat, a bitter green leaf that acts as a stimulant when chewed. Tibo asked around. Lots of people knew Mohammed Anyule. He was a petty merchant now, and often worked as a delivery driver for one of the national newspapers. During the recent elections, he'd been President Museveni's local campaign agent.

Tibo walked to the place near the town mosque where he'd been told Private Anyule lived. The house was small, with mud walls, and shaded by a large, leafy mango tree. Peeking around the back, Tibo could see the skeletal remains of what had once been a much larger brick home. It had no roof and a fringe of bright green weeds had sprung up from atop its cracked walls. The liberators had sacked the whole province in 1979. These ruins were everywhere. Tibo also noticed the frames of several junked cars: a Land Rover, a Morris Minor, but no Volkswagen Beetle.

Tibo knocked at the door. The woman who answered said that Anyule was not home. She offered Tibo some water, explaining that Anyule was off at a funeral and might not return for some time. Tibo told her it was no problem. He'd come back soon.

The detective returned to Kampala and told Duncan what he'd discovered. Duncan, impressed by his work, decided to reveal the full story of the Volkswagen and its missing owner. At the end of the conversation, Tibo said he was willing to set aside his tribal loyalties and see the case through to its conclusion. But if the matter was this serious—if he might be investigating a murder—he'd have to involve his senior partner, Alfred Orijabo. He was better with the rough stuff.

Orijabo was a gaunt man in his late thirties, with sunken cheeks and a high, reedy voice. He'd lived a rambling and quarrelsome life. Like both his partner and the suspect, Orijabo was a member of the northern Lugbara tribe. In 1979, as a teenager, he'd fled to Sudan with his older male relatives. He'd fought in a rebel army for a time. He liked to show people a scar, a thin black line along his index finger—"my trigger scar," he called it. He claimed to have been a spy and an assassin who had later moved into law enforcement, which in Uganda wasn't such a dramatic departure. "You see, a person of the Lugbara tribe," Orijabo liked to say, "we are naturally police. God-made police." To solve cases, Orijabo placed mystical faith in the power of dreams and omens. He believed he could tell a guilty man just by looking him in the eye.

The private investigators told Duncan that it was time to get the police force involved. Mohammed Anyule had to be arrested and interrogated. Duncan went down to the station near Uganda's parliament building, filed a handwritten affidavit, and met the detective superintendent in charge of the serious crimes squad. Duncan explained the situation. The detective superintendent had never investigated a case like this before, but then again, he'd never met a complainant who was so fixated. Duncan was also known to have political connections, and the police force was, at that very moment, in the midst of a highly publicized shake-up. For whatever reason, the detective superintendent told Duncan he'd help, which was a surprise. He said he could only spare one man to accompany the detectives, a corporal, and Duncan would have to foot all his travel expenses. But if the men found Private Anyule, they could bring him back to Kampala for questioning. There was no statute of limitations for murder.

On April 15, 2001, the private detectives and the police corporal set off for Yumbe together. The corporal complained the whole way. The last leg of the trip, from Arua to Yumbe, skirted territory controlled by a rebel group, the last revanchist remnant of Idi Amin's old army. The corporal demanded a fifteen-dollar bribe from the detectives before he'd risk the road. They took a bus partway, then hired a pickup truck. The road was rocky and only wide enough for one vehicle in most places. They wound past cornfields and palm groves and tall brick towers used for curing tobacco. They crossed rivers and streams over bridges made from a few nailed wooden planks. The corporal worried aloud about a guerrilla ambush. The mountains of Yumbe loomed bluish in the distance.

The three men arrived in Yumbe in the late afternoon, dusty from the long journey. They waited for Mohammed Anyule near a market he was known to frequent. At dusk, they spotted him, walking home from evening prayers: a thin man with an angular face and a gray goatee, wearing a round knit cap and carrying a walking stick. Employing a little subterfuge—they told him they were working for someone who wanted to hire a professional driver—the detectives talked Private Anyule into the rented truck. They took him to the local jail and had him locked in a cell overnight.

Anyule was confused and outraged. "I am a campaigner for His Excellency, Yoweri Museveni!" he protested, rattling the bars of his cell. He was sixty-eight years old, an aged and respected man, a hajji. This was all very undignified. He was hungry and his clothes were dirty. He wasn't even wearing any underwear.

The private detectives told him someone in Kampala, someone important, wanted to talk to him. Something about a car—there might be a job in it for him.

The skeletal remains of Mohammed Anyule's house in Yumbe (a relative stands in the foreground) ANDREW RICE

"It seems you are intelligence officers," Anyule said, resignedly. Then he went to sleep.

At dawn the next morning, the detectives loaded Anyule into the pickup truck, took him to Arua, and brought him on a small commuter plane back to Kampala. Before they boarded, Orijabo bought the old man a soda and tried to put him at ease. He sat next to him on the flight and engaged him in friendly conversation. He had nothing to fear, the detective said. They were kinsmen, brothers.

Duncan was waiting at the airport when the plane touched down. Anyule climbed into the back of his car, along with the rest of the party, and they drove to the police station. The mood was oddly cordial. The suspect and the son made small talk in Swahili. Anyule was not in handcuffs. He still wasn't sure why he'd been brought to Kampala.

At the police station, the corporal escorted Anyule into his boss's office for interrogation. The atmosphere was informal. The private detectives and Duncan were allowed to sit in. Duncan could barely believe what was unfolding, that this man was here before him. The detective superintendent asked Anyule a few preliminary questions in Swahili, the only language both he and the suspect understood. Then he told the former army driver that they were looking for a Volkswagen Beetle with the license plate number UYO-010. Anyule snapped, a little too quickly, that he'd never owned a Volkswagen. He stuck to his story under questioning.

The private detectives eventually persuaded the police to let them talk to Anyule. Few cops spoke Lugbara, an obscure language, and the detectives had managed to develop a rapport with the suspect. They brought Anyule a change of clothes and underwear and took him to lunch in the station canteen. They told him the police would probably treat him as a cooperating witness if he confessed.

Anyule confided in them as tribesmen. "I am a hajji," he said. His conscience was clean. He said he was only the driver.

Orijabo had a tape recorder running.

"Tell us the whole truth of how these things happened from the start," the detective said.

"I will not tell you a lie, in the name of God," Anyule replied. "I have never killed a person." At the time of Amin's coup, Anyule confessed, he was a private in the army, stationed at the barracks in the western town of Mbarara. "I was recruited into the intelligence service," he said. "I would drive the intelligence officers to do their work." Sometimes he would ferry a condemned man to a secluded place for execution, he said, but he swore he'd never pulled the trigger himself. He had tried his best to uphold his high moral standards. "I always say it is not good to kill a human being," Anyule told the private detectives. "I say people should be taken to court."

On the morning of September 22, 1972, Anyule recounted, he was at the Mbarara barracks when a sergeant in the intelligence service summoned him. "He was called Nasur Gille," he said. "He was a ruthless person." The sergeant told the driver that they'd been ordered to pick up a county chief. "I did not know that man," Anyule maintained. "It was Nasur who knew him." According to Sergeant Gille, informers from the area had identified this chief as a rebel collaborator.

Anyule said he, the sergeant, and a local informant crammed themselves into his small car and drove forty miles north to the town of Ibanda. They found the chief in his office. They told him he was wanted for questioning at the barracks. The chief went without protest, driving his own Volkswagen Beetle. The sergeant sat beside him in the passenger seat, holding a submachine gun. The two cars traveled in tandem back toward Mbarara. About halfway there, at the edge of a cattle ranch, the Volkswagen pulled to the side of the road. It was a secluded place. There was no one in sight. The sergeant ordered the chief out of the car and walked him through the underbrush at gunpoint. Anyule got out of his car and followed them.

The chief put up no resistance. In front of an immense anthill, the sergeant told him to stop and lie facedown in the tall grass.

"Nasur was always telling me to kill, and I always refused," Anyule recalled. This time, pulling rank, the sergeant insisted. "He gave me the gun and I tried to shoot it. But the bullet did not come out." The gun had jammed. "God must have made it happen," Anyule continued. "Nasur told the man to move forward. He shot him in the head, dead."

Anyule claimed that he had only come into possession of the chief's Volkswagen months after the killing. It had been sitting around the barracks, rusting, he said, and an officer had given it to him as a gift, a reward for a job well done. He'd repainted it light blue and driven it as if it was his own, even going so far as to reregister the car in his own name. But then it had broken down and Anyule hadn't seen it since he fled into exile.

"I am pleased with the way you have treated me," Anyule told the detectives. "You buy me food and clothes and you come to console

me." Now, he believed, they could see the whole matter was just a mis-
understanding. The man they were looking for, the real killer, was
Sergeant Nasur Gille. He could be found in Arua. "He repairs bicycles
under a *minikini* tree," Anyule told the detectives. "He has large ears and
a curved back."

After the conversation was over, the private investigators escorted
Anyule back to the detective superintendent's office. Duncan was there.
Anyule told the police he was willing to testify against Nasur Gille at
trial in return for leniency. He repeated the whole story. A profound
sense of relief came over Duncan as he listened: finally, some answers.

At some point, someone told Anyule that Duncan was actually the
dead chief's son. He was shocked. Duncan seemed so cool, so lacking in
animosity. But then again, the hajji told the detectives, he really should
have known. Duncan looked just like his father.

The detectives found Nasur Gille exactly where his old driver said he'd
be, at the base of a gnarled fig tree, just past a sewage ditch, amid the
reed stalls of Arua's town market. He was sitting on his box of bicycle
repair tools, drinking tea from a cheap tin cup, when the police surrounded him. Orijabo asked the local cops not to handcuff the suspect,
and he walked next to him on the way to the police station, explaining
the charges as they went. When Orijabo told him he was suspected of
killing someone in 1972, the detective later recalled, Sergeant Gille just
laughed and said, "Which one?"

It didn't take long before Sergeant Gille's relatives heard he was
arrested, and that night they surrounded the police station, shouting
for his release. Many in Arua thought Gille was the victim of unjust per-
secution. His crime was having served in Amin's army, they believed,
and belonging to the wrong tribe. The next morning, to avoid a riot,
the police bundled the sergeant into the back of a pickup truck, rushed
him to the Arua airfield, and put him on a plane to Kampala.

Once again, Duncan picked the suspect up at the airport. He hadn't
felt scared escorting Mohammed Anyule to the police station; the hajji
seemed like a harmless fool. Gille, by contrast, was a chilling presence.
He was a decade younger than Anyule, sinewy and strong, with cal-
loused hands and yellowish, snaggled teeth. But it wasn't just the way
he looked. It was how he carried himself, cavalier and remorseless.

Within the army, Gille had been famed for his precision as a marks-
man. He'd once competed in an international shooting competition

Nasur Gille at work in Arua

in Ghana. He'd been a bodyguard to a high-ranking officer, another Lugbara, at the time of Amin's coup. After that, he'd been recruited into the intelligence service. In 1979, he'd fled to Sudan, but he'd come back after Museveni took power. He'd been pleading for years for his army pension, and shortly before his arrest, the government had finally granted him about one thousand dollars, which he'd used to purchase a modest farm.

Alfred Orijabo interrogated the suspect at the police station. At first, he was uncooperative.

"Who told you these things?" the sergeant yelled.

Then Gille tried to tell the private detective that two other soldiers—he claimed to remember only their first names, "Charles" and "William"—had been responsible for the chief's execution. The suspect said he was feeling feverish.

Orijabo offered to buy him some aspirin. Anyule had already confessed to everything, the detective told him. He talked of an immunity deal in return for a confession that implicated his higher-ups. Orijabo may or may not have made some promises and threats—later on, this would become a significant point of contention.

Eventually, Gille broke down. He told the detective he was just following orders. "In fact, the thing is, we were summoned," the suspect said. "They wanted us, the intelligence officers, to come. So we went to see the Big Man at the Lake View Hotel. . . . He said rebels had entered with their collaborators. He gave orders to the intelligence officers, saying we should go out into the field. He gave us a long list of people. We went to pick up that man with Anyule. We picked him up and killed him, as we were ordered to do."

Afterward, Gille confessed, he had driven Laki's Volkswagen Beetle back to the barracks, as "proof" that the chief was dead.

"We went to park it in the Big Man's yard," the suspect said.

"Who was this Big Man?" the detective asked.

"Gowon," Gille replied. "It was Gowon himself who sent us."

4

THE BIG MAN

At dawn on Tuesday, April 24, 2001, the morning call to prayer rang out from a green-trimmed hilltop mosque in the Kampala suburb of Ntinda. The muezzin's warbling voice, amplified by a tinny loudspeaker, echoed across the valley, and off the rusted sheet-metal roof of a small brick house. Yusuf Gowon awoke to the clangor of the stirring morning. Roosters crowed, hammers hit metal, the conductors of passing minibuses shouted their destinations: "Nakawa . . . Kampala Road . . . Nakawa . . . Kampala Road." As the sun rose in the sky, soft light seeped through the cracks in Gowon's splintery wooden shutters, illuminating the fine dust that hung in the air.

Ntinda was a fashionable suburb, home to many high government officials. One of its planned communities was known as the "ministers' village." But Gowon's residence was several notches below the norm in grandeur: a collection of low-slung buildings constructed around a muddy courtyard in haphazard fashion, as if from ill-matched spare parts. The main house's cramped sitting room, where Gowon spent his mornings, was decorated with tattered signs bearing devotional sayings (THE QUR'AN HAS THE ANSWER) and pages from old newspapers, pasted up like cheap wallpaper. Via a doorway covered by a thin white curtain, the room adjoined his son's bicycle shop, which brought a little money into the house. Gowon needed it. He was nearing sixty-five, a *mzee*, or elder, as they say in Swahili. But his compound was filled with a plentiful and ever-shifting cast of dependants. He had twenty-eight children by four different wives and twenty-two grandchildren.

Gowon dressed and readied himself for the day. He planned to go downtown to make his rounds, calling on old friends to cajole scraps of business. He would walk there, as usual. It had been a long time since he had owned a car.

It was one of those ironies of African politics that back when he was young and vigorous, Gowon had never been forced to tax his feet. He'd commanded a whole fleet of Land Rovers and Mercedes-Benzes. Little Ugandan flags had fluttered from their fenders. In those days, he'd been Major General Gowon, the chief of staff of the Ugandan army, which had made him the second-most-powerful man in the country after President Idi Amin. Now, two decades later, Gowon was a private citizen, and he had to hoof it everywhere. Men who'd known him in his majestic days could hardly believe the old general's deflated circumstances. Even his former boss had poked fun from exile in Saudi Arabia. "I hear Gowon, a whole major general, walks from his house in Ntinda to town and has no car," Amin chortled to a Ugandan newspaper interviewer in 1995.

Gowon didn't let the jibes bother him. He was cheerful by disposition, with a ready smile and playful almond-shaped eyes. He told his friends he liked the exercise. He needed to lose weight. With age, his belly had expanded to spill out far over his belt.

Gowon walked outside and headed toward the intermittently paved road that skirted the left side of his property. Almost as soon as he was out the door, a Toyota sedan pulled up alongside him. The passenger-side door opened, and a short young man bounded out of the car. Gowon stuck out his hand in greeting. The young man clasped it with two hands, a traditional gesture of respect, and shook it vigorously.

"*Mzee*, excuse me," the young man said, and introduced himself, saying his name was Brian Tibo. He worked as a private investigator. He said they had met once a few years before, through a mutual friend. They came from the same northern province.

Gowon apologized for not recognizing him.

"Where are you going?" Tibo asked.

Gowon said he was walking to town.

"Mind if I give you a lift?"

Gowon didn't mind. He wasn't one to pass up a free ride. So he thanked the polite young man and hopped in. The Toyota took off.

Before long, Gowon noticed that the car wasn't heading toward his destination, a nearby market. He thought that a bit strange. But he assumed his new friend must have some errand to run. Tibo was whispering into his cell phone.

Gowon didn't make a stink about it. At his age, he was seldom in any great hurry.

The car pulled up before a fenced-in official building not far from Uganda's parliament. Gowon didn't know where he was. "Why are you taking me here?" he asked.

The building was a police station. Tibo explained that the cops wanted him, just to talk. "You are a Big Man," he said. "You have a lot of wisdom."

Still confused, Gowon followed the young man into the building. He led Gowon into the basement office of the detective superintendent in charge of the police force's serious crimes squad. There were several other men sitting in the small room when he arrived: a couple of officers, another private investigator, and a lawyer named Duncan Laki. The detective superintendent said he and Gowon needed to talk alone.

Gowon assumed that the policeman wanted to discuss his philanthropic work. Since he had returned from exile in Congo in 1994, amid great fanfare, the old general had become a self-appointed advocate for peace, and was engaged in retraining former rebels in useful occupations. He'd worked with a Quaker group called the Alternatives to Violence Project. He was a political supporter of President Yoweri Museveni and had campaigned for his reelection.

After some initial pleasantries, however, the detective superintendent began asking Gowon odd questions. He wanted to know about his army days. About a rebel attack on the military barracks in Mbarara, a western town, back in 1972, when he was just a major. About a county chief named Eliphaz Laki.

Laki had disappeared shortly after the rebel attack, along with his car, the policeman told Gowon. Two men had recently been arrested for his murder. They had confessed. The man who ordered Laki killed, they claimed, was the second-in-command of the Mbarara barracks at the time of the attack, one Major Yusuf Gowon.

Gowon admitted that in 1972 he had been a major and stationed at the army battalion in Mbarara. But he had never heard of anyone named Laki, he said, and he knew nothing about a killing. These two men who'd accused him, a private and a sergeant, they were just *takataka*, riffraff. They would never have interacted with a high-ranking officer.

The policeman informed Gowon he was under arrest for murder. Gowon protested: President Museveni himself had invited him back to Uganda under an amnesty! He had the documents to prove it! The policeman told the general that he had looked into the legal details of the matter, and the immunity deal did not cover crimes committed before 1986, when Museveni had taken power.

Major General Gowon was ushered into another room at the police station, where he was allowed to give a statement. "I never gave an operational order to Nasur Gille and Mohammed Anyule to go and kill anybody in Mbarara," he told the officer who recorded it. At the bottom of the page, Gowon added a capitalized postscript in his own loopy handwriting: "I KNOW NOTHING ABOUT THE MURDER OF ELIPHAZ LAKI."

PART 2

5

DECENT REST

The Nile Hotel, Idi Amin's favorite spot in Kampala, stood on spacious grounds along a tree-lined avenue in the center of the capital, alongside a connected conference center, a hexagonal slab of port-holed concrete designed and built by Yugoslavs. Amin presided over the completion of the hotel complex, a feat he considered to be among his greatest accomplishments. He was so proud that he sometimes claimed he'd been born on the site, where a barracks had once stood. (That was just one of several conflicting accounts Amin gave of his birth.) The Nile Hotel was the place where the dictator would fete visiting heads of state. It was the scene of many of his audacious publicity stunts. The hotel's expansive lawn was also where Uganda's Anglican archbishop, the Reverend Janan Luwum, was tried on trumped-up charges of arms smuggling in 1977, before a horde of thousands of soldiers chanting, "Kill!" Amin kept a hideaway office and private living quarters on the hotel's second floor. Several other suites—room 305, room 311, room 320, room 326—doubled as torture chambers.

The Nile Hotel survived Amin's fall and the wars that followed it, but it never quite shook its dark associations. At the time I lived in Uganda, most locals avoided the place, though its outdoor bar still attracted a meager clientele of soldiers, intelligence agents and other shadowy types, who appreciated the atmosphere of faded menace. In 2004, an international luxury hotel chain bought the property and announced plans to renovate it, adding amenities such as a pool and a twenty-three-foot waterfall. While excavating the basement, a local newspaper reported, construction workers unearthed three skeletons. The new owners rushed to hush up the story, but Ugandans thought they discerned a glint of truth. The Nile Hotel could be remade and renamed, but its past would not stay buried.

There were many places like that in Uganda. If you followed one major highway eastward out of Kampala, you reached a borderline where the unruly sprawl of the city dissipated, giving way to farm plots and banana groves. There was a Coca-Cola bottling factory on one side of the road, and on the other, a field covered with flowery brush and populated by flitting yellow weaver birds. The area was called Namanve. During Idi Amin's time, all of Namanve had been a dense forest and one of the military's favorite corpse-dumping grounds. The local villagers had done a lucrative business as professional body find-ers, charging fees of hundreds or even thousands of dollars to the searching families of the disappeared. Right after Amin fell, there was a plan to turn Namanve into a national cemetery. "Every family which lost [a] member will be able to put a date and inscription on [a] grave in memory of their dead," Uganda's transitional president declared in 1979. "We do not like Ugandans to forget these things." But that president was quickly overthrown, and the initiative never came to anything. The forest was cleared. In the 1990s, Yoweri Museveni's gov-ernment announced plans to develop the site as an industrial park. But as much as Uganda tried to focus on progress, the bones kept turning up, from beneath farm fields and building sites and new roadbeds, the unidentifiable remnants of untold vanished souls.

Duncan Laki had heard all the stories about these discarded remains. He wanted a more dignified ending for his father. With the apprehen-sion of Mohammed Anyule and Nasur Gille in April 2001, he glimpsed a tantalizing opportunity to discover the answer to the question he'd been asking for most of his life: Where was Eliphaz Laki?

The two former soldiers had given nearly identical accounts of the killing. Neither of them showed much remorse. They were just soldiers, there was a war on, these things happen, they told the police. The two suspects said they'd shot the chief in a cattle pasture not far off a high-way. They hadn't touched the body or even covered it with underbrush, which outraged Duncan almost as much as the murder itself. "This was a person," he said. "You don't even get a banana leaf and cover him?" But initially, Duncan had to tamp down his anger and even feign gratitude toward the men who'd confessed to killing his father. Their very shame-lessness meant they were valuable to Duncan, because both suspects made it clear that if he asked the right way, if there was some leniency in it for them, they might be willing to help him find Eliphaz Laki's body.

Duncan and the police both needed to locate the chief's remains, though for different reasons. The police needed evidence. At this juncture, the prosecution was principally focused on building a case against the highest-ranking defendant, Major General Gowon, who was seeking bail and talking to lawyers and appealing to influential friends in the government, claiming that the charges against him were supported by little substantiation other than the word of a couple of self-interested criminals. If Gowon's prosecution was to move forward, it was essential to recover the body of his alleged victim. In the interest of assuring their assistance in recovering Laki's body and their willing testimony at trial, the police and the prosecutor's office considered the possibility of dropping the charges against Gille and—in particular—Anyule. What the authorities actually told the retired soldiers is a matter of dispute, but it is clear that the two suspects believed that they were being treated as cooperating witnesses. Through the spring of 2001, they guided Duncan on a series of strange pilgrimages to the scene of his father's death.

Anyule was Duncan's companion on the first trip. They drove out west in a police pickup truck, with a couple of detectives in tow. Duncan was eager to see Gowon prosecuted, but gathering evidence was not his primary motivation. Most of all, he wanted to bring his father back home to Ndeija, to give him the decent rest his family so desired. A convivial atmosphere prevailed on the trip. Anyule acted like an enthusiastic participant in the investigation. Though he was still officially a prisoner, he was not handcuffed and was even allowed to stay at the home of some relations in Mbarara, without police supervision. Duncan bought all of his meals.

On that trip Anyule retraced his steps. He took Duncan to the county headquarters in Ibanda, where a pair of elderly men—the last living witnesses to Eliphaz Laki's arrest—identified Anyule as the man who had escorted the chief out of his office back in 1972. Then they drove toward Mbarara, following the same route Eliphaz Laki had taken to his death. Along the way, Anyule told them to pull over at several promising spots, none of which proved to be the right one. Finally, at an abrupt twist where the road rounded the foot of a hill called Nyampike, he said, "I think this is the place."

They got out of the police pickup and walked into a pasture, a quiet corner of a vast cattle ranch. Duncan knew the place—it had once belonged to a man named Rwakanuma, another chief from the 1960s era, and since his recent death the land had passed to his children. To Anyule, however, it was just an anonymous patch of grass. The former army driver was an outsider to Ankole. On the day of Laki's killing, he'd relied on a local informant, a man named Salim Sebi, to guide him to Ibanda and back. Maybe Sebi had picked the pasture, but Anyule couldn't remember, and he could not pinpoint the exact spot where Laki had been killed. He was pushing seventy, after all.

Frustrated, the search party returned to Kampala. Eleven days later, Duncan and the investigators returned to Ankole with Nasur Gille, the triggerman. He turned out to be an ideal witness—he recalled even small details with unsettling clarity. Calmly, methodically, Gille reenacted the crime, leading Duncan to the precise place where he'd shot the chief: just past a trench, next to an anthill. There was no immediate sign of Laki's remains, which was not surprising after such a long time. Maybe someone had taken it upon himself to bury the corpse, Duncan thought, though if that was the case, he had to wonder why no one had ever informed his family of the grave's location. Eliphaz Laki, after all, had been a well-known figure in his day. Duncan pushed that riddle out of his mind, however, and began making preparations for an exhumation.

Even as he did so, however, Duncan had to contend with opposition from an unexpected quarter: his own family. One evening, he was visiting the home of an Anglican minister, a friend of his father's, when his cell phone rang. It was his older sister Justine, calling from her home in America. She'd heard about what her brother was doing. She was not comforted at all by his discoveries, and questioned the whole venture. "Don't you think this is dangerous?" she asked him. "Don't you think these people have their own sons?"

The disappearances of the 1970s had scarred an entire Ugandan generation. Children had been robbed of their fathers; families had been ripped apart. Some Ugandans had responded by descending into depression or alcoholism; some had retreated into a cocoon of passive defiance; some had taken up arms to seek revenge; some families had simply dispersed into exile. The Laki family had been fortunate, relatively speaking. They'd survived, gone to universities, done well. Many of them now lived abroad, scattered across Africa, Europe and North America. They kept in fairly close contact, however, and Duncan's decision to investigate their father's disappearance had caused a wrenching dispute among them, carried out in e-mails and international phone calls.

"Some of them were outraged—negative," Duncan said. "You see, during Amin's time, it was terror. I mean *terror*." His mother had never allowed the children to discuss their father's disappearance. "It was as if even the household help was probably planted" by the secret police, Duncan explained. "And so I think it became a tradition, something we grew up with, never to talk about those things."

In 2005, long after the trial had ended, I met Duncan's sister Justine at her white clapboard home in Barrington, Illinois, a Chicago suburb. "We didn't all agree that we should start the whole thing," she told me. "We didn't know how far it would go." Justine, a short-haired, slender, circumspect woman who works as a geriatric nurse, showed me a picture of her grown son, who still resided back in Kampala. This child, she seemed to be telling me, mattered more than any personal quest for justice.

Justine was ten years older than Duncan, and the disappearance of her father had shaped her life differently. In September 1972, Duncan was just a boy and somewhat sheltered from the reality of Amin's Uganda. Justine, in her third year of nursing school in Kampala, realized how afraid she should be. After she heard the soldiers had taken her father, Justine tried to continue with her studies as if nothing had happened, but she found herself paralyzed by unspeakable grief. When the concerned headmaster asked her what was going on, Justine told him, but she swore him to secrecy. At that point, fairly early on in his regime, Amin was still popular with many Ugandans, including her classmates. "I only mentioned it to three people," Justine said, "because I knew the reaction would be: 'He deserved it.'"

"There was no peace at home," said Joyce Laki, another of Duncan's older siblings, "because everyone was so sad about Dad." A soft-spoken woman in her fifties, Joyce, like her sister Justine, now works as a nurse in the Chicago area. "There are times when you find yourself as if you are in the middle of an ocean, in a boat," Joyce reflected. "The waves are coming from this side and that side, and you have to be in the middle, waiting for whatever takes place."

Duncan's older brother, Dennis, had his own way of coping: He decided to make himself strong. In the 1980s, he graduated from Makerere University and joined the Ugandan military, which was then fighting a civil war against Museveni's rebels. After the government fell, his professional reputation allowed him to make a smooth transition into Museveni's reconstituted national army as an artillery specialist, and he eventually rose to the rank of colonel. Some in the family questioned his choice of such a rough vocation. "People always say, that guy, he joined because he wanted revenge, but it wasn't that," Dennis said. He saw himself as a pragmatist, trying to change the country's most powerful institution from within. "If I study Shakespearean literature, will that transform society? I say no," he said. "You have to have a stake in the power base. These things showed us that education is not enough. That is what I realized at an early age."

Dennis said that when he'd heard that his younger brother had found the name of some army private in the registration file, he'd called Duncan to ask why he was following the trail of clues. He didn't trust the legal system the way Duncan did, and he could even feel some sympathy for the men who'd been arrested for his father's murder. He didn't think they could really be held responsible. "I've got no problem with Gowon," Dennis said. "Me, I know what he was thinking, because I know what soldiers do. He wanted to please his boss."

Among the Laki children, only Joyce strongly supported Duncan's efforts to investigate their father's disappearance and to find his body. "It was tug of war," she said. "My brother was in a struggle. In the family, he was alone." But Joyce thought their father would have approved. She remembered that once, when one of Laki's own uncles drowned, he'd scoured the river for the body, long past the point of hope. If he could just find an arm, a bone, Eliphaz had told his daughter, he could bury it and rest.

Justine, like most of the other siblings, saw things differently. Her mother's dying instructions had been to leave the past alone, and now that she had a child of her own, she was convinced that this was the wise course to take. "Maybe she thought it was a hopeless case," Justine said of her mother. Then she reconsidered: "Not that it was hopeless, but that it would bring us bad memories, bring us tears. And besides, we couldn't trust anyone. I think she was protecting the boys, protecting the family. If you're trying to figure out who killed your father, the people who are suspects, eventually they will get to you, and they will kill you. My mother didn't want us to go through that. And I supported her, because it's a small world."

Duncan ignored his sister's warnings, though, and kept pressing forward with his search. He went to visit the owners of the ranch identified as

Joyce Laki with her father's portrait ANDREW RICE

the site of Eliphaz Laki's execution. He was slightly acquainted with the family. Yonasani Rwakanuma, who had died just the year before, had been a colleague of his father's from the provincial government, and all the children of Ankole's elite knew one another. Duncan was surprised, therefore, that when he informed them about the details of his father's death, they were initially hostile and defensive. They knew nothing about a killing on their property. Eventually, the Rwakanuma family understood that Duncan wasn't making an accusation, and invited him to keep looking for his father's grave on their land. But no one remembered anything about a body turning up in the pasture Nasur Gille had pinpointed, which was curious. It didn't seem like the sort of occurrence easily forgotten.

For his part, Gille was certain that he'd correctly identified the spot where he'd shot Eliphaz Laki. The former army intelligence officer prided himself on his remarkable memory. Once, when Duncan said something about his father having been shot in the head, Gille had corrected him: No, he'd shot Laki at the place where his neck met his shoulder blades. The sergeant had fixed the spot of the killing easily, because he remembered that around that same time, some rebels had been massacred on a hill across the way. Maybe animals had eaten the body, he suggested.

The police were ready to accept that explanation, but Duncan couldn't. The pasture was out of the way, but not so isolated that people never passed through it. A corpse, even picked clean to the bone by hyenas, wouldn't have just vanished. One of Duncan's uncles had searched along the road that ran past the ranch back in 1972, looking in every pond and stream for a floating corpse, asking the local cattle herders to be on the lookout for the missing chief. Duncan was certain: Someone had buried his father's body somewhere in that field. He dug more holes, but none of them yielded a trace of resolution.

April passed, then May and June. The news of Duncan's investigation and Yusuf Gowon's arrest broke in the local newspapers. As the details of what Duncan had learned and where his search had taken him became public, a nervous shudder went through Ankole. It wasn't so much the identities of the suspects that worried people: Yusuf Gowon and his ilk had no power anymore, and as angry as his tribesmen might be, they lived in a faraway region of the country. They no longer had the reach to hurt people in Ankole. What caused the disquiet, then, was not a few old soldiers, but a sinister sense that more intimate enemies existed, agents of harm who remained unrevealed. Everyone in Ankole knew that many collaborators had worked with Amin's regime, some publicly and some furtively. It was rumored that some of those who were complicit were influential figures, people with connections to the present government and the military—with the power, perhaps, to suppress any inquiry that strayed from the straightforward issue of Eliphaz Laki's whereabouts and broached the more threatening question: Why did he disappear?

This question was so laced with intrigue that whenever I broached it, in my many conversations with people who'd known the missing chief, a pall inevitably fell over the conversation. The subject inspired palpable fear. I saw it in the face of an old colleague of Laki's from the local government, who'd later become a university dean, who swore that he could tell me nothing. "All that I know," he said, "is that I am probably alive because I wasn't interested in politics in Ankole." I heard it in the voice of an eminent former officeholder, white-haired and half-deaf, who turned cold and inhospitable when he realized what I wanted to know, seeing me out of his house with the words, "They are all murderers."

"I don't want to create another situation. Some of these things are terrible," said a friend of Laki's, a man who proudly displayed on his wall framed pictures of independence era heroes like Patrice Lumumba. He carefully maneuvered around the question: "We've reconciled. All these things, we are calling them a past chapter. . . . At one time the president of Kenya, Jomo Kenyatta, said, 'We are forgiving but we are not forgetting.' That's us. We forgive, but we will not forget."

The reality—the almost unspoken truth—was that everyone in Ankole assumed Eliphaz Laki had been done in by something more than a mere gunshot. *Betrayed* was the word his family always used. But Laki had not known the soldiers who had taken him away, and familiarity is a necessary ingredient to betrayal. We are betrayed by those we know the best: the ones we love, the ones we trust. Our neighbors, our friends.

To understand why Laki had died, one had to understand how he had lived. In fact, the events that led to the chief's death had followed seamlessly from the work of his life: politics. A rift divided the west of Uganda, an ethnic split. In the years after independence, it had opened wide, and it had swallowed men and their ideals. Idi Amin had killed Eliphaz Laki, but other forces, nearer forces, had determined his fate.

6

THE BRIGHTEST STAR

On July 1, 1891, on a rough patch of scrubland cleared especially for the purpose of a summit, a slight, walrus-mustachioed British army captain met a robed emissary of the African kingdom of Ankole and formed a bond of blood brotherhood. In keeping with the local custom, they pricked their stomachs with knives and ate blood-soaked coffee berries out of each other's palms. Having ritually established their friendship, the captain presented the representative of the king, Ntare V, with a treaty, as well as the flag of his employer, the imperial British East Africa Company, and a gift of some colorful textiles. "We had a very long talk, and all the usual protestations were made, that all his country and everything he possessed were now mine, &c. They were most intelligent men," the captain wrote in his diary afterward. "If I appear liberal in my presents . . . it is because I know there is a quid pro quo. Ankole is a *huge* country, annexed by a present of a load of cloth!"

The captain's name was Frederick Lugard, and he was most assuredly a man of his era, when almost by accident, Britain built an African empire. He was thirty-three years old, the son of missionaries to India and a veteran of military campaigns in Afghanistan and Sudan. Five years before, he'd had his heart broken by an alluring divorcee, and in keeping with what one biographer calls "the odd, but generally accepted, convention of contemporary fiction that rejected suitors should go to Africa," he'd set off for the territory of Nyasaland, where he'd been seriously wounded in a battle with Arab slavers. In 1889, he'd been hired by the British East Africa Company, a quasi-governmental entity, to extend its dominion over the unexplored environs around Lake Victoria. The mission originated more from a sense of imperial competition with Germany and France, which had lately been making incursions, than out of any financial interest or strategic plan. Captain Lugard appeared just the sort of man to perform it: a cold, resourceful, orderly officer, utterly convinced of his nation's right to rule the world.

Captain Lugard and his small contingent of British officers moved through the interior over crude footpaths. Behind them, their porters carried an immense quantity of trade goods such as beads and cloth, as well as a wheeled precursor of the machine gun called the Maxim. Though better armed than the natives, Lugard's men were terrifically vulnerable, both to attack and to diseases like malaria, which killed many nineteenth-century European visitors within months of their arrivals in Africa. Years later, after a long career in the British colonial service, Lugard—by then Lord Lugard—would write that the practical application of "indirect rule," a theory that he codified and popularized, was born in Uganda. Indirect rule sought to extend Britain's influence by enticing African kings and chieftains to become partners in their own subjugation. The reward Captain Lugard offered King Ntare of Ankole was really much more than a load of cloth. It was the promise of British recognition, British goods and—most importantly—British guns. The consequences of the deal forged in blood that day in 1891 would be felt for decades, shaping generations, creating the riven world into which Eliphaz Laki was born.

One of the first things Lugard noticed when his expedition marched into Ankole was that there was a division among the inhabitants of the western kingdom. The people, known collectively as the Banyankole, were split into two ethnic subgroups. They spoke the same language and shared the same land, but they dressed differently, practiced different customs, believed in different gods and did different kinds of work. The king's ethnic group, the Bahima, was made up of nomadic cattle-keepers who dressed in cured calfskins and measured their wealth by the sizes of their herds. The royal court, a collection of beehive-shaped grass huts, was centered on a paddock where the king lived with multiple wives and many hundreds of stately longhorn cattle. The Bahima people shunned meat and vegetables and survived by drinking the milk and blood of their animals. Perhaps because of this diet they had a distinctive physical appearance: "Tall, thin and lithe, with high foreheads and most intelligent faces," Lugard later wrote. "The eyes piercing, the features sharp, the nose often aquiline." The Bahima made up a minority of the population, however. The vast majority of the Banyankole were members of another ethnic subgroup, the Bairu, who worked the land as farmers. But coming from his own hierarchical society, infused with notions of racial superiority and social Darwinism, Captain Lugard looked at the Bahima and saw a ruling class. In his diary, he dismissed the agriculturalists as "extraneous races."

After signing the treaty, Lugard marched on to the north, toward Ibanda, a mountainous area that was ruled by an obese enchantress, whose power stemmed from her reputed ability to metamorphose into a cow. "Here we found a huge plateau covered with beautiful grass, and cultivation and villages," the captain recorded. "The soil was very good, and two rills of beautifully clear water flowed along the top and descended into a gorge. The men were saying to themselves that here was the place to build another Kampala!" But it was at this juncture of his exploration that Captain Lugard first encountered the unwitting victims of his alliance. The people in this area were Bairu, not Bahima. They considered themselves enemies of the kingdom Britain had allied itself with, Lugard later wrote in his memoir, *The Rise of Our East African Empire*.

"My appearance caused a great alarm. The warriors rushed for their spears and shields, and began to collect for war—others drove off the goats, and the women fled," Lugard recounted. The captain invoked the name of King Ntare, saying that the two of them had made a pact of friendship, but assured the alarmed people that "even at his wish I would attack no one, till I had heard the rights of the story: certainly then we should not do it for any lesser man, for we British were men of peace. . . . Nor were we merely passing travelers, but we had come to arrange the country, and to build and settle in it." Lugard's words did nothing to calm the agitated Bairu, however. "In spite of my assurances," he wrote, "the foolish people, seeing the size of the caravan, ran away."

Lugard had no idea what was going on, because he didn't understand the complexities of the social arrangement he'd stumbled into, which had no corollary in his European experience. There was really no such thing as a "Banyankole" identity, at least not before Lugard arrived; this anthropological notion of "tribe" was something the British applied inflexibly everywhere in Africa, often for reasons that suited little besides their political objectives. There were in fact people who considered themselves to be Bairu or Bahima, but even these classifications were fluid—they could change from generation to generation. An individual could alter his ethnicity by marrying outside his group, or even by moving, the same way someone born in Iowa can become a New Yorker. Lugard called Ankole's ruler a "king," and his Bahima people an elite, but he'd actually happened into a far more ambiguous system of governance. It was true that the Bahima exercised some degree of social control over the agriculturalist Bairu—the word *bairu* translates roughly as "serfs"—but it was a weak form of dominance. Those Bairu who opposed the king could move to one of the many areas of the west where he exercised no real control. With the coming of British rule, however, the situation was about to change. Lugard and his successors would turn their misinterpretations into realities.

Captain Lugard left Ankole a few days after his encounter with the farmers, continuing on his journey north toward the Great Lakes and the Mountains of the Moon in search of his ultimate quarry, a garrison of Sudanese soldiers who'd been trained and then abandoned by an eccentric German doctor. He hoped to muster them into a native army. (That's another story—Yusuf Gowon's.) Back in Ankole, meanwhile, the appearance of the white man was beginning to seem like an evil portent. There was an outbreak of rinderpest, which had first reached Africa in 1887 along with a shipload of exotic cattle imported by Italian missionary priests. The disease devastated the Bahima's cattle herds. Then a human smallpox epidemic, perhaps brought by the foreign explorers, killed off many members of the royal clan. Finally, the king himself died. Into the leaderless chaos stepped a clever young chief, who realized quicker than most the lasting implications of the British arrival. He would become, as one historian put it, the "arch-collaborator."

His name was Nuwa Mbaguta, though he would be known to the people of Ankole simply by his noble title, the *enganzi*. The word, derived from traditional astrology, literally means "the brightest star near the moon." Within the royal court of Ankole the office was traditionally reserved for the king's designated favorite. Mbaguta, however, seized command of the kingdom by overseeing the installation of a fat, dimwitted teenager on the throne, which allowed him to exercise effective control. Through this arrangement, Mbaguta was able to dominate Ankole for more than four decades.

Only in his twenties himself, stout and powerfully built, Mbaguta had first made his reputation at tribal wrestling tournaments and later as a brave warrior in cattle raids against the neighboring people of Rwanda. As the king's chief minister, he vastly expanded and strengthened the kingdom. The introduction of advanced tools of coercion allowed Mbaguta to transform his domain into the very thing Captain Lugard had imagined it to be: a strong monarchy. From behind the throne, Mbaguta ruled like a haughty despot, consolidating the cattle-keepers' power over the Bairu.

There are many conflicting theories about the origins of Ankole's stratified society. The Bahima tell stories of a godlike line of kings who swept down from the north, ruled the land through magic and finally disappeared into a crater lake. One of these beings remained behind with the royal drum, it is said, to become the founder of the cattle-keepers' dynasty. Recent archaeological and linguistic research suggests that environmental factors, such as droughts, may have played a decisive role. But the best-known theory, even in Ankole today, is a bit of colonial-era crackpot anthropology. The first British visitors took a look at the Bahima's sharp features and relatively light skin and decided they must have originated from Ethiopia, making them members of a superior "Hamitic" race. At some time in the distant past, the hypothesis went, they'd migrated south and conquered the agriculturalists, primitives with dark skin and "Negroid" features.

This narrative, of course, comfortingly echoed Britain's colonizing project. One early colonial administrator called the Bahima "born gentlemen." In 1901, a decade after Captain Lugard's first visit, Mbaguta brokered an agreement with the British by which the lands of the west were absorbed into the newly formed Protectorate of Uganda, which also encompassed the neighboring kingdom of Buganda and a patchwork collection of other territories. Ankole was divided into counties overseen by chiefs appointed by Mbaguta. He and his allies were ceded huge land-grant estates, introducing a conception of individual land ownership previously unknown to the culture.

In the old days, there'd been some mobility within the social hierarchy. A brave warrior among the Bairu could be accepted into the chiefly class. Once the British came, however, the Hamitic myth was incorporated into local folklore, and the Bahima became firm believers in their own inherent superiority, while the agricultural people were seen as inferior beings. A social distinction hardened into an immutable difference of race. The Bahima, who viewed cultivating the land as dirty work, employed the Bairu as tenant farmers on their plantations, or as servants, who performed tasks such as cleaning out chamber pots. The Bairu's resentment showed through in their proverbs. "Befriend the Bahima," one went, "and they'll end up making you bury their dead."

Over time, as Mbaguta filled the ranks of chieftaincies with young Bahima who'd been educated at the new British mission schools, the colonial-era elite became alienated from the nomadic ways of their forbears. They wore Western suits, lived in houses furnished in the Victorian style and liked to sip brandy and play tennis. They hunted elephants for sport. They collected taxes and demonstrated beneficence through shows of charity.

In the early decades of the twentieth century, life didn't promise much for those born outside of this Bahima elite. Attaining literacy was unlikely and political influence was almost out of the question. But there were some fortuitous exceptions. Africans, then as now, had their own kind of social-welfare system. The chiefs sponsored schooling for promising children, with the expectation that these "pages" would be their devoted protégés, giving back "homage and gifts," one Ugandan political scientist wrote, "as from a loving son."

One day, sometime in the 1930s, a big red Studebaker passed through a swampy village called Ndeija. The car, the only one for miles around, belonged to a chief named Ernest Katungi, Mbaguta's son-in-law, and one of the most influential figures in the kingdom. Katungi was known for holding fairly progressive views on education, at least for that time. He paid for the school tuition of many bright Protestant boys, even members of the Bairu underclass. In Ndeija, someone pulled aside the chief's driver and pointed out a poor, fatherless fourteen-year-old. The child needed to learn to read—he was the smartest boy around. The driver said he could come and live at the chief's residence, miles away. And that was how Eliphaz Laki ended up going to school.

Born around 1920, Eliphaz Laki had never known his father, who had died within a few years of the boy's birth. He grew up something of an outcast. Tribal custom dictated that upon the death of his father, his paternal uncle was supposed to marry his mother, assuming responsibility for the family. But for some reason the remarriage didn't occur, and Laki's mother was left to fend for her family alone. She did the best she could, peddling millet, sorghum, beans, peanuts and fruit around the village of Ndeija. But to other villagers she was an unattached woman, an object of scorn. They ridiculed her, referring to her as the "widow"—a slur that combined overtones of both "useless" and "witch." They called her son Eliphaz an orphan.

Ndeija was a harsh place back then, before the swamp was drained. The valley was weedy and rife with mosquitoes. Laki's family lived in a round grass hut placed high on a hillside. As a child, he worked the fields and played the usual boyhood games, kicking a soccer ball made from wrapped banana fibers and pretending to hunt elephants with toy spears. At the time, young men from Ndeija typically grew up to be migrant laborers, working on the colonial tea and coffee plantations.

That would have been Laki's life, too, if not for the appearance of Ernest Katungi's red Studebaker. For several years, he lived with Katungi's driver in the servants' quarters at the chief's official residence, performing household chores and attending primary school. (At the time, when education was considered a rare privilege, it wasn't unusual to see a fourteen-year-old in a first-grade class.) To Laki, the chief must have seemed wealthy beyond imagination. He owned the car, for one thing. His cows, the traditional measure of income and status, numbered perhaps three hundred. Another boy who grew up in the chief's home, a lifelong friend of Laki's, said Katungi was a benevolent guardian who treated his wards "like his own children." But he was also aloof and

Mbarara, the cattle-keeping heart of Ankole
ANDREW RICE

old-fashioned. He would greet the lower-caste Bairu boys around the house with a tap of his walking stick, so as to avoid touching them with his hands. Bahima superstition held that Bairu skin was unclean.

After completing primary school and scoring well on his exams, Laki was admitted to Mbarara High School on a government scholarship. The school, founded in 1911 by Protestant missionaries, was the training ground for the kingdom's future leaders. Originally, that had meant the sons of the Bahima chiefs. But by the time Laki was a teenager, more Bairu were receiving educations. Agriculturalists vastly outnumbered the cattle-keepers in Ankole. In the 1930s, a census counted 224,000 Bairu and just 5,000 Bahima. And farming was suddenly far more profitable, due to economic changes. The colonial government had introduced cash crops to Ankole, distributing free coffee seedlings, for instance, along the main road through Ndeija. Some of the migrant workers who'd gone to work on the plantations to the east had returned with knowledge of commercial farming. Throughout Ankole, some Bairu had become rich landowners. They could afford to send their children to school.

Mbarara was the seat of Ankole's government, and as such the heart of the cattle-keepers' society. (Even today, a concrete statue of a long-horn bull stands at the entrance to the town.) Many of Laki's classmates were Bahima and disdainful of interlopers from the inferior ethnic group. But there were other scholarship students like him, and more important, a handful of sympathetic Bairu teachers. Laki and some of his classmates started a Bairu fraternity, with a name derived from a local proverb that went, roughly, "The children will grow up one day." In response, the Bahima students started their own exclusive group. They'd split up in the dining halls and conduct meetings after meals. "Laki was one of the leaders," recalled a classmate. "He was a man who didn't want to be despised. He said why do they despise us? We shall one day even beat them, because they are smaller in number."

Laki graduated from Mbarara High School with the equivalent of a ninth-grade education, about as much as he could have hoped for at the time. He attended a course in public health in Kampala and then took a job as a roving health inspector for the colonial government. He married and started a family. He became a familiar figure on the dirt roads of Ankole, which he traversed on his bicycle, always wearing a gray suit, a white shirt and a tie. A fastidious man, he taught the villagers the importance of hygiene, told them to build pit latrines and to dig wells instead of simply drawing water from impure natural springs.

Sometimes Laki traveled from town to town with an acting troupe, dramatizing the importance of cleanliness through plays.

Laki was part of a rising generation of Bairu teachers, reverends and civil servants. "Their clean oiled bicycles, their pressed khaki shorts, their coloured ties worn during Sunday service had made them heroes of the rural community," a western Ugandan novelist wrote. They were conscious of prejudice because they'd achieved some small measure of privilege. As they came of age, they began to demand an end to Ankole's system of institutionalized inequality.

It was not just in Ankole that things were changing. The Second World War was over. Many Bairu had come back from fighting for the British army in Eritrea and Burma. Anticolonial ideas were bubbling up in places like India. The very word *independence* had a contagious effect, which was spreading even to Uganda. Parties were forming, platforms were being drafted, new leaders were emerging.

In Ankole, resistance to the established governing arrangements started to manifest itself in 1946, when Laki's patron Ernest Katungi was nominated to be the new chief minister, the office that had been held for so long by his father-in-law Nuwa Mbaguta. Educated Bairu, now confident and assertive, mobilized to thwart the appointment when it came up for approval by a council of chiefs and the local British administrator. They began gathering for secret meetings at night. According to the traditional rules of patron and client, Laki owed obedience to the chief who had raised him. But he found his sympathies migrating instead to the leader of those night meetings, a fellow member of the Bairu. He was a tall, commanding man in a tweed jacket, a schoolteacher. In clipped sentences, he delivered lessons on the subjects of equality and usurpation.

Kesi Nganwa, the schoolteacher, liked to do things quietly. When he wasn't in class he wrote children's books in the vernacular, and they can be read as parables of his political style. The stories pitted his protagonist, Mr. Hare, against fearsome lions and hyenas, which he inevitably outmaneuvered through tricks and subterfuge. The weak could overcome the strong, Nganwa seemed to be saying, only if they were nimble and cunning.

Nganwa was the rare man of his generation and class who'd made it through the colony's prestigious Makerere University. He'd been singled out for advancement because he was a talented long-distance runner.

Nganwa had gone on to become an instructor at Mbarara High School, where he'd educated many members of the new Bairu elite. A subsequent job, as a supervisor of schools for the Native Anglican Church, gave him cover to pursue his true avocation: politics. He traveled to Ankole on his bicycle, recruiting followers into a clandestine nonviolent resistance movement. "He could look at you and see your talents," said one supporter, now in his mid-seventies. The movement was a secret shared among Laki's educated peers. Word from Nganwa was whispered from person to person, at funerals or wedding receptions or in meetings after church.

They called their organization *kumanyana*, or "getting to know one another." In the beginning, meetings took place at Nganwa's home, sometimes lasting late into the night. The men, many of whom had traveled long distances on their bicycles, would gather in his living room or outside among the livestock in his pasture. They'd slaughter a goat for dinner. Then they'd drink tea and talk. Nganwa peppered his conversation with traditional proverbs, in the manner of a tribal elder, but his overall message was a modern one: With democracy, the Bairu could take over Ankole.

Laki cut a striking figure at these meetings. Tall, thin and balding, he was a slow speaker, not hotheaded like some of the men. The others were impressed with his intelligence and political savvy. Laki, in turn, found fellowship among a group of ambitious young people who shared his views. Over time, their surreptitious bond deepened into close friendship. The men spent holidays at each other's houses. Their wives socialized, and their children played together. They went into businesses together. They made pacts of blood brotherhood. One of them was godfather to some of Laki's children.

Across the Empire, pressure for self-rule was building. In the neighboring province of Buganda, there were nationalist demonstrations and boycotts. Britain appointed a new, progressive-minded governor. When, in 1955, the position of chief minister of Ankole came open again, the colonial administrators decided to change the bargain they'd made with the Bahima nobles a half century before. The chief minister would no longer be picked by the king—with these reforms, he became largely a figurehead—and confirmed by the local British commissioner, but he'd instead be elected by a parliament representing the entire province, like a prime minister. The Bairu managed to attain a small majority in the parliament. As Ankole's new leader, they chose Nganwa.

The night of his election, Mbarara erupted in jubilation. The Bahima representatives walked out of parliament in protest and demanded an audience with the king. He told them he was helpless to change the election results. The animosity between the two ethnic groups, which had so far been confined to covert meetings and anonymous letters, suddenly burst into the open. Paranoid rumors circulated that Nganwa would be assassinated before he could take office, and his supporters met to make their own preparations, drawing up lists of prominent Bahima to be murdered in reprisal. In the end, however, tempers cooled and Nganwa was inaugurated without incident. The leader of the down-trodden was now the *enganzi*, the brightest star.

Kesi Nganwa's election marked a sharp turn in Ankole's politics. Many Bairu were appointed as chiefs and elevated within the civil service. A multitude of social programs were brought to fruition. Schools were built in Bairu areas, scholarship funds were set up for Bairu students and advanced cultivation techniques were introduced on Bairu farms. Nganwa promoted the establishment of agricultural cooperatives and local welfare societies, which were intended to bring the cause of Bairu advancement down to the village level. Perhaps inevitably, however, victory was accompanied by a conflict over its benefits. The large pro-portion of the Bairu population that was Catholic felt they were being allotted a meager share of public jobs and patronage. Under British rule, the Catholic Bairu had suffered even more discrimination than the Anglican Bairu, and they resented the bourgeois Protestants—Nganwa's core supporters—at least as much as the Bahima.

For their part, Laki and his friends pledged undying loyalty to Nganwa. They called him *Ruterengwa*, which roughly meant "the incomparable one." In the early 1960s, however, their leader fell ill. Cagy to the end, Nganwa didn't reveal to anyone what the doctors told him, that the cancerous cells in his bloodstream were dividing and dividing, sapping his lithe runner's body of its strength. One day, he quietly checked himself into a hospital in Kampala. He underwent an operation and died. He was only in his late forties.

Nganwa's death deeply shook the men who'd followed him to power. His funeral, held at the St. James Cathedral in Mbarara, had the air of a state occasion. Children were given the day off from school. Laki and the rest of his group attended. Many of them wept openly. The doctors said it was leukemia. But before the Europeans and their science had come to Uganda, traditional culture possessed no concept of natural death—only of evil spirits and witchcraft—and in politics especially, no leader's demise could be ascribed to something so arbitrary and mysterious as cancer. Among themselves, Nganwa's men whispered: "poison."

It was the tenor of the times. Nganwa's death coincided with the turbulent run-up to independence, when the colony's ethnic divisions took the form of party politics. By the early 1960s, two parties had formed in Uganda: the Uganda People's Congress (UPC) and the Democratic Party (DP). There were some nominal ideological differences between the two groups: The UPC, which grew out of the trade union movement, was modeled on Europe's social democratic parties, while the DP was more conservative. But what really separated the parties, at least in Ankole, were the factors of ethnicity and religion. The UPC, which was associated with Anglicanism, naturally drew the veterans of Nganwa's movement. The Catholics gravitated toward the DP. Even though they were mostly Anglicans, the Bahima likewise joined the DP, making an alliance of convenience with the Catholics against the upstarts who'd dislodged them from power.

Prior to independence, Uganda conducted a series of elections on both the local and national levels, and power swung dizzyingly between the two newly formed parties. The campaigns in Ankole were nasty. Public rallies often descended into name-calling and shoving. One side would try to drown out the other's voices by banging metal tins. There was little debate about issues or economics, only personal attacks and naked ethnic appeals. UPC leaders warned farmers in the countryside that if the DP won, they'd go back to serving Bahima, and peddled old tales about the humiliations the king had inflicted on their ancestors. The DP spread the rumor that if the socialists of the UPC took over, they would confiscate people's private property and extra wives. A small Muslim minority was up for grabs, and the Protestants tried to woo it by accusing the Catholics of worshiping idols and savoring pork.

To call this "tribal politics" is somewhat deceptive shorthand. In a very real sense, politics created the tribes, not the other way around. All over Uganda, factions were coalescing around whatever differences existed among the people, whether regional, religious, cultural or linguistic. Tribalism was a convenient way to pick sides for the most elemental of political struggles, the competition for the spoils of government.

On October 9, 1962, Uganda gained its independence. The country's first prime minister, handpicked by the British shortly before the initial handover, was the UPC leader Apollo Milton Obote. Not yet forty years old, he was widely considered to be one of the most promising politicians to emerge from the African anticolonial struggle. "Dr. Obote," as his followers called him—though the doctorate was only honorary—was an austere, intelligent and unassuming man, with a crisp, high-pitched voice and a distinctive swept-back hairstyle. He claimed to have adopted the name he went by, Milton, after reading *Paradise Lost*. Obote liked to smoke a pipe and to talk politics over sips of whiskey. "He seems happiest when he is relaxing at home, dressed in an open-necked shirt, and shrouded by a cloud of tobacco smoke," said one early magazine profile. His calm, cerebral style appeared to be a living rebuke to those Europeans who said Africans were too savage and backward to govern themselves.

Obote's professorial exterior masked a knack for ruthless politics. In Ankole, a round of elections for the provincial parliament had been held shortly before independence, and the results had gone against the UPC. Now that he had taken power, Obote called for yet another vote. Determined to crush the DP in Ankole, the central government gerrymandered electoral districts in the UPC's favor, working from voter lists compiled by Anglican parish priests. UPC activists canvassed hut-to-hut across the province in government-owned cars. The way the balloting system worked, each voter was supposed to step behind a curtain and drop a slip of paper into one of two boxes: one for the UPC, and the other for the DP. A top DP official, then working as an election monitor, told of visiting a polling station in Ndeija on election day and finding his party's box "completely empty," and the local DP organizer "chased away." (Elders in the village said they recalled no such shenanigans.) Though outnumbered by the Catholic-Bahima alliance, the Protestants of the UPC nonetheless won the election handily.

After much intrigue and infighting, the Ankole provincial parliament elected a new chief minister, one of Nganwa's most able lieutenants. James Kahigiriza, an affable government land surveyor, was a member of a well-off Bairu family, and he'd been educated at the colony's finest boarding school, King's College. He owned a car, an Austin A10, and was a bit of a dandy. He was also Eliphaz Laki's closest friend in politics. The two men had met during the secret meetings of the 1950s, and their careers had advanced together. Kahigiriza served as Kesi Nganwa's deputy in the provincial parliament, which led to Laki's own appointment to a series of important administrative positions. When one of those promotions required Laki to move to Mbarara, he

*James Kahigiriza, Eliphaz
Laki's closest friend in
politics* ANDREW RICE

lived at Kahigiriza's home. When it came time for Laki to get his own
place, he bought a house almost next door. When Laki fell sick and his
wife was far away in Ndeija, it was Mrs. Kahigiriza who nursed him back
to health. When the Kahigirizas had difficulty conceiving children, Laki
sent one of his own daughters to live with them for a while. The two
men did business together, and even held a joint bank account.

Kahigiriza was inaugurated in Mbarara in June 1963. More than ten
thousand supporters came to hear his speech over loudspeakers that
had been erected outside the provincial parliament building. Inside,
Kahigiriza, dressed in the traditional robes and fez, was handed the ceremonial walking stick that symbolized the office of chief minister.

He assured the figurehead king, who was in attendance, that his
government pledged to treat the monarchy with dignity and deference. He told his audience they'd been called to battle "three gigantic
enemies"—poverty, ignorance and disease. "Tribal factions of the Bairu
and Bahima must cease forthwith," he said. "For the good of the country, such factions, tribal, religious or otherwise, must remain private
matters and must in no way interfere with public duty." Afterward, a
three-hundred-car motorcade proceeded to the St. James Cathedral for
a prayer service.

That evening, there were raucous celebrations. Even these moments
of triumph, however, were tinged by portents of what was to come. A

few days after Kahigiriza's inauguration, a newspaper reported that amid the revelry, a mob chanting "UPC!" had attacked a leading Catholic politician's house with stones.

For Eliphaz Laki, James Kahigiriza's ascension to Ankole's highest office meant only good things. Shortly after his election, Kahigiriza made his friend a county chief. Laki was posted to the same small town where he had grown up as a ward of Ernest Katungi. The elderly chief had built the official county residence on his own estate, as if he anticipated that his descendants would rule like barons forever. But now his former servant was the master of the house. Katungi retreated to his nearby private ranch, where he lived out his days in the company of his beloved cows.

Laki, as was customary, assumed some of the old chief's aristocratic habits. He grew wealthy, at least by local standards. He acquired his own cattle. He dispensed with his bicycle and bought a car, a Volkswagen Beetle, with money he obtained via a special government loan program for public officials. The chief's big house was always full of children, including many orphans and poor relations. As he well knew from his own upbringing, the chief was expected to act as a one-man social safety net. One villager would plead for a few shillings to fix a bike, another for help seeing a doctor.

The chief tried to instill strength and discipline in all his children. When they went away to boarding school, Laki wrote them letters in

Eliphaz Laki (left), *sworn in as county chief.*
Kahigiriza is at his side.
LAKI FAMILY

Laki, the chief (left), *"was expected to act as a one-man social safety net."* LAKI FAMILY

meticulous cursive, warning them against lapses in concentration. His daughter Joyce suffered from scoliosis, a deformity of the spine that hunched her back. At the hospital in Kampala where she went for treatment, Laki would point out children crippled by polio, to show her she could be much worse off. "He would tell me, 'Never show people that you are in pain,'" Joyce later recalled. "Because when you show people that you feel pain, that you cannot do this, you cannot do that, they will always look at you as a useless person. . . . He encouraged us like that, that we should never give up."

These were the good years—and not just for the Laki family. The whole country, it seemed, was rushing to catch up with the developed world. Milton Obote's government had launched an ambitious program for social and economic advancement. Promising young people were winning scholarships and getting government jobs. A policy of "Africanization"—essentially, replacing white managers with black managers—was being promoted in national ministries and private enterprises. In Ankole, the government increased the pace of hospital and school construction, largely in Bairu-dominated areas. Laki had a factory to cure coffee built near Ndeija. A public program eradicated disease-carrying tsetse flies from the eastern part of the province, opening its ample grasslands to habitation. With four million dollars in funding from the United States Agency for International Development, local officials carved the land into ranches. Many Bairu, seeing a chance to own cattle for the first time, banded together to form cooperative ranching societies, which they gave brave names like *Abatahuunga* (Those Who Never Retreat). Laki himself took advantage of the program, joining with a group of friends to obtain a five-square-mile tract, which they stocked with cattle.

In 1964, again with U.S. funding, James Kahigiriza took a delegation of leaders to Colorado to study ranching techniques. The chief minister brought along his friend Laki, who was very impressed with the United States, especially with the nonviolent civil rights movement led by Martin Luther King Jr. After Laki came home, he began greeting his friends and family with the 1960s salutation: "peace."

The contented interlude couldn't last. As the 1960s passed, religious rivalries, tribal grievances, personal grudges, greed—all the great maladies of African politics—conspired to drive Ugandans to opposition, as if by some insidious mitotic process. Movements split into parties, parties into factions, factions into cliques. Rhetoric turned violent, and soon actions did too. The promise of independence wasted away.

Even as he extolled freedom and democracy, Milton Obote cleverly undermined all potential electoral competitors. With parliament firmly under UPC control, he offered lucrative ministerial jobs to DP leaders, and the defectors nearly trampled each other in their haste to cross the aisle. Then, once the opposition was hobbled, Obote's loyalists began to question its reasons for existence. In Ankole, James Kahigiriza gave a speech endorsing the creation of a one-party state, calling such a system "a real African government," and saying people were "disgusted" with frequent elections.

Though he belonged to a socialist party, and he liked to cast himself as a champion of the common man, Kahigiriza, once in charge of Ankole, ruled much like his royal predecessors. Though only in his early forties, he took to carrying a walking stick, that totemic symbol of wisdom and status. He toured the province in a motorcade, opening factories and attending UPC rallies, handing out heavy envelopes of cash. He had prison laborers tending his garden. When the beleaguered opposition attacked his administration for using public funds to supply its leaders with houses and cars, and for doling out scholarships and chieftaincies on the basis of religious and ethnic ties, Kahigiriza responded by threatening to arrest "subversive" elements, saying he wouldn't allow them to "wreck the country." The fact that he had forged close ties to Obote—he was godfather to one of the prime minister's children—only enhanced his aura of power.

In Uganda, power and patronage are linked so deeply that the relationship is embedded in the language. As in many poor countries, weight is equated with wealth: A man who has power is said to be "eating," and a worthy leader makes everyone fat. But in the mid-1960s, the focus of the country's political class started to shift, as providing became less important than depriving. If one group was feasting, its opponents had to starve. Factional infighting led to campaigns of reprisal, as chiefs, teachers and other government workers were fired or transferred to undesirable postings simply because they came from the wrong religious or ethnic background. With livelihoods at stake, politics became increasingly vengeful.

Eliphaz Laki's personal papers, preserved at his farmhouse in Ndeija, show how the bright hopes gradually darkened. A letter one unfortunate schoolteacher wrote the chief in 1965 is indicative. "Sir," it petitions plaintively, in English. "I was transferred one hundred and sixty miles from my home, and this school is 30 miles from the main road without means of transport but wild beasts. Sir, I am quite confident to put forward that life is quite more unbearable to my family, my fellow men, and I."

The writer goes on to say that his wife has left him and that his children are languishing without care. Then, in a long postscript, written in the local language, he explains that he "converted" from the DP, that he is now "strong UPC," and that all he desires is to be transferred nearer to home. He refers to members of the DP as *abazigu* (enemies) and as *ebyata*, an untranslatable ethnic slur. "What annoys me most," he writes, "is that these *ebyata* DP are rubbing it in, saying what did I gain from changing to UPC?"

James Kahigiriza would later say he did his best to hold the province together. "I saw myself as the *enganzi* of all Banyankole, whether Bairu or Bahima, Roman Catholic or Protestant," he wrote in his autobiography. He resisted radical elements within the UPC who pushed for a wholesale purge of DP officeholders. He succeeded in luring many of these opposition leaders, including some Bahima, to the UPC. In return, Kahigiriza accepted compromises. The program to divide eastern Ankole into ranches, financed by the United States government, was transformed into an elaborate scheme to win over the Bahima elite, as much of the land, originally meant to be distributed for the public good, was instead turned over to members of the old aristocratic class. Kahigiriza and other UPC leaders also staked out ranches for themselves, leading to a diplomatic incident, as the project's American funders expressed "deep concern" about corruption.

That controversy came to nothing. More troublesome to Kahigiriza, however, was a symbolic issue: the monarchy. Though various institutional reforms had deprived the king of most of his power, he remained an emotional rallying point for the Bahima. Many Bairu in the UPC leadership wanted to see the monarchy abolished. Kahigiriza, recognizing the explosiveness of the issue, once again tried to conciliate. He pushed a resolution through the provincial parliament that required all chiefs to take a pledge of fealty to the king. He presided over an elaborate yearly celebration where thousands of children paraded past the royal palace. Kahigiriza believed these ceremonial measures promoted ethnic comity, but many of his old comrades started to call him a turncoat.

To them, it seemed like power was inflating the chief minister. Once, at a public ceremony, Kahigiriza spoke wistfully of a prior era when ethnicity was less divisive. He cited an antique proverb that said that once a farmer managed to amass a herd of fifty cows, he shed his inferior status and could rightfully consider himself one of the Bahima. To the Bairu who'd fought so long to dislodge the traditional system, it sounded like Kahigiriza was talking about himself—he was saying he wasn't one of them anymore. "He had been elevated to prime minister, this royal thing," one of them said decades later, the disdain lingering in his voice. "He was going to cling to it."

Across Uganda, tensions were rising and allegiances were growing shaky. At independence, in order to forestall regional disputes between the country's north and south, the British had brokered an awkward power-sharing agreement. After Milton Obote, a northerner, was elected prime minister, he arranged for the most powerful of the southern kings, the *kabaka* of Buganda, to be installed as the country's president, its ceremonial head of state. But the conciliation was short-lived. Tensions between the two leaders mounted for three years, until Obote, citing "an attempt to overthrow the government," ousted the *kabaka* from the presidency in February 1966. Obote pushed a new constitution through parliament and assumed all executive powers. He had a group of his own ministers, alleged coup plotters, arrested at a cabinet meeting and imprisoned. Buganda threatened secession. In May, Obote declared a state of emergency and ordered the army, under the command of Colonel Idi Amin Dada, a northerner, to shell the *kabaka*'s palace on Mengo Hill. Buganda's king fled into exile in London, where he lived in a shabby docklands flat until his death two years later, of alcohol poisoning. Obote assumed the presidency and turned the royal palace into a military barracks.

In Ankole, the national turmoil caused a local split in the UPC. The generation of politicians that had grown close while listening to lectures about equality once again began meeting secretly, but this time to plot against each other. James Kahigiriza, who'd been tightly associated with one of the cabinet ministers imprisoned by Obote, was now seen as vulnerable. Those who were disgruntled with Kahigiriza's concessions toward the Bahima coalesced into a hard-line faction, calling themselves the *enkomba*, or "the concentrated," after a term for thickened millet porridge. Those who stayed with Kahigiriza were known as the *omufunguro*, "the diluted."

The leader of the hard-liners, a firebrand named Nekemia Bananuka, embodied the fractious Uganda emerging in the late 1960s. After graduating from high school, he'd turned down a clerical government job when his prospective boss, the traditionalist chief Ernest Katungi, had declined to shake his impure hand. He'd prospered in business instead, peddling exotic foodstuffs like cabbage and cauliflower to the small European community in Mbarara. Brash, ambitious and impatient, the vegetable salesman openly boasted that he intended to lead Ankole one day. On the issue of the monarchy, he was a fervent abolitionist. He drove a powder-blue Ford Fairlane, a splendid machine he nicknamed *omugabe nankizaki*, which meant: "Does the king have wheels like these?" The king drove a clunky Ford Zephyr.

Bananuka had been the tactical mastermind of the UPC's controversial electoral victory in Ankole in 1963. He'd been passed over for the chief minister's job, however, because many of his counterparts were concerned about his hostility to the king. "We feared this man, although he was leading us," one of the moderates later recalled. "He had that kind of radicalism." Out of political necessity, Kahigiriza put Bananuka in charge of the important Ministry of Health and Public Works. But he had never stopped maneuvering for the top job.

It would be difficult to imagine two rivals more suited to antagonism. Bananuka was thin and severe, with a long, vulpine face. Kahigiriza was pudgy and dapper, with a well-tended mustache. Bananuka was self-made, popular with the illiterate peasantry. Kahigiriza's father had been a county chief, the rare man among the Bairu who'd risen above his caste, and his well-educated son mixed easily with the Bahima elite. Bananuka was a rabble-rouser. Kahigiriza was gregarious and refined. At first, his social graces had worked to his advantage, but now they opened him up to charges of class betrayal. Bananuka played the populist, using his position at Health and Public Works to build roads and hospitals and making sure to take the credit. Kahigiriza, annoyed, moved him to a less-visible job. Bananuka responded with a campaign of insults and innuendoes. With each slight, the dispute grew more spiteful, sophomoric and overt.

There is no way to know now what Eliphaz Laki thought as the political, religious and ethnic strife worsened around him. In all likelihood, he abhorred it. Those who knew him say he was unprejudiced and courteous even to those with whom he disagreed. "Laki was a gentleman," recalled one Catholic politician then active in the DP. "He was not like Bananuka. He was not rough. He was not rude." A cousin who knew him well said: "He took religion to be something alien that had come to our communities. He was of the view that people shouldn't be divided because of a religion that had just come yesterday."

Nonetheless, by the mid-1960s, sectarian conflict had come to infect even the most routine interactions. For years, Laki carried on a campaign of bureaucratic warfare with the chief administrator of the province, a Catholic civil servant. The two men traded allegations of financial impropriety and dereliction of duty. The chief administrator accused Laki of participating in an "unholy" campaign to undermine the local Anglican bishop, who was from a cattle-keeping background and thus suspected of DP sympathies. (The bishop eventually resigned, unhappily, and was replaced by a solid UPC man.) Kahigiriza did not back Laki in this feud, and the Catholic bureaucrat held on to his job. Perhaps for this reason, or perhaps because Laki was dismayed at Kahigiriza's rightward drift, or perhaps because of some other disagreement lost to history, their once close relationship grew chilly. By early 1966, the chief minister was hearing from his spies—he had many of them—that Laki, the friend he'd raised to such heights, was holding surreptitious nighttime meetings with Bananuka.

The discovery that his own appointees were turning against him infuriated Kahigiriza. On May 3, 1966, he fired off a memorandum to all government officials in Ankole:

SPREADING OF RUMOURS AND UNDERMINING YOUR OWN
GOVERNMENT AND CHARACTER ASSASSINATION

The last two months, i.e. March and April 1966 have been months of
creating and spreading rumours by some of our civil servants and even
going to the extent of mudslinging and character assassination of the
Heads of this Government and some of our colleagues.

This sort of thing will not be tolerated any longer and steps are being
taken and will be taken also in the future to deal with any civil servant
who may be found to be endulging [*sic*] in politics, causing hatred
among our people and making public the secrets of Government.

The new Constitution has been made to bring about closer unity of
this country and Ankole is no exception to this. There is no reason
therefore why some of us should continue to play about with this dangerous weapon of creating hatred and disunity among our own people
in this kingdom.

We must now strive hard to labour for things that will unite this
country rather than labour for those that divide it.

Afterward, Kahigiriza finally ousted Bananuka from the government,
accusing him of intrigue and corruption. As a final petty rebuke, the
chief minister sent a police tow truck to impound Bananuka's treasured
Ford Fairlane. But firing his opponent only exacerbated the rebellion.
Some of Kahigiriza's onetime allies resigned from the government, saying that he'd acted unfairly. The Ankole parliament descended into
rowdiness. After each screaming session, delegations from both factions
would jump in their cars and speed to Kampala, like bickering children
running to their father, each rushing to be the first to tell President
Obote about the other's outrageous behavior.

Eventually, Obote made his choice. In March 1967, he visited
Ankole for a rally at the Mbarara soccer stadium. Kahigiriza introduced
the president, who proceeded to slyly ridicule him before thousands of
cheering UPC supporters. "It is the well-to-do who think they are superior. These are the people that know the more there is division, the better for them," the president said, in a clear reference to Kahigiriza.
"Certainly some money has been dished out in secret. . . . I am just
wondering how many people in Ankole ate it. I guess, and I think I am
right in saying, that just a handful of people ate it. The masses did not
taste it at all."

Obote's next move erased several enemies at once. The president declared Uganda a republic, abolishing all the traditional kingdoms. The measure was primarily aimed against restive Buganda, where monarchist sentiment was still running high, but it also had the effect of eliminating all royal offices in Ankole. Technically, the chief minister had been appointed by the king, so the abolition order effectively removed Kahigiriza from power. He was given three days to vacate his government-owned residence. The Ankole branch of the UPC assumed the administrative powers that Kahigiriza's office had previously exercised, and the man in charge of the local party apparatus was its secretary general, Nekemia Bananuka. In September 1967, Bananuka had the royal family evicted from its palace in Mbarara. Ankole's new leader confiscated the monarch's robes and jewelry, along with the royal drum and throne. Everything was loaded onto a pickup truck and hauled away to a government warehouse.

Uganda was descending into one-party dictatorship. When his repressive measures catalyzed domestic unrest, Obote turned to the military, more than quadrupling the size of the army. Violence, once rare, began to corrupt every organ of society. Gangs of armed bandits terrorized the cities and towns. It was said they bought their guns from soldiers. In 1969, Obote announced a "Move to the Left," marking a sharp departure from previous policies, which had tended to be in line with British and American interests. In December of that year he delivered an address outlining a new socialist program to a group of UPC stalwarts at a stadium in Kampala. As he triumphantly left the venue, to a marching band's rendition of the party anthem, "Uganda Moving Forward," an assassin stepped from behind a tree and shot him in the face. Obote escaped serious injury, losing only a few teeth. The assassin, quickly apprehended, turned out to be a taxi driver, an angry nationalist of the Baganda tribe. Yet there were insinuations of the wider conspiracy.

After the assassination attempt, Obote banned all serious opposition groups. He then announced a series of internal party elections. In October 1970, James Kahigiriza attempted a quixotic comeback in Ankole, mounting a campaign for the local UPC leadership against Nekemia Bananuka. The vote was held in public at the Mbarara soccer stadium. The two men were sent to opposite sides of the field. Delegates were told to line up behind their choice. According to Kahigiriza's autobiography, "to the surprise of all those present, a column of soldiers suddenly appeared in the stadium, and ordered all the delegates to line up behind Bananuka."

There is no mention of this incident in contemporary newspaper accounts, though that doesn't mean it didn't happen, since Obote had also curtailed the press. Regardless, Bananuka won. That evening, President Obote, who was on hand for the vote along with the chief of his intelligence service, held a party at the presidential lodge in Mbarara. Despite the electoral victory, the president's mind was troubled. After leaving Ankole, Obote was supposed to travel to Tanzania for the ceremonial opening of an East African railway, but he decided to cancel the trip. Since the assassination attempt, he'd become reluctant to leave the country. He worried that the army was turning against him.

Only a year earlier, Obote had declared that he was the one leader in Africa who did not fear a military coup. Now he was wracked with paranoia. Obote suspected that his army chief, Major General Amin, had somehow been involved in the attempt on his life. Uganda's first leader, like the British before him, had consolidated his power through a strategy of divide-and-rule, but the factious process had acquired a momentum even its instigator couldn't control. Obote and Amin were both from the north, but they belonged to different tribes. Each man commanded a faction within the military, but neither felt strong enough to risk a showdown. Finally, in January 1971, Obote forced the issue by secretly ordering Amin's arrest. Then he departed for a summit of the leaders of the Commonwealth nations in Singapore, leaving Amin, who was still at large, an opportunity to strike.

Early in the morning of January 25, 1971, tanks rumbled down the road past Eliphaz Laki's house toward Uganda's western border. Laki, like everyone else, turned on the radio. The BBC said there had been a coup. Radio Uganda played nothing but martial music. Then, at around 3:45 p.m., an unfamiliar soldier's voice came over the airwaves.

> It has been necessary to take action to save a bad situation from getting worse. We give here below examples of matters that have left the people angry, worried, and very unhappy.

The soldier went on to list eighteen justifications for the army's actions, among them, "the creation of a wealthy class of leaders who are always talking of socialism while they grow richer and the common man poorer," "the lack of freedom in the airing of different views on political and social matters" and the absence of fair elections.

"Long live Amin!" The coup, 1971 THE NEW VISION

The announcement concluded:

Power is now handed over to our fellow soldier, Major General Idi
Amin Dada, and you must await his statement, which will come in due
course.

We have done this for God and our country.

When the coup announcement came, many residents of Mbarara fes-
tooned their cars with tree branches in a fluttering demonstration of
joy. President Obote and his ruling party had long since lost the faith of
most Ugandans. Major General Amin, they believed, could restore stability and maybe even right some old wrongs. Among those who took
to Mbarara's streets that day, I was told, was James Kahigiriza.

"I saw him with my own naked eyes," said an acquaintance of Eliphaz
Laki's, more than thirty years after that day. "He was carrying a flag
around town, celebrating the fall of Obote. . . . He was praising Amin,
praising the army, praising the overthrow of that guy."

7

A SERIOUS YOUNG MAN

On the morning of January 25, as rumors of troop movements swirled, the streets of Kampala stood deceptively silent. At a public housing complex on the outskirts of the city, a bespectacled young man opened the front door of his tiny flat, no. 35, and walked out into a changed nation. At first, Yoweri Museveni didn't even notice the difference—the absence of all the usual cacophonous traffic. He could be that way: oblivious to the world outside his head. Acquaintances often snickered at his solitary habits and his bookworm radicalism, at his rumpled khaki fatigues with their missing buttons. He held himself above petty material concerns. "The leader of a revolutionary movement," Museveni had recently written, must "lead a pure, exemplary and, most preferably, ascetic life." He abjured frivolity; he was purposeful in all things. On this morning, a Monday, he was on his way to his job at the office of President Milton Obote.

"HEY!" A voice pierced Museveni's preoccupation. He looked around. People were gathered on crowded verandas, wearing confused expressions, trading fretful chatter. "Someone shouted after me to ask where I was going," Museveni recounted in his autobiography, *Sowing the Mustard Seed*. "I said that I was going to work, but he told me that I should not proceed towards town as there had been some problems during the night."

The upheaval had started the previous afternoon, a languorous Sunday in the hottest month of the year. People who lived near the army barracks on Mengo Hill, formerly the palace of the *kabaka* of Buganda, had heard the first sign of trouble, a flurry of gunshots. Then, around the time bar-goers were draining their last beer of the weekend, tanks and armored personnel carriers had begun rumbling down the streets of the capital, taking up positions around parliament, the radio station and all the strategic traffic intersections. There'd been another, more intense, round of gunfire at dawn. Not far from Museveni's apartment, two factions of soldiers had clashed.

At the time, though, all Museveni knew for certain was that his bus wasn't running. He walked back to his dim concrete flat and turned on Radio Uganda. Instead of news, it was broadcasting only the tinny strains of a recorded military brass band. Museveni went to visit a neighbor, a friend of his from high school, another recent university graduate. They spent a few cooped-up hours listening to the same tired marches, waiting for a definitive announcement. After lunch, they decided to check things out. Museveni's friend, who worked at a bank, owned a white Peugeot, which they drove downtown.

Even before the two young men reached the main road into central Kampala, they encountered the jubilant throngs waving fistfuls of flowers and banana leaves. The Baganda had hated Milton Obote ever since he'd driven out their *kabaka*, and now they were celebrating. Just to be safe, the two friends stopped, fetched some tree branches from the side of the road and tied them to the exterior of the Peugeot. By the time they reached the parliament building, where Museveni's office was located, it was clear he'd never be returning to work. There were soldiers everywhere. Thousands of people—the most they'd ever seen in one place—were cheering the army, climbing atop tanks, joining in chants of "Long live Amin!"

Already, Yoweri Museveni knew what he was going to do.

A little before 4:00 p.m., a soldier came on the radio to announce that the military had taken over. He concluded by saying, "We have done this for God and our country." Just as Major General Amin was making his way to the radio station in an armored convoy, preparing to give his own speech justifying the coup, Museveni arrived at the suburban home of an acquaintance, where a group of friends and classmates had gathered to discuss the stunning news. They were professionals in their twenties. Most of them were socialists. Many, Museveni included, were from the province of Ankole. They discussed their political options. "We were just like academicians debating," one of those in attendance later recalled. Some suggested that they join Amin, a man without apparent ideology, and push the new regime to the left. Others argued, tentatively, for resistance.

But only one of them had a plan. Of all those present at that shell-shocked meeting—indeed, of all the Ugandans who experienced that upended day—only twenty-six-year-old Museveni seems to have seen clearly, instinctively, the danger and the possibilities of the moment. He exhorted his friends to consider the coup an opportunity: their chance to radically transform the country. "To say that one can introduce fundamental changes without a violent shake-up," he'd written the year before, perhaps foreseeing just such an eventuality, "is to say that one can turn ore into iron without melting it." He told his friends he would go to Tanzania, where he'd attended university, where Milton Obote was fleeing, where he knew he could buy guns.

The rest of the men were skeptical. They didn't want to rush into any hasty decisions. They had salaries and futures to consider. Museveni, however, insisted on leaving immediately. He planned to cross the border out west, passing first through his home province. He knew he could rely on the assistance of some sympathetic local politicians. One of them was a chief named Eliphaz Laki.

Museveni asked his neighbor, the banker, for a little travel money. The banker reached into his pocket, gave his friend a fistful of shillings and told him good-bye. With that, the young man slipped off to mount his revolution.

In the firsthand accounts of this downcast moment, retold many times and reshaped retrospectively, Yoweri Museveni comes off as certain, decisive—even curiously elated. With Amin's coup, he had lost his job, and he would soon lose his homeland, but he had acquired a cause, which was the one thing for which he had always longed. "People, I understand, . . . state that I am ambitious," Museveni once said. "My answer is that for us, we are fighting for principles. Someone who is ambitious never fights, because if he fights, he may die."

Museveni had always felt destined for a life of violent struggle. Even his name presaged a future at arms. His father's surname was Kaguta, but in keeping with Uganda's flexible naming customs, his parents called him "Museveni," the "seven" honoring the local soldiers of the Seventh Battalion of the King's African Rifles. Born during the waning days of World War II, Museveni was reared in Ankole, just a few miles down the road from the village of Ndeija. His people were Bahima cattle-keepers. His father was a simple man, a bit of a drinker, who never took to Christian ways. His mother was from a chiefly lineage, devout and puritanical. Museveni took after her.

In Bahima society, where one is judged by the size of his herd, Museveni's father was a man of little standing. He'd inherited a substantial number of cattle, but due to disease and neglect, they'd dwindled to about fifty by the time of Museveni's childhood. The family shared a single round hut. Museveni's mother dressed him in the skin of a premature calf. He was put to work by the age of four, grazing calves and cleaning dung from the stockade. He was taught to milk the family cows, to massage them and to chase away the birds that pecked at their hides. Like all good Bahima children, he learned to revere the cow as an exquisite giver of sustenance. He regarded the ones he tended "like cousins and sisters," he wrote in his autobiography. The Bahima rarely slaughter their cattle. Museveni's family subsisted on a diet of dairy products.

By and large, the Bahima held that European-style education was of dubious value. Boys belonged in the pastures, it was thought, not in the classroom. (This cultural prejudice is one reason why, in the run-up to independence, farming people supplanted the cattle-keepers as Ankole's ruling class.) Museveni's father, however, saw promise in his eldest boy and sent him to primary school. Museveni learned to write letters in the sand with his finger. Later, he was admitted to a missionary academy in Mbarara. He was still a raw peasant child. One classmate recalled that he arrived at boarding school barefoot.

"You could describe him, even at a very early age, as rebellious," recalled a childhood acquaintance. Museveni challenged his teachers,

Yoweri Museveni (right).
"You could describe him, even at a very early age, as rebellious." THE MONITOR

who sometimes beat him for his impertinence. In high school, when the white missionaries who ran the Scripture Union told him a Christian should not involve himself in worldly matters of politics, he stormed out of the organization, saying the God he worshiped didn't want him to be meek.

After classes, Museveni and his friends took to hanging around the provincial government headquarters, where they became acquainted with all the local notables. They immersed themselves in the calamitous politics of the mid-1960s. Museveni led public debates about the crises in Rhodesia and Congo. He and his schoolmates nicknamed each other after African leaders. His best friend grew a goatee, emulating Patrice Lumumba. In contrast to earlier generations, the students at his school did not divide up along ethnic or sectarian lines; they thought of themselves as Ugandans foremost. They were outraged when Obote suspended the country's constitution and attacked the *kabaka* in 1966. They mounted a protest before Ankole's leader, James Kahigiriza, who advised them to leave politics to the grown-ups.

At graduation, Museveni and his cohorts all applied to one place of higher learning, University College, Dar es Salaam. "This is not so much because I was interested in going to a college as in coming [to] Dar es Salaam—to Tanzania," Museveni subsequently wrote in a student publication. At a time when his own country was sinking into authoritarianism, Tanzania seemed to be soaring. Under the rule of President Julius Nyerere, an erudite man universally known by the honorific *mwalimu*, or "teacher," the country was in the midst of an ambitious attempt to create something called "African socialism." Nyerere's charismatic leadership and visionary-sounding pronouncements about a self-reliant and unified continent exerted a romantic pull on youthful African nationalists like Museveni. "I looked on Tanzania as Africa's Prussia," he wrote as a student, "and President Nyerere as our Bismarck."

Museveni arrived in Dar es Salaam in 1967, crossing Lake Victoria by steamer and taking a train to the coast. He had never left Uganda, had never seen the sea. Dar es Salaam was a busy port, situated on a turquoise bay, with a rapidly growing population of around three hundred thousand. Its skyline was dotted with palms and minarets. A sultry wind blew in off the ocean. Down in its sandy market streets, Arabs, Indians and Africans haggled and commiserated in a rapid-fire patter of Swahili and slang. The place had a port city's air of ferment and licentiousness. Museveni arrived on campus to find that, contrary to his exacting expectations, most of the student body was less interested in politics than in "drinking, dancing, and watching decadent Western films."

The university culture changed radically, though, in the time Museveni was there. Young people from across the continent flocked to Dar es Salaam to take part in Nyerere's socialist movement. They read Mao and Frantz Fanon, colonial Africa's theorist of violent liberation. They addressed each other as *ndugu*, a Swahili word for "brother," used as an equivalent to "comrade." They staged plays by avant-garde African writers in a common area they called Revolutionary Square. "In Dar es Salaam," said a classmate of Museveni's, "you could not help but be infected by the liberation virus."

With a group of like-minded associates, Museveni founded an organization called the University Students' African Revolutionary Front. The Front met on Sunday mornings—ideology had replaced religion in Museveni's life—and hosted famous militants like Stokely Carmichael, the father of Black Power, and Walter Rodney, the Guyanese leader of the Pan-Africanist movement, who was a university faculty member. Museveni organized a campuswide commemoration of the death of Che Guevara—who'd actually passed through Dar es Salaam in 1965 and '66, while organizing an ill-fated rebellion in Congo—and mounted a protest against a speech by the American senator Edward Brooke, a black Republican, whom he labeled "the arch Uncle Tom." When a visiting American lecturer had the temerity to criticize Frantz Fanon, Museveni stood up in class to denounce him and later led a campaign to have the professor kicked off the faculty and deported. "He was an impressive young man," the professor recalled, decades later, adding that he still gave Museveni the highest grade in the class. "This was a Big Man in the African sense—a natural leader." According to one oft-told anecdote, Museveni would sometimes write the following graffito on lecture hall chalkboards:

MARX WAS A GREAT MAN. MARX IS DEAD.
LENIN WAS A GREAT MAN. LENIN IS DEAD.
FANON WAS A GREAT MAN, AND NOW FANON IS DEAD.
I AM NOT FEELING TOO WELL MYSELF.

A young man who possessed such aspirations couldn't remain confined to campus politics. It was 1968, the year of the Paris riots and the Chicago Seven, and Dar es Salaam was a fulcrum of leftist struggle. On the streets, bearded liberators from all over the continent rubbed shoulders with Chinese men in Mao suits, spies of many nations and peddlers selling copies of the Little Red Book. Several armed movements fighting white-ruled governments in southern Africa had their headquarters in the city. Museveni, through his student organization, was able to endear himself to the founder of the Mozambican rebel group FRELIMO. The rebel leader put the enthusiastic student to work as an errand boy and propagandist. As a reward, over the Christmas holidays in 1968, he sent Museveni and a few other students to visit FRELIMO's bases in the mountainous north of Mozambique, where the guerrillas were battling the country's Portuguese rulers.

Everything that followed for Museveni was shaped by this single revelatory experience. He and his comrades crossed into Mozambique in small boats and traveled to a rebel encampment, where they spent three weeks as guests of a man who called himself Commander Notre. They trained with the guerrillas. They sang rebel songs and watched dance performances that dramatized heroic ambushes. They met comely female fighters who saluted them crisply in greeting. They observed how the rebel officers slept in the same kinds of huts, on the same crude beds of underbrush, as frontline soldiers. They sat in on tactical briefings where Commander Notre, standing before an earthen mound shaped like Mozambique, outlined his plan of attack. On Christmas morning, instead of a church service, they attended an ideological lecture, where the commander compared the rebels' sacrifices to the one that Jesus made on the cross.

When Museveni returned to Dar es Salaam, he turned his observations of FRELIMO into a senior thesis. It read like a personal manifesto. Museveni argued that armed struggle, and only armed struggle, could bring an end to Africa's tribalism, dispel superstition and reverse "backwardness," creating a "new peasant" and "a purified society" without crime and immorality. What most intrigued him was the gun's power to transfigure its holder. The paper opened with a quote from Frantz Fanon—"At the level of individuals, violence is a cleansing force"—and went on to describe Museveni's encounter with a rebel officer, a man who had once worked as a servant for whites and was now killing them.

There we were, university undergraduates, probably reactionary puppets of neo-colonialism in the making, with more than one and a half decades of Western "education," getting rudimentary lessons in the science of liberating our people—who have been oppressed by Imperialism for centuries—from a man who was considered but a grown up child in the colonial days. There he was watching over us and patiently correcting our faultering [*sic*] moves in the handling of the mother of liberation—the gun. Our long stay in the Western Citadels of "learning" notwithstanding, there we were learning the ABC of national liberation, of history making, from a former "house boy." This is what authentic national liberation means—making the first last and the last first. This commander had become a history-maker while we were history-students.

In 1969, Museveni traveled to North Korea for a journalism conference. While he was there, one of Kim Il Sung's colonels taught the eager student to shoot.

The next year, Museveni graduated from college and returned to Uganda. Kampala was not Dar es Salaam, but it had its own small radical subculture, and Museveni stormed right into it. Skinny and boyish, with a wispy mustache and heavy black-framed glasses, he was a "Marxist of almost Maoist virility," recalled one acquaintance. He idolized Che Guevara and dressed in Cuban-style military fatigues. His brash style took aback many of Uganda's student socialists, who were more oriented toward the establishment, and considered President Obote a friend of the movement. Around the time Museveni came home, Obote announced his "Move to the Left," nationalizing industries and foreign-owned companies. His speeches started to take a bellicose tone toward Western powers with whom he'd previously enjoyed good relations, particularly Israel and Britain. "We are not going to have puppets ruling us," the president vowed. Museveni, however, used to joke that this "Move to the Left" was about as heartfelt as a traffic lane change. He gathered a small cadre of like-minded militants around him.

One of this group's few surviving members is a blustery thickset man with the euphonious name of Zubairi Bakari. He says he still remembers the night when Museveni, whom he'd only met once, came knocking on the door of the shack where he lived, down a dirt alley in a Kampala shantytown. Bakari, who worked at a bakery, was one of a number of proletarian types who hung around the leftist students. When Museveni dropped in, he joined in a card game Bakari was hosting and earnestly began to preach revolution. The young firebrand was to become a regular visitor. Museveni brought pistols over and furtively taught Bakari and his friends how to use them. "You see, he was already plotting to overthrow Obote," Bakari said. "He had already told us he was going to rule this country one day."

Even then, however, Museveni was a man of contradictory impulses. At the same time as he was covertly urging President Obote's overthrow, he was also making preparations to run for parliament in Ankole as a candidate of the UPC. While preparing the political ground-work, he came into contact with many of the ruling party leaders in his home province, including its secretary general, Nekemia Bananuka, and the county chief Eliphaz Laki. "We were not very interested in fighting, per se," Museveni explained in 2005. "If we could also push our programs peacefully, we could also try that." He laughed off Bakari's anecdote about the pistols, saying, "That was the 1960s."

Most of Museveni's school friends had found work as lawyers, bankers or civil servants. Realizing that he too needed to make a living, Museveni applied to the Foreign Service. His interviewer, impressed, redi-rected the promising applicant to the president's office, where he was offered a position in a newly founded agency called the Department of Research. The department, which was headed by a recent graduate of Moscow State University, was officially meant to function as the ideo-logical apparatus of Uganda's budding socialist state. Many Ugandans believe that the office's true mission was something else entirely. "He was working in 'Research,' but I don't know what they were research-ing," joked Museveni's oldest friend, a longtime cabinet minister. "Really," he added archly, "it was called the General Service Unit."

The GSU was Obote's domestic intelligence apparatus. After the 1969 assassination attempt and Obote's ban of opposition parties, the agency stepped up surveillance of dissident activity. Some of Museveni's own friends had been thrown in prison. Though Museveni has long maintained that his job consisted of little more than clipping magazine articles, his contemporaries are nearly unanimous in their belief that he was doubling as an intelligence agent. At the time, Obote was looking for informants on the left. It is difficult to reconcile such careerist calcu-lation with the young man's vehement anti-establishment posture, but at heart, for all his genuine moral courage, Museveni had always been and would always be a pragmatist.

Amin's coup seems to have had a clarifying effect on Museveni, resolving whatever confusion he felt about his proper path to power. At long last, he had a real enemy to fight. He also had a real reason to flee. In one of his first actions, Amin announced that he was disbanding the GSU and commanded its agents to report to the local police. Hundreds of GSU operatives were rounded up in the days after the coup, and many were transported to a camp where soldiers bayoneted and bludgeoned them to death.

Two days after the coup, Zubairi Bakari and a friend picked up Museveni at his government-owned flat. The newly minted rebel bounded out the door, carrying a small bag containing a jacket and sweater. The three men caught a bus heading west. They made their way to a farmhouse outside Mbarara, the home of Nekemia Bananuka.

Bananuka had taken in the news of the coup in the company of his loyal UPC supporters. The evening of January 25, Eliphaz Laki and others gathered at his house. Together, they listened, via the radio, to the thick-tongued voice of Major General Idi Amin Dada.

> Fellow countrymen and well-wishers of Uganda, I address you today at a very important hour in the history of our nation. A short while ago men of the armed forces placed this country in my hands. I am not a politician, but a professional soldier. I am therefore a man of few words and I shall, as a result, be brief. Throughout my professional life I have emphasized that the military must support a civilian government that has the support of the people, and I have not changed from that position.
>
> Matters now prevailing in Uganda force me to accept the task that has been given me by the men of the Uganda armed forces. I will, however, accept this task on the understanding that mine will be a thoroughly caretaking administration, pending an early return to civilian rule. Free and fair general elections will soon be held in the country, given a stable security situation. Everybody will be free to participate in these elections. For that reason political exiles are free to return to this country and political prisoners held on unspecified and unfounded charges will be released forthwith. All people are to return to work as usual.

Laki and his friends were not persuaded by Amin's conciliatory rhetoric. They could now see that all the triumphs of the past two decades had come to nothing. The leader of their party was gone. "When you lose a government, it's like when you lose a parent," one of the group later recalled. "We were all saying, 'What's going to happen to this country?'" Someone raised the example of Nigeria, where the military had overthrown the government in 1966, with bloody consequences.

"West African countries were having coups," the attendee said, "and we were hearing bad, bad things."

When Yoweri Museveni came bounding up Bananuka's front steps, two days later, he brought reports from the capital that worsened their fears. Museveni looked scared. "He was just trying to save his life," said one of Bananuka's friends, who happened to be sitting on his porch that day. "As a student of politics, he knew exactly what happens when a government is overthrown." Inside, Museveni briefed Bananuka about what he'd witnessed in the capital, and told the party leader that he had to get to Tanzania to see Obote, who had headed there after learning of the coup.

Bananuka knew Museveni well. He was familiar to members of Ankole's political class; he had been a prominent character since his high school days, and he was also a friend of one of the party leader's sons. Everyone considered Museveni serious and dedicated; he'd joined Obote and the UPC even though he was a member of the Bahima. Bananuka decided to help the young man and set out to find someone to take Museveni to Tanzania. He came back to the house with Eliphaz Laki.

Over the years, Laki had become one of Bananuka's most trusted subordinates, a relationship that was solidified by their ties to the same tribal clan. That morning, Bananuka found Laki in town, where he had gone to buy milk and butter for the family. Now, after some hurried preparations, and without a word to his wife or any other family member, the chief got into his Volkswagen Beetle and set off for Tanzania with Museveni, his comrade Zubairi Bakari, and two other political activists.

It was near dusk when they left. The little Beetle was crammed, and the bumpy drive down the dirt road jolted and jostled the passengers. The route Laki took ran through a little border town called Kikagati, winding through eucalyptus groves and marshes, past scrubby flatlands where buffaloes grazed under the stalking gaze of leopards and lions. Finally, late that night, the travelers crossed the river that forms the boundary between Uganda and Tanzania. They slept at a border town hotel. In the morning, Museveni thanked Laki for the ride, and told him he could find his own way to Dar es Salaam. But the soft-spoken chief insisted on continuing. Like Museveni, he was hoping to secure an audience with the former president.

Obote had received the final word of his overthrow as his plane home from Singapore was in the air over the Indian Ocean. Rather than landing in Uganda, he had flown on to Dar es Salaam, where Julius Nyerere had welcomed him like a wronged hero, sending a Rolls-Royce to the airport to pick him up. Soon afterward, Nyerere had organized a huge rally, where he'd vowed not to recognize Amin's regime. "How can I sit at the same table with a killer?" he'd asked the crowd. Outraged Tanzanians had waved banners reading: GIVE US THE ARMS TO FIGHT.

Obote was staying at Tanzania's State House, a whitewashed, Moorish-style building originally erected to house the colonial governor. Nyerere had even allowed him to raise the Ugandan presidential standard on the flagpole above the building. Museveni, Laki and their little delegation were granted an audience there. They were escorted through a lush garden of bougainvillea and frangipani, and up to a second-floor sitting room. It overlooked a white palm-fringed beach and a terraced lawn where peacocks roamed.

Obote looked confused and crestfallen. The ousted president, clearly long exiled from reality, seemed not to believe the reports of widespread celebrations after the coup. He pressed the men for firsthand descriptions of the mood within Uganda.

After a while, Nyerere showed up, dressed casually as always in a simple collarless suit. Obote had been pressing him and other African leaders to give armed support to an immediate invasion to drive out Amin. Tanzania's president, who knew Museveni from days at the university, pulled the young militant out on a balcony and asked him what he thought of the idea. Museveni argued for patience, saying that he was capable of organizing a guerrilla war from within.

The talks went on for several days and ended with an understanding that Nyerere would finance a rebellion, if Obote and Museveni could work together to prepare it. Laki, Museveni and the other three men set off for home again. They stuck together as far as the border, where they all split up. Before the travel companions parted, Museveni told them all, "I will contact you."

8

SINGAPORE

In Uganda, all history is political, and so are the secrets. Some surround pain, some surround shame, but the heaviest silences obscure the powers of the present day. Duncan Laki's investigation yielded the simple facts of his father's murder, but in a way that was the easiest part of the crime to explain. When it comes to the question of motive, what Eliphaz Laki did to attract the army's attention—and clearly he did something—the story recedes into the murk of speculation. Most of those who fought Amin in the underground resistance perished in the struggle, so firsthand testimony is scant. Survivors are often reluctant to speak openly, even though their nation now considers them heroes. Their lives once depended on discretion and such habits are persistent, but there are other reasons for the generalized reticence. As president, Yoweri Museveni has closely tended the legend of those days, portraying himself as an unfailingly resolute resistance leader. Old comrades who cross the president find themselves written out of the past. Museveni's biography is regarded as a matter of state interest, guarded by a watchful cadre of government propagandists, intelligence operatives and guerrilla war veterans, who attempt to steer any attempt at deeper inquiry back to the president's own writings. It is little wonder then, with their long experience of capricious rulers, that Ugandans are reluctant to speak about events—even laudable ones—that might depart from the authorized narrative. "These matters involving the president are . . . ," said one friend of Laki's family, pausing for a long time to consider his words, "very . . . *sensitive*."

Fragments of Laki's role in the resistance can be gathered from the scant documentary record and many piecemeal memories. The chief returned home from Tanzania one day in early February 1971. His clothes were grimy, and his face, which he usually kept shaven, was covered with a scraggly beard. In Africa, the man of the house is seldom questioned, and Laki didn't say where he had been. But his long absence had not gone unnoticed. At home, he found a letter waiting from the government, dated the day he had left for Tanzania, reporting that the new regime had canceled all leaves of absence and ordered all civil servants back to work. Upon his return, the chief sent the provincial government a terse handwritten note, dated February 6, saying he was back in his office and had "resumed duty accordingly." But the delay was suspicious. Gossip flourishes in the countryside, and word went around that he had gone to see Milton Obote.

With Obote gone, those who felt they'd been wronged by the UPC were suddenly emboldened. One night soon after the coup, someone dumped a pile of banana fibers out front of the home of Nekemia Bananuka, as if to say: "Tie your things up and go." A military governor soon replaced Bananuka as Ankole's leader. The new provincial authorities summoned all the chiefs to Mbarara, where they were required to swear allegiance to General Amin. Laki took the pledge, but as a known UPC loyalist, his actions were scrutinized. A civil servant like him couldn't easily be fired, but he was transferred to the remote town of Ibanda, far from his family. He was certain that spies were watching him—the military government had informers all over Ankole—and he was acutely aware of the dangers of discovery. Yet Laki continued to work covertly to undermine the new regime.

Contemporaries report sighting Yoweri Museveni around Laki's house and office on many occasions after the coup. At the time, the young revolutionary was regularly slipping in and out of Uganda, often disguised as a university student or in white Muslim robes. Museveni was spiriting able-bodied opponents of Amin into Tanzania for military training. Chiefs like Laki made ideal recruiters. They also played useful roles by raising funds, providing safe passage and offering logistical help. At the time, Museveni's group was seeding Uganda's hinterlands with caches of Chinese-made armaments.

"These fellows knew how to work underground," said one of Laki's friends. Another told me, "Laki was not a radical person, but he was a very, very brave guy." They were fighting an unfashionable struggle. In the beginning, it seemed to many Ugandans that Obote was the tyrant and Amin the reformer. "Indeed," read one congratulatory letter printed in a Kampala newspaper a few days after the coup, "God has nominated you to save your people from the ghastly haunt of Obote's scratching paws."

Amin's initial moves were calculated to please the disenchanted. He announced that there would soon be new elections. He disbanded the General Service Unit and released political prisoners at a rally in Kampala attended by tens of thousands. He zoomed around the capital in an open jeep, waving to people, sometimes offering them lifts. "I never thought I would live to see this," one overjoyed academic wrote in an anonymous column published shortly after the coup in the respected African journal *Transition*.

> The situation is remarkably calm. We know there are "mopping up" operations taking place here and there, but it is hard to credit that less than two weeks ago the coup took place. I personally believe, as do many of my friends and colleagues, that this atmosphere of "back to normal" is largely the result of General Amin's own personal statements, conferences and discussions with various sections of the public at large and his personal untrammeled, unguarded appearances everywhere—Kampala streets, shops, barracks and even Makerere campus. You will know that he makes constant reference—whenever the occasion presents itself—to the need for brotherhood, unity, love and no victimization, and indeed this, above all, contributes to the atmosphere of normality that prevails.

In the first months after the coup, Idi Amin barnstormed across the country in his camouflage-painted helicopter, holding rallies where he gave off-the-cuff speeches, promising new roads, schools and hospitals, even though the country was deeply in debt. The crowds chanted the name Dada, which also colloquially means "grandfather." When Amin's victory tour reached Mbarara, a crowd of thousands greeted him at the local soccer stadium. A delegation of Bahima elders presented him with a gift of one hundred longhorn cattle as a gesture of gratitude and submission. The province's police commander, one of the many Bahima who'd been appointed to high office since the coup, fell to his knees to kiss the general's feet.

Wearing a casual field uniform and garrison cap, Amin presided over a military parade. "They are here this afternoon," the general said, gesturing to his troops, "to show you your security is fully guaranteed."

Amin told the crowd that he was aware that the people of Ankole had been divided by "tribalistic and religious differences" in the past. He said he'd been informed that some local politicians were once again holding nighttime meetings, where they were plotting to reinstall Milton Obote.

"I have always said that the Government of Uganda is under full control and as such any force to disrupt the Second Republic of Uganda will be met with maximum force," Amin warned. "It is your duty therefore, you, the people of Ankole, to cooperate with security forces and to report any person whose activities are suspected to be that of a guerrilla now being trained in Tanzania, or people spying on Uganda."

The crowd cheered Amin riotously. Then the general said good-bye and climbed back into his helicopter. After it lifted off, local entrepreneurs swarmed the landing site, digging up clods of turf. People bought them, thinking Amin's dirt would bring them good luck.

One afternoon a few weeks after Amin's appearance, the Reverend George Nkoba, a friend of Laki's and the headmaster of the Ibanda primary school, was sitting in his farmhouse, having his usual after-work cup of tea, when he saw an olive green Land Rover coming along the road. It pulled up to his house, and three armed soldiers got out. Nkoba walked out his front door to see what the soldiers wanted, and before he could say a word, they threw him in the back of the jeep. Nkoba fell with a soft thud on top of someone else's prone body. He couldn't see who it was. Then he heard Eliphaz Laki's voice.

"Have you also been arrested?"

The soldiers took Laki and his friend to the barracks in Mbarara. After a day or two of captivity, a soldier—the same one who'd originally announced the coup over Radio Uganda, as it happened—arrived at the Mbarara barracks. The officer told the prisoners they were accused of collecting a million Ugandan shillings to send to Obote in Tanzania. The sum was preposterous, the equivalent of almost $700,000 today. The men were loaded into military vehicles and taken to a Kampala barracks called Makindye.

By way of greeting, the soldiers at Makindye flogged the new arrivals with canes covered with rough hippo skin. They made them hop around the grounds crouched on their haunches, like frogs. Laki and the others were placed in a cramped, dark and fetid cell. It had no toilet, just a bucket, and an excrement-filled trench ran the length of the concrete floor. That first night, the men's captors prepared a dinner for them, huge helpings of meat, more than any person could possibly consume. The soldiers kicked the men in their backs. "Eat your food," they told the prisoners. "This is the last supper you will have on this earth."

It was just a cruel trick. Laki and his friends weren't killed. They were exposed, instead, to continuous physical and mental torment. Throughout their months in the prison at Makindye, new batches of prisoners kept arriving: disloyal army officers, members of Obote's Langi tribe, other perceived enemies of the military regime. Each night around midnight, soldiers would come to the cell doors and read out a few names. The men they called were taken away to another cell called "Singapore," so nicknamed because, like Obote, prisoners who went there never came back.

One morning, the guards called Laki and his cellmates to Singapore and ordered them to clean it up. The cell was strewn with corpses and the walls were splayed with blood and grayish brain matter. The dead men were bludgeoned beyond recognition. It was a routine: to save bullets and shift the burden of killing, the soldiers typically forced a few prisoners to smash the others' skulls with hammers and pickaxes. When they had finished the job, they were bayoneted or shot. The Ankole group was henceforth assigned the daily job of loading the bodies onto trucks for disposal. "When they had been hammered, you would be called to lift them," one of Laki's cellmates recalled. "If you were not strong, you would also be killed."

On Sundays, the prisoners were allowed a few visitors. Friends and family made the five-hour drive from Mbarara. When Joyce Laki first saw her father, his face was swollen almost beyond recognition. The visitors brought small things: bread, underwear, toiletries. Sometimes the gifts got through; sometimes the guards confiscated them. On one occasion, as a group of family members were waiting to be ushered inside the barracks, soldiers pulled two new arrivals from the trunk of a car, shot them, and then ordered the Ankole prisoners to haul off the corpses, in full view of their horrified loved ones.

The men from Ankole were convinced they'd eventually be killed. "Each of us, in his own way, prayed to God to take his breath away so this torture would end," one of them said. But then, in his unpredictable way, Idi Amin decreed that Laki and his cohorts had been forgiven for their dissension. Over the course of the summer, they were gradually released. On the day Laki was let out, he and some other freed captives went to a photo studio on Kampala Road. They had

On the day he was released from Makindye, Eliphaz Laki (standing second from right) *posed with fellow prisoners and family*
LAKI FAMILY

not bathed, shaved or changed their clothes, but they posed for a group photograph with some members of their families.

"It was a landmark in their lives," said Kenneth Kereere, a cousin of Laki's who was sitting front and center in the picture, a framed copy of which he still displays in his home. "Many other Ugandans were imprisoned at the time. Very few got out."

Kereere, then a foreign service officer, owned an apartment in Kampala. That night, Eliphaz and Jane Laki stayed there. The freed prisoner took his first shower in months, and then they all ate dinner. They talked through the night. Jane, saying little, stared at her husband. He looked weary and emaciated. For the first and only time, Laki spoke about what he'd seen in Singapore.

"It had nearly driven him mad," Kereere recalled. At the time, he didn't believe the army was done with Laki. "I had watched Amin's style," he said. "He would get hold of people he intended to kill, put them in prison. After a while he would announce that he had forgiven them . . . they had now become good citizens. And then, quietly, he would go after them. So I told Laki, 'This fellow is capricious. He will give you some sense of security. Then after that, when you no longer expect anything to happen to you . . . you will disappear quietly.'"

Kereere urged his cousin to think about going into exile. Laki refused to consider the idea, not wanting to leave his thirteen children. He had faith that God had a plan for him. "He said, 'Let them kill me—they will also die someday, just like me.'"

• • •

Of all the men in Laki's group, only one fled to Tanzania while he still had the chance. The rest stayed and tried to settle into low-profile lives. Laki returned to Ibanda, his backwater posting, and resumed his duties as chief. Some of Laki's friends, out of their government jobs, opened shops or went back to farming. Nekemia Bananuka started a bus company. "When we were released, we thought it was all over," said one politician of the time. "We thought they had rehabilitated us."

Broken might be a better word for it. Laki had never been inclined to talk about his emotions, but after he was freed from prison, he became even more reserved. For long spells, he would just sit, silently, his head down, his arms folded and his feet stuck out, crossed at the ankles. He seemed to be remembering things he didn't want to speak aloud. It is difficult to say for sure, but Laki appears to have curtailed his involvement in the underground resistance. Like many Ugandans before and since, he learned to swallow his outrage. When Idi Amin passed through Ibanda on one of his tours, the chief dutifully presided over an evening of music and traditional dances in the general's honor.

Not everyone was willing to make such accommodations. Compromise had never been Nekemia Bananuka's strong suit. One day, a taxicab driver named Yoasi Makaaru, formerly an influential member of the provincial parliament, was passing through Mbarara when Bananuka flagged him down. He got in the back of the car and told his friend to drive to a small house he owned. There, the taxi driver saw a slim, familiar figure waiting: Yoweri Museveni.

The young rebel had come with a friend, another leftist student. They all went inside and talked. "They told us that Amin had a plan to finish us all," Makaaru recalled in a 2003 interview. "They said that unless we arranged for him to be toppled, Amin would not leave any stone unturned." Amin's intelligence service was already gaining a reputation for malevolent effectiveness. The taxi driver became nervous. He had been to prison once, and he knew what would happen if anyone found out he had met with the rebels.

Museveni, sensing his uneasiness, pulled out a pistol. "You people are so timid for nothing," he said disdainfully, as Makaaru remembers it. "You see this pistol? I got this from the barracks." Museveni said he had secret sympathizers in the army. When he was finished taunting Makaaru, Museveni dismissed him curtly: "You are going to be finished off."

The taxi driver left. Bananuka stayed behind.

To the south in Tanzania, preparations for an invasion were continuing. Obote had established a military training camp on a parched patch of government property in the center of the country. A group of around three hundred men were training in hand-me-down uniforms, with beat-up rifles, under the command of a pair of exiled army captains. The fighters, however, soon fell into the same politicking and ethnic squabbles that had afflicted Uganda before the coup. One of Bananuka's sons, Fred, was among those who trained there, with his father's blessing. "I was in Obote's camp for seven months, and I could see that things were going wrong," he told me. "We were doing nothing."

By 1972, Museveni was taking steps to distance himself from Obote. "I do not think that having to choose between Obote and Amin is a pleasant choice for many Ugandans," he told a journalist. "What many people want is a fresh beginning." He established his own rebel group, which he named the Front for National Salvation. Technically, he was still working in concert with Obote—they were both receiving financing from the same source, the Tanzanian government—but the superficial alliance masked an underlying rivalry between the exiled president and his ambitious former aide. Museveni modeled his organization on a Marxist liberation movement. A core group of followers, mostly old schoolmates, traveled to a military camp in southern Tanzania, where they trained alongside guerrillas from Mozambique. Museveni made arms-dealing contacts with the Mozambicans, the Tanzanian intelligence service and a Congolese warlord, whom he met in his mountain lair after a treacherous canoe journey across Lake Tanganyika. Within a few months, Museveni was commanding some seventy devoted men.

The Front for National Salvation established cells in northern and southwestern Uganda, as well as Kampala. There was also a small group in Mbarara. Museveni and his comrades, having finished their training, would sneak across the border from Tanzania to conduct rudimentary lessons in guerrilla warfare. At a safehouse in Kampala, a group of young recruits, referring to each other only by code names, met at night to learn to handle guns, playing loud music to cover the noise as they drilled. Museveni also acquired a small plot of land in Ankole, right along the Tanzanian border, which he used as a base for smuggling in rifles and grenades.

The authorities soon became aware of Museveni's activities. They struck back hard against his suspected operatives. One of the three men who had sat in the backseat of Laki's Volkswagen on the trip to

Tanzania, a UPC activist named Yuda Katundu, disappeared in fall of 1971. He was sitting in his car outside the hospital in Mbarara, waiting to pick up a friend, when soldiers came and forced him to drive off to the barracks. The rumor circulated that Katundu had recently been seen with Museveni.

After their friend went missing, Laki and three associates drove to Kampala. They had heard that they were going to be picked up next. They met with a sympathetic official from the Ministry of Internal Affairs. "Because of this rumour they became frightened and had to run to this office for rescue," the official wrote in a letter to Ankole's police chief, Ephraim Rwakanengyere. "They of course need assurance from your Security Committee that so far there is nothing to make them panic unduly."

In reality, the police chief—the same man who'd knelt to kiss Amin's feet at a rally in Mbarara—was perhaps the last person from whom Laki could have expected reassurance. A long-standing ally of James Kahigiriza, Ankole's former leader and Laki's estranged friend, Rwakanengyere had been ousted from his previous job as Ankole's chief jailer during the political purges of the 1960s, an event that had left him "permanently resentful," according to a former subordinate. He was one of a number of prominent members of Kahigiriza's faction who were now serving the Amin dictatorship with enthusiasm. The police chief was a man so famously subservient that people joked that he'd throw his body in front of his boss to shield him from a stiff breeze.

"Our enemies took advantage," said a friend and former cellmate of Laki's, by tapping the army's strength and fulfilling its needs. "They kept their eyes on us."

On the morning of Sunday, September 17, 1972, the Anglican bishop of Mbarara, Reverend Amos Betungura, was saying mass when he heard several trucks rumble down the main road through town, heading toward the army barracks. "We heard guns," the bishop recalled, three decades later: the sound of a battle taking place at the town's army barracks. The church emptied in a terrified rush, as everyone, including the bishop, ran in the opposite direction of the gunfire. Shots and explosions were heard for several hours, in fierce, gut-wrenching bursts. Then, as abruptly as it had begun, the firing was over. Several trucks sped back down the road in the direction of the Tanzanian border.

It was the long-anticipated rebel attack. Fleeing townspeople spread the news across the countryside. When word reached Ibanda, Laki was flabbergasted. The timing was terrible. Amin was still so popular. Neither Museveni nor anyone else had sent advance warning. Laki's disbelief turned to anger as it became clear that the disorganized rebels, outgunned and outnumbered, had been routed. Sitting in his office, listening to the military's triumphant updates on the radio, the chief began to recognize the consequences of the debacle. Furious with Museveni, Laki yelled to a friend, "This man is going to get us killed!"

The attack proved to be just the provocation Amin needed to eliminate all his remaining opponents. Over the next few weeks, the army rounded up nearly all the major figures in Ankole's branch of the Uganda People's Congress. One chief, the godfather to some of Laki's children, was taken from his office. Another, the man who'd stood next to Laki in the post-prison group photograph, was picked up from the hospital. He'd just undergone a circumcision after making a hasty conversion to Islam, Amin's religion, in the hope that it might save him.

At the time of the assault on Mbarara, Nekemia Bananuka was at his farmhouse, not far from the army barracks. When the rebels scattered, a few wounded stragglers came to him to seek shelter. Bananuka gave them food and water, and told them to hide in some woods on his property. Soldiers came, killed the rebels and fired on his house.

Bananuka fled to his sister's home. The soldiers came there riding in Bananuka's own bus, which he had started operating when he lost his job. His driver, a Muslim, was behind the wheel, escorting his pursuers. It is said that after Bananuka was captured, he was taken to the barracks, where soldiers cut off his penis, lit it on fire and stuck it in his mouth, like a cigar. Then they killed him. His body, like the remains of most others, was never recovered. Soldiers raided about one hundred thirty cattle from his ranch and confiscated his bus, which they later used to ferry army children to school.

Three of Bananuka's sons, aged nineteen to twenty-six, tried to make a run for it. They escaped on foot to Ibanda, more than forty miles away, where they had relatives and knew the local chief. When they arrived at Laki's house, they discovered that he was worried for his own life. He told them it was not safe to stay near him. So they hid in a nearby village. Soon the soldiers came, again led by a local man. They took the boys to a spot outside of town, near a well, and shot them, instructing the local people not to bury the bodies. The corpses lay out in the sun for days.

Nekemia Bananuka (seated). *Three of his sons pictured
here were shot* FRED BANANUKA

When Laki returned to his house for lunch the same afternoon, a friend told him Bananuka's sons were dead. "There hasn't been anyone looking for us?" Laki asked, with weary resignation. Numerous people came to visit him in his last days, suggesting that he try to get out, flee the country. Instead, the chief wrote his will. Laki's daughter Joyce rushed to Ibanda when she heard of Bananuka's death. Laki told her, too, that he wouldn't run: He wanted to die in Ankole. "He had given up," Joyce recalled. "He saw all his friends had been killed."

That evening, Laki said he wasn't hungry. He just wanted to get into bed. "We prayed together," Joyce said. "I took some water for him to bathe, but he said no. And Daddy was a person who never, ever slept without bathing. But that night, he said, 'Let me sleep. Let us pray and then I sleep.'" The next morning, Joyce caught a bus back home. She never saw her father again.

Laki wrote a letter to his wife, telling her he loved her, and asking her to take good care of their children. He wrote one to his daughter Justine, too, giving her a last piece of paternal advice: Stay out of politics.

He tried as best as he could to put off the moment he believed to be inevitable. He kept out of sight and stayed away from the office, finding excuses to visit farmers in far-off places. One day shortly before his disappearance, as he was walking home from church, Laki ran into another civil servant from the area, a man named George Kahonda.

"He and I decided to take another route, a shortcut from the church to the [county] headquarters," Kahonda remembered. "Not a shortcut as such, but a path that avoided the main road, because the army officers traveled the main road, and you could not be sure whether you would get home. So we took the path. Before we got to the headquarters he told me one thing I will never forget. He said, 'My dear friend, I fear my heart is too heavy to be contained in my chest.'"

9

A SHALLOW GRAVE

Francis Kwerebera was cutting weeds by the roadside when he first saw them coming. It was a sweltering late-morning at the end of the dry season, when the western hillsides turn from shades of green to hues of sand and ash. Kwerebera, then twenty-four, was bent over, working with a scythe, barefoot, wearing just a T-shirt and shorts. He heard the dull rumble of an automobile—in 1972, still a somewhat exotic noise in the Ugandan countryside—and looked up.

A small car, a Morris Minor, was moving fast down the dirt road, kicking up a fine fog of dust in its wake. It tore through the heart of tiny Ibanda. Past the strip of Indian shops, now forlorn and abandoned since their owners had been ordered out of the country by Idi Amin, past the low, red-roofed county headquarters. The car abruptly skidded to a halt right in front of the spot where Kwerebera was cutting weeds. He could see three men sitting inside.

The driver threw the car into reverse, backed up and parked in front of the county headquarters. He got out and walked inside.

Kwerebera was a relative of Eliphaz Laki and had been living with him in Ibanda for about a year, doing odd jobs around the house and farmwork in the nearby banana groves. He looked up to the chief—his uncle, the Big Man. Yet Kwerebera had noticed that since the attack on Mbarara five days before, Laki had become a different person, no longer the poised and commanding patriarch. His lean frame sagged, as if beneath the weight of some great sorrow.

That morning, September 22, the chief had been late to work, which was unusual. He had a reputation for punctilious adherence to routine: at his desk by 7:30, home for lunch at noon, back to work at two, home again at five. But on this morning he had tarried over his breakfast, seeing his son Duncan off to school, giving him a shilling to buy ink. Then, at around 9:00 a.m., he'd walked across the street from the chief's official residence to the four-room county headquarters.

For the last few hours, Laki had been shut in his office, a small room with a view of the rambling mountains beyond the town. The county cashier was sitting across from him, doing the books. Outside his closed door, in the headquarters' spare concrete-floored anteroom, several men were passing the time in idle conversation. When a stranger walked in, everyone hushed. He was a tall wisp of a man with bloodshot eyes, dressed nondescriptly in a white shirt and black trousers. The men noticed the stranger's skin was charcoal-dark, and they guessed he was from Uganda's north, Amin's home area.

The stranger flashed a card identifying himself as a military intelligence officer. One of those lingering around the headquarters, a policeman, snapped his head back and looked away. Back in those days, he later said, seeing a soldier, and especially an intelligence officer, was "like seeing a snake." The stranger asked to see the chief. The men gestured at the closed door to Laki's office.

Inside, the cashier heard a knock. "Come in," Laki said. The stranger entered. He and Laki talked for a moment in Swahili, a language the cashier did not understand. Then Laki stood up.

"Let's go," he said.

Laki was led across the street and up the steep driveway leading to the chief's residence. One of the strangers asked Laki where he kept his car. The chief objected. If he was going to be killed, he said, he didn't want his family to lose its most valuable possession. He asked where he was being taken. To the army barracks, the strangers told him. There was an officer there who wanted to see him. Just to talk. He'd be fine.

They walked around the spacious veranda that ran along the front of the house to the back door. Laki asked to go inside to change his clothes. Whatever was going to happen, he wanted to be dressed for the occasion. The stranger allowed him to enter the house and waited by the door. Laki went into his bedroom, grabbed his best coat and put it on over his white shirt and tie. He picked up his car keys.

When Laki emerged from the room, his maid asked him what was going on. He said only that he had to leave. Laki called to a nephew,

James, who lived in the house. He dug some bus fare out of his pocket and gave it to James. Then he instructed him to go to the family farm in Ndeija and tell his wife that soldiers had summoned him to the barracks. He'd come back soon, he promised.

Laki walked back outside. One of the three visitors had opened up the wooden door to his garage and was pushing the Volkswagen Beetle out into the backyard. This man was not a stranger—he was a local. Laki recognized him. It was Salim Sebi. Before the coup, Sebi had been a bus driver. Now he was working with the army as an informer.

Laki got into the Volkswagen and turned the ignition. The vehicle wouldn't start. It was out of gas. No problem—the soldiers had brought a full can, just in case. They poured the fuel in, and Laki turned the ignition again. Once more, the Beetle wouldn't start.

Someone clapped, loudly. Francis Kwerebera, who was still cutting weeds down by the road, knew that was a signal to him. He and a few other men working nearby walked up the hill to the chief's house. Laki asked them to push-start the car. This time, it roared to life.

Out of the corner of his eye, Kwerebera noticed that one of the strangers, a tough-looking man with yellowed, snaggled teeth, had a machine gun slung over his shoulder. Salim Sebi and one of the strangers got into the Morris Minor. The other, the snaggletoothed man with the gun, opened the Beetle's passenger-side door and sat down. The Morris Minor peeled off ahead impatiently. Laki was ordered to follow. As the Beetle passed the bamboo groves at the bottom of the driveway, the chief turned back and waved to one of his sons, Peter, who was kicking a soccer ball around the yard.

A few miles from Ibanda, Laki pulled over in front of the office of a local chief, one of his subordinates. He sent someone inside to fetch him. When the local chief came outside, Laki, efficacious to the end, handed over his set of keys to the county headquarters. Then he sped off. Laki was last sighted about twenty miles further along the route to Mbarara, by a friend who, even thirty years later, still recalled his terrified expression. Then he was gone, disappeared down the dirt road.

The snaggletoothed man told Laki to pull over at the edge of a cattle ranch. Laki must have recognized the place—it belonged to an acquaintance, one of the old-guard Bahima chieftains. Laki's passenger, still carrying his machine gun, walked around the car, opened the driver's-side door and told the chief to come out.

The Morris Minor had pulled up behind them. The tall stranger got out, holding his own rifle. The man with the gun jabbed the barrel into

Laki's back and ordered him into the bush. Salim Sebi stayed with the cars. The chief was marched into the tall grass, across a drainage ditch, and told to stop before an enormous anthill.

"Lie down," the snaggletoothed man said firmly in Swahili.

Eliphaz Laki put his face to the ground. The man turned to his accomplice and ordered him to fire. There was a harmless click as one gun jammed. The two argued in Swahili over who was going to kill the chief.

Then the snaggletoothed man shot Laki in the back of the neck.

One Friday a few months after Eliphaz Laki's disappearance, James Kahigiriza received a message summoning him to Kampala to see General Amin. The politician considered fleeing into exile. "Since extra-judicial killing had become Amin's official policy," Kahigiriza wrote in his autobiography, *Bridging the Gap*, "I feared that by going to Kampala I might suffer the same fate as thousands of other Ugandans who had already 'disappeared.'" But Kahigiriza decided that trying to escape was too risky. He presented himself at the president's office at the appointed time. When an official car arrived to take him to Amin, who was elsewhere, Kahigiriza handed his walking stick to his personal driver, giving the man instructions to return the prized possession to his family if he never came back.

The presidential car took Kahigiriza a short distance across town, to a hillside mansion just past the golf course, the private residence Amin called his Command Post. Kahigiriza was ushered into the general's spacious home office. The curtains were drawn. Amin was seated in a chair in the corner, his immense proportions submerged in shadow. He gestured for Kahigiriza to sit down. "The first thing he told me," Kahigiriza recalled, "was that he had been told that Ankole was now calm and free."

Then Amin revealed the reason that he'd called Kahigiriza to Kampala. He'd decided to make him an ambassador. Politely as he could, Kahigiriza tried to deflect the job offer. He knew that Amin was fickle about his ambassadors; those who displeased him often ended up dead. He stammered out excuses, family business that wouldn't allow him to leave the country. Amin said he understood.

"What about if I give you another job," the dictator asked. "Will you refuse?"

"Your Excellency," Kahigiriza replied. "I am ready to serve."

It was the only acceptable answer. A few weeks later, Kahigiriza returned to Kampala at the president's command. Amin took him for a ride aboard his helicopter. The rusty roofs of the city fell away as the camouflage-painted chopper took off. Kahigiriza and the president bobbed over the lushly foliated hills of central Uganda. Down below in the patchwork fields, peasants craned their necks to catch a glimpse of the president's wondrous flying machine. The helicopter would touch down periodically so that General Amin could make public appearances, and at each stop his entourage was greeted in the customary way, with chants, songs and trilling choruses of ululation. They flew northeast, into the volcanic mountains along the Kenyan border, and stayed for the night at a remote lodge. In the morning, Amin called for Kahigiriza and delivered the news. He'd been appointed the chairman of the Uganda Land Commission.

Kahigiriza could not help but feel pleased. In Uganda, an agricultural society, landownership is an important measure of wealth and status, and the commission oversaw vast tracts of public property. The post entitled him to a generous salary and ministerial perks, including a residence in Kampala. Only one thing dampened Kahigiriza's satisfaction. Almost as soon as his appointment was announced, rumors started circulating back home in Ankole. There were those who speculated that such a plum job could only have been secured by performing some sinister favor.

"What was clear to me was that rumor mongering and suspicion had gradually permeated public life in Amin's Uganda," Kahigiriza wrote in his autobiography. "It was becoming increasingly difficult to distinguish fact from fiction, truth from falsehood."

For several days after Eliphaz Laki's death, his body lay in the pasture where the soldiers had shot him, untouched. Eventually, his corpse grew bloated and foul-smelling, and some cattle-herders discovered it. The herdsmen alerted the land's owner, Yonasani Rwakanuma. The rancher came out to the pasture to see his employees' grisly discovery. He must have recognized the dead man. Rwakanuma knew Eliphaz Laki well. He, too, was active in politics, but he was from the other side of Ankole's ethnic divide, one of the Bahima. An ally of Kahigiriza, Rwakanuma had once been the chief of Ibanda himself until Laki's hard-line faction of the UPC had conspired to remove him. He was apparently embittered about the affair.

The rancher wanted the body moved because the trench it lay near drained into a pond where the cows drank. He ordered his herdsmen to dig a grave and bury the body, and he instructed them not to speak of the incident. Rwakanuma lived until 2000, two decades after Amin's overthrow. But even after Amin was gone, he never told anyone about what had become of his successor, the vanished chief of Ibanda.

10

EXHUMATION

For nearly three decades, Eliphaz Laki's body remained hidden beneath a few feet of soil. Then, in April 2001, the two ex-soldiers who'd confessed to killing him—the tall army private Mohammed Anyule and the snaggletoothed sergeant Nasur Gille—led the dead chief's son to the place where they'd committed the murder. But they failed to locate Laki's grave. Duncan Laki kept returning to the pasture, digging holes, prospecting for his father's bones. Nothing panned out. He'd been so close, he felt, but now he began to wonder whether he'd ever know what had finally become of his father.

Then one day an elderly worker from a nearby ranch showed up at the pasture. He'd heard about Duncan's search. The old ranch hand revealed a secret kept for many years, recounting a story about a body found and hastily buried there in 1972. He told Duncan that he even knew the name of one of the men who'd dug the grave.

It took several months, but someone finally tracked down the gravedigger. The man was recalcitrant under questioning by the local police—he, too, said he knew nothing. He was afraid of being set up for murder charges. Duncan offered a large reward, but the gravedigger still refused to talk. So the police threw him in jail for obstructing justice, informing the man that they were taking the case very seriously. After the arrests of three men for the resistance hero's murder, President Museveni himself had written Duncan a letter endorsing his efforts and offering him financial support.

Not even the president's involvement, however, could shake the gravedigger from his denials. The man's relatives pleaded, saying they could persuade him to tell his secret. The authorities eventually released him on the condition that he would lead Duncan to the gravesite. The Laki family soon received a call telling them to come to the pasture. The gravedigger's people said they had found someone else who could guide them to the correct spot.

At the appointed time, a boy appeared in the pasture. Dressed like a witch doctor, in a leopard-skin cape, he whirled and danced, singing an incantation. The Laki family members looked on incredulously. What was this hocus-pocus? Then the boy stopped and pointed to a spot beneath a short *oruyenje* bush.

The family dug. A few feet down, the shovel hit something. Duncan, who was still rushing from Kampala, heard the news on his cell phone and begged his relatives to wait. He arrived on the scene with a friend, a doctor. Carefully, they pushed away the soil. "It wasn't even a body, really," Duncan said later. The bones were brown and badly decayed: a femur, a rib, a skull. The moment was curiously anticlimactic. An onlooker offered to perform a traditional African mourning ritual, which would have involved Duncan smearing himself with herbs. Duncan refused. He was a firm Christian, like his father, and he didn't believe in such superstitions. Instead, Duncan carefully placed Eliphaz Laki's remains into a cardboard box.

His search was over. He did not cry.

On August 18, 2002, a long feature about the Eliphaz Laki murder case appeared in the Sunday edition of the *Monitor*, Uganda's largest and most respected independent newspaper. It recounted the story of Duncan's investigation, from his discovery of an unexpected clue at the motor vehicle registry to the disinterment of his father's remains, which had subsequently been sent to the United States for conclusive identification via DNA testing. "That is one mystery solved," the article concluded, "but how many more families wait with incomplete puzzles?"

The article created a sensation around Uganda. The idea that someone could find a body three decades later, and reclaim it from anonymity with a DNA test, struck many Ugandans as miraculous and exotic. The news coverage of the Laki case inspired other children of the disappeared, and over the next few years there were a string of similar exhumations in locales all over the country. "Laki was the first," said

Conrad Nkutu, a newspaper editor who managed to recover the remains of his own father, a government minister murdered in 1973, from an unmarked pauper's grave in a public cemetery. "During Amin's time, nobody told me that my father had been killed—they said he had gone away somewhere," the editor recalled. "I think all these cases have provoked a historical flashback."

Yet, not everyone was eager to see history revisited, particularly in Ankole, where the atrocities of the past still tinged present-day politics. At first glance, the region's ethnic divisions appeared to have been laid to rest under Museveni's regime. The president himself came from a Bahima background, but his government was populated—disproportionately—by people from both Ankole ethnic groups. Westerners who belonged to the ruling elite now identified themselves as "Banyankole," not Bahima or Bairu. There was a sense that everyone was too busy making money to worry about who'd killed whom in the old days. Yet if you dug beneath this surface comity, particularly in conversations with the generation that lived through Amin's terror, you soon hit an unsettling substratum of conspiracy theories and resentment. Those at the very top level of Uganda's current government—the generals, the inner-circle advisers, the intelligence agency chiefs—were mainly Bahima. The president himself might have offered support to the family of Eliphaz Laki, the victim's contemporaries said, but what of the people around Museveni? Were they really interested in excavating the past?

A typical story was recounted by a doctor whose uncle, another UPC chief in Ankole, disappeared in 1972. When I met the doctor in 2003, he confided that he, too, was trying to determine his relative's ultimate fate—but he felt he had to proceed very cautiously. "I think the risk is still perceived," he explained, "because Museveni is one of the Bahima." If fellow Bahima were involved in the killing, the doctor said, "people are not convinced that Museveni can be tough enough."

As was so often the case in Uganda, the language of ethnicity was being employed to describe a more complex political reality. In Ankole, it was universally held that the killings of the 1970s were the fruits of the rifts of the 1960s. Amin's army had recruited collaborators within Ankole, many of them politicians who calculated that the UPC's loss would be their own gain. Sergeant Nasur Gille, the intelligence officer, told his interrogators that in September 1972, the army was working from "a long list of names" of people who opposed the military coup. "I don't think Amin on his own would have known" who opposed him, not "without the assistance of the local people," said one cabinet minister, a former leader of the resistance—an assessment Museveni himself echoed.

Duncan Laki wasn't interested in making accusations about his father's betrayal. "I think he was betrayed by our system," he said with characteristic reserve. Yet many others wondered why, of all the lonely pastures the soldiers could have chosen for the chief's murder, they had picked one that belonged to Yonasani Rwakanuma, a political figure from the other side of the ethnic divide. There was no evidence that Laki's killers chose to stop along that stretch of country road for any reason other than its isolated topography, and the rancher would have had rational, innocent reasons to quietly bury the body—speaking up about such a discovery could be dangerous in Amin's time. Why, though, had he stayed silent for so many years afterward? "What is not clear," said a close relative of Laki, "and what some of us think is doubtful, is that he did not know who it was."

That was as far as Duncan's family members would venture in airing their private suspicions. Other children of the disappeared, however, were willing to press the question of responsibility further. One of them was Sarah Bananuka, who lost not only her father, Nekemia, the UPC leader of Ankole, but also three brothers in the purges of 1972. Bananuka's daughter, middle-aged and serving Museveni's government as a local administrator stationed in Mbarara, read the newspaper story about Duncan's quest to find his father and started to consider her own family's tragedies. She had heard that her father's dismembered body had been tossed into a mass grave and therefore assumed it was beyond reclamation. But her brothers David, Herbert and Edward, who'd been shot somewhere near Ibanda, might possibly be found.

"I want to bury them," Bananuka said one morning as she sat in the farmhouse outside Mbarara where her father had raised her, which was still gouged with bullet holes from the fighting of 1972. She wore a long *kitenge* dress with a white shawl knotted stylishly around her neck, and spoke with a tone of blunt determination, a family trait. A funeral, she said, was only the beginning of the reckoning she wanted. Wiping tears from her eyes with a paper napkin, Bananuka explained that a local man had guided the army to her brothers. She knew his identity: He was a respectable reverend now. "For a long, long time, there was—and there still is—jealousy and intrigue" in Ankole, she said. She had decided it was time to name names. Earlier that year, while attending a routine county council meeting in the course of her duties as a government official, Bananuka had stood up and pointed at one of the elected members, Ephraim Rwakanengyere, saying the man had been complicit in her father's death. The councilman, who had once been Amin's local police commander, angrily denied the charge.

Bananuka's rare public accusation had become a big story in the local Mbarara newspaper, causing intense concern among the survivors of her father's generation. "One could construe it as trying to revive the old politics," said one such elder. "If five or so others come out with this accusation, where will we end up? Naturally, you arouse some sentiments which we were trying to bury."

Bananuka was unapologetic. "It was all those associated with my father" who disappeared, she said. How, she wondered, did Amin's people know who to go after? She told me to write down a name, one that was known all over Ankole. "This is the man," she said, "who is really responsible for the death of all our people."

When he was young, and so was his nation, James Kahigiriza was fond of carrying a carved wooden walking stick. In a culture where age signified status, it was an indicator of the power and eminence he possessed so precociously as the chief minister of Ankole in those early years of independence. By the age of eighty-four, however, Kahigiriza's cane had come to hold more than symbolic importance. He kept it close at hand as he whiled away his days inside a musty living room decorated with faded black-and-white photographs. Kahigiriza's wood-framed ranch house was situated at the end of a grassy path, atop a hill that oversaw a lovely anthill-speckled savanna, but the home's proprietor could no longer appreciate his view. His eyes were failing him, along with his ears, his kidney and his prostate. Positioned in an overstuffed chair, surrounded by pillows, his left leg propped up on a stool, Kahigiriza greeted a visitor without standing, speaking in a faint, raspy voice.

"Laki was a great friend of mine," the elderly politician said. "He was almost like a brother." History had conspired, however, to set the two friends on opposite sides of Ankole's political divide. On the armrest of Kahigiriza's chair sat a copy of a memoir he'd published some years before, entitled *Bridging the Gap: Struggling Against Sectarianism and Violence in Ankole and Uganda*. In it, he had told the story of his life-long political migration. Since his start in the Bairu equality movement of the 1950s and '60s, Kahigiriza had gradually moved away from his youthful beliefs. Now, in his old age, he led an organization that advocated for the restoration of the abolished Bahima monarchy, at least in a ceremonial form—or as he put it in his book, "reviving the culture of Ankole." With its ethnic overtones, the monarchist movement remained highly controversial, and as its leader Kahigiriza had earned the contempt of many former comrades. Kahigiriza saw his ideological turnabout, by contrast, as the natural culmination of what he believed to be his life's work: healing ethnic divisions.

"Some diehards still think in terms of ethnic differences. Me, I think that's useless," Kahigiriza explained. "I thought everybody should be mixed together. . . . I have no problems with the Bahima. Even now, they still call me the *enganzi*."

Kahigiriza's third wife, Mable, a doting and vivacious woman a couple of decades younger than him, served him a tall gray glass of millet porridge, which he told me he drank for its restorative properties. "I had some operations," Kahigiriza said. "I couldn't even stand up as I am now able to. Now I have improved a bit." His face, always pudgy, had acquired a jowly gravity, but the rest of his body appeared lumpy and misshapen, flabby in some places and hollowed-out in others. At times, his memories were fuzzy; his autobiography was there by his side in case he forgot any details.

About Idi Amin's coup, which others had said they'd seen him celebrating, Kahigiriza's recollection was clear. "I would frankly say that I was one of the group that was happy," he readily admitted. "Obote had a way of making people hate each other." The evening of the coup, Kahigiriza told me, a group of his friends and political supporters, some of them Bahima notables who'd opposed the UPC, had gathered at the very house where he was now sitting. "I remember that I gave them a cow—a bull—and they roasted it," the retired politician said, laughing softly. "They were so happy. These were people that Obote had not done well by. They had been against him."

Kahigiriza served in Idi Amin's government for five years as chairman of Uganda's land commission. In *Bridging the Gap*, he had described the vertiginous experience. Those who were within Amin's circle of influence, as Kahigiriza was, enjoyed access to wealth, rare luxury goods and most of all, a measure of the military's reflected power. But Amin was also a diabolical master. When the dictator decided that some subordinate was no longer useful—and one never knew when or why that might happen—the unlucky person's body would often wash up on the far side of the Nile's Karuma Falls.

Kahigiriza's turn came on February 15, 1977. That morning, he was working in his government office, right across the street from parliament, when three secret police agents burst through his door and informed him that he was wanted for questioning. They pushed Kahigiriza out his office door, down a flight of stairs and into an unmarked car. They handcuffed him and threw him into a narrow, bloodstained basement cell, which was jammed so tight that its occupants sat face-to-face, their knees touching in the darkness. He was held there for several miserable weeks. One of his cellmates was the Reverend Janan Luwum, the Anglican archbishop of Uganda, who after a brief period of confinement was taken away and executed on Amin's orders. Kahigiriza never really knew why he'd been arrested, though eventually he was questioned by an interrogator who accused him of involvement in a nonexistent subversive organization called the Intelligentsia Group. Kahigiriza professed his innocence, and to his surprise, he was eventually released. After a few days' rest, he went back to work, and continued to serve the regime until Amin's overthrow in April 1979.

After the Amin regime fell, Kahigiriza returned to the ranch. He found the place had been ransacked by looters, and most of his cattle stolen or slaughtered. Ankole's new rulers were his old adversaries, the UPC hardliners—at least those of them who'd managed to outlast Amin—and it was rumored that they wanted to kill him. "I was warned . . . never to frequent the town, Mbarara," Kahigiriza later said. "I had to keep on my farm."

A year after Yoweri Museveni took power in Uganda, Kahigiriza testified about his harrowing experiences before the Commission of Inquiry into Violations of Human Rights. He told the commission that the malignancy that afflicted Uganda, the cancerous habit of faction, had developed long before Idi Amin. "When I became *enganzi*, in fact, there were some people who were supporting me thinking that when I come I will fight Bahima," he said. "When I did not do it, it annoyed them. They said, 'Oh, this one is one of them.' This is how the split started in UPC." When Kahigiriza concluded his testimony, the commission members applauded his "refreshing" candor. "You are a respected citizen not only of Ankole but of this country," one of them said, "and your evidence, views, opinions are of great value."

Back in Ankole, however, some viewed Kahigiriza not as a respected elder, but as a traitor. He and his allies were never able to shake the insinuation that they'd been complicit in the deaths and disappearances of Amin's regime. The accusation was seldom voiced, at least publicly. But

names of the suspected informers were whispered like deadly confi-
dences. Kahigiriza was the one Sarah Bananuka had singled out. Others
repeated her charge, identifying him as Ankole's chief collaborator.

"Kahigiriza was the architect of the whole thing," said Edward
Rurangaranga, one of Eliphaz Laki's friends and political allies. "He was
the one creating all this mischief," said Kesi Nyakimwe, leader of the
Banyankole Cultural Foundation, an organization of Bairu dedicated to
fighting Kahigiriza's efforts to restore the monarchy. "All these people
who were arrested, he was pointing them out." Some of those who
made the accusation had obvious grudges against Kahigiriza, but I also
heard it voiced by many who had no stake in Ankole's feuds: history
professors, cabinet ministers, even those who'd sided with Kahigiriza in
politics. "During the invasion," said Francis Bantariza, a former member of parliament who'd belonged to the opposition Democratic Party
during the 1960s, "the Kahigiriza people were the ones killing, to eliminate the other side."

The allegation was difficult to prove. But there was at least one individual who was positioned to know something close to the truth.
Brigadier Ali Fadhul was the commander of the barracks in Mbarara at
the time of the September 1972 invasion. In 1987, during the brief
period between Yoweri Museveni's rise to power and the government's
decision to make national reconciliation its overriding policy, Fadhul
was arrested. His trial took place over the course of two years in a
Mbarara mansion that had been converted to public use as a courthouse—as it happened, it had been the brigadier's own residence back
when he'd been the local commandant—and culminated in a conviction and a death sentence. Well over a decade afterward, however, Fadhul was still sitting on Uganda's death row, thanks to a series of appeals
that had staved off his execution.

Fadhul met me in a dingy prison visiting room. Though he was now
in his sixties, he was still an imposing man, who wore white Muslim
robes and a graying goatee. The brigadier tried to explain the difficulties
he'd faced as Amin's army commander in Ankole. To the south in Tanzania, Milton Obote was making warlike speeches. Rumor had it that
some area UPC leaders were sending men and money across the border
to rebel training camps. An elusive militant named Yoweri Museveni
was known to be sneaking around the province. Amin had issued strict
orders to stamp out such threats. Yet Fadhul, a northerner, was essentially a foreigner to Ankole. He didn't know the people, understand the
culture or speak the language. He needed locals to guide him, to gather

the gossip, to tell him who was really on his side. "The civilians were very helpful," Fadhul said. "As a new person, newly transferred to Ankole, I didn't know the area. It was a big area. So it took me a long time to know these people. My job was to keep in touch with all of them."

And James Kahigiriza? He "was helping, but indirectly," Fadhul said. "As a person of high reputation, he could not show his involvement."

Kahigiriza said he knew Eliphaz Laki to be "an innocent fellow." His recollection beyond that, he confessed, was not as sharp as it used to be. He said he wasn't sure why Laki had been killed. "You know, it could be that his friends" were involved with the resistance, he said somberly. "So many other people were killed in this way, through false allegations." Kahigiriza paused periodically, as if lost in private thoughts. The words came to him slowly, and at times he drifted into inaudible mumbling.

"We had been friends from down below," he continued. "There was even one time when he fell sick with a certain blood fever and he came and stayed with me and my wife, and my wife took care of him, and she looked after him and he recovered. No, I didn't have anything against him. He was quite warm. He was a friend of mine, but then . . ." The sentence trailed off.

"What happened?" I asked.

"You know, politicians are attracted by some funny, funny things that sometimes draw their attention away from what they should have been doing," Kahigiriza replied. "I think some of my friends thought, what they thought I would *do* was not what I *did*, you see." For instance, the former chief minister explained, some UPC hardliners wanted to fire all the Bahima officeholders, but Kahigiriza had resisted. "They thought that by not going with them on the side of hating the Bahima, I was betraying them," Kahigiriza went on. "Some of these people were my friends, but they were easily taken in. They betrayed me because they thought I had betrayed them."

"I heard that many of these people were ousted from their positions after Amin's coup," I said, as gently as I could. "They were even put in prison for a while."

"Yes, there were people who were arrested. But I had no hand. I didn't even know," Kahigiriza answered, responding to a question that I hadn't even put to him. "I don't want to . . . sorry . . . to enter into something on which I am not concrete. I am not concrete on this." He murmured something I couldn't understand. "There were people who I respect from here, some they used to arrest. But I wouldn't know . . ."

One of his cows mooed outside the window. Kahigiriza tried to collect himself. The accusations against him, he said, were all politically motivated. "Those ones who call themselves the Bairu, the strong UPC fellows," he said, "they hated me, and maybe there are those who are still in the habit of hatred. If they see me together with the Bahima, there is that grudge. I am still bitter and unhappy to see the Banyankole divided."

Kahigiriza's face suddenly looked ashen. "Excuse me," he said, standing up abruptly and reaching for his cane. He hobbled a few steps toward the bathroom, listed hard to the left side and then collapsed in a heap on the floor. His chest was heaving. Mable came running into the living room. "I'm sorry," she said as she tried to hoist her husband back to his feet. "He has been sick for so long."

I excused myself and walked out onto the ranch house's porch. After a decent interval, I went back inside to say good-bye. Kahigiriza was sitting in his chair, a bit recomposed but still weak. He said he was happy to see that people were still interested in his achievements. Then he repeated a roundabout proverb about old age, one that conveyed the lesson that mortality was unforgiving.

Very few of his contemporaries, however, had been afforded this gift, the humiliations of a long life. Many years before, antagonism born of grievance and ambition had created circumstances in which men who knew each other well, who had been schooled together, who worked together, who ate together and went to church together, had turned against their friends with frightening ferocity. Only one side had survived. Whatever Kahigiriza had done, he had managed to live long enough to write his own history—one that would endure, he hoped, long after he was gone. It might have been incomplete, or full of lies, but it was impossible to say for sure. Certain truths were no longer retrievable. They existed only in the old man's memories, and even those were dimming now, flickering like frayed filaments in a dying bulb, passing into oblivion with the rest of a generation.

PART 3

11

THE PRISONER

Luzira Prison, like Sing Sing and Alcatraz and many other storied houses of detention, occupies an incongruously sunny piece of real estate, a commanding bluff overlooking the serene blue waters of Murchison Bay, a northern-jutting finger of Lake Victoria. The facility, surrounded by a high fence, consists of a number of squat cinder-block structures that run upward along a steep potholed road. The level of security rises as you climb. At the topmost point of the hill stands a massive crenellated fortress known as the Upper Prison. Constructed by the British in 1928 to hold "the most hardened, difficult, and refractory type of prisoner" (in the words of one colonial-era report), the Upper Prison still functions as Uganda's maximum-security penitentiary. Before independence, many of the country's foremost nationalists did time there. In the present era, the facility has become a repository for captured rebels, treason plotters, scoundrel politicians and Islamic extremists, as well as many hardened criminals. Designed for a population of around six hundred fifty inmates, it now holds well over three times that many.

Major General Yusuf Gowon, the lead defendant in the Eliphaz Laki murder case, was remanded to Luzira on July 17, 2002, after the magistrate presiding over a preliminary hearing ruled that prosecutors had amassed enough evidence to proceed to trial. Gowon, who had been free on bail for most of the fifteen months since his initial arrest, reported to the courthouse that day prepared for an extended prison stay, carrying a rolled-up papyrus sleeping mat and a blue plastic bag filled with belongings. Despite the seriousness of the circumstances, the general—short and bald, with a copious belly and a gray-speckled mustache—wore a wide smile and a cheery tropical-patterned shirt. He was trying not to worry too much. As he neared the age of seventy, Gowon had grown accustomed to his uncommon life's dizzying pattern of rises and reversals.

Here, at last, was someone to take the blame. Laki's betrayers were unidentifiable, and Idi Amin was far away, but Gowon, a central figure in the dictatorship, was one man who could be brought to account. Once Amin's second-in-command, he had been charged with Laki's murder on the strength of confessions by two lower-ranking soldiers, an assessment of responsibility that was altogether rare in Uganda, where guilt was usually apportioned to groups—tribes, parties, religions— rather than to individuals. Gowon's case had marked a dramatic departure: an unlikely investigation leading to a singular prosecution. Whether this turn of events represented justice, however, was a matter of fierce internal debate. "Ugandan history is told through different lenses," explained a prominent journalist, whose own father had disappeared during the Amin regime. "Which tribe are you from? Which religion are you? Which region are you from? What regime are you affiliated with, and is it still in power? That last one is the most important."

Duncan Laki and his supporters might have felt that Gowon's arrest was a victory for truth and right, but the general's tribesmen, who inhabited the poor northwestern region of West Nile, saw the prosecution as a show trial, just one more episode in a decades-long campaign of vengeance against the people of Idi Amin. They looked at Yoweri Museveni's support for the Laki family as sectarian meddling, a case of the president siding with his tribe against the national interest. Like all the high-level Amin regime figures who had returned to Uganda at Museveni's invitation, Gowon had been led to believe that such a prosecution was impossible—otherwise, he never would have left the safe haven of exile. So why was this happening?

None of it made much sense to Gowon. Inevitably described as a "simple man" by his friends, he had little education and less understanding of the concept of justice. He assumed his arrest had to be the result of some opaque government vendetta. Unable to comprehend, powerless to resist, Gowon resigned himself to staying in Luzira for the duration of his trial, which was scheduled to begin in the fall of 2002.

Because of his advanced age and his former high status, Gowon was accorded a few special privileges. While most Luzira inmates were kept in overcrowded common cells, the general was given one to himself, roughly the size of a broom closet. While most prisoners slept on coarse blankets or sheets of cardboard, he had his sleeping mat. (He later upgraded it to a hard foam mattress.) Still, Gowon had to contend with difficult conditions. His cell had no toilet, just a plastic bucket. Sanitation was poor throughout the prison, and disease, including HIV, was rampant. Prisoners were fed one meal a day, typically a bowl of *posho*, a starch made of corn flour, occasionally augmented by a helping of weevil-riddled beans. Gowon rapidly shed more than thirty pounds.

Uganda had very retributive sentencing laws; they prescribed an automatic death sentence in cases of murder. Gowon tried not to dwell on the prospect. He was not overly given to introspection. He tried to make the best of prison life, spending his afternoons shuffling around the prison's walled, muddy exercise yard in cheap plastic flip-flops, chatting up new acquaintances as the younger inmates played soccer. Though he'd once been feared, Gowon was disarming in person. He possessed a natural warmth and a jolly laugh that put one at ease. He even struck up a friendship with a former enemy, a bitter opponent of Amin who had gone on to commit his own ghastly crimes while serving a subsequent regime. Now on death row, he'd become a born-again preacher.

The people Gowon had to avoid were the ones he knew best: those who had served alongside him in Amin's army. The men whose confessions had implicated him, Private Mohammed Anyule and Sergeant Nasur Gille, were also imprisoned at Luzira. Though they'd been charged with the same crimes as Gowon—the tentative cooperation deal they'd struck with the prosecutors had fallen through—it still appeared possible that they would eventually testify against him in return for leniency. The facility held a few other Amin-era officers, imprisoned over the years for various crimes, but Gowon couldn't count on the sympathy of his former peers. They reviled him as a tactical blunderer, the one who'd caused their defeat in the 1979 war that thrust them from power. One ex-general, whose antipathy toward Gowon traced back to ancient palace intrigues, went so far as to offer comfort to the turncoats Anyule and Gille, inviting them to stay in his cellblock, where they could enjoy his physical protection and a private supply of food.

Despised, deserted by his natural allies and confined to a lonely cell, Gowon had time to look back and consider his failings. In these moments of reflection, the general never dwelled on his actions during the time he possessed power, never displayed the slightest guilt. Rather, Gowon believed his true mistake had come in a moment of weakness, a point in his life when he'd possessed one overriding desire: to return home.

In 1979, when Amin was ousted, Gowon scampered into Congo atop a Honda motorcycle, never imagining he'd be gone for fifteen years. A disastrous war was in its dying moments, and the general needed a temporary refuge. He found a Congolese customs officer and promised the man a car in return for safe passage. The officer, a pliant fellow, took Gowon to some kindly Catholic missionaries, who offered him shelter. Gowon, finished with fighting, began to build a civilian life. He managed to get a few trucks he owned brought across the border from Uganda, and started a business renting them out. He also did a little smuggling. He eventually bought a comfortable house in the Congo town of Bunia. Two of his wives joined him and kept him well fed.

Gowon originally thought he'd return to Uganda as soon as the fighting burned itself out. But there was no end to the bloodshed. There was a long civil war, which was really many civil wars: There was Yoweri Museveni's movement, and a Baganda nationalist movement, and a movement led by a northern soothsayer who claimed she was possessed by the Holy Spirit. The chaos pushed an estimated 250,000 to 350,000 refugees from West Nile across Uganda's borders into Sudan and Congo. Some of Gowon's former colleagues from Amin's high command recruited refugee armies and set themselves up as warlords, with guns and plunder and concubines. But Gowon didn't follow their example. He wanted to be left alone in peace.

As the years passed, though, a sense of disconnected longing gripped him. Gowon missed the sound of a familiar language, the companionship of his extended family, the dungy smell of his farm fields. It all lay so frustratingly close. Then, one day in 1994, a visitor arrived from the other side of the border, an old girlfriend. She'd come as an emissary from President Yoweri Museveni, for whom she worked as an adviser. The emissary told Gowon that things had changed at home. The president wanted him to return. To the exiled general, it sounded like the promise of deliverance.

There was a letter, written on presidential stationery and signed by a senior military aide to Museveni. It explained the government's new amnesty policy.

I wish to assure you and through you other former officials, and indeed all Ugandans currently in refuge/exile, of the [Museveni] government's commitment to the policy of national reconciliation. . . . I wish therefore to encourage you and through you all Ugandans still in refuge/exile to come back home and participate in the democratization and development process going on.

Museveni had declared that it was time for Ugandans to put an end to their endless cycle of violence and retribution. He wanted to sign treaties with rebel forces and bring the exiles home, to stabilize the country and reinforce his image as a peacemaker ahead of upcoming free elections. In return for submission, Museveni was offering significant inducements: government jobs, government houses, government cars—and most important, the government's pardon. It was never explicitly stated, but the tacit understanding was that when it came to the crimes of Idi Amin's regime, there would be no more questions asked: not by the government's faltering truth commission, and certainly not by the police or the courts.

Gowon was not a rebel leader, but he was still a major general, and Museveni's government imagined his safe return would set a high-profile example. It announced his repatriation deal in March 1994, just as Ugandans were going to the polls to vote for representatives to an assembly that would write a new constitution. When Gowon finally crossed back over the border that December, he came as the head of a delegation of twenty-five former military officers and some ten thousand civilian refugees. A picture of a happy, healthy Gowon, reunited with his family, was published in the state newspaper for all to see.

The government did all it could to make the old general feel welcome. The night of his return, he was checked into the best hotel in Arua, the White Rhino, and a party was held in his honor. Gowon gave a speech in which he lauded President Museveni for his commitment to peace and reconciliation. A few days later, Gowon was flown to Kampala, where he and a few comrades met Museveni in the parliament building. Sitting in a thronelike chair at the head of a long conference table, the president told the returnees they had nothing to fear, that "Uganda was home for all Ugandans."

Afterward, Museveni pulled Gowon aside. "Gowon, do you know me?" the president asked, as the general remembers it. "I was the one who attacked in 1972 but came back alive." The two men cheerily reminisced about fighting each other in Mbarara, in the battle that led, indirectly, to Eliphaz Laki's execution.

Gowon decided to settle down in Kampala, where the government rented him a house in a desirable suburb of Ntinda and provided him with an allowance equal to several hundred dollars a month. "When I came back Museveni was very, very happy," Gowon later said. "We came back under this government to serve this government." In 1996, when Museveni first stood for election—ten years after taking the presidential office by force—Gowon traveled the country making speeches on behalf of his campaign. "I sought Gowon's support," one of the ruling party's political strategists recalled. "As an ex-army chief of staff, I was under the impression he would wield the support of his fellow former soldiers, and so deliver them to Museveni."

After the election, Gowon met with the president and told him about an idea he had, a scheme to get into Uganda's biggest growth industry, the relief business. He was starting a nongovernmental organization called Good Hope. The NGO's stated mission was to assist former rebels in adjusting to civilian life. The plan was that they would be trained to work at private enterprises such as a bus company and a fishing outfit—businesses Gowon would own and presumably profit from. Museveni approved the idea and promised Good Hope several hundred thousand dollars in public funding.

But the money never materialized. This was the beginning of a mysterious series of reversals. Gowon's government stipend stopped coming. Then so did his rent. Gowon's landlord evicted him, and he had to relocate to a far more modest residence in back of a bicycle shop run by one of his sons. Jobless and broke, he found himself spending a lot of time hanging around a place called the Slow Boat Pub, wondering what had become of his good fortune. He could only assume some powerful force was working against him. Then he was arrested.

Death row occupied the innermost cellblock of the Upper Prison. Yusuf Gowon wasn't housed there, because he was still awaiting trial, but the place loomed ever-present in his mind, like a suppressed dreadful thought. At the time Gowon was imprisoned in Luzira, there hadn't been a hanging in three years, because President Museveni maintained a policy of merciful neglect when it came to signing death warrants. But the preserved memories of past executions, horror stories retold around the exercise yard, were enough to send a shudder through any man facing judgment. When the warrants were handed down, they usually came in batches. With their arrival, the prison would suddenly be engulfed in morbid activity. Inmates would be put to work making wooden coffins and sewing black hoods. For several nights, as the preparations went on, the sleepless voices of the condemned, singing Christian hymns, would float across the prison. Then, one by one, the doomed prisoners would be taken to the gallows and hanged. It was an unpleasant way to die: Even with a broken neck, a hanged man would often remain conscious for excruciating minutes until dying of asphyxiation, and sometimes his head would snap clean off from the force of his fall. This latter, grisly occurrence happened most commonly, according to one report, in the cases of "old inmates aged above 60."

Facing the gallows, and figuring he had nothing to lose, Gowon agreed to meet me in October 2002 for what was to be the first of many interviews. I can't be certain why he opened himself up to examination, but I know he felt lonely and powerless and saw himself as a political prisoner. He hoped that by telling his story he would bring attention and sympathy to his plight. Most of all, Gowon wanted to keep me around, because he calculated, not without reason, that my very presence as a conspicuous—that is, white-skinned—observer in the courtroom would act as a check on his country's unreliable justice system. "He thinks it is such a good opportunity," Gowon's defense attorney, Caleb Alaka, told me as we set out for Luzira Prison to meet his client.

The lawyer and I passed through a series of checkpoints on foot, where guards in beige uniforms transcribed our names into heavy ledgers and confiscated our cell phones and wallets before allowing us to proceed to the Upper Prison at the top of the hill. As we waited outside in a long line of doleful visitors, we could look out over a precipice and see fishermen casting their nets into the lake from wooden canoes, as the afternoon sun glinted off the water's surface in a long rippled ribbon. Eventually, with the loud clack of a bolt, a wooden door swung open and we were admitted into the prison.

Guards ushered us down a dank corridor. Its water-stained turquoise walls were decked with peeling posters exhorting rehabilitation and warning against tuberculosis. Hanging from a high spot was a small portrait of President Museveni. We were led through a passageway to a darkened, unused office. One of the guards jiggled the light switch. Nothing happened—another blackout, a frequent occurrence in Kampala. The guards shrugged and left us to wait for the prisoner to appear.

Through one small window, I could see a bruised band of thunderheads rolling in off the lake.

After a few moments, Gowon walked in and took a seat on a short wooden bench. He wore a weathered blue golf shirt, blue slacks and flip-flops, and looked tired and worried. His small eyes were bloodshot. The dim light gave a shiny cast to the prisoner's face, and I noticed a set of three faint, vertical scars along each of his cheeks, the marks of a childhood initiation rite of his northern tribe. It was Idi Amin's tribe too.

Gowon carried with him a small bundle of tattered newspaper clippings. One was the recent feature from the *Monitor* about Duncan Laki's long search for his father's killers. Another was an article President Museveni had written for the state-owned newspaper to commemorate the thirtieth anniversary of the rebel attack on Mbarara. Gowon had underlined and annotated passages that he thought might help exonerate him. He began to explain details of the military command structure, trying to make the case that he wasn't really in charge during the harsh repressions that followed the rebel attack of 1972.

"I was the second-in-command, the administrator at the barracks," Gowon said, giving an earnest account of his duties during the fighting. "My work was to see how to get coffins, doctors to treat the wounded, and to see that food got to the locations where the war was going on." He denied any involvement with intelligence operations, which he said were the province of his superiors. "I had no knowledge about these chiefs, I had no knowledge of Laki," Gowon said, his voice gathering passion until it crescendoed into a shout. "I really told the police I did not know anything about it. These people were civilians. They could not have been killed. This is what I *know*."

As fat drops of rain began to clatter off the sheet metal roofs of the prison complex, Gowon said he was still perplexed about the cause of his arrest. "They said there is peace. They talked about amnesty," the general complained. "They said, 'Mr. Gowon, you have no problems. You can come back home.'" Now Gowon felt that he'd been betrayed, led into a trap by unknown conspirators. How else could he explain why he had been singled out for prosecution despite the government's assurances?

The truth was less fantastic and more heartening. The reality was that Gowon had simply lost his political leverage. His usefulness to the government had always been symbolic; unlike those who had commanded rebel movements, he couldn't call on any fighters to rise up in his defense. As the insurgencies in West Nile had abated in intensity, the balance of expediency had shifted slightly away from reconciliation and toward accountability. The judiciary had acquired some independent power, and prosecutors, who could read the news from the Hague and Arusha, were getting their own ideas, ones that might, just possibly, fit within the widening bounds of discretion allowed by Museveni. In a country where events had long been dictated by a single man at the top, things were loosening up. No one had realized exactly what was now possible, however, until a random occurrence—Duncan Laki's discovery of a clue in the motor vehicle registry—had led the authorities to Gowon. Duncan's success, which had surprised even him, was an unanticipated indicator of an untested freedom to seek justice.

To Gowon, though, his impending trial was nothing but a cruel, tribal exercise. During the time of our acquaintance, a period that started with one interview and stretched into years, I think I came to understand how things looked from where he sat. Our relationship was naturally hemmed by circumstance. Sometimes we talked in Luzira, where he reminisced for hours outside the presence of his lawyer. On other occasions we discussed things through the bars of a holding cell in a courthouse basement. We snatched moments of conversation during the many breaks, recesses and delays in his trial, sitting beside one another on hard courtroom benches as his guards looked on. Through it all, the imprisoned general never wavered in maintaining his absolute innocence.

On one level, the claim was preposterous. No one who had served Amin at Gowon's level could honestly deny responsibility. Yet Gowon was not standing trial for complicity with a criminal regime. He was accused of the murder of Eliphaz Laki. When it came to the narrow issue before the court—whether Gowon had really sent two soldiers to Laki's office with orders to kill—the verdict was no foregone conclusion. A judge would have to confront serious questions: Were Anyule and Gille telling the truth about the execution order, or was it possible that they were trying to deflect the prosecution's focus to a high-profile target? What had investigators really promised those two in return for implicating the general?

Ugandans asked more searching questions. What would constitute a just resolution to this case? If Gowon was hanged, would that punishment really redress an evil that seemed more like a national sickness than an individual crime? Even in Ankole, there were those who felt conflicting emotions about the prosecution. Many remembered Gowon as a relatively rational and humane army officer: the best of a bad lot.

There were numerous accounts of Gowon's mercy, told by people who recalled being harassed by soldiers or threatened with death, only to be freed after an audience with him. "Let no one deceive you," said one of Laki's associates. "Gowon saved a lot of lives."

In 1995, shortly after Gowon's return from exile, the town of Mbarara had even thrown the general a homecoming celebration. In a picture of the event, the scene is recognizable to anyone who has lived in Africa—one of those daylong, sweaty, speechifying affairs, held on a stage beneath colorful patriotic bunting. Dozens of notables are assembled on risers: judges, soldiers, politicians and their wives. As the guest of honor, Gowon is seated at a table set with flowers and bottles of orange soda, wearing a contented look. He could be excused for thinking that he had been forgiven.

"When I heard of Gowon being implicated in Laki's disappearance, it surprised me more than it would have were it anyone else," said Zeddy Maruru, a retired army officer and a distant relative of the Laki family. Maruru described how he had fled to Kenya in 1977 to avoid death at the hands of fellow soldiers who doubted his loyalty and went on to become a leader of the liberation army that removed Amin. Having served alongside Gowon and having fought against him, Maruru saw the general not as a monster but as one of those workaday attendants who populate every dictatorship, a normal man with human failings who had been plunged into monstrosity almost by chance. Like Laki, the chief who'd allegedly died by his order, Gowon's life had followed a course dictated by a force larger than himself: the vengeful history of a marginal and downtrodden people who were carried to power on a convectional current of resentment.

"I always looked at Gowon as one of the more reasonable of Amin's soldiers: a one-eyed fellow among the blind," Maruru concluded. "He just happened to be born at a bad time. He came from that place, and from that tribe."

12

AMONG THE CANNIBALS

Later on, they blamed the Turks for bringing the demons up the river. The Turks, who ransacked their villages; the Turks, who dragged the strongest of them back to Khartoum in chains; the Turks, who captured slaves and marked their cheeks with three vertical scars. The Turks were bad enough. But then one day the Turks came paddling upstream in a wooden boat, into the country of the river people, and this time they brought three black-cloaked demons, hideous to behold, with ashen faces and unruly hair. For generations, the people of the river had passed down tales of pale spirits who held the power to bring sickness, banish the rains, kill off their livestock and, most dreadful of all, carry their children away, not to force them into servitude but to feast upon them as cannibals.

The boat moored itself by a tree near a village and the demons waded ashore. The villagers gathered around them in stricken horror. One of the river people, a stooped elder, stepped forward. He held out an arm laden with iron and ivory bracelets and touched one of the demon creatures, finding it was made of solid, clammy flesh. A frightened murmur went through the crowd. Then another brave man stepped forward and, with a bold thrust of his arm, waved the demons away.

"Back to the boat," the river people yelled. "Back to the boat!"

The demons hastened back on board, and the Turks paddled them away, back toward Khartoum. That night, the river children slept safely on their mats of grass. The people felt lucky—they'd chased off a curse.

There were many more where the demons had come from, though. What the river people could never understand was the power of that ancient name, the *Nile*. Far away, on a continent they knew nothing of, the very word acted like a magnetic force on loose filaments, drawing dreamers and restless spirits south against the great river's current. Europe's journey of rediscovery began in Egypt, with Napoleon's military campaign at the turn of the nineteenth century, and continued along the Nile's route through Sudan, a march that ultimately led into the river's remote wilds and a region called Equatoria, a province of tenuous Ottoman suzerainty that encompassed a large portion of present-day northern Uganda. The first white visitors to this area were less tangibly threatening to the natives than the Ottoman merchants who had harvested them as human cargo for export to Arabia. But in those bewildered moments of initial contact, the newcomers were taken to be a menacing alien force.

The demons of the indigenous people's imaginations were actually a group of Italian priests, members of a Khartoum-based mission that sent several expeditions along the Nile during the 1840s and 1850s. About a year after the missionaries' first recorded appearance, a single one returned, Father Angelo Vinco. A report subsequently published by church authorities in the priest's native Verona vividly describes the terror his arrival unleashed. All along his route upstream, when Vinco's wooden boat would pass, the natives ran away, fearing that the stranger was about to devour them. The missionary would shout for them to come back and listen, tossing valuable beads onto the riverbank, but few heeded his pleas.

Vinco eventually came ashore at a settlement ruled by a rainmaker called Nyigilò. The rainmaker had done business with the previous group of Italians, as well as with the Ottoman slavers; he was not one to let superstition get in the way of a profit. In exchange for an extortionate sum—some fine clothing, two brass bells, a mirror and other precious items—and the missionary's commitment to pay him regular tribute in the form of beads, the rainmaker allowed the visitor to stay in his lands, provided that no one fell sick or got eaten. Just to be safe, however, he sent the stranger inland, where the curious people, reassured to learn that he would use his magical powers on their rainmaker's behalf, greeted him with great interest, caressing his skin and tugging at his beard.

That year, the rains arrived safely, and the people of the river saw their crops and livestock thrive. They stopped fearing the stranger, whom they affectionately nicknamed "Maneater." At first, he seemed insensate to them, but he gradually learned a bit of their language. The priest told the people that he'd been sent from the north by a god they didn't know, one who had created the sun, the moon, the stars, their cattle, the trees and even the river itself. The people were eager to learn more about such wonders, but before the curious pale creature was able to explain he caught a fever and died.

Over the coming seasons, however, the Europeans became a regular presence along the river. At first, they came in wooden boats, like the slavers. Later, they plied the river in smoke-belching crafts made of iron. Over time, they established protectorates and colonies, state structures that meant little in practice to the people along the river. Far into the nineteenth century, they lived in relative ignorance of the outside world, grouped in insular clans ruled by rainmakers. They wore little clothing; they kept their bodies shaved; they pierced their lips and earlobes with iron pins; they wore bracelets of ivory and python skin. They fit perfectly, in other words, the white man's notion of a "savage" society. European anthropologists even asserted that they practiced that most transgressive of all primitive customs, cannibalism.

Of course, the river people speculated that the whites engaged in the same heinous conduct; in their languages, the word for "European" literally meant "evil spirit." But the indigenous people traded with the outsiders, and sometimes even served them as their guards and porters, although they continued to live as they always had—at a wary distance from European civilization. That all began to change in the summer of 1877, when a slight, willful and extremely nearsighted German doctor sailed into this atmosphere of mutual incomprehension aboard a rickety thirty-eight-ton screw-steamer. His arrival set in motion a chain of events that would one day propel Yusuf Gowon, a humble farmer, to power.

The doctor went by the name Mehemet Emin. As his boat chugged south, at a pace of four miles an hour, he jotted down meticulous observations of the Nile: the rocky reefs that split it and the long-necked herons perched atop them; the tall palms along its banks, waving in the merciful breeze; the water lilies and the blue-green snakes that glided across the surface of the water. Emin tooted his steam whistle and watched the tall grass rustle along the riverside. His unwitting subjects emerged, naked, carrying firewood that they offered to trade for beads. This land that he'd been given to rule, Equatoria, was really just a word on the map, an imaginary state, but Emin intended to build it, alone, according to the dictates of his eccentric ambition.

He had been born Eduard Schnitzer, in the Prussian province of Silesia, to a bourgeois Jewish family in 1840. But he'd long since shed both his German and Jewish identities, choosing an itinerant life that, through many exotic twists and turns, had finally taken him into one of the last unknown precincts of the earth. During his initial stay in Khartoum, he'd converted to Islam, taking his new name, and before long, despite lacking any evident aptitude for statecraft or warfare, he'd managed to secure himself an appointment as pasha, or governor, of Equatoria. Technically, Equatoria was a province subject to Egypt, which was in turn a vassal state of the Ottoman Empire. That only began to describe its complex status: Emin's boss, Sudan's governor, was the famous British general Charles "Chinese" Gordon, who was freelancing on behalf of the Egyptian khedive, who owed allegiance to the Ottoman sultan and, more pressingly, large sums to British and French banks, which had financed the enormous cost of constructing the Suez Canal. The further south Emin sailed, however, the less any of that mattered. Then, as now, the sway of law and government seemed to grow feebler as he reached a frontier where borders did not so much come together, or overlap, but fizzle out.

Emin Pasha, as he is known to history, remained on the Nile for the next dozen years, overseeing a string of stations along the river, neat square forts surrounded by moats and earthen walls. He proved to be an able administrator, drawing up ambitious plans for the advancement of agriculture and combating the evils of the slave trade, while sending immense quantities of ivory back to his superiors in Khartoum, who shipped it on to Europe and America. In the late nineteenth century, there was a sharp increase in demand for ivory in the West, as the purveyors of luxury living sold it to the moneyed classes in the form of billiard balls, snuffboxes, piano keys and inlaid pistol handles. Emin did not think of himself, however, as someone motivated by such crass commercial interests. He sent a series of long letters to well-placed correspondents in Europe, meant to describe his civilizing project to the outside world.

To extend his influence over the natives of the interior—and their ivory trade—Emin also created an army of about 1,400 men. The provenance of these soldiers is somewhat mysterious. A few officers, it seems, were cast-off members of Ottoman armies, but the vast majority of the force appears to have been conscripted from the tribes surrounding Emin's stretch of the Nile. Many of the soldiers were former slaves, bought or otherwise freed from captivity, and their cheeks still bore the three parallel scars that the slavers used to mark their chattel. They were from disparate tribes and spoke a variety of unrelated tongues, but they adopted Islam as their religion and a pidgin form of Arabic as a common language. In one of the letters he sent upriver, Emin extolled the virtues of his "willing and brave" native army. "There is no better and more workable material for soldiers in the world," he wrote a German friend, "than our Sudanese."

In September of 1882, a comet appeared in the sky, one so bright that it could be observed even during the daytime. It blazed like a momentous omen. To the north of Emin's territory, a youthful Sudanese boatwright was raising a rebellion. Drawing on Islamic eschatology, he called himself the Mahdi, or "redeemer," and he promised to liberate his people. Within three years, he'd vanquished all but one of Sudan's foreign governors, beheading General Gordon, Emin's immediate superior. Emin, the lone holdout, fought on in the far south. Cut off by the rebellion, surrounded by his shelves of books in his thatched-roofed residence, he penned a series of increasingly forlorn letters to Europe, little knowing if they'd ever reach their destination.

It seems the Negroes . . . have had enough of being regarded as "things" from which every possible service is to be extorted, and which are then maltreated in return for the work they have done. After many years experience of the Negroes, and intimacy with them, I really have no hopes at all of a regeneration of Negroes by Negroes—I know my own men too well for that—nor have I yet been able to believe in the hazy sentimentalism which attempts the conversion and blessing of the Negroes by translations of the New Testament and by "moral pocket-handkerchiefs" alone; but I do not on that account despair of the accomplishment of our task, viz., the opening up and consequent civilization of the African continent. It will no doubt be a work of time, and whoever devotes himself to the task must first give up all thoughts of fame and of his services being acknowledged. But Europe possesses energy for anything, and if one man dies, another will take his place and carry on his work.

Marooned, with only a motley handful of similarly desperate Europeans to keep him company—a Russian-born doctor, a Greek merchant, an Italian captain and his pet chimpanzee—Emin vacillated wildly between demonstrations of giddy affection for his African subjects and deep melancholic spells. One day, he'd be swearing to martyr himself— "I shall in no case abandon my people," he vowed in a letter—and the next, he'd curse them and turn his attention to tending his collection of stuffed birds. As Emin obsessively stockpiled a hoard of ivory, worthless since the rebellion had shut the trade routes to the north, his soldiers' uniforms grew tattered, and the army was forced to forage for food. The Africans worried that their leader was losing his mind, a concern Emin seems to have shared. "During the many years I have sojourned here my mental acclimatization, *i.e.* my degeneration into the Negro and the egoist has proceeded apace," he wrote in a letter to one friend, "so satisfactorily that at times I am quite alarmed."

One day, a contingent of Emin's soldiers encountered a group of white men along the shores of Lake Albert, at the far southern end of their territory. These newcomers were dirty and bedraggled, having just hacked their way through several thousand miles of Congolese jungle. It turned out they were the advance party of a group called the Emin Pasha Relief Expedition, which had been organized in Europe in response to the doctor's letters. As word of the rescue party's arrival spread up the Nile, Emin's African soldiers grew restive. They worried that their commander was preparing to evacuate. The soldiers even briefly imprisoned Emin, calling him a traitor for contemplating the idea of leaving them. Emin persuaded the soldiers to release him, assuring them that he could never abandon his men. Then he did. While the African soldiers fanned out across the countryside to prepare for a mass retreat, Emin and his impatient rescue party set off for Lake Victoria and the coast. When the soldiers returned to the rescue party's camp, with their families and packed belongings in tow, they found the place deserted.

Emin Pasha's "rescue" from Africa was one of the first great publicity stunts of the modern media age. In 1890, the leader of the expedition sent to find Emin, the swashbuckling journalist Henry Morton Stanley, published *In Darkest Africa*, a highly embellished account of how he slogged and shot his way through an exotic land of pygmies and cannibals on his mission to fetch the noble German doctor. The book was a bestselling sensation. Its depiction of a lone white intellectual surrounded by horrific savagery was a probable source of inspiration for the novelist Joseph Conrad, who was then working on a Congo riverboat and pondering themes of inner darkness. The story also made a strong impression, for altogether more practical reasons, on Captain Frederick Lugard, who was about to become the first British administrator of colonial Uganda.

Lugard considered himself a different caliber of explorer than the oddball Emin or the self-promoting Stanley, privately scoffing at the latter's tales of "the Dark Forest and dwarfs." If they represented that first wobbly wave of Europeans in Africa, the captain, a priggish, pith-helmeted imperial officer with a walrus mustache, was an exemplar of the final stage, when discovery gave way to organized domination. What had most intrigued Lugard about Stanley's book, which was published the same year he set off into the African interior, was its description of the strong and ready African soldiers Emin had left behind.

Lugard didn't come to Uganda via the Nile, like Emin had, but rather marched overland in a caravan from the Indian Ocean, accompanied by a few other fever-addled British officers and some of the same African guides that Stanley's recent expedition had used. Lugard's objective was Buganda and the other African-ruled kingdoms that lay around the Nile's headwaters, some 250 miles south of Equatoria. In his own conception, at least, he was journeying there not for personal glory, but to build the British Empire in Africa. Lugard would later describe his method for accomplishing that goal with a succinct formula: "Thrash them first, conciliate them afterwards." Before he could thrash anyone, though, the captain needed an army.

Arriving in Buganda, Lugard found the kingdom verging on a civil war incited by competing Christian missionaries. The Ingleza, as the African converts to Anglicanism were known, were battling the Fransa, or Catholics, as well as Muslims and a pagan group known as the Bangi because they smoked "bang," or marijuana. Lugard set up camp atop a hill in what is present-day Kampala, within sight of the thatch-roofed palace of the *kabaka* of Buganda, with whom he hoped to sign a treaty. The king, however, had sided with the Catholic faction, and was arming himself with the assistance of a gunrunning Irish missionary. Warriors began parading menacingly around the British encampment, waving a French tricolor. Realizing that his position was tenuous, Lugard decided to march out of Buganda in search of reinforcements— Emin's soldiers.

Lugard's search first took him west, into the kingdom of Ankole, where he stopped long enough to conclude a pact of friendship with the local ruler, an event that would reverberate through the life of Eliphaz Laki. Then Lugard turned north, enduring several months of difficult passage over the unmapped mountains of the Western Rift. Finally, he reached Lake Albert, where he came upon the lost army.

As the captain's exploration party marched toward the soldiers' camp, over tracks flattened by elephants through the vast, thorny grasslands, he was met by a deputation of Emin's men flying a white flag of truce. Captain Lugard presented himself to their commanding officer, a sergeant major. The soldier took his hand, kissed it and pressed it to his forehead, a local gesture of welcome. Lugard took note of the African officers' makeshift uniforms, which they'd tailored themselves from local cotton, as well as the dirty animal skins worn by more recent recruits. They were not much to look at, the English captain thought, but they would have to do.

Unbeknown to Lugard, the African soldiers had faced a series of difficult trials since their abandonment. Most had originally been conscripted from lands far to the north, in present-day Sudan, and in the absence of their leader they had fallen into squabbling about whether or not to return home. One faction had advocated going back to their tribal lands, while others had argued that it was their duty to maintain Emin's forts along the Nile. In the ensuing infighting, many soldiers had been killed and both of the army's steamships had sunk. When the battles finally quieted, the majority had decided to stay, turning to agriculture and taking local wives. By 1891, when Lugard happened into their settlement, they were planting fields of cotton and sorghum and harvesting salt from the brackish shallows of the lake.

Given the opportunity, however, the men were more than happy to enlist in another military campaign. After a few days of negotiation, a thousand or more African soldiers agreed to join Captain Lugard's force. On September 17, 1891, they mustered at the British camp, parading in formation before their new commander to the sound of drums and bugles. They were still flying the flag of Egypt, as they had under Emin Pasha. "It was a sight to touch a man's heart to see this noble remnant who were fanatical in their loyalty to their flag," the captain wrote in his diary that night, "scarred and wounded, many prematurely grey, clad in skins, and deserted here in the heart of Africa—and I *do* thank God (as I said in my speech) that it has fallen to my lot to come to their relief."

Lugard told the African soldiers that if they served their British offi-

cers loyally, they would find them to be "kind and considerate masters." He promised that he would issue them proper uniforms and feed
them regular meals. The captain was planning to place them in gar-
risons all over the territory he administered, where they would serve
as the shock troops of his colonizing project. In the coming years,
Buganda and the other southern kingdoms would be brought to heel,
and Emin's province of Equatoria would be divided up, with a substantial portion incorporated into the new colony of Uganda.

When he finished speaking, Captain Lugard wrote, "All seemed very
delighted." A few days later, his new army marched south with him,
into the Ugandan heartland.

Most people, and even many Africans, take what we call "tribes" to
be ancient and immemorial groupings. But just as a person living in
Ljubljana can one day be Yugoslavian and the next a Slovene, African
tribal identity is really not so static. The Africans who encountered the
first Italian missionaries, and who were later ruled by Emin Pasha, never
had any conception of a common identity larger than their extended
families and clans. During the colonial era, such people had tribes more
or less invented for them by white anthropologists, artificial groupings
they were placed in, in part, because a large tribe was easier to administer than many small clans. But this process could work the other way,
too. The men of Emin's army essentially created a new tribe for themselves, one that was to play a central role in the tumultuous events to
come.

By the turn of the twentieth century, Uganda had been pacified and
incorporated into the empire. Their fighting done, most of Emin's soldiers chose to stay in the colony, settling in the familiar environs of
their old territory, the southernmost portion of what had once been
Equatoria. The area, ceded to the Uganda Protectorate in a colonial land
swap, was now known as the province of West Nile. Names changed,
but the soldiers' pacifying role remained the same. Some were
appointed to administer the territory as chiefs in the colonial service,
proxy rulers the British referred to as "sultans."

Emin's soldiers married and had families, mixing with the local populace. But they retained the contours of their underlying identity. They
were bound together by a common religion, Islam, a common language,
an Arabic creole, and most of all, by a shared sense of exile. To commemorate their journey, they and their descendants would customarily

mark their children's faces just as the Ottoman slavers had, appropriating the scars as a signifier of communal pride. They called themselves "Nubians," a name that harkened back to their origins in Sudan.

They proved to be a remarkably fluid ethnic group. As time went on, it wasn't necessary to be descended from Emin's troops to be a Nubian. If you were from one of the indigenous West Nile tribes—the Lugbara, the Alur, the Kakwa—you only had to practice Islam, speak a little Nubian, profess a desire to be a Nubian, and then you were one. And because the Nubians were preferred collaborators of the British, and joining the group offered opportunities for advancement within the colonial hierarchy, many men did choose to become Nubians, among them Yusuf Gowon's father.

The whole culture of West Nile was built around respect. The most prominent elders were referred to as "men whose names are known." Gowon's father, Ibrahim, was one such man. He owned a great deal of land and much livestock. Though he was born a Catholic and a Kakwa, he converted to Islam sometime before Gowon was born, adopting a Nubian identity. He was subsequently, and surely not coincidentally, appointed a chief in the colonial administration. After his son Yusuf was born, around 1936, Ibrahim cut the distinctive marks of the Nubians into the child's cheeks. To a great extent, this single symbolic act would determine the course of Yusuf Gowon's life.

West Nile is flat, grassy country, crisscrossed by muddy streams and punctuated by abrupt outcroppings of rocky hills. It was ignored during colonial times, even as the British developed other regions of Uganda as centers of trade or cultivation. About the only Europeans who went there were ivory poachers and adventuresome tourists. Winston Churchill shot elephants and rhinos in West Nile, and pronounced the place a "hunter's paradise." Carl Jung visited in order to observe the primeval psyche. "Both chiefs and people are primitive in their outlook," a British administrator wrote in a report around the time of Gowon's birth, "and profess to be almost fanatically opposed to any change."

When Gowon was a boy, his people still lived much as they had for generations, in homesteads of clustered huts surrounded by hedges of thornbushes. They slept on beds of sticks and grass. While some younger denizens of West Nile had adopted European clothing, most of the older generation still favored traditional dress: The men wore animal skins, and the women were naked except for tufts of leaves worn around their waists like loincloths. Some people worshipped the God of Christianity, some the God of Islam, but they all retained a measure of the age-old belief in the power of nature spirits and in the rainmakers who communed with them. Most political decisions were made at the level of familial clans, by councils of elders.

The people of West Nile subsisted on finger millet, which they also used to make beer. They kept livestock and caught fish from their streams. In the rainy season, women beat the earth to harvest white ants, a local delicacy. Gowon spent his childhood working in the fields, looking after his family's goats and cattle and hunting small game with bows and arrows. He and his friends played in a river near their village. As a chief's son, within the context of his time and place, he was a child of some privilege. He wore such sharp modern outfits that the other village children nicknamed him "Goan," because the best tailors in colonial Uganda were Indian immigrants from the city of Goa. The moniker stuck so well that, with a slight change of spelling, Gowon eventually adopted it as his last name. (His given name is Yusuf Mogy.)

Gowon's father sired a great many children. "I was the only one who volunteered to go to school," Gowon said. "But I did not go very deep. My father had many cows, but he could not care about education." When his father reluctantly sold a few cattle to pay his son's school fees, the clan elders gave him a stern lecture about wasting his money. Everyone knew that there was no work for the learned in impoverished West Nile.

Gowon was determined, however, and he managed to wheedle a few years of tuition out of his father. He attended an Islamic school in Arua, the provincial seat of West Nile, sharing a bed with another boy in the home of a family friend. He earned his keep by doing household chores and work in the fields. His classmates remember him as a merry child, a prankster, who entertained them with ribald jokes and renditions of local songs.

Arua was a creation of the colonial era, a garrison town. One of the first structures built there had been a military stockade—hence the town's name, which literally meant "little prison." Arua's streets were always full of soldiers, local youths serving in the King's African Rifles, the colonial army, who'd come back to town on their leaves. Gowon and his friends, like schoolboys everywhere, were fascinated with all things military. They used to gawk at the soldiers, watching the way they wore their crisp uniforms, the way they walked with such purpose.

"The people in this area are very brave. Brave, brave soldiers," one of Gowon's classmates recalled. "Every boy here had the feeling that he wanted to join the army when he was grown."

They idolized one soldier in particular, a strapping and handsome young sergeant major. He would often talk to the starry-eyed children. Though he was only in his twenties, he had already begun to accrue such respect that his name was known across West Nile. Like many young men of his generation, he'd been named for that curious German who'd first led the Nubian people into a life of arms. In his case, because of the vagaries of Arabic transliteration, the name Emin, meaning "faithful servant," was spelled Amin.

Africa the place is forever obscured by the shadow of Africa the notion. If one historical figure could be said to embody the continent as it is stereotypically imagined—dark, dangerous, atavistic and charged with sexual magnetism—it would be Idi Amin Dada. He is remembered today as a villain straight from a comic book, a monstrous, malaprop-spouting tyrant in a medal-bedecked field marshal's uniform, an archetypal brute with immense and depraved appetites. Much mythology surrounds the circumstances that formed him. According to popular literature, West Nile province is a barren, lawless and violent place, home to "a warrior tribe" that lives on the margins, "as marine slugs," says one British writer, "are part of the life on the edge of the sea." In fact, West Nile is relatively fertile, its tribes never fought much, and before Amin came to power, the province had one of Uganda's lowest homicide rates. Tellingly, the most persistent bit of folklore surrounding Amin says that he ate his enemies, in keeping with "blood rituals" supposedly common in West Nile, but there is not a shred of reliable evidence that such cannibalism was ever practiced. The "man-eating myth," as the anthropologist William Arens memorably called it, is one of the oldest slurs in the world, an excuse to dominate other peoples. It "sweeps them outside the pale of culture," Arens writes, "and places them in a category with animals."

"Truly, I never saw Amin eat anyone, and I never heard of him eating anyone," Yusuf Gowon told me, laughing heartily at the very thought of it. Then he pointed out the irony: "You know, our people used to say that it was you whites who were cannibals."

It's distasteful to defend a murderer like Amin from slander. But to ascribe his behavior to some cultural predisposition, to some savage nature that dwelled within him, is not only to deny his humanity, but also to obscure the West's role in making him what he was. Long before Amin led an African nation, he was a soldier in a British regiment, led by British officers, in a distant outpost of the British Empire, and it is that experience that formed him. Like his underling Gowon, like every Ugandan of that time, Idi Amin was a creature of politics and the deforming history of colonial rule.

From the very beginning of the colonial era, the people of West Nile were targeted for recruitment into the British army. This was a cornerstone of Captain Lugard's policy of "indirect rule," which persisted long after its author had left Uganda. The tribes of West Nile were more kin to their neighbors across the artificial colonial borders with Sudan and Congo than they were to the peoples of Uganda's south. That made them useful to the British, who needed to pacify the southerners, who were considered more advanced. Later, white anthropologists studied the situation white administrators had created, and decided that the peoples of Uganda's north were culturally "warlike."

The British authorities regarded West Nile as little more than a vast reservoir of cheap labor. They took deliberate steps to retard the province's development, discouraging the introduction of cash crops like cotton. Young West Nile men who might have preferred to stay home and farm their own fields were instead transported to work on the vast sugar plantations of the south, where they were given hazardous, backbreaking jobs cutting cane. The only other way to make a decent income was by joining the army. Over time, the Nubian force recruited by Lugard evolved into the King's African Rifles, a regiment of the British army. During the First World War, when Britain needed soldiers to turn back a German campaign in Africa, the colonial government imposed a flat "hut tax" on West Nile, forcing men to enlist in search of the necessary cash.

This African regiment distinguished itself, fighting the Germans across the continent until the Armistice. It expanded and mobilized again when the Second World War broke out in 1939. ("The less advanced tribes were particularly anxious to take an active part in the hostilities," a contemporary colonial administration report recorded, "and some of their proposals to help were rather embarrassing to the local district officers.") Around seventy-seven thousand Ugandans, about 10 percent of the able-bodied male population, served in the war, doing battle with the Italians around the Horn of Africa and the Japanese in Burma.

After the war, the King's African Rifles shrank to a more manageable size, but Uganda's north continued to provide its manpower. Teams of officers traveled around the northern provinces on "recruiting safaris." They gathered unemployed young men, put them through races and rudimentary drills, gave them physicals and measured them with a stick that was cut with a notch at five feet, eight inches, the required minimum height for African troops. The most promising physical specimens were inducted into the army on the spot. Sometimes, if their quota was low, the recruiters would throw a few unwilling conscripts into the back of their truck. The recruits often signed their induction papers with a thumbprint, because many couldn't read or write or even speak English. That didn't bother the British recruiters. In their army, white men did the thinking, and they gave their orders in Swahili. The British officers' view of the northern soldiers, whom they sometimes called "Sudis" because of their supposed Sudanese lineage, was captured by this King's African Rifles marching song.

> It's the Sudi, my boy, it's the Sudi,
> With his grim-set, ugly face:
> But he looks like a man and he fights like a man,
> For he comes of a fighting race.

In the south of Uganda, a bright young man like Eliphaz Laki could learn to read and write at missionary schools. There were few such schools in the north. Not surprisingly, the southerners soon developed a superior attitude toward the northerners as well as a prejudice against service in the army. "They looked down on soldiering as a job of failures," said a rare southern officer of that era. "If you failed at everything else, why not try the army?"

As disdained people often do, the northerners seized on the negative stereotype and made it their own. They became a warrior people. Until independence, the soldiers serving in the King's African Rifles continued to wear the Ottoman red fez for ceremonial occasions, as a reminder of the lineage they traced to Emin Pasha. Men who'd served in the regiment returned to West Nile and, like old soldiers everywhere, regaled children with their war stories. Every boy Yusuf Gowon grew up with had a father or uncle or brother who had served in the army. And they all seem to have known, from a young age, the promising soldier named Idi Amin.

According to the legend, Idi Amin was a child of the barracks. It is said that his mother was a soldier's concubine and a witch, and that little Idi grew up peddling sweet biscuits along a dirt road outside a military installation. In fact, very little is known for certain about Amin's early life. It seems he was born sometime in the mid-1920s, somewhere in the northern corner of West Nile, near the borders with Congo and Sudan. But his first reliable appearance in the historical record does not occur until December 20, 1946, the day he was inducted into the army.

Amin was in his twenties. World War II had just ended with the Allied triumph. No one yet imagined that Britain might soon divest itself of its empire, least of all the white officers of the King's African Rifles. "Corporal Idi," as his British superiors called him, was their kind of African soldier, tireless and eager to please. From the beginning, he stood out because of his appearance. "His physique was like that of a Grecian sculpture," Major Iain Grahame, Amin's Scottish commander and mentor, wrote in a memoir. British officers put great stock in their soldiers' performances in athletic competitions, and Amin was peerless. He won sprints and anchored his battalion's tug-of-war team. He held the army's heavyweight boxing title for years. He played forward on an otherwise all-white rugby club. Sometimes, when the team traveled to play against clubs with whites-only policies, Amin would obligingly wait on the team bus after the match while his teammates took part in postgame festivities.

Amin hid his resentment. He fought for the British against the Kenyan Mau-Mau insurgency, proving to be a skilled tracker and an excellent shot, though he was a bit trigger-happy. He was tireless on long marches and popular with his fellow soldiers. He had this deep, resonant, enveloping laugh. One former Ugandan general told me that when he first entered basic training—he said he didn't enlist in the army so much as he was shanghaied, whisked off one day when he went to town to buy medicine—the first friendly face he encountered was Idi Amin's. He greeted the new recruit in their common language, Nubian, and comforted him, telling him he was among friends and kinsmen.

Eventually, Amin was promoted and given command of a platoon. However, because he could hardly read and struggled with spoken English, his superiors considered him unfit for a higher position. "Idi Amin, we all agreed, had reached his ceiling," his Scottish mentor recalled. But as independence became inevitable, British officers made a hasty effort to groom African successors. Major Grahame instructed his protégé Amin on the proper etiquette for using a knife and fork and helped him to open a bank account.

"On many occasions I endeavored to steer our conversation round to the subject of the future of Uganda," Grahame subsequently wrote, with an illustrative air of condescension. "A worried expression would then come over his large, moon-shaped face, the tribal scars behind his eyes would stand out, and he would repeat his distrust of all the soap-box orators from the south. It was not his nature, however, to dwell on matters beyond his comprehension, so he would quickly change the conversation."

In July 1961, Idi Amin was one of two Ugandan soldiers promoted to the rank of lieutenant. Fifteen months later, at a parade ground in Kampala, he took part in the ceremonial end to colonial rule in Uganda. As darkness fell that night, a contingent of the King's African Rifles, wearing their distinctive red fezzes, filed onto the field to the tune of a military band's rendition of the "Bab-el-Mandeb March." Bag-pipers played, howitzers were fired and an army helicopter delighted the crowd with an aerial display. Near midnight, an honor guard, dressed in the quaint old uniforms, handed their regimental colors over to the Duke of Kent, who was there on the queen's behalf. Lieutenant Idi Amin stepped forward from a phalanx of soldiers wearing modern khakis and green berets. The duke handed over a new flag to the highest-ranking African in the independent Ugandan army. The band played "God Save the Queen," the Union Jack was lowered for the final time and the night exploded with fireworks.

A century after Europeans had first appeared along the headwaters of the Nile, the soldiers of Uganda were finally serving one of their own. Far away, back in West Nile, young Yusuf Gowon began to feel the inexorable pull of Idi Amin's charisma.

13

THE LIONS

Unlike many of his school friends, Yusuf Gowon initially resisted the call to arms. "I didn't want to be a soldier," Gowon said. "I was a farmer." He enrolled in an agricultural college, where he learned to drive a tractor, and tried to work his own land, but it was tough to make a living that way in West Nile. So in 1964, amid the rapid public-sector expansion that followed independence, Gowon joined the government's prison service. He was posted to a northern penal farm, where work gangs of inmates were turning fallow brushland into fields of cotton. A British overseer on the project took a shine to his eager young understudy and taught him to fix farm machinery. In retrospect, Gowon would later say, this was the happiest time of his life.

But the lure of the military proved too strong to resist. There was nothing romantic about Gowon's career decision: It was purely financial. In 1964, there was an uprising at an army barracks in the eastern town of Jinja. The mutinying soldiers demanded a pay increase and the quick replacement of the handful of British officers who'd stayed on to oversee the transition to self-rule. Uganda's defense minister caved in to the troops' demands, and military service, once a lowly occupation, became a lavishly paid one. Overnight, even the lowest-ranking soldier was making fifteen times more than the average Ugandan. And because the holdover British officers were hastily departing, a promising enlistee could count on fast promotion, provided he had the right connections.

After the Jinja mutiny, Idi Amin was promoted to colonel and placed in charge of army recruitment. Gowon knew he had an in with the rising commander. He and Amin came from the same remote stretch of West Nile, and in addition to identifying themselves as Nubians, a sort of umbrella ethnicity, they both belonged to the same minuscule tribe, the Kakwa. With the benefit of this close relationship, Gowon could count on being placed on a promising career path—one more lucrative, at least, than working on a prison farm. In 1968, at the age of about thirty-two, he enlisted as a private.

After World War II, the British had dramatically decreased the size of the King's African Rifles, and at the time of independence the regiment had been further subdivided among Britain's three East African colonies. Uganda's share had amounted to an army of only around one thousand men. Gowon joined up amid an ambitious recruitment drive, which drove a sevenfold increase in troop strength. All over West Nile, parents were telling their boys to join the army and "serve Amin." The wording was significant. Uganda's first prime minister, Milton Obote, was also a northerner, but he was a member of an unrelated tribe from the other side of the Nile. The president was the *kabaka*, the king of the Baganda, the country's largest ethnic group, which had long occupied a superior position in the country's regional pecking order. They tended to treat northerners like they were unwashed bumpkins. But as the 1960s went on and democracy faltered, it gradually became apparent that power in independent Uganda would rest with the men who held the guns. The northerners would have their chance to even the score with the southern tribes. In 1966, amid rumblings of secession, Obote ordered Colonel Amin to attack the *kabaka*'s palace on Kampala's Mengo Hill. The king fled into exile, Obote assumed the presidency and unchallenged political power and Amin was promoted to major general.

By the time Gowon joined the army, though, the clapped-together alliance between the president and his top general was swaying beneath the weight of their accumulating mutual suspicion. Obote, wary of Amin's ethnic power base within the army, launched his own recruitment effort. Officers loyal to Obote rushed to enlist soldiers from the president's home province of Lango and the neighboring region, Acholiland, and these soldiers were swiftly promoted. The more power Obote's tribesmen gained within the army, the more tenuous Amin's grip on it became.

Amin countered by creating a new secret unit made up mostly of Nubians. Private Gowon was assigned to it. The enlistees underwent training at a boot camp located near a large Nubian enclave just north

Yusuf Gowon, more farmer than fighter
RADIO UGANDA

of Kampala. When Obote found out, he ordered the unit disbanded, fearing that his army commander was creating a force to overthrow him. Amin grudgingly complied, dispersing the troops to other units. Private Gowon was reassigned to a military police battalion.

The intrigue, however, only mounted. The night that a would-be assassin shot and wounded the president, Amin behaved strangely, fleeing his house in bare feet, jumping his back fence and hitching a ride to the same garrison town where his secret unit had undergone training. Obote suspected that the general had somehow been involved, and soon afterward stripped him of most of his official powers. Amin assumed that it was only a matter of time before the president took more drastic action. He consulted someone he trusted, Colonel Bolka Bar-Lev, the Israeli military attaché in Uganda. At the time, Uganda was an important strategic partner of Israel's. Uganda controlled the headwaters of the Nile, Egypt's vital artery, and it bordered Sudan, which had lately been tightening its ties to other Arab-led governments. Obote had allowed Israel to use Uganda in the past as a staging point to funnel arms and other support to rebels in southern Sudan, but the alliance had soured. The Israeli colonel thought Idi Amin would be a more reliable friend, so he gave him some advice. Muster some six hundred trusted and able men, he told Amin. Station them near Kampala. Give them commando training and make sure they have access to armor and jeeps. Such a force, the Israeli colonel said, could easily overwhelm a much larger army.

Soon after the conversation, Amin began transferring Nubian soldiers to a new elite unit, the Malire Mechanized Battalion. Its headquarters was the *kabaka's* old palace on Mengo Hill. Amin stationed the army's modest store of heavy armor there, including six Sherman tanks that Israel had captured from the Arabs in the 1967 war and had then given to Uganda. The installation was also home to a paratrooper school. Sometime around 1969, Yusuf Gowon was sent there for advanced military training, under the tutelage of Israeli instructors. At the end of the course, Gowon and his comrades were awarded Israeli paratrooper's wings. Amin affectionately dubbed them his "Suicide Squad."

Obote saw the threat and moved to neutralize it. He reshuffled the army, replacing Amin's loyalists inside the officer corps with his own. The Malire Mechanized Battalion was placed under the command of a lieutenant colonel close to Obote, and soldiers of the president's Langi tribe were transferred into the unit to counterbalance the Nubians. Gowon and several others were sent to Greece for an extended training course, effectively putting them out of action. Feeling more secure, Obote departed on his fateful trip to Singapore. Dueling rumors swept the capital: Amin was to be arrested; Obote was to be assassinated. Both sides moved. Amin was faster.

Weekends were typically lazy times around the barracks on Mengo Hill. It was customary for soldiers of the Malire Battalion to spend them with their wives and children, who often lived in and around the installation. But on this particular Sunday, there was odd activity. Some of the Nubians stationed at the barracks noticed that others, Obote's tribesmen, were putting on their uniforms and picking up guns. Then they locked the armory. Word spread that a contingent of Langi soldiers was going to Amin's home to arrest or kill him, and that all the Nubians were about to be massacred.

A fire alarm sounded. All officers were called to gather in the mess hall, where the battalion's commander, the Obote loyalist, stood before the assembled men and began ranting about unnamed elements within the army that were organizing a "bloodbath." Outside the mess hall, a group of Nubian enlisted men decided it was time to fight. Obote's forces within the battalion had taken the precaution of hiding the keys to all the armored vehicles. But the Nubian soldiers knew a trick. They used nails to hotwire the ignition of an armored personnel carrier. One jumped behind the wheel and rammed the vehicle into the locked armory doors. He and his comrades snatched up guns and ammunition, and the barracks was soon consumed in a full-scale firefight.

At a bar in a nearby neighborhood, a staff officer from army head-quarters who'd been enjoying a Sunday afternoon drink heard the shooting and placed an urgent call to the Malire Battalion. "There is total confusion here," the panicked switchboard operator told him. "What followed was chaos," the former staff officer later said. "But within the chaos was order." With an efficiency that suggested long preparation, the Nubian soldiers commandeered armored vehicles and fanned out to key points all over town: the radio station, parliament and the main roads into the city. Inside an office at parliament, a group of Obote's key cabinet ministers, army officers and police officials were meeting to plan Amin's arrest, unaware that they'd already been outmaneuvered. The president, in Singapore, managed to reach the group over the telephone.

"They said there was an attempted coup but they had incapacitated it," Obote recalled in a newspaper interview shortly before his death in 2005. "They said they had alerted loyal army officers. . . . 'Oh dear, Oh dear,' I told them on the phone, 'it's already too late, it's already too late!' And two hours later, Amin's tanks surrounded the parliamentary building and began to shell it."

Amin called his friend, the Israeli colonel, and told him, "The revolution has started."

That same day, in Washington, D.C., an urgent confidential memo arrived at the White House office of Henry Kissinger, national security adviser to Richard Nixon. "Uganda's President, A. Milton Obote, on his way back from the Singapore Commonwealth Conference, appears to have been overthrown today by a military *coup d'etat*," it began. The memo went on to describe the day's chaotic events in Kampala to Kissinger. "It is not clear how solid Amin's position is," the memo said, but it concluded that his ascension to power might not be an altogether unwelcome development. "The statements of the new leaders," the memo went on, "suggest they would seek a government of national unity that might be more conservative than Obote's both in national and international issues."

Milton Obote went to his grave believing that a cabal of Western intelligence agencies was responsible for his overthrow. In fact, the available evidence suggests that only one foreign power—Israel—may have played a direct role. Recently declassified documents indicate Britain and the United States were taken by surprise. The morning of the coup, Britain's befuddled high commissioner had to rush to the Kampala residence of Amin's friend, the Israeli defense attaché Colonel Bolka Bar-Lev, to learn why tanks were on the street. Over the next few weeks, the Israeli colonel was seldom far from Amin's side. He acted as an emissary between Uganda's new leader and Western diplomats, describing the general's plans to hold multiparty elections and relating how "all potential foci of resistance . . . had been eliminated." In Washington and London, however, there was much debate about whether to recognize the military government. The coup set off several days of frantic transatlantic diplomacy between the two allies, as they struggled to divine the character and intentions of Major General Idi Amin.

To the British, the coup was unexpected but by no means dismaying. The Africa specialists in the Foreign Office had hated Obote for what they perceived as his lack of deference. "I fear his subconscious is a festering mass of ancient grievances and suspicions," one diplomat had written in a confidential memo shortly before the coup. Idi Amin, by contrast, appeared the very model of an obedient colonial soldier. An internal assessment by the Foreign Office concluded: "We now have a thoroughly pro-Western set up in Uganda of which we should take prompt advantage. Amin needs our help."

The United States was more cautious. Two days after the coup, the State Department cabled America's ambassador to Uganda, saying the government was "seriously concerned" about the "disruptive effect" a coup might have "in what has been one of the most stable areas in Africa." The ambassador was ordered to London with instructions to propose that a mediator be appointed to broker a negotiated settlement that would allow Milton Obote to return to power. After talking the idea over with his Foreign Office counterparts, however, the American ambassador sent a blunt telegram back to Washington.

> Mediation between Obote/Amin not in US interests in Uganda or in our interests in the rest of Black Africa. US interests Uganda will be better served by less "progressive" GOU likely to emerge under whoever real power is. . . . Moreover, likely center of gravity new GOU certainly will blunt influence SOVS and CHICOMS. . . . I believe crucial problem

and real possibility is counter coup or intra-coup from Obote followers or other rivals for power who have capacity to govern (which Amin decidedly has not).

It would not be the last time Idi Amin was underestimated. At this juncture, inexperience and obscurity were his great advantages. He had no known political opinions, and that allowed everyone, both inside and outside Uganda, to project their own desires upon him. The Israelis thought Amin would be a helpful ally against Sudan and the Arab nations. British and American diplomats judged Amin dimwitted but manipulable—a useful corrective to Obote's querulous socialism. The Ugandan public thought he was a nationalist, a unifying figure who could restore stability. In time, of course, Amin would spectacularly betray every initial expectation. But initially he was judged to be, as one Foreign Office official put it to a reporter, "a decent chap." British diplomats were heartened when Amin wrote "a very nice letter" to Queen Elizabeth II and requested a signed portrait of Her Majesty.

The foreign press also took favorable measure of the burly general. The *New York Times* described him as "a simple, bluff man who still seems like a sergeant and a boxing champion." London's *Telegraph* wholeheartedly endorsed the coup, saying it was a "good reason that might be advanced for holding Commonwealth conferences more often," while a columnist in the *Spectator* wrote, "If a choice is to be made between quiet military men and noisy civil dictators then I prefer, in Africa at least, the military." The foreign correspondent corps in Kampala appreciated Amin from the start. The consensus, one journalist later wrote, was that he "was none too bright, but he was available"—always good for a colorful quote when you found him poolside at the Imperial Hotel.

Ugandans were duped just as badly. In contrast to the tweedy Milton Obote, with his pipe and his European affectations, Amin styled himself according to the traditional image of a chief, physically powerful, openly polygamous, above ideology and democracy's crippling factions. The poor heard his earthy laugh and his stumbling speech and thought he was a peasant like them. Intellectuals saw his first cabinet, which was made up of technocrats, and supposed he was a man with whom they could reason. Many on the left heard Amin talk about African empowerment and a "people's coup" and concluded that he was a rough-hewn socialist. The Baganda took him for a royalist when he declared that the body of the late *kabaka* would be flown back from

Idi Amin Dada, "a decent chap" THE NEW VISION

London, where he'd died in exile, for immediate reburial with pomp and honors. "Amin *oyee!*" the adoring crowds chanted in those early days—"praise to Amin."

In July 1971, Amin made a triumphal state visit to Britain. The general paid a call on Buckingham Palace, where he met the queen and the Duke of Edinburgh, whom he chummily called "Mr. Philip." Amin pledged his undying loyalty to the nation that had trained him as a soldier. Then he asked for the government's assistance in obtaining heavy weapons, including sophisticated new Harrier fighter jets.

Meanwhile, at that very moment back in Uganda, the first purges had begun.

Yusuf Gowon returned home from his training course in Greece in the middle of 1971. In his absence, his country had changed entirely, and in his favor. Officers who backed the wrong side in the coup were mysteriously disappearing from the upper ranks of the military, while the winners were reaping their rewards. Idi Amin had promoted himself to full general and had assumed the title of president of Uganda—as a caretaking measure only, he'd assured the public. Within the army, his loyal tribesmen were being rewarded with rapid promotions. Privates were becoming lieutenants, and sergeants were becoming colonels. As soon as he returned from Europe, Gowon was promoted to major and assigned to Mbarara, as the deputy commander of the Ugandan army's western battalion.

Gowon's fast rise created considerable resentment within the ranks. For one thing, since he'd been in Greece, he hadn't risked his life for the coup. For another, he was widely disdained as a latecomer to the army. His fellow officers snickeringly called him "the tractor driver." They weren't sure what General Amin saw in this ignorant farm boy. They scoffed at Gowon's behavior in Amin's presence, which they judged overly fawning, even by the standards of servility prevailing within the Ugandan military. Soldiers who served with Gowon in those days told me he boastfully spoke of Amin as his *uncle*, a word that, in this context, would have meant a tribal patron.

"The element of tribe, ethnicity, leaning in his favor in advancing his career was very clear," a general who served as defense minister during Amin's regime told me. Gowon's promotion from private to major, this officer said, was "a very, very big jump. He was not prepared for commissioned officer status in any way. But he was specially favored and specially selected for prominent service in the military."

On paper, Major Gowon was only the second-in-command in Mbarara. But the battalion's top officer, Lieutenant Colonel Ali Fadhul, was a close confidant of Amin's and was often away in Kampala. He left Gowon in charge of the unit's day-to-day operations. Amin had chosen his protégé for the post because he believed that this particular battalion needed close supervision. By the time Gowon arrived in Mbarara, it had already been the scene of a series of violent incidents. At this stage, when Amin had not yet consolidated power, he still worried about his international reputation. It was critical to Amin that the First World powers kept viewing him as a conciliatory leader with broad public support.

After Amin took control, there was a lot of talk in the foreign press about a "bloodless" coup, but that wasn't really true. "Lots of blood flowed," one soldier wrote in a memoir—particularly within the army, where divisions between Obote and Amin were the starkest. The killings started off relatively selectively, targeting high-ranking officers. Then the purges widened into wholesale slaughter. During the latter years of Obote's rule, Nubian soldiers had found themselves being sidelined and passed over for promotion, while members of the Langi tribe and the related Acholi were given favorable treatment. Now Amin's men inflicted their revenge. In one barracks in Kampala, Langi soldiers were locked in a room that was then dynamited. Elsewhere, they were machine-gunned or hacked to death.

Some of the gravest early atrocities took place in Mbarara. The soldiers there had a reputation for violence and indiscipline. Many of them had been hastily recruited and poorly trained. Some were not even Ugandans. After the coup, Amin greatly expanded the army by enlisting an estimated four thousand mercenaries from southern Sudan and eastern Congo, many from tribes that were ethnically related to those of West Nile. These men had learned to fight in rebel movements in their home countries. Amin gave the unit the name Simba Battalion, after the Swahili word for "lion."

The Simba Battalion barracks was situated a few miles outside the center of town, across the road from a eucalyptus forest that lined the highway to Kampala. Painted on the outside wall of the base's guardhouse was a brightly colored mural depicting two ferocious-looking big cats. One day in late June 1971, a month or so before Gowon was posted to Mbarara, a truckload of soldiers arrived from the capital. These soldiers compiled the names and tribal affiliations of everyone stationed at Simba Battalion. An alarm sounded, signaling that all soldiers were to gather on the barracks parade ground. The Langis and Acholis were separated out. Then their fellow soldiers set upon them with clubs, bayonets and hippo hide whips.

The massacres themselves were not what caused Amin to shake up the leadership of Simba Battalion. In fact, he almost certainly ordered them. "The army did not go out of control," one retired general told me. "What happened within the army was planned and coordinated at the command level, on the commands of Amin." The problem, rather, was that the killings in Mbarara were neither efficient nor quiet. Trucks full of bodies rumbled down the open highway. Hundreds of wailing widows congregated at the local bus park. Rumor that something terrible had happened out west swiftly made its way back to Kampala, and to an American journalist named Nicholas Stroh, a thirty-three-year-old freelancer who wrote for the *Philadelphia Evening Bulletin* and the *Washington Star*.

Stroh persuaded a friend, an American professor who was researching a book on missionaries, to ride out to Mbarara with him. On the morning of July 9, the journalist left his friend behind at their hotel and drove his Volkswagen Beetle to the Simba Battalion barracks. Wearing a light blue nylon shirt, tan Hush Puppies and the scruffy beginnings of a beard, he presented himself at the barracks. Stroh talked to a major and must have said something that angered the officer, because within a few minutes, soldiers were pushing the muddy, roughed-up journalist across the barracks yard. Then he was shot. A carload of soldiers descended on the hotel where Stroh was staying and picked up the journalist's travel companion, the professor. They murdered him too. Afterward, the major who had ordered the killings told his fellow soldiers that he'd been annoyed by the journalist's impertinence. "These white men think that we Africans are savages," he said.

The killings occurred while Amin was on his overseas visit to the queen. When he returned, he found himself besieged with frantic inquiries from the U.S. embassy. The missing journalist, it turned out, was also an heir to the Stroh brewing fortune. It was one thing to murder thousands of Ugandans, but the disappearance of a wealthy foreigner was not something the world could overlook. Amin ordered a hasty cover-up. The two murdered Americans' bodies were unearthed from a shallow grave, burned and cast into a river. The major who had killed Stroh, who'd been driving the journalist's Volkswagen around Mbarara, had the car torched and pushed into a ravine.

Amin, still furious, relieved the troublemaking major of his command and replaced him with Gowon, who was assigned to lead a special board of inquiry set up to solve the mystery of the missing Americans. Naturally, the investigation never went anywhere. Gowon's real mission was to restore order in Mbarara. In particular, the army needed to mend its relationship with Ankole's civilian leadership. Many members of the local political class had welcomed the coup, particularly members of the Democratic Party and UPC apostates like James Kahigiriza. But the working relationship had become strained because of the behavior of Simba Battalion's soldiers, who were brandishing their newfound power, acting rude and unruly around town. Gowon imposed some appreciated discipline.

"He was one of the best," remembered an elderly Ankole politician. "He was more polite and liberal than the others."

Under the emerging structure of military rule, the locus of political power in Mbarara shifted from the provincial government headquarters, in the center of town, to the Simba Battalion barracks on its outskirts. Whoever ran Simba was effectively the governor of the western province. Major Gowon took on the role once occupied by politicians of the ruling party, and before that by the ministers of Ankole's king, distributing patronage, arbitrating squabbles, even intervening in legal disputes over land. He was also a religious leader of sorts. The battalion raised funds for the local mosque and sponsored gatherings where hundreds of Christians converted to Islam.

Since as far back as early colonial times, Uganda had been stratified not only by tribe but also by religion. Anglicanism, the faith of the British establishment, enjoyed the highest status, followed by Catholicism. Islam, the religion of the Nubian outsiders, was considered lowest of all, the poor man's faith. But Amin's rise to power upset this traditional order. All over the country, young men were donning white robes and packing into mosques, embracing Amin's religion and calling themselves Nubians, altering their religious and ethnic identities so that they might catch the prevailing political wind.

In today's Uganda, it is often said—by those born south of the Nile—that Amin's was a "northern" regime. But a broad cross-section collaborated with the dictatorship, at least in the early years. In that first brief flush of power, Idi Amin was more popular than any leader of Uganda before or since. His collaborators included policemen and politicians, the lowly and the highest born. One Ugandan-born political scientist concluded that the "several thousand full-time agents" of Amin's secret police, "plus several times as many part-time informers, came from every nationality and religion of the country, and from both sexes too."

Amin found his most vociferous support, however, within the country's Muslim population, which found itself privileged as never before. In Ankole, when officeholders from the Protestant elite—men like Eliphaz Laki—were imprisoned shortly after the coup, Muslims were appointed to replace them. The government distributed patronage through mosques and used public funds to sponsor trips to Mecca, creating a new elite class of hajjis. Across the countryside, where Christian and Muslim villagers had long coexisted as neighbors, mutual suspicion built. Those who benefited were naturally inclined to cooperate with Amin's widening domestic intelligence network. Some informed on their neighbors out of a genuine, if misplaced, affection for the regime. Others were motivated by what Swahili speakers call *fitina*: greed, jealousy, bitterness.

One of the most notorious of Ankole's collaborators was a man named Salim Sebi. A Muslim and a Nubian, Sebi had lived in Mbarara for as long as anyone could remember, and he was married to a local woman. He was a towering, muscular man; people said he looked very much like Amin. Before the coup, Sebi had been a bus driver who used to hang around the provincial government headquarters. He seemed to be an agreeable man of little consequence, a barnacle. No one ever knew what ill-defined grievances set his transformation in motion. But after Amin came to power, Sebi loudly declared that he was a "brother" of the general, in the tribal, not familial, sense. He began working as an informer for the army intelligence service, which suddenly gave him mighty influence.

Sebi used the hunt for traitors as a pretext to pursue his own personal agendas, avenging old slights with ruthless disproportion. He orchestrated the disappearance of a local cattle trader to whom his father-in-law owed a large sum of money. He blackmailed other members of the elite. "He would arrest people he knew were rich, so he could take their money," one victim of Sebi's shakedowns told me. Another recounted the following incident. Early one morning, Sebi came to this man's house and told him he'd been ordered to take him in for questioning at the Simba Battalion barracks. The man, certain he was about to be murdered, knelt and said a brief prayer with his family. Sebi stood over them, mockingly praying along, drawing out the second syllable of *amen*, so that it sounded like: *Amiiin.*

General Amin loved to visit Simba Battalion. So often did his helicopter swoop over Mbarara on its way to the barracks that one resident of the town, writing in his diary, wryly described it as the president's "favorite watering hole." One evening in August 1971, shortly after Major Gowon arrived at the battalion, Amin hosted a banquet at the Simba mess hall to honor some special guests, a team of British military advisers who had been sent to cement the friendly ties between their government and Uganda's new military dictatorship.

Simba Battalion's troops may have been undisciplined, but they knew how to put on a party. The unit's jazz band was the tightest in the army, and an attached dance troupe was famed for its acrobatic routines. That night, as Amin and his foreign minister, a London-trained Ugandan lawyer, held court at one end of the mess hall, the band played, the beer and liquor flowed freely and the British officers danced with some scantily clad women who had been brought in for their amusement. At one point, the music stopped and Amin picked up his accordion and played a calypso tune.

Less than a month later, Amin expelled the British advisers, accusing them of spying on Uganda. It was perhaps the first sign that he'd soured on his Western admirers. The break was carried out in the language of ideology, with Amin playing the Third World liberator, but the real issue was arms sales. While the British and the Israelis were being stingy, asking him to pay cash, another prospective patron had emerged, one with deep pockets and no scruples: Libya's firebrand ruler Colonel Mu'ammar al-Gadhafi.

In February 1972, Amin flew to Tripoli, where the oil-rich Libyan leader promised him huge amounts of economic and military aid. The price, which Amin was more than willing to pay, involved turning against Israel, the country that had done more than any other to help him seize and consolidate power. At the close of the visit, Amin and Gadhafi put out a joint communiqué in which Uganda pledged its support for the Palestinian struggle. Within a few weeks, Amin ordered all Israelis to leave Uganda. When they were gone, he handed the country's vacated embassy over to Yasir Arafat and the PLO.

Amin turned against Britain next. The move that precipitated the final sundering of their relationship was also the single most popular policy Amin ever adopted. In August 1972, Amin announced plans to expel some forty thousand residents of Indian, Pakistani and Bangladeshi descent, a community that native-born Ugandans commonly called the "Asians." The history of their relations with the black population was infused with covetousness, racism and cultural antagonism. "They were, in other words, ideal targets," one Amin-era government official wrote in a memoir.

The Indians had first come to Uganda at the end of the nineteenth century, when many were brought over by the colonial authorities as indentured laborers working on the East African railway. Later, the British had made the Indians the middlemen of colonialism—the clerks, the shopkeepers—while actively discouraging Africans from going into business. This policy had suited British interests because it had prevented the emergence of a homegrown middle class, which might have begun to question foreign rule.

The British had denigrated their Indian underlings, calling them "coolies." Many Indians had mistreated the Africans in turn, reproaching them as stupid and lazy. Black Ugandans bridled at the mistreatment. The men of West Nile, many of whom had toiled under harsh

Indian foremen as migrant laborers on the sugarcane plantations, developed a particular animus. Throughout the 1950s, as the independence movement brewed, political activists had staged boycotts against Indian businesses, which sometimes had turned into race riots. After independence, the call of "Africa for the Africans" had grown louder. But wealthy Indian businessmen had always known whom to bribe. No politician had been willing to challenge the economic system's persistent inequalities—until Amin.

Amin told his people that God had come to him in a dream to tell him to seize the nation's riches for Africans. "No country can tolerate the economy of a nation being so much in the hands of non-citizens," Amin said in the nationally broadcast address in which he announced his plans. Then, in ringing language that many Ugandans recall wistfully even today, he declared his country would finally be free of foreign domination:

> Ugandan Africans have been enslaved economically since the advent of the colonialists. They have suffered in their own country. They have been laughed at by foreigners. The Africans have been regarded by these foreigners as second-class citizens in their own country. They have been humiliated in their own country. My government has therefore decided that time has come to emancipate the Ugandan Africans in this republic. My government has decided that the only way to liberate Ugandan Africans in commerce and industry and therefore to achieve true independence is to declare [a] War of Economic Independence.

The Indians were given ninety days to leave the country. The government announced that it would confiscate their properties and shops for redistribution, it was promised, to the Ugandan people. Many of the Indians held British passports, and so, through the late summer of 1972, the world's newspapers were full of pictures of women in saris arriving at Heathrow Airport. Britain's ill-prepared government had little desire to handle this influx of brown-skinned refugees. Somewhat hypocritically, it attacked Amin as a racist. But Ugandans were overjoyed. They resented the Indians and were jealous of what they owned. Idi Amin was going to help them get even.

Amin had discovered that, for all his lack of formal education, he had an intuitive feel for populist politics. It was around this time that he began sending his famous telegrams, the wildly impolitic missives that alternately amused and horrified the world. Amin taunted Richard Nixon. He made lewd suggestions about the queen. The "inevitable confusion that followed," one acquaintance of Amin's wrote, "appealed vastly to his own sense of humor." Amin also had a gift for outrageous publicity stunts. He forced expatriate British businessmen living in Uganda to kneel before him and swear an oath of allegiance to the army, and had himself carried into a party on a litter by a group of white men. Every time the British recoiled at one of his outrageous statements or the foreign newspapers ridiculed his intellect and his poor grammar, Amin's status as a folk hero inflated. To regular Ugandans, he was one of them—and he was no one's lackey.

The newspapers couldn't get enough of the story. In September 1972, the final month of Eliphaz Laki's life, a London tabloid splashed a surly looking picture of Amin across its front page, underneath the giant headline: HE'S NUTS!

No, in fact, he wasn't.

14

SEPTEMBER 1972

On the evening of September 2, 1972, at the Summer Olympics in Munich, a long-legged Ugandan named John Akii-Bua strode onto the track to compete in the final of the 400-meter hurdles. He was wearing a pair of two-year-old shoes, one of which was missing a spike. Akii-Bua, a policeman, had only competed in one other major tournament, and his name was unfamiliar even to track-and-field cognoscenti. The favorite in the race, to his right in lane 5, was David Hemery of Great Britain, the world-record holder in the event. But when the starting gun fired, the Ugandan proved he was the fastest.

With sleek, loping strides, Akii-Bua, in bright red togs, blew past the tiring Hemery in the final 50 meters, winning the gold medal, his nation's first ever. After crossing the finish line, Akii-Bua glided over a few more hurdles for good measure, waving joyously, as if he never wanted the race to end. When the scoreboard flashed up his time, he clasped two hands over his gaping mouth: 47.82 seconds, a new world record.

When the news of Akii-Bua's triumph was announced over Radio Uganda, people poured onto the streets of Kampala and staged impromptu celebrations, drumming and singing songs of praise. "Akii-Bua," went one refrain, "is building the nation." His victory on the track seemed symbolic of something larger. A decade after independence, and eighteen months after Idi Amin's coup, it appeared that Uganda was finally growing into self-confident adulthood, and Amin was setting the tone. His "Economic War" was proceeding. Thousands of Indians were lining up at Entebbe International Airport, carrying only their battered suitcases, as the government confiscated their homes and businesses in preparation for a public lottery.

Two days after Akii-Bua ran, the Munich Olympics were eclipsed by tragedy, as eleven Israeli athletes were killed in a Palestinian terrorist attack. Amin responded to the incident by sending the following message to the secretary general of the United Nations:

> Germany is the right place where when Hitler was the Prime Minister and supreme commander, he burned over six million Jews. This is because Hitler and all German people knew that Israelis are not people who are working in the interest of the people of the world and that is why they burned the Israelis alive with gas in the soil of Germany.

The world reacted with predictable outrage. Amin's "obscene comment on modern history's most atrocious genocide," the *New York Times* wrote in an editorial, "will make it difficult for other countries to deal with him as a civilized—or even a sane—representative of his unhappy land." But many Ugandans just laughed. People loved it when Amin played the provocateur. No faraway violence could dim the glory of Munich for them. On September 14, John Akii-Bua returned to the country along with the rest of the Olympic team. The next day, the runner, dressed in his team-issue red blazer, carried an enormous Ugandan flag through the roaring streets of Kampala. At a state dinner that night, Amin praised Akii-Bua, saying it particularly pleased him to note that he'd captured the world record from an Englishman. The giant headline atop next day's edition of the state newspaper read: UGANDA PUT ON THE WORLD MAP.

Five nights earlier, beneath the bloodless sliver of a three-day-old moon, a group of men, about twenty in all, pushed a column of bicycles along a lonely dirt road. Their clattery bikes were laden with suitcases full of guns. As the furtive group wound through the lush riverine valley that forms the border between Tanzania and Uganda, their leader, the twenty-eight-year-old Yoweri Museveni, kept an eye out for headlights. Having made many missions like these, to deliver weapons to clandestine armories in Ankole, he knew Idi Amin's soldiers often patrolled the border at night.

Museveni sniffed something acrid—gas fumes, he thought. He held up his hand, bringing the column of bicycles to a halt. The smell might be nothing, Museveni realized, but it could also indicate the presence of an army jeep ahead. He led his men off the road and into the underbrush. Museveni believed in prudence, both in this operation and the movement as a whole. He advocated patience and a careful massing of forces, believing that Amin would eventually reveal his true nature. Marxist doctrine held that a soldier of colonialism could only govern like a fascist. But for now, while Amin was so popular in Uganda, his enemies would do best to prepare for a long guerrilla war.

Back in Dar es Salaam, Milton Obote saw things differently: He wasn't seeking change so much as a restoration. The exiled president was living in a private oceanfront mansion, sipping whiskey late into the night with his tight circle of followers, dreaming up plans for a quick strike that would return them all to their rightful places. But Museveni disdained such "putschist solutions." He'd been schooled in the mythology of African liberation movements and Mao's Long March. He called his force the Front for National Salvation. It was a small band of a few dozen fighters, university-educated soldiers trained in guerrilla tactics at camps in Mozambique. His operatives were already forming cells in towns across the country. They camouflaged themselves among the country's unemployed young people, rendezvousing at bus stations and safehouses, recruiting in college dorm rooms, making gun runs in rented cars to a farm in the far south of Ankole, where their comrades stashed weapons spirited in from Tanzania.

When the sun rose, Museveni crept back toward the source of the gas fumes and found there was nothing to fear, just a commuter taxi parked along the road. He and his men pushed their bicycles onward. They had little reason to worry about being spotted by civilians, who would naturally assume they were smuggling black market goods, like so many others who were capitalizing on the shortages in Uganda brought about by the expulsion of the Indian merchant class. In the afternoon, Museveni and his men arrived at the farmhouse that was their secret armory, where they deposited their loads of weapons. They rested for a day. On the morning of September 14, after a long overnight march, they returned to their rear base in Tanzania, where Museveni found an urgent message waiting for him. He'd been summoned to the nearest town, a port on Lake Victoria, for a meeting with the Tanzanian minister of defense.

Museveni hopped into the Tanzanian army jeep that had been sent to fetch him. As it bounded through the marshy flatlands surrounding Lake Victoria, Museveni wondered what development could possibly merit a summons from the defense minister. It had to be important. Tanzania's socialist president, Julius Nyerere, was Amin's sworn enemy and Museveni's patron, but he preferred to keep the guerrillas at a deniable distance.

At the meeting, the defense minister got right to the point. The moment to attack had arrived. There were rumors that the British were preparing to invade Uganda in order to halt the Indian deportation, and Nyerere, as a leader of free Africa, could never tolerate such an intervention. Africans had to strike first. The defense minister explained that the plan was already in motion. A plane was in the air; military trucks were on their way to the Front for National Salvation's camp. Museveni and his men were going to war.

The attempted invasion of Uganda in September 1972, one historian has written, "constitutes one of those rare events in military history: a perfect failure." The battle plan, worked out in strict secrecy by Milton Obote and his supporters in the Tanzanian military, called for a three-pronged attack, principally carried out by the ousted president's so-called People's Army, a force of 1,300 Ugandan loyalist soldiers who had escaped into exile. In the plan's first phase, a hijacked DC-9 airplane piloted by a Ugandan civilian was to fly to a landing strip near Mount Kilimanjaro, where it would pick up eighty commandos. They were to seize Uganda's international airport at Entebbe before driving on to the capital twenty-five miles away, where they would take the national radio station and play a tape of Obote calling on Ugandans to rise up against the military. As the commandos completed their mission, a far more extensive ground invasion would begin. A thousand men would cross the border and assault Masaka, a strategically important town midway between Kampala and Mbarara. A third force of around 350 was to attack the Simba Battalion in Mbarara.

That's where Museveni's band of guerrillas came into play. At this point, the inexperienced rebel leader remained a small player, not yet important enough to be considered a rival to Obote for leadership of the resistance. (Though Obote still distrusted him, and Museveni was only informed of the invasion plan at the last possible moment.) But Museveni had assured his Tanzanian handlers that he'd built an extensive network of supporters in Ankole, and the battle plan presumed that these covert fighters would join the attack on Simba Battalion. Once the installation was taken, the rebels were supposed to raid it for weapons to distribute to the general populace.

But everything went wrong. "The so-called 'invasion,'" Museveni wrote in his autobiography, in a rare chastened moment, "was in reality an encounter between two groups of fools: Amin's group on one hand, and ours on the other." Sheer incompetence foiled the elaborate plan to take Entebbe International Airport. The pilot Milton Obote selected for the mission, the son of a friend, turned out to be unfamiliar with flying a DC-9. After stealing the plane off the Dar es Salaam tarmac with the connivance of the Tanzanian intelligence service, the pilot failed to properly retract the plane's landing gear. When he landed near Mount Kilimanjaro, he did so at far too high a speed, and the plane's tires exploded. The damaged DC-9 could not take off again, so the commando raid was scrubbed. A sympathizer on the ground in Entebbe, who had rented buses to carry the rebels to Kampala—his cover story was that they were intended for revelers celebrating John Akii-Bua's return from Munich, which was scheduled for the same day—was forced to abandon his fleet near the airport.

With that, the rebels squandered their only advantage, the element of surprise. The same day that coverage of Akii-Bua's parade filled the front page of the *Uganda Argus*, a smaller article, headlined PILOT VANISHES IN DC-9 MYSTERY, relayed a sketchy but suggestive report about the botched hijacking. If that news report didn't put Amin on alert, it appears that informants did, for he responded to the first reports of a ground incursion with uncommon alacrity. At around 4:30 a.m. on the morning of the attack, Amin ordered Lieutenant Colonel Fadhul, the commanding officer of Simba Battalion, to investigate reports that a rebel column was entering Ankole. Fadhul rushed off toward the border in his own private car, leaving his second-in-command, Major Gowon, in charge of the defense of Mbarara.

At that moment, Yoweri Museveni was once again nearing the Ugandan frontier, this time on the back of an open Bedford truck. He'd been up since the night before, when the invasion force had mustered with great fanfare at a camp in Tanzania. Before they departed, there had been courageous speeches and yelping war dances and heady talk of homecoming. But already, by dawn, their surprise attack had turned into a lumbering fiasco. Since they had set off in a convoy of twenty-seven trucks there'd been wrong turns and rest stops and countless inexplicable delays. After crossing the bridge over the Kagera River, which represented the international border, the two sections of the invasion force split. Nine of the trucks, including the one holding Museveni's contingent, headed up the road that ran to Mbarara. They were running hours behind schedule.

From the start, the force's progress was hampered by the clashing styles of its leaders. Museveni's guerrillas were wearing civilian clothes, so as to better blend in with the population once the attack began. Obote's men, former soldiers, were dressed in army-issue fatigues, with red sashes tied through their epaulettes. They expected a swift and painless operation. The more levelheaded members of the invasion force, however, could see the trouble ahead. "We are too few," some officers grumbled. The rebels' guns were old and grease-caked. Some of the men were completely unarmed. On its way up the road, the force surprised and destroyed an outnumbered detachment of Ugandan soldiers, but even this brief and successful engagement was enough to spook some of the more unseasoned rebels, who ran into the hills. As they proceeded north, the convoy happened to pass the civilian vehicle that Lieutenant Colonel Ali Fadhul, the commander of Simba Battalion, was driving toward the border on a reconnaissance mission. The enemy officer sped past them, unrecognized, and radioed Amin with vital details about the invaders' location and strength from an army border outpost.

At the sight of the rebels, a few sympathetic civilians raised the black, red and blue party flag of the Uganda People's Congress above their houses. Contrary to expectations, though, no one joined their attack. The convoy lurched into Mbarara at around 10:30 a.m. The rebels blew through a couple of roadblocks, fired on and overturned a jeep and advanced toward their ultimate objective, the army barracks on the far outskirts of town.

On the other side of the lines, Major Yusuf Gowon had spent the morning making frantic preparations for Simba Battalion's defense. At around 9:00 a.m., a bugler had sounded an alarm call, alerting all the soldiers inside the barracks, who assembled on its parade ground. Gowon told his men that their country had been invaded. He ordered each company to take up defensive positions around the barracks, and he dispatched several jeeps to guard the main road, including one mounted with a 106-millimeter recoilless gun. The major then took up a command position inside the barracks' orderly room.

When the rebels reached the eucalyptus forest that stood across from Simba Battalion, the jeeps Gowon had dispatched opened fire, blowing up one of their trucks. "That one shell," Museveni later wrote, "changed the course of the whole adventure." Inside the barracks, the Ugandan soldiers saw the invaders jump from their vehicles and scamper into the nearby woods. At this point, the assault fell into disarray. The rebel commander, a former army captain, disappeared from the fray. Museveni rallied a group of around thirty fighters and led them toward the barracks gate, where they took cover behind tall anthills and exchanged fire with Gowon's men. Another group occupied an elevated position near the town mosque, from which they lobbed a few mortar shells into the barracks. A third contingent of men rushed toward the fence that surrounded the installation. They might have been able to get through the barbed wire if they had been equipped with wire cutters, but instead they had to climb over it. Tangled up, the rebels made easy targets, and their bullet-raked bodies piled up around the perimeter.

After an hour or so, Gowon's men had pushed the rebels back into the eucalyptus forest. There, Museveni gathered the leaderless remnants of the invasion force and argued that they had to retreat. Some of the men resisted—rumor had it that their compatriots had taken Kampala. Museveni turned on a transistor radio he had brought along. The national radio station was still broadcasting Idi Amin's propaganda. Their hopes dashed, the remaining rebels climbed into three trucks and set off back toward Tanzania. Museveni's vehicle was almost out of gas, so he stopped to fill up on his way out of Mbarara. He escaped town just ahead of Gowon's counterattacking soldiers, who, finding the invaders were gone, killed the gas station attendant instead.

For days afterward, the civilian population of Ankole stayed huddled behind locked doors, listening to radio bulletins. At first, there were reports that the rebels had taken three towns near Masaka, and that Simba Battalion was surrounded by hostile forces. A "military spokesman"—a pseudonym for Idi Amin, everyone knew—issued bellicose statements, conveyed by radio announcers, assuring the public that the fighting would be "the hottest ever experienced by the enemy." Within a day or two, it was clear that the slapdash rebellion had been routed. On the Masaka front, the invaders had run out of ammunition before they had even advanced halfway to their objective. On the Mbarara side, just 46 of approximately 350 rebels had made it back to Tanzania. Only a few had been killed in the initial attack on the barracks. The rest were scattered and on the run.

Three captured rebel leaders, including the captain who had been in command of the Mbarara attack, were paraded before Amin and the press at the general's Kampala residence. Amin scolded them: "You have been killing one another when Obote is drinking Bell [Beer] and listening to the BBC in Dar es Salaam." The three were then taken away and executed. The next day, Amin released details of what was alleged to be a copy of an invasion plan extracted from the rebel captives, claiming that it called for the wholesale massacre of several tribes, as well as the elimination of political and religious leaders, and members of certain occupations, such as taxi drivers. That last detail was an especially diabolical touch, since any rebels still at large would likely be looking for taxis to Tanzania. The invasion had so shaken Uganda that it hardly mattered that the supposed "plan" was a blatant forgery. The logic of kill-or-be-killed took hold. "After that," one then-resident of Mbarara recalled, "that was when the hunting started."

All over the Ankole countryside, rebel stragglers were lynched by angry villagers or turned in by friends who'd promised to hide them. Soldiers fanned out across Ankole, throwing up roadblocks, stopping cars and buses, and interrogating suspect wayfarers. On Radio Uganda, the "military spokesman" commanded all citizens to cooperate with the regime's intelligence agencies. "The government wants to make it absolutely clear," one statement warned, "that anyone harboring any of these people will be putting himself in the same position of the guerrillas." There was no doubting the threat's implication.

Amin publicly boasted that he had obtained "a full list" of rebel sympathizers. Throughout the country, neighbors turned against neighbors, often for scant or selfish reasons. Yusuf Gowon recalled that the day after the invasion, some Muslim civilians brought a truckload of battered people to the Simba Battalion barracks. These men, fellow residents of their town, were Christians and onetime supporters of Obote's party. The Muslims claimed that the prisoners had been seen hoisting a UPC flag and slaughtering a goat after hearing news of the invasion. "Some of these people, I knew them," Gowon said. "They were businessmen. What could they be having to do with the rebels?" The Christians were petrified. "They said to me, 'Some of us brought Bibles. Let us pray first before you kill us.' I said, 'You will not die, or I will die together with you.'"

As Gowon told the story, he ordered the captives returned home and reprimanded those who had brought them in. The Muslim leader in the area of western Ankole where the informants came from was notorious for using the army to settle business disputes, deploying soldiers, for instance, to eliminate his rivals within the leadership of a local tea-growing cooperative. "Most of these killings during Amin's time were exactly because of this," Gowon said, disapprovingly. As outsiders ignorant of Ankole's internal divisions, he explained, the army could be easily duped into intervening in matters that had nothing to with the rebellion. "Those were the people who were just feeding us false allegations," he said. "The Ankole people knew themselves, who was who."

Gowon denied that he personally had any involvement in the killings that followed the attack. When asked about them, he theatrically put his hands over his ears. "Something about civilians—I didn't hear that," he said. As the second-in-command of a battalion, he claimed, he was consumed with vital logistical duties. "What I knew is that my war ended at the barracks. I did not know about anything going on outside that wall."

In reality, during the first few days after the invasion, when Simba Battalion's commanding officer Ali Fadhul was tied down in the south, mopping up rebel remnants, Gowon had absolute authority over Mbarara, the barracks and the captured fighters that soldiers regularly brought in, along with civilians who were believed to have collaborated. Several witness accounts say the major presided over an ad hoc court in his office to handle all the arrests, where he had the final say in sorting legitimate from spurious accusations. Gowon reluctantly confirmed this version of events, portraying the tribunal as his attempt to curb unwarranted reprisals. "There was allegation after allegation without proof," he said. "I was not the commanding officer, but I interfered."

During that terrifying September, when soldiers arrested civilians in Mbarara, people begged to be taken to see Major Gowon. The word was that he was reasonable—you stood a chance with him. Decades later, a retired politician named Yoasi Makaaru recounted being picked up by an army detachment at a shop he owned. "The soldiers said this was the last sun I would ever see," he recalled. At the barracks, he said, he and several other prisoners were "brought into the council of Mr. Yusuf Gowon," who saved their lives.

"Gowon asked someone to introduce us to him, to say why we had been brought," Makaaru recounted. One soldier claimed that he had been recruiting young men to train as rebels in Tanzania. "Then Gowon wanted to know if they had any evidence. This fellow did not have any evidence. He asked if he had any exhibits, anything that would show that I belonged to that particular rebel group." The soldiers stammered that they didn't have anything.

"Why did you pick these ones?" Gowon yelled, as the politician recollected it. "They're not on the list."

The major ordered them all freed. "When he was asking those questions in my presence, I thought it was God," Makaaru said. "Military fellows don't ask."

His flashes of mercy aside, though, Gowon surely knew what kind of war the army was waging. For days, a mounting pile of rebel corpses moldered in the Simba barracks yard. They weren't hidden. The army wanted the public to know the costs of resistance. One day, an army photographer took pictures of the corpses for propaganda purposes. Dozens of broken bodies were laid from head to toe in several rows, beneath the vigilant eyes of the two lions painted on the battalion's guardhouse wall. A group of soldiers in combat gear posed around them, brandishing their rifles. On September 21, 1972, the grisly photograph appeared on the front page of Uganda's official state newspaper, beneath the headline: THE MBARARA INVASION THAT FAILED.

That picture of carnage became one of the enduring images of Idi Amin's rule. It was picked up by the UPI wire service and transmitted around the world. The Sunday after the rebel invasion, it appeared at the top of the front page of the *New York Times*. What was happening in Uganda could no longer be ignored. Amin's soldiers were also detaining foreign journalists and rounding up expatriates. Britain began planning a military operation to evacuate its citizens.

At 7:42 p.m. on September 21, 1972, the day the famous photograph of Simba Battalion was published—and the last full day of Eliphaz Laki's life—President Richard Nixon placed an agitated call from the White House to his national security adviser, Henry Kissinger. Naturally, it was taped.

"I want hard action," the president said. "Now, goddamnit."

"That will be ordered today," Kissinger replied.

"Now we—I think you will agree, Henry, we have really had a double standard on this thing."

"Oh, sure."

Nixon launched into a diatribe against the Africa Division of the State Department, where seasoned diplomatic hands were urging restraint. "Do we care when these damn Africans eat a hundred thousand people?"

"The Mbarara Invasion That Failed"—the Simba Battalion barracks, September 1972
CORBIS

the president asked. "I mean, it's really gone too far. What do you think?"

"I couldn't agree more," Kissinger replied.

Nixon spent that weekend at Camp David, and though he had many important matters to ponder—peace talks with the North Vietnamese, his reelection campaign, the indictment of two aides on charges relating to a burglary at the Watergate—he was still dwelling on the killing in Uganda. Kissinger called the president that Sunday morning to tell him that the State Department was once again trying to foil British plans to intervene militarily in Uganda, because of opposition from other African nations.

"Screw State!" Nixon bellowed. "State's always on the side of the blacks. The hell with them!"

The president embarked on one of his rambling soliloquies. "Don't you feel—I mean . . . let's be totally honest," he asked his national security adviser. "Isn't a person a person, goddamnit? . . . I'm getting tired of this business of letting these Africans eat a hundred thousand people and do[ing] nothing about it."

"And . . . all these bleeding hearts in this country who say we like to kill yellow people," Kissinger replied.

"That's right."

Nixon went on. "Isn't it awful what these—that this goddamn guy at the head of Uganda, Henry, is an ape."

"He's an ape without education," Kissinger concurred.

"That's probably no disadvantage," the president said, as Kissinger burst into laughter. "I mean, you figure that asshole that was the head of Ghana"—he meant Kwame Nkrumah—"had a brilliant education in the United States."

"That's right," Kissinger said.

"I mean, so, let's face it. No, no, no, what I mean is he's, he's—he really is. He's a prehistoric monster."

"Yeah," Kissinger replied.

"Let the British know we're going to help," Nixon said before hanging up. "The idea that we're going to stand still on the ground that any African government that . . . overthrew a colonial power thereby becomes lily white by our . . . standards and thereby beyond criticism is ridiculous. The damn double standard is just unbelievable."

"Out of the question," Kissinger replied.

Three months later, after the threat to expatriates subsided and Britain set aside its intervention plans, Kissinger presented the president with a policy memorandum recommending that, with no vital American interests at stake, "no decisions need to be taken concerning Uganda, particularly aid levels." At the bottom of the document, Nixon scrawled his initials next to the word *approve*.

After a few days, the several dozen enemy corpses that were stacked at the entrance to the Simba Battalion barracks began to swell and stink. A gang of inmates from the local prison were pressed into service as gravediggers. The prisoners loaded the bodies onto trucks and took them to a secluded patch of farmland not far from the barracks, where they were tossed into a six-foot-deep trench. A tractor pushed the upturned earth back over the mass grave—the final resting place, it might be said, of organized resistance to Idi Amin. The grave was not marked and has never been exhumed.

Amin's war against his internal opponents had entered a new subterranean phase. For a dictator eager to consolidate power, the attack proved to be, in the words of one former official, a "pure gift." Anyone suspected of the slightest disloyalty could now be eliminated under the pretext of national security. "It was a matter of policy, naturally," said one of Amin's generals. "The net had been widened, and so many people started getting picked."

Fame and eminence offered no protection. Security men grabbed the chief justice of the Supreme Court from his chambers, walked him to their car at gunpoint and took him to a military prison, where he was shot—some say by Amin himself. Professors, businessmen and journalists were dragged from their homes or offices, or waylaid as they dropped their children off at school. One evening, a popular newscaster was taken from a bar on Kampala Road where he was having a drink with a girlfriend. When people wondered why, they remembered that once, as a young heavyweight, he had floored Amin in a boxing match. "What is now occurring in Uganda," a CIA analyst wrote in a classified report on the consequences of the failed invasion, "is the destruction of the Ugandan elite: the judiciary, the top civil servants, the academics, a limited professional class, and the senior army and police officers who do not come from a West Nile tribe."

Such a wide-ranging purge required the support and assistance of thousands of civilians. In Ankole, one of the key participants was the intelligence informant Salim Sebi. A former bus driver, he knew all the roads and he knew all the targets. Sebi had once been a well-regarded member of the community, but the invasion seemed to unlock some malignancy in his character. "Sebi was a great friend of mine," said one associate of Eliphaz Laki's. "But I think power corrupted him. I think he wanted his kith and kin to retain power."

Boniface Byanyima, a now-elderly leader of the Democratic Party in Ankole, described an unannounced visit that Sebi had paid to the politician's Mbarara home sometime after the 1972 invasion. "He told me he was a brother to the president," Byanyima recounted. Sebi launched into his usual extortion routine, accusing the politician of harboring thieves. He coolly offered Sebi a drink, and they sat down to talk, and after the second beer the former bus driver seemed to lose interest in squeezing his host for money. As he grew drunker, Sebi boasted about his role in tracking down subversives. "He told me his job was to hunt the bad people and kill them, and clean the country," Byanyima said. "He said they had cleaned many people." Sebi went on to list some names, including Eliphaz Laki's.

Sebi, whose old bus route had run to Ibanda, was the one who allegedly guided Nasur Gille and Mohammed Anyule to the county headquarters on the morning of September 22. When Anyule fetched Laki from his office and walked the frightened chief across the street to his residence, Sebi stood guard at the bottom of the hill, keeping a close eye on several locals who were hanging around on the county head-quarters' veranda and watching the scene unfold. At one point, one of the witnesses, a policeman, also crossed the street, just to see what was going on. Sebi stopped him at the bottom of the driveway. He knew the policeman well—they'd been friendly back in the days when he drove a bus.

"Where are you going?" Sebi barked.

"The chief forgot his keys," the policeman replied, making up an excuse for his curiosity.

"Forget it," Sebi told him. "Where he's going, he won't need keys."

After a long drive, Sebi stood lookout while the soldiers marched Laki into the brush of Yonasani Rwakanuma's ranch. A gunshot rang out across the pasture. Then the soldiers reappeared. Sebi took the wheel of the dead chief's Volkswagen, and the two cars continued their tandem journey to Mbarara. At the Simba Battalion barracks, Sebi parked the Beetle in front of Major Gowon's office.

"I . . . told Gowon that we accomplished the work he assigned us to do," Sergeant Gille said in his 2001 confession, adding that he offered Laki's Volkswagen to the major "as a proof." Gowon allegedly com-mended the soldiers for their work, ordered them to fall out and told them to get some rest. There would be many more missions to perform.

On the final day of September 1972, the residents of Mbarara were startled to hear the thwacking sound of a helicopter's blades spinning overhead. It was General Amin, hovering above them, making an aerial inspection of the front. Inside the cockpit, the president was enjoying his view immensely. He was in an invigorated mood when he landed at the Simba Battalion barracks, where he was welcomed by Lieutenant Colonel Fadhul and Major Gowon. As the president climbed out of the military chopper, his soldiers surged forward and surrounded him, reaching out to touch him, to kiss his immense hands.

The next day, Amin conducted a walking tour of Mbarara in the com-pany of his military police chief and his baby son, Moses. Amin and his child wore matching camouflage jackets. Father carried a simple wooden walking stick and son a toy machine gun. Outside a shoe store, they were swarmed by grinning townspeople. Amin enjoyed a luncheon

Idi and Moses Amin (far right) *in Mbarara, after the rebel incursion* THE MONITOR

banquet back at the barracks and then presided over a memorial service for the seventeen soldiers of Simba Battalion who were killed during the invasion. He announced that all the men would be awarded the new Uganda Independence Medal. Amin also bestowed one on himself, along with ten other commendations: the Distinguished Service Order, the President's Commendation, the Operational Service Medal, the Efficiency Decoration, the Long Service and Good Conduct medal, the Republic of Uganda Medal, the Mau Mau Campaign Medal, the State Combat Star, the Victorious Cross and the Most Excellent Order of the Source of the Nile.

In his speech, Amin praised the bravery of the soldiers of Simba Battalion, who sat before him cross-legged on the ground. He said the cowardly rebels had not just been defeated, but humiliated. Some of them, Amin claimed, had been rounded up by women armed only with sticks and knives. (It was a tale his propagandists had invented.) Others were reported to have been torn apart by lions as they fled unarmed through the bush. Playing on the meaning of the Swahili word "simba," Amin declared that "many yet will be prey to the lions which are now hunting them."

He was particularly fulsome in his praise for Major Gowon, the defender of the barracks. Amin presented him with a new automobile, an olive green Land Rover. By the end of the year, Gowon was promoted to lieutenant colonel and within a few more months he was given sole command of Simba Battalion.

All this time, allegedly, Eliphaz Laki's Volkswagen Beetle sat idle in the driveway of Gowon's home. Now that he had that fancy new Land Rover, Mohammed Anyule felt emboldened to ask for his own reward. He made an appointment to see the lieutenant colonel. He later recalled that he flattered Gowon, employing a proverb that likened him to a great and generous hunter. He asked, "Do you have any meat for me?"

Gowon understood him, Anyule later alleged in his confession. Gowon handed over the keys to the Volkswagen and advised the private to get it repainted before he took it out. The pleased private drove away in his new car. He went downtown and, forging Laki's signature, completed the paperwork necessary to have the vehicle reregistered under his own name.

15

BAD OMEN

Yoweri Museveni returned to exile defeated, but not chastened. In early 1973, his Front for National Salvation published a manifesto entitled "An Indictment of a Primitive Fascist," which included some of the first detailed descriptions of Idi Amin's atrocities.

> People have been choked with their genitals, their heads bashed in with sledgehammers and gun butts, hacked to pieces with *pangas*, disemboweled, blown up with explosives, suffocated in car boots, burned alive in cars and houses after being tied up, drowned, dragged along roads tied to Land Rovers, starved to death, whipped to death, gradually dismembered. The luckier ones have simply been shot—and what luck is that?

The manifesto was filled with combative rhetoric. It was all bluster. In actuality, the failure of the invasion had effectively destroyed Museveni's rebel group, along with all other forms of resistance. Most of Museveni's underground cells had been uncovered. One of his key operatives, a young college professor, was captured after a gunfight at his Kampala apartment. He was executed by a firing squad in a square in Mbarara, before a large, boisterous and approving crowd. A few months after the publication of the manifesto, Amin once again appeared in Mbarara, accompanied this time by an American admirer, the black nationalist Roy Innis. The dictator took the opportunity to directly rebuke Museveni and his supporters, saying that far from being true anti-imperialists, they were in fact tools of the Israelis and the CIA. "The organization is not only spoiling the good name of Uganda," Amin said, "but the whole of Africa."

Back in Dar es Salaam, Amin's opponents were disheartened. After the invasion debacle, strong international pressure was brought to bear on Julius Nyerere, the president of Tanzania, who had sponsored the rebels. He reluctantly signed a peace agreement in which both Uganda and Tanzania pledged to "end all hostilities" and to cease harboring "subversive forces." Britain and the United States protested the killings in Uganda but took no substantive action, while the Arab states and the Soviet Union pledged to supply Amin with arms. Milton Obote became an increasingly remote and pathetic figure. Prohibited from talking to the press by his Tanzanian hosts, he spent his days in the living room of his oceanfront mansion, listening for news from Uganda on his shortwave radio. His community of sympathizers mostly dispersed, gathering only for occasions like the ex-president's birthday party.

Museveni tried to keep up the struggle, but the invasion and the publication of the manifesto had raised his profile, and he could no longer move around Uganda inconspicuously. On one occasion, he only barely escaped capture by Amin's operatives; a close friend and comrade was killed in the encounter. Museveni curtailed his activities after that. He settled down in Tanzania, taking a job as a schoolteacher. He married and had a child, though with characteristic secretiveness, he kept the news from his friends. His wife earned a little extra cash by peddling homemade marmalade. For the time being, it seemed, the possibility of returning home was vanishingly remote.

Lieutenant Colonel Yusuf Gowon, the hero of Mbarara, was being groomed for a commanding role. Pleased with his valiant service on the battlefield, Amin made sure that Gowon received promotions, publicity and opportunities for personal enrichment. After the Indians were expelled in 1972, the military government formed a number of committees to reapportion the departing merchants' houses, businesses and valuables. Gowon was appointed to head one of them. At the time, Amin proclaimed that the lottery system would enrich all Ugandans. In fact, the military monopolized the loot. Gowon allotted himself a hotel near the taxi park in Kampala and gave other confiscated properties as gifts to friendly soldiers and their families. For an officer on the rise, it was an invaluable way to build goodwill within the ranks.

Since the days of the British, Ugandan society had been defined by a fairly rigid class system, dominated by a southern upper crust educated at missionary boarding schools. The rise of Amin upended this traditional hierarchy, and Kampala filled with swaggering young northerners. The locals nicknamed these newcomers the "one-elevens," after the three vertical slash marks that so many of them bore on their cheeks. For generations, the people of West Nile had been denied access to education and good jobs and were treated with disdain by the southern tribes. Now that roles had reversed, Uganda's military rulers took great pleasure in tormenting the elite. The president bullied Makerere University into awarding him an honorary law doctorate and declared that henceforth he was to be called "Dr. Amin." His men made themselves rich by looting the state. Individual officers took over the national bus company, the national coffee concern and government-owned sugar plantations and mines. These new managers saw no reason to export through legal duty-paying channels, not when it was so much more profitable to smuggle. A culture of impunity set in. "The life we passed through was very difficult," one former army officer said. "In those days, Big Men, they could say anything."

Amin, the most formidable of them all, took to calling himself "Big Daddy," a nickname originally coined by the British tabloids. He played the warm patriarch when it suited his purposes, but as a judge who served during his regime later wrote, he "could turn from laughing fat man to evil-minded sadist in a moment." He meddled in the most intimate details of his subjects' lives. He issued decrees banning miniskirts, wigs and straightened hair, which he labeled as examples of "imperialist style." He regarded beards as suspicious leftist affectations, so all men had to shave. He proclaimed that "everybody in Uganda must act as a member of the intelligence service."

Gowon had a place in the tier of influence just beneath Amin, among the officers that made up the dictator's high command. This nebulous and ever-shifting clique was embodied by a mysterious organ called the "Defense Council," which had no known membership roster. "Amin could take one officer, they may go to Entebbe, they go swimming, they decide something there," one general later recalled. "He comes back and [announces] that the Defense Council has taken such a decision." Those within this inner circle were mainly rough and uneducated soldiers, many of them hastily promoted from menial jobs because of their personal ties to the president. General Mustafa Adrisi, the fantastically corrupt vice president, had served alongside Amin in the colonial army but he could not read or write. The psychopathic Colonel Isaac Malyamungu, a cousin of the dictator's, was a former sugar plantation gatekeeper. Other cronies conveyed their brutal qualifications via noms de guerre: Lieutenant Colonel Christopher "Gore," commander of the Masaka Regiment, who was seldom seen without a marijuana spliff in his mouth; Lieutenant Colonel Juma "Butabika," a battalion commander who took his name from a mental hospital on the outskirts of Kampala. One notorious officer called himself Captain "Kill-Me-Quick."

Amin's toxic spirit seeped into every corner of the country. In Mbarara, Salim Sebi became an agent of Amin's principal domestic intelligence organization, the Bureau of State Research. Though the bureau's Orwellian name suggested a certain level of evil sophistication, State Research agents were actually flagrant and fairly incompetent. They dressed conspicuously in bell-bottoms, floral-print shirts and dark sunglasses. "Their intelligence, in both senses, is minimal, inaccurate and misleading, and often directed against people with whom they have quarreled," a contemporary resident recorded in his diary. Decades later, at the very mention of Salim Sebi's name, a farm caretaker in Ankole pushed up his sleeve to show me a scar on his forearm. "This was Sebi," he said. Apparently, the caretaker had once parked a car somewhere Sebi didn't like, so Sebi had lashed him with barbed wire.

Men like Sebi were accountable to no one. On one occasion, he was charged with assault after a fight with some soldiers in a Mbarara bar. Sebi returned to the police station in the company of Gowon, who ordered the police to withdraw the charge and transfer the arresting officer to another town. A police superintendent later told an investigatory commission that he'd had no choice but to comply with Gowon's demands. "All I know is he would not have been happy" had the police not dropped the charges, the superintendent said. "He could have done anything."

"I was not a friend to Sebi," Gowon countered in a prison interview. He claimed that he, too, feared the secret police agent and was powerless to stop such men. "My boss Amin had special units around him that had power, more than commanding officers," he said. "If they went to your area, you could not arrest them. They were allowed to do their research"—a euphemistic way to say "murder."

"We had no voice," Gowon claimed. "Any uniformed battalion commander . . . he was just under fear." No one discussed the disappearances, he insisted, and no one tried to stop them. To speak out against the terror would have invited the death squads to one's own door. "Any commanding officer who defended them . . ." Gowon's voice trailed off. "When you defend," he finally continued, "you become a collaborator."

Gowon soon found he had good reason to be afraid. In 1974, a Catholic general from West Nile led a coup attempt that very nearly succeeded in deposing Amin. Afterward, someone—in these situations, it was never clear who—circulated the rumor Gowon was secretly Christian. "They denied me," Gowon said. "They said I had converted." He was placed under house arrest, but the vice president, General Adrisi, pled for his life. Adrisi had been Amin's close friend since they were young soldiers combating the Mau Mau uprising in Kenya together. His intercession convinced the dictator to spare Gowon. The message had been sent, however: No officer was above Amin's wandering suspicion.

Amin loved to drive rally cars, and he often staged road races across Uganda in which he and his generals competed. That was what it was like to serve him: all high-speed maneuvering and fiery crashes. The officers within the high command were constantly scheming to keep Amin's favor, a state of affairs the dictator encouraged. He never placed too much trust in any of his generals, and he tried to keep them off balance. He'd favor one for a while and then abruptly accuse him of corruption or malfeasance. The dictator was fond of awaking his subordinates with 3:00 a.m. phone calls, sometimes to issue orders, sometimes to charge them with disloyalty. "It would happen quite often," one general said. "He would pick on one person, then another. He was a very clever man."

Lieutenant Colonel Yusuf Gowon (left) *with Vice President Adrisi* GOWON FAMILY

By the mid-1970s, however, Amin was no longer the muscular, vigorous, populist general who had taken power. He was fat, isolated and angry. Where he once mixed freely with the people, he now often disappeared from public view for days or weeks at a time, as he recuperated from hypochondriacal ailments. His stomach expanded to gargantuan proportions, as did his ego. In 1976, Amin proclaimed himself "President for Life." That same year, a team of Palestinian-aligned terrorists hijacked an Air France flight that had originated in Tel Aviv, diverting the plane to Uganda, where Amin received them with sympathy. In the predawn hours of July 4, 1976, as Americans were celebrating their bicentennial, a team of Israeli commandos flew into Entebbe International Airport and rescued 102 passengers. Twenty Ugandan soldiers were killed, and the military was humiliated. Afterward, a group of air force officers tried to kill Amin, ambushing and destroying his Mercedes limousine. Amin escaped with minor injuries only because he had chosen to ride in another car in the presidential convoy. This was one of several times when Amin narrowly averted assassination. His invulnerability became the stuff of folklore, as people told tales about the magical powers he'd supposedly picked up from witches in the wilds of Kenya, back when he was fighting in the colonial army.

No black magic, however, could keep the gangster economy from collapsing. Inexperienced soldiers were running their confiscated shops into the ground. Staples like bread, salt and tea were disappearing from the country's shelves. Legal exports were declining dramatically as trade goods were diverted to the black market. Farmers could no longer fetch a decent price for cash crops, so they grew only what they needed to subsist. As trade shrank, so did the government's reserves of hard currency. "Amin could not grasp this fiscal reality," wrote a former minister of his. "By his definition countries could not go broke, because they printed money and could always print more." Amin increased Uganda's money supply by 600 percent. Hyperinflation turned the banknotes that bore his face into valueless scraps of paper. Soap cost the equivalent of five dollars a bar.

Amin's next move was to turn decisively against the country's Christians. Muslims made up only a small proportion of Uganda's population, perhaps 10 or 15 percent, and they had long occupied an inferior position in society. But Amin began to govern as if Islam was the established state religion. He started construction on a gargantuan mosque at the top of Old Kampala Hill, on the grounds of a historic fort once occupied by Captain Frederick Lugard. He outlawed all but a handful of churches, focusing his crackdown on the increasingly popular evangelical sects. In villages across the country, Muslims were appointed to replace Christians as local chiefs. Tensions between the two faiths, which dated back to the colonial era, took on a new intensity.

On one occasion, Gowon, as the top army officer in Mbarara, confronted the town's Anglican bishop, accusing him of sheltering American and British spies. "They were not spies," the bishop told me. "They were missionaries." Another time, a Muslim leader from Ankole objected to his daughter's engagement to a Christian doctor. He went to Gowon, asking him to stop the marriage, and Gowon took his case all the way to the president. Amin declined to intervene, but he did listen with concern when Gowon reported that the groom's emissary to the bride's family, James Kahigiriza, had made snobbish remarks about Muslims. Afterward, Kahigiriza began to notice suspicious vehicles in his rearview mirror. He was eventually imprisoned by the Bureau of State Research, for reasons that were never disclosed to him.

In 1976, Anglican Church leaders quietly dropped a routine prayer for the president's well-being from the Sunday service. That Christmas, in his holiday radio broadcast, Amin attacked them for preaching "bloodshed" and undermining the government. Two months later, he ordered the arrest of the Reverend Janan Luwum, Uganda's Anglican archbishop, on charges of treason. A day later, a brief boldfaced bulletin appeared in the state newspaper, the *Voice of Uganda*, tersely relating that the archbishop and two veteran cabinet ministers had been killed in a car accident while attempting to "fight and overpower" an army officer "who was driving them away for interrogation." In reality, the archbishop had been killed with a pistol shot through his mouth. For Amin, it was an act of desperation, marking the beginning of the regime's final paranoid phase.

By this time Gowon had been promoted again, to brigadier general, and was commanding an infantry brigade in eastern Uganda. But that didn't protect him from the Bureau of State Research. One day, the secret police arrested him, after another general had whispered to Amin that Gowon was sending messages to rebels in Tanzania. Gowon and General Adrisi, his longtime patron and protector, were brought to the president's office in Kampala, where Amin confronted them with the report.

Amin initially ordered Gowon out of his sight. Gowon was certain he was going to be summarily executed. Adrisi crept to Amin on his knees, pleading that Gowon was innocent. Amin softened, brought

Gowon back into his office and told an orderly to bring everyone tea. As Gowon cradled his cup with trembling hands, Amin said he'd spare him. But Amin also warned him that the next time he received such a report, they wouldn't be taking tea.

Shortly after that, the army chief of staff, a Christian graduate of the prestigious British military academy at Omdurman, announced his surprise resignation while addressing a summit of regional heads of state. He left for West Nile and didn't return. The general's official explanation was that he wanted to take time off to build a house for his mother. In fact, he'd likely caught wind of Amin's plans to set a climactic purge in motion. To carry it out, the dictator appointed Brigadier Gowon to be the new chief of staff.

Through his rise, Gowon had acquired a reputation as a ruthless infighter. "Gowon was capable of saying one thing to you and then going to Amin and saying something different," one former colleague told me. "I think when you have a person who finds himself enjoying a lot of favor, who has some post for which he is not qualified, in my experience such a person is capable of telling lies." Another of Gowon's old rivals, still roused to fury by the mere mention of his name, sputtered, "He was a snake!"

One of Gowon's first moves was to sideline the leaders of two intelligence services who were feared to have amassed too much influence. Then, in April 1978, Amin called a meeting of his cabinet, army command and other notables, including Gowon. The president launched into a tirade against "big-headed" cabinet ministers, singling out one in particular, Brigadier Moses Ali, the finance minister and one of the original conspirators in the 1971 coup. Amin charged Ali with mismanaging the Bank of Uganda and other misdeeds, growing so enraged that he hurled an ashtray at him.

The finance minister had become very popular in his own right as the leader of an Islamic charity. Amin ordered an investigation into its finances. At a religious gathering, Gowon announced that he had discovered that Ali had embezzled 77 million shillings from the charity, adding that "no one except the president is above the law." Ali snuck out of the capital in a civilian car and retreated to his home in West Nile, where a group of armed men attacked his house. Ali fought them off with a machine gun. He would always blame Gowon for engineering both his downfall and the attempt on his life.

At around the same time, General Adrisi was nearly killed in a car accident. Most people assumed it was no accident at all. Adrisi, who had support within the army that rivaled Amin's own, was said to be disgusted with the disappearances of many army officers and also annoyed with the president's attempts to move in on some of his business concerns. (He was one of the country's richest coffee smugglers.) Amin had learned that Adrisi was planning a coup. By a stroke of fortune, though, Adrisi survived his arranged car wreck, and his supporters managed to get him on a plane to Cairo for medical treatment. Gowon went to the airport to see his stretcher loaded on the plane.

In May, Gowon was promoted to major general. The *Voice of Uganda* carried a front-page photograph of the chief of staff toasting Amin's long life at a military reception. Over the course of his eight years in power, Amin had first eliminated his real enemies, then his imagined ones, and then he had turned on his allies and friends. Through this brutal process of elimination, he had finally found a henchman fit for his insecurities. Yusuf Gowon was from his tribe. He was thought to be reasonably loyal. He had no power base within the army. He seemed to lack the imagination necessary to mastermind a coup. In short, he was not a threat.

None of these qualities, of course, equipped Gowon to fight a real war against a real army. And as fate would have it, one was about to begin.

On October 9, 1978, the sixteenth anniversary of Uganda's independence, a small detachment of Amin's soldiers crossed the border into Tanzania, burning down two houses. Such skirmishing between the two countries had been going on for years. It was not the sort of incursion that seemed likely to set off a major war. But for some reason, Idi Amin seemed determined to have one. There are many theories about the reason for this catastrophic miscalculation: Perhaps Amin needed to distract an increasingly mutinous army; perhaps he had become intoxicated by the legend of his invulnerability; perhaps he was just spoiling for a fight. "It started very, very small," Gowon reflected in one of our interviews. "The leader as a commanding officer maybe was . . ." The general considered his words. ". . . showing off."

"Showing off?" I asked.

"Showing off," Gowon repeated, more emphatically. "It caused a lot of chaos. Thousands of people died."

In response to the initial Ugandan assault, the commander of a small detachment of Tanzanian troops along the border ordered his artillery to open fire. Amin's propaganda machine roared. TANZANIA

TROOPS ATTACK UGANDA, blared a headline across the front page of the state-run *Voice of Uganda*. For days afterward, the radio carried reports of an imaginary invasion from the south. Amin made a tour of the front—posing for a picture before a frontier road sign reading REPUBLIC OF TANZANIA—and professed his commitment to peace. The *Voice of Uganda* further reported that Amin, though "now referred to by many people as the King of Africa," had no ambition to conquer "his children" in Tanzania.

In late October, Amin visited his troops in the border area again, accompanied by Major General Gowon. Then, on the morning of October 30, approximately three thousand Ugandan troops crossed the border in trucks. Facing only token resistance, the invaders swiftly occupied a seven-hundred-square-mile swath of northern Tanzania. Amin claimed that the entire operation took merely twenty-five minutes. The pages of the state newspaper were filled with photographs of Gowon in battle fatigues, commanding the troops. In one, he stood with his hands stuffed casually in his pockets as he inspected a Tanzanian corpse, supposedly a soldier's, sprawled in the high grass.

Throughout the occupied region, Ugandan troops gang-raped Tanzanian women and killed civilians with abandon. An estimated 1,500 perished. One of the army's main objectives seems to have been looting the local sugar factory. Drunken Ugandan soldiers stripped it bare, set

Chief of Staff Gowon with his patron. "Gowon was capable of saying one thing to you and then going to Amin and saying something different." RADIO UGANDA

up mortars and demolished it. Similar pillaging occurred across the occupied area, as soldiers carted off everything of value: livestock, pots and pans, even the tin roofs from Tanzanian houses. Witnesses noted that Gowon gleefully took his pick of the spoils, making off with tons of valuable sugar. When one captain refused to give up a tractor Gowon fancied, the general is said to have summarily demoted him. (Gowon admitted that incident happened, but explained that he commandeered it only because the captain didn't know how to drive it as well as he did.) Thirteen thousand cattle were rustled away from a government ranch and driven ninety miles north to Mbarara, with such relentless disregard for their well-being that the pastoralists of Ankole would attribute Amin's subsequent misfortunes to a bovine curse.

Gowon's men blew up the bridge over the Kagera River, which separated the captured area from the rest of Tanzania. Amin announced its annexation and declared victory. In early November, Gowon returned to Kampala to brief his commander and to attend a celebration for the troops. "In a jubilant mood," a newspaper account of the event reported, "President Amin said that if he had met Nyerere at Kagera he would have kissed him to show him exactly who President Amin is."

"Gowon came back very pleased, as if that was it," recalled a fellow member of the army high command. "He could not see how the Tanzanian army could ever cross after he took that little bridge. He thought, *That's it, I have finished the war.*"

In Dar es Salaam, Amin's exiled opponents were still squabbling and disorganized. Over the past six years, the focus of the resistance had shifted from training to talking, with political life revolving around a number of loose-knit Marxist "discussion groups." Yoweri Museveni was involved at the margins of these meetings. ("I remember he never spoke," said one participant. "Except on military matters.") But he cut an enigmatic figure among the Ugandan exiles. Still only in his midthirties, Museveni cultivated an air of studied mystery, adopting aliases and disguises. It was a running joke among his acquaintances that no one knew where he lived. It was rumored that he was on the Tanzanian intelligence service's payroll, and had moles inside Amin's Bureau of State Research. Yet for all his veiled references to secret operations, Museveni's rebel organization, the Front for National Salvation, seemed to exist solely to issue bellicose communiqués.

When he launched his invasion, Amin inadvertently galvanized his enemies. "Never since Amin's coup in 1971," Museveni later wrote, "had I felt so buoyant." Seeking to prove his seriousness, the leader of the Front for National Salvation volunteered the force's services to the Tanzanian military. It was hardly an army: just around thirty young men who had been trained at leftist rebel camps in northern Mozambique. But Tanzanians knew the participation of Ugandan exiles was essential. Nyerere did not want the Ugandan public to perceive his coming counterattack as a foreign invasion.

Museveni wasn't the only one spurred to action. From all over the world, Ugandans descended on Tanzania to join the struggle: professors and soldiers, monarchists and Maoists. Nyerere visited Milton Obote at his oceanfront residence, and told his friend, "This is the opportunity we have been waiting for." Several hundred of Obote's former soldiers had settled down at the site of their onetime rebel camp in western Tanzania, growing prosperous by farming and producing charcoal. Obote traveled west and told the exiles, some of them now pushing fifty, that the resistance needed them. He raised eight hundred volunteers.

Tanzania's military was one of the weakest in the region. Nyerere had always been more interested in building a socialist society than in financing a force that might ultimately overthrow him. Amin was certain that the Tanzanians could never mount a serious counteroffensive. His propagandists spread the story that Nyerere's soldiers were drowning and being eaten by crocodiles as they attempted to cross the Kagera River. The dictator held a party for the army high command at his lakeside villa, where he announced that he was creating a new medal in honor of the army's conquest, which he naturally awarded to himself. Then he and his generals danced to a funk band's rendition of a special number called the "25 Minute Battle of River Kagera Operation."

In fact, Nyerere was assembling a formidable army, which included tens of thousands of Tanzanian peasant militiamen who had been pressed into emergency service. Ultimately, around forty-five thousand Tanzanians and a smaller number of Ugandan exiles would fight in the war. The Tanzanians constructed a pontoon bridge over the Kagera River. When they crossed it, Amin's occupying army fled back over the border, taking some two thousand Tanzanian women and children with them as hostages. Amin called for a truce and international mediation, proposing that he and Nyerere might be able to settle their differences in a boxing match refereed by Muhammad Ali. Nyerere declined the invitation. Instead, his army launched a furious artillery barrage against Uganda's border defenses.

. . .

On the front line, the Ugandan troops were hunkered down in trenches, hungry and shell-shocked. The earsplitting screams of Tanzania's rockets, Russian-made Katyushas, were like nothing they had ever heard. The terrified Ugandans called the weapons *saba-saba*, after the name of a Tanzanian national holiday, and credited them with supernatural accuracy. "There was now propaganda that the enemy had very sophisticated weapons that could follow you wherever you were," said one Ugandan officer who fought in the war. "That made the soldiers weak and mindless cowards."

A Ugandan major named Bernard Rwehururu, who commanded some of these forward troops, sent desperate messages to his superiors, warning that the Tanzanians were preparing to cross the border. One day, the army commander himself, Major General Gowon, came to Rwehururu's headquarters to assess the situation. The major spread a map out on a table to point out the likely course of the Tanzanian attack. "What's wrong with you?" the contemptuous general said, according to Rwehururu's recollection. "You are always thinking of maps. Do you fight with maps?"

Gowon had risen through the ranks on the basis of his subservience, but now, facing a capable opponent, he was flailing. He was unwilling to deliver any disturbing news to Amin. Major Rwehururu and others told Gowon that the army was in great danger and pleaded for heavy weaponry to counter the *saba-saba* rockets. Gowon dawdled. At a crucial meeting, another general berated the chief of staff until he agreed to call Amin and request money to buy artillery. Once asked, the president readily agreed. One of Uganda's foreign ambassadors was sent several million dollars to buy the arms, but he promptly absconded with the money.

Amin's aura of invincibility was dissipating, and with it his capacity for intimidation. None of the rank-and-file wanted to keep fighting, and disgruntlement was spreading up the ranks. "Quite a few Ugandan army people had acquired a lot of money," one officer reflected. "And they did not think of dying and leaving their money." Meanwhile, the generals continued with their petty feuds. Some of Gowon's counterparts felt he was more concerned with outmaneuvering his internal rivals than he was with planning to fight the Tanzanians. "Very often, we'd get an outburst from Amin that was coming, as far as we could see, from out of the blue," a general recalled. "Normally, you'd come to know these utterances, these outbursts, came after a meeting with the chief of staff."

"He is the person who messed up each and every thing," said another high-ranking officer. He added that Gowon annoyed many of his colleagues by "prowling in other officers' affairs," going outside the chain of command to give orders to front-line units. Gowon's critics within the high command considered him to be a rube without any aptitude for strategy or tactics. Behind his back, they still called him "the tractor driver."

In mid-January 1979, Amin traveled to Saudi Arabia to make a frantic appeal for military aid. Back in Kampala, rumors of a coup circulated. Various African radio networks reported that a group of disgruntled generals headed by Gowon had attempted to overthrow the dictator. When, a few days later, Amin presided over the public commemoration of the eighth anniversary of his coup at a soccer stadium in Kampala, Major General Gowon was standing at attention behind him. But then Amin abruptly dispatched his chief of staff to the front, a move widely interpreted as a punishment.

Shielded from reality, Amin couldn't accept the military's setbacks.

Gowon (right) *briefing Amin at his villa on Lake Victoria* RADIO UGANDA

The Tanzanians had crossed the border and were now advancing swiftly north along the rim of Lake Victoria. Ugandan soldiers were fleeing from their border positions, abandoning their expensive military hardware to the enemy. If sending the chief of staff to the front lines was supposed to boost the troops' spirits, it didn't work. For some reason, whenever Gowon visited the trenches, a missile barrage seemed to follow. The superstitious enlisted men nicknamed him *bisirani*, or "bad omen," and tried to keep him away.

On February 24, 1979, the key town of Masaka, eighty-five miles west of Kampala, fell to the Tanzanians. The next day, farther west, eighty Ugandan rebels led by Yoweri Museveni marched into Mbarara. The hilltop barracks that had housed the retreating Simba Battalion had been reduced to rubble by intense shelling, as had much of the rest of the town. But the people of Ankole were overjoyed. In just a few days, Museveni recruited more than two thousand volunteers. Tanzanian military officers had been openly dismissive of Museveni, whom they considered a campus radical, and they thought his guerrillas had been next to useless in the field, but the Front for National Salvation had suddenly grown into a formidable force.

The largest remaining section of the Ugandan army fell back to a position on the far side of an enormous marsh that skirted Lake Victoria. It was there that Amin decided to make his last stand. At this dire moment, Amin removed Gowon and appointed himself army chief of staff, taking personal command of the defense. According to Gowon's version of the story, Amin sent an emissary to the front who informed him that he'd been fired. Then the emissary mounted a tank and gave a speech to the beleaguered troops, accusing Gowon of betraying his country to the enemy.

The ousted commander took the hint. Gowon fled to Kampala, hopped on an inconspicuous Honda motorcycle and rode north, back to the relative safety of West Nile. His excuse was that he was mustering reinforcements. Soon some other out-of-favor officers joined him in the town of Arua. "They had slipped back into West Nile, and they were sitting there, drinking and planning their escape to Zaire," said a former colleague of Gowon's. (Zaire is the former name of the Democratic Republic of Congo.) He recalled that they seemed "very eager to enter a new country and make it their new home. They didn't care what happened to Uganda."

By the end of March, the invaders had laid siege to Kampala. Rumors of Gowon's apparent desertion were circulating down through

The end of the Amin regime, 1979 THE NEW VISION

the ranks, with predictable effects on morale. "Major General Gowon, has disappeared," an anonymous soldier wrote in a letter to the African magazine *Drum*. "Only hell knows where he is." As artillery shells fell on the capital, Amin issued a scathing radio communiqué.

> Dr. Idi Amin Dada, VC, DSO, MC, Conqueror of the British Empire, has expressed deep appreciation for the soldiers who are not—repeat, are not—cowards, but who defend their families' home and are now on the front line doing very well indeed with the determination to die for their motherland, Uganda. He . . . said that he is very, very happy with the action they took, unlike those soldiers who are confused and taken up only with rumor-mongering and loitering about while doing nothing for the nation.

It was no secret that Amin considered Gowon to be one of the "cowards." One rumor even suggested that Gowon was willfully responsible for the army's defeats, that he'd sold a copy of the Ugandan war plan to the Tanzanians. At some point, a detachment of soldiers happened upon their former commander in West Nile. They arrested him and took him to a military barracks. "All my things were taken," Gowon told me. "I was only about to die. They said they had got information that I was collaborating with the Tanzanians."

Once again, luck was with him. A helicopter appeared overhead. It was General Adrisi, recuperated from the injuries he'd suffered in his suspicious car wreck. He landed at the barracks and came to Gowon's rescue one last time, ordering the soldiers to free the fugitive general. Then he advised Gowon to get himself out of the country.

Gowon got on his motorcycle and rode to the far northern corner of West Nile, to a place where the international border was marked only by a dirt road. One side of the road was Uganda. The shops on the other side of the road were painted with the chipped word *Zaire*. Sudan lay just a few miles farther north. Gowon couldn't decide where he was headed. "I didn't know Zaire, I didn't know Sudan," he recalled. But the outcast general had been informed that most of Amin's men—the ones who wanted to kill him—were planning to head for Sudan.

Yusuf Gowon turned his motorcycle west, toward Congo, and rode on into exile.

16

THE SCARS

Kampala was ruined by bombardment and celebration. When the invaders captured the capital, people took to the streets, liberating its shops and offices of anything of value. They called it "the night of the wheelbarrows." Afterward, the city's roadsides were littered with typewriters, couches, refrigerators, ceiling fans and other bulky things of doubtful value, left where the looters discarded them. It was reported that one man had died of exhaustion beneath the weight of a one-hundred-pound sack of sugar. An angry mob ransacked the headquarters of the Bureau of State Research. Inside, among cells filled with bludgeoned corpses, an arsenal of guns and explosives, piled back issues of the *Economist* and plentiful quantities of marijuana, they discovered files that implicated several thousand Ugandans—at least—as secret police agents or informants.

Yoweri Museveni returned to Kampala and took up residence at a luxury hotel. The city was teeming with former exiles, who congregated in the few places of lodging available in the fortified center of the capital. They were Uganda's new leaders: a fractious collection of aggrieved and mistrustful men. A few weeks before Amin's fall, the exiles had held a hurried unity conference to determine the shape of a transitional government. The meeting had turned into a raucous mess as dozens of anti-Amin organizations—some of them marginal or previously unknown—staked competing claims for representation. Milton Obote had chosen to boycott the meeting, mostly because it would have required cooperating with Museveni. As the commander of the Front for

National Salvation, an army that now numbered some nine thousand men, Museveni argued that he should be treated as an equal to the former president. Obote disagreed, contending that he was still Uganda's rightful ruler. The delegates to the conference chose as transitional president an innocuous former university professor, who in turn appointed Museveni to be his minister of defense. Obote, furious, decided against returning home to participate in the liberation government. Instead, he dispatched his loyalists to Kampala with instructions to undermine their rivals and to lay the groundwork for a comeback.

The capital was no longer the stately British-designed city that Museveni had left. Its streets were pocked with shell craters, its homes were ruined and roofless, its storefronts were burnt-out. On pulverized sidewalks, half-starved peddlers squatted before crumpled packs of bootleg cigarettes. Great mounds of trash had collected everywhere; there was hardly an intact window in town. Museveni had hoped that liberation would mark the start of a societal transformation. In one of his contributions to the unity conference, he had spoken of the need to "raise political culture" to eliminate "this notion of politics . . . which considered tribalism as 'natural.'" Yet that mind-set had proven to be a more tenacious enemy than Amin. The liberation government immediately split into familiar factions. At night, by the light of cracked lamps and flickering candles, politicians met in hotel rooms to cut deals and plot coups. There were four governments in just over a year.

The instability in Kampala spread outward into the provinces. In Ankole, men loyal to Museveni took up important administrative positions, but these officials soon found themselves challenged by a coterie of hardline supporters of Obote and the Uganda People's Congress. They called themselves "the Syndicate." The loudest member of this group was a liberation army officer named Major Edward Rurangaranga. A short man with a thick beard, built like a stubbed-out cigar, he'd served as a sort of roving political commissar during the war, working to convince the rank and file that they were fighting for Obote rather than for some nebulous idea of revolution. This had provoked several confrontations with Museveni, who believed the major was trying to sow ethnic dissension by spreading scurrilous rumors about him among the Bairu of Ankole.

The speaker of the provincial parliament in the years before Obote's overthrow, Rurangaranga had always been a UPC firebrand, suspicious of all Bahima, and he was not about to let one of them reassert control over Ankole. Many of his friends had died at the hands of Amin's soldiers, and he himself had been abducted, shot and badly wounded in 1972. Though he had been lucky enough to survive and make it into exile, he still bore scars from the encounter, and he'd display them to anyone who questioned his right to lead, calling them "my C.V." With some canny bureaucratic maneuvering, Rurangaranga quickly managed to displace the Museveni ally who had been appointed to oversee the western half of Ankole, his home area. In his new domain, Rurangaranga instituted his own brand of justice, traveling in the company of an armed entourage. "They claimed that they came all the way fighting from Tanzania," remembered a contemporary observer. "There was a lot of threatening, a lot of talk about shooting, killing and whatnot."

Almost immediately, troubling reports began to filter back to Kampala. "Ankole is divided up on the basis of religion and tribal factions," a civil servant stationed there wrote in June 1979, in an urgent memo to his bosses in the central government. Under the heading "Security Hazards," the memo went on to describe a series of violent incidents that had recently taken place in Rurangaranga's zone of administration.

> It is alleged that during Amin's regime, the Muslims were instrumental for the indiscriminate killings and disappearances of the Christians in that area. The Muslims used Amin's Military Police to whisk away people from the village, never to be seen. . . . Such a state of affairs lasted during the Amin days, but hate and intense animosity was brewing in the Christians. When the country was eventually liberated and Amin and his soldiers were no longer on the scene, is when the Christians took the law in their own hands, to revenge on the Muslims.

The first acts of retribution were spontaneous. As Amin's soldiers retreated up the main road toward Congo, pillaging local shops along their route, Christians celebrated by chopping down Muslims' banana groves. Then two hundred local Muslims were rounded up and jailed on suspicion of working for the Bureau of State Research, even though that was not legally grounds for imprisonment. Many of those imprisoned were innocent: The most notorious secret police agents, like Salim Sebi, had already fled to Rwanda and Congo. (Sebi apparently died in exile, of natural causes.) The prospect of capricious arrest was enough to scare many Muslims out of Ankole. They sold their farms at cut-rate prices, or just abandoned them to their Christian antagonists, and fled to another town in a neighboring province that had a large Muslim population. After that, several accused collaborators who had chosen to stay in Ankole were found murdered.

Resentment had motivated the organizers of the 1971 coup; a similar vengefulness now inspired rounds of reprisal across the country. Mob logic said that "Amin's people" had benefited collectively and they should pay collectively. On the streets of Kampala, anyone with darker-toned skin—a supposed indicator of northern heritage—was in danger of being lynched. The liberation government announced that all Nubian civilians were required to register with the police. Names and ID photos retrieved from the files of the Bureau of State Research were published as a daily feature in the new government-run *Uganda Times*. Readers wrote letters to the editor demanding the informers' home addresses. "Such people, when they were killing Ugandans and being paid highly for it, did not think that their turn to suffer would come," wrote one correspondent. "Everything has got an end."

The biggest villains were out of reach. When the liberation army occupied West Nile at the beginning of June, the remaining soldiers of Amin's army fled to safety in Sudan and Congo, carting along a comfortable amount of booty. (One general took eleven tractors with him to Sudan, while another drove three thousand cattle across the border.) A militia made up of men from the once-persecuted Acholi tribe rampaged through the undefended province, destroying mansions belonging to Amin's henchmen and killing civilians indiscriminately, in a campaign so bloody that a newspaper later described it as "genocide."

Museveni was horrified to see what liberation had unleashed. "Amin was totally defeated," he wrote in a 1980 essay, "but Amin-ism remained."

One day in the spring of 1979, in the village of Kiziba, in western Ankole, Bashir Semakula received a visitor at his home. Bashir, a Muslim in his twenties, belonged to a well-known local family. His father, Dauda, was a former official in the provincial government and a prominent member of the Democratic Party, and his family owned one of the village's finest pieces of land. Bashir had played no role in the crimes of Idi Amin. But his neighbor, a Christian, informed him that he had nonetheless been judged guilty. A village council had voted to levy "taxes" on all Muslims as reparations. Bashir was told he owed one bull and two jugs of millet beer.

Kiziba was not a remarkable place or a strategic one, and it had not suffered disproportionately at the hands of the military regime. The village had a relatively large percentage of Muslim residents, but nothing made its sectarian tensions inevitable. Before Amin, its residents had always gotten along, in the communitarian spirit of rural African life. Christians had lived alongside Muslims, working the same land, growing the same crops, attending the same weddings and funerals. Through the years of the dictatorship, most of the area's Muslims had remained very poor, and only a handful had ever assisted the secret police. Nonetheless, with Amin's fall, Kiziba became a focal point of vindictive reaction.

In resolving to seek reparations, Kiziba's village council cited a number of purported offenses, grievances that had accumulated over the Amin years. The Christians of the area, for instance, believed that the Muslims had used the promise of government patronage to lure their children into converting to Islam. But Bashir didn't think he had done anything wrong. He considered the fines to be harassment, so he refused to pay them. Most other Muslims gave in, and urged Bashir to reconsider for the sake of his safety. But the young farmer was stubborn. Eventually, some of Bashir's Christian neighbors came in the night, destroyed his crops and burned down his home.

What really enraged Bashir was that he knew these people. One of the chief instigators of the reprisals was a man named Machote. He lived up on the hill that overlooked Bashir's farm. He and Bashir's father had been good friends. Before Amin's overthrow, Machote had worked for a time as a security guard at a gas station in Kampala, and when Bashir had attended school in the capital, he had occasionally stayed in Machote's home. Machote was a tall, argumentative braggart, but he'd never showed the combative side of his personality to Bashir or his father. He invariably deferred to those above him in the social hierarchy. But now, with Amin gone, Uganda had changed, and so had Machote.

Still, Bashir knew that someone like Machote would never act on his own. He thought his neighbor had to have the backing of some higher authority.

Around this time, the new regional government held a public meeting in a town near Kiziba. Bashir and his father attended, along with peasants from all over the countryside. The meeting was held outdoors, and it had the air of a political rally. Major Edward Rurangaranga addressed the crowd, stepping forward with a perceptible limp. In a bellicose speech, he told his audience the story of his injury.

Edward Rurangaranga
ANDREW RICE

Rurangaranga was a familiar figure to the villagers. During Milton Obote's regime, he had represented them as an elected official. Like so many others, he had been targeted after the 1972 rebel attack on Mbarara. Soldiers had stuffed Rurangaranga into the trunk of a car. They had left him confined there while they'd eaten lunch at a restaurant belonging to a sympathetic Muslim businessman, Hajji Abbas Kayemba, who had advised them that Rurangaranga was like a safari ant: a biting insect that had to be exterminated. The soldiers had then taken their prisoner to the wooded banks of the Rwizi River, where he had broken loose. He'd been shot multiple times as he made a dash for the water. Left for dead, his pelvis shattered, Rurangaranga had floated downstream, and had found his way home before managing to escape to exile, where he had nursed his wounds and his grudges for seven years. Now he was back in Ankole and seeking redress. Though it went unmentioned at the rally, everyone in the audience knew that Abbas Kayemba was one of the local Muslims who'd recently been murdered.

Rurangaranga finished his speech with a rousing call to action, telling the villagers that it was time for them to do their part to eradicate Amin's legacy. "We have felled the tree," he said, repeating a local proverb. "It is up to you to cut the branches."

A few days after the speech, not far from Kiziba, a mob of Christians attacked the homestead of a well-off Muslim farmer, chanting, "We are going to cut the branches." They hacked the farmer to death, disemboweled his brother with a spear and hanged his son from the rafters of the house.

Things quieted down for a while after that. Then, in late June 1979, someone attacked one of the Christian leaders of Kiziba's village council. The man apparently had no shortage of enemies. (One popular theory holds that he was a victim of a murder hit sponsored by his mistress's jealous husband.) On his deathbed, however, the Christian named some Muslims as his assailants. The night he died, as his relatives gathered to mourn, Kiziba's Christians massed and armed themselves.

Bashir Semakula was not in Kiziba on June 26—he'd moved away after his house was torched. But his father, Dauda, was at home, along with his wife and much of the family. The mob came in the late morning, when Bashir's mother was out in the front yard peeling plantains for lunch. They were peasants mostly, barefoot and ragged, and they wielded peasant weapons: machetes, spears, stones. The majority were male, but there were women too, running ahead, ululating, urging on the men. Bashir's family recognized most of the faces in the crowd. A few of them were their in-laws.

One of Bashir's brothers, a mute, ran into the house, waving his arms wildly. Dauda walked outside and realized the house was surrounded. His onetime friend and neighbor Machote stepped forward, brandishing a spear. Machote ordered Dauda to turn around and then hit him from behind. He tied Dauda's hands behind his back. The mob cut down Dauda's crops and set fire to his house. It then went from homestead to homestead, rounding up the rest of Kiziba's Muslims.

"Where are you taking us?" a young mother asked one of the mob leaders.

"To Idi Amin," he replied.

About one hundred Muslims were brought to the home of the local imam. There, Machote called for the captives to be harnessed together with ropes. Then the mob marched the Muslims out of Kiziba, down the country roads that led to the Rwizi River about four miles away. It was a hot, cloudless, dry season day. Near the river, the mob stopped and separated the prisoners into groups of twenty and led the first group, which included Bashir's family, down to the riverbank. The mob assembled itself into a "V" formation, with the Muslims' backs to the river. Then they attacked their neighbors with machetes. The mob went for the imam first. His falling body knocked Dauda into the river. As

Bashir's father floated away unharmed, he heard one of his neighbors scream, "Machote is killing me!" The massacre continued for hours, with the Christians working in shifts.

Early the next morning, before dawn, Dauda appeared at the house where his son was staying, some distance from Kiziba. He was still dripping wet. Bashir rushed to Mbarara, where he reported news of the massacre to the local authorities and convinced some Muslim townspeople to accompany him to the Rwizi River. At the scene, they chased away a half-dozen members of the mob who had stayed behind to ward off any search for survivors. Bashir crossed a wooden bridge to the far bank of the river. The grass there was slicked with blood. He saw the body of a girl—his niece. In the water bobbed the corpse of a neighbor, a mother who still had an infant strapped to her back. Bashir took off his clothes, waded into the river and began to retrieve bodies. Later on, on two sheets of notepaper, he and his father compiled the names of the sixty-two people who had perished: thirteen men, twenty-two women and twenty-seven children.

The day after the massacre, the liberation government sent a military detachment to assist in recovering the dead. A young soldier, one of Yoweri Museveni's recruits, reported what he'd witnessed to his superiors. Museveni was alarmed. Within a few days, an emergency meeting was convened at a government building a few miles from Kiziba. The surviving Muslims—who thankfully included all of Bashir's immediate family members—assembled to give their account. Extraordinarily, many of the village's Christians also chose to attend. They weren't ashamed of the mob's actions. On the contrary, they vocally endorsed them, reciting insults they had endured during Amin's time and naming many Christians who'd disappeared. Bashir's father rose to question whether the government had incited the massacre, saying some in the mob had even invoked the minister of defense. Museveni, aghast at hearing his own name associated with such actions, asked the Muslims to point out the leaders of the mob. He ordered their arrests and also dispatched a soldier to find and detain Edward Rurangaranga.

Immediately after the massacre, Rurangaranga had obstructed a team of investigators sent by the liberation government, telling them that they had no authority to ask questions in his area. Then he had run off to Kampala. Museveni's agent looked for him there, but before long, he was told to call off his search. "I could not pursue the matter," the soldier later testified, "because it had become political." Museveni's influence within the government was limited; there were opposing

forces at work. Before long, the ringleaders of the massacre were mysteriously released from jail, and Rurangaranga returned to Ankole.

Milton Obote's long sojourn in exile came to an end in May 1980. He
made his triumphant homecoming at a rally held in Ankole, just a few
miles from Kiziba. Edward Rurangaranga, who organized the event,
proclaimed it to be "the greatest occasion in the whole history of our
country." The country was preparing to hold a presidential election,
which was intended to restore stability after a series of brief-lived governments, and Obote had decided the time was right to reenter the
political fray. Museveni declared his intention to run against the former
president, pledging to bridge tribal and religious barriers and to "heal
old wounds."

Museveni captivated Uganda's young intelligentsia with his promise to break the country free of its tortured history. Other candidates in
the large field made similar calls for a fresh start. Obote, by contrast,
appeared cynical, embittered and entirely unreformed. When reporters
asked him how he hoped to avoid repeating past mistakes, the former
president replied that he couldn't recall having made a single error. Ever
the consummate political schemer, however, Obote was able to manip-
ulate the election, using allies he'd advantageously placed in the transitional government to gerrymander districts and stuff ballot boxes. Even
so, he managed only a narrow victory.

During the campaign, Museveni promised to "meet intimidation
with intimidation, violence with violence." On February 6, 1981, he led
twenty-seven men in a raid on an upcountry military barracks. The
attack signaled the beginning of his long-contemplated "people's war."
Museveni's force quickly gained size and popularity and took control of
an area just north of Kampala. In that occupation zone, Museveni instituted a form of grassroots democracy by replacing appointed chiefs
with elected "resistance councils." He set a code of conduct for his soldiers that mandated the death penalty for rape, and he forbade stealing
anything from the populace, even "sweet bananas or sugar cane." He
issued a Ten-Point Program that promised to banish dictatorship, tribalism and corruption.

Outside the occupation zone, however, the cycle of violence only
continued to whirl. President Obote launched a crackdown, repressing
internal opponents and promoting unsavory allies. Edward Rurangaranga
was put in charge of the cabinet ministry that oversaw local govern-

ment. In turn, the mob leader Machote was appointed to be the chief of Kiziba and its surrounding area. For the few Muslims who'd stubbornly chosen to stay on their land, including Bashir Semakula and his family, the civil war brought constant abuse. For more than a year, Bashir was held in jail on invented charges of subversion.

Finally, in January 1986, Museveni's rebel army took the capital. The day he was sworn into office, wearing a foot soldier's simple green fatigues, Uganda's new leader promised his people a "fundamental change." He assured the uneasy audience that gathered to hear his inaugural speech that he was a modest man. "Personally, I do not like being called 'Excellency,'" he said. People in the liberated areas, he told the crowd, just called him Yoweri, or by a vernacular sobriquet that roughly translated as "Mr. Fix-It."

Museveni tried to mend the wrongs done in Kiziba. The Rwizi River Massacre, as the infamous incident came to be called, was held up as an example of the kind of retribution the new government would end. Six people, including Machote, were tried and convicted for their roles in the killing, while Rurangaranga was arrested on murder charges related to a separate set of reprisal killings and held in prison for several years. Justice Arthur Oder's Commission of Inquiry into Violations of Human Rights investigated the Rwizi River Massacre and concluded that Rurangaranga was one of the "key architects of this tragedy." Eventually, however, a judge dismissed the murder charges against him for lack of evidence. In Ankole, that decision met with anger and confusion within the traumatized Muslim population.

In Kiziba, Christians and Muslims continued to reside next to one another, but you couldn't really say they lived in peace. After the massacre, all the villagers ringed their homesteads with high hedgerows of euphorbia shrubs, their tangled, poisonous spines forbidding a glimpse from the road. More than two decades after the massacre, as he guided a visitor down narrow dirt paths lined by yellow-blooming cassias, Bashir Semakula pointed out the homes of the mob's leaders. A stone cross stood next to one well-kept cottage, marking the grave of one of the perpetrators who had passed away naturally in Luzira Prison. Machote had also died behind bars. But a lingering sense of disappointment remained: The more important culprits had avoided justice.

"They were organized from the top," Bashir said. "There were some government heads organizing them."

Now fifty, slight and wiry, Bashir wore a gray jacket that was threadbare in patches and kept the cuffs of his khaki pants rolled up to keep them free of the mud, a farmer's habit. We were driving from his home, a squat concrete house tucked inside a dense grove of banana trees, to the scene of the massacre, accompanied by his younger brother Noor, a thickset man with a furrowed forehead. Near the river, the terrain became flat and rocky. A ridgeline hovered in the middle distance. The village of Ndeija was a few miles away, just on the other side of the hills; the Rwizi River ran right by Eliphaz Laki's farmhouse. Ducking through a fence constructed of stripped branches, the brothers walked into a glade surrounded by eucalyptus trees. Peering down from the steep riverbank, you could see that the Rwizi was really more of a stream, winding and mud-brown, and lined by tufted papyrus plants.

Noor unbuttoned his light blue shirt and pulled it down around his shoulders to show the deep scars of several machete gashes along his back and chest. He was a survivor, one of the last living eyewitnesses to the massacre. He explained that the mob had hacked him several times, but then he had fallen into the river. He had floated and waded around three miles downstream, where a good samaritan had cut the ropes that bound his hands. Noor said he knew who had inflicted his wounds. The man who had tied his hands, for instance, lived just down the road. When they ran into each other, they'd exchange salutations as neighbors, never speaking of their shared history.

"We greet each other, we get water from the same well," Noor said. "We cannot forget what happened, but we have to forgive. Revenge doesn't work. Life goes on."

Edward Rurangaranga had gone on with his life, too. He operated a hotel in a bustling market town near Kiziba, out in the hill country surrounding the Western Rift. "Some people want us to go back to that life in grass thatched huts," he said in greeting when I went to visit him. He explained that he, like Eliphaz Laki, had fought for equality as part of the Bairu political movement of the 1960s. "This house is mine," Rurangaranga continued, leading the way through the hotel's low-lit bar to a back room where he took a seat along a long wooden table. "A man who has a house like this one, you cannot sit on him."

At seventy, Rurangaranga still looked stout and unyielding. His beard, once full and dark, was now gray and neatly trimmed. Since his release from prison in 1991, he had been attempting to rehabilitate his reputation. A year after Rurangaranga was freed, his old constituents had once again elected him to one of Ankole's ruling councils. "I can proudly say I am popular," Rurangaranga said. He had remained active in politics, voicing strong opposition to Museveni's government. The accusation that he had incited murder, he contended, was nothing more than a smear concocted to discredit him.

"It was all political," he said indignantly. "I had nobody killed. I live with Muslims!"

Without prompting, Rurangaranga stood up from the restaurant table, undid his belt, untucked and unbuttoned his maroon oxford shirt and ran his index finger along a shiny black spot on the left side of his abdomen—a bullet scar. In grim detail, he described the wounds he had suffered. "Those were the bullets," he concluded, with a gruff edge of anger undiminished by time. "It is thirty years ago now."

Every vendetta has to begin somewhere. Rurangaranga traced his back to the same events that had claimed the life of Eliphaz Laki. He said he was eagerly following the trial, then just getting underway in Kampala, of Laki's accused murderers. Rurangaranga had known the chief well; he said they "were close to brother and brother." But he had more than a sympathetic observer's interest in the case. He recounted that, on the day that soldiers took him away, a major from the Mbarara battalion had accompanied them to his farmhouse: Yusuf Gowon, the very man who now stood accused of ordering Laki's murder. Years later, Gowon denied having anything to do with the killings of 1972, but Rurangaranga described a vivid scene. "He gave instructions to the soldiers: 'Take him, kill him, don't take him to barracks'—in front of my children, in front of my father, in front of my stepmother, in front of my wife," Rurangaranga recounted.

"I knew Gowon," he said. "I saw Gowon."

On and on they came, in a long, lowing procession: brown cows, dappled cows, longhorns and short, their tails swishing behind haunches branded Y.K.M. General Yoweri Kaguta Museveni, the president of Uganda, sat regally in a padded plastic chair, a ceremonial cattle prod stuck beside him in the ground, watching with an expression of transported delight. Cattle are prized all over Africa as symbols of wealth and status, but the animals had a particular hold on Museveni's imagination. Born among the cattle-keepers of Ankole, Uganda's president grew up tending his family's herd, and for all the world-shaking rhetoric he'd mouthed back in his Dar es Salaam days—the talk of creating a "new peasant" and discarding "backward" traditions—he had never truly jettisoned the ways and values of his ancestors. As the cattle parade proceeded across the acacia-dotted pasture, Museveni, dressed in casual clothes, combat boots and a floppy hat that shielded his shiny pate from the sun, rose from his chair to point out his favorite bulls. The president had around four thousand head of cattle at this ranch, one of two he owned, and he claimed to know every one by name. "I had to leave my cows to chase Amin," he shouted. "But this is my way of life. I can't forget my children just because I'm working for the regime . . ." He paused a beat, reconsidering his choice of words. ". . . for the *government.*"

I was tagging along with a delegation of Ugandan journalists who had been invited to one of the president's country estates to chronicle a day in his life as a gentleman-rancher. Museveni liked to style himself as Uganda's benevolent herdsman, guiding his people out of the dangers of the past. He had first taken the presidency by force, but he had since won two elections. He often likened politics to cattle-keeping, and he had developed a method of governing much like the one employed by the slim Bahima in threadbare clothing who patrolled the pasture, keeping the herd before him orderly. He beat the grass with sticks, to let

Yoweri Museveni, herdsman ENOCK KAKANDE

the animals know which path to follow. When one strayed out of line, he chased it down and rustled it back with a solid thwack to the side.

A quarter century had passed since Idi Amin's fall. The rebel of the 1970s was now the longest-serving leader his nation had ever known. He was no longer a skinny Marxist ideologue. His face had grown pudgy, his mustache was flecked with gray, and he had eased into the time-honored role of leader-as-patriarch. Everywhere Museveni went, he was followed by a cadre of scurrying aides and bodyguards, uniformed soldiers and plump private secretaries. He no longer eschewed grand titles, and his advisers typically addressed him as "Your Excellency." Those who knew him more intimately referred to him as *mzee*, or reverently called him—when out of earshot—"the Big Man."

Sitting behind the wheel of a bulletproof Toyota Land Cruiser, Museveni made his morning rounds about the ranch, careening from one fly-swarmed field to another. The president relished the pleasure of driving himself, one he was rarely allowed elsewhere due to security concerns, and he deliberately chose a roundabout route that passed through some surrounding villages. His subjects rushed to the roadside at the sight of his vehicle, waving their hands in adulatory greeting. Every so often, Museveni pulled to the side of the road and spoke to a wide-eyed villager. Everyone had a problem. A group of widows needed money for food. Some recent high-school graduates, wearing garlands of dried banana fronds—a ruling party symbol—petitioned for seed money to start a business. One man complained that a soldier had run off with his wife. At each stop, as the president listened, an aide would run up from a trailing car to jot down the supplicant's particulars on a yellow legal pad. When one teenaged girl begged for money for school, Museveni reached out and tenderly caressed her cheek.

Museveni regarded himself, quite literally, as the father of his nation—a personalized state he'd molded in his own image. He was the commander of Uganda's army, its economic guru, its house moralist and its lecturer-in-chief. He penned long letters to newspapers on subjects ranging from military reform to linguistics, archaeology and banana cultivation. He was fond of turning press conferences into long-winded history lessons and disquisitions on his accomplishments, which were many and real. He had presided over the enactment of a new constitution meant to protect human rights. He'd reversed Idi Amin's racist economic policies, welcoming back expelled citizens—and new investors—of Indian descent. He'd promoted an open political culture, and he'd been one of the first African leaders to talk honestly about AIDS. He'd rebuilt the ruined economy, though in order to do so, he'd had to forsake socialism for the sort of free market policies mandated by Western aid donors. Most importantly, he'd brought his country stability, putting an end to its looping litany of vengeance.

Museveni dominated every institution, made every serious decision, influenced every aspect of national life. He often liked to say, to the consternation of his political opponents, that he was the only Ugandan with a vision for his country's future. Asked if it was true, as many old comrades maintained, that he had always imagined that he'd be president, Museveni offered a hearty laugh. "*No*, not the president," he replied. "I couldn't fight to be president. You know, to kill so many people and have so much trouble, just to be president, is really madness. But to get rid of killers: that was the plan I had all along."

To be sure, his successes were not complete. A long-running civil war in the north still flared up occasionally, and in the 1990s, a force of Muslims based in western Uganda—the adult survivors of earlier reprisals—had mounted an uprising against the government. Museveni had succeeded in putting the Muslim rebellion down, but imams still evoked the killings at the Rwizi River in fiery fundamentalist sermons. Yet these were conflicts at the margins. Museveni had given Uganda more peace than it had known in decades.

It was a hollow kind of peace, though. It was a peace born out of fear—fear of war and of the kind of retributive violence that had consumed places like Kiziba. And while General Museveni was far gentler than General Amin, Uganda was still a militarized state. It was a peace that all too often required the silence of those who had suffered abuses. Some Ugandans believed that the peace had cost too much, that their enforced reconciliation was a mere artifice built over stifled truths and outright lies. But Museveni believed forbearance had ultimately proved worthwhile.

In the late afternoon, as thunderheads were rolling in across the savanna, Museveni beckoned me and a couple of Ugandan journalists to hop into his Land Cruiser for the ride back to his ranch house. The rain broke out of the clouds and the presidential vehicle skidded through mud puddles, while Museveni spoke of the "spirit of forgetting the past."

"But is it always better to forget?" I asked.

"I don't think it's good to forget the past and to cover up mistakes," Museveni replied. "But since some of our people think so, and since it was mostly our supporters who were injured by those killers, and since we defeated them, then we could sacrifice and move on. We say okay, we resisted evil. We won."

Outside the window, women in long traditional dresses were standing in front of thatched huts and brick shacks, clapping rhythmically in the downpour as His Excellency passed.

"The minority who were involved in making mistakes, it would have been better if they could see their mistakes," Museveni continued. "Since, however, they don't seem to see their mistakes, and we have also not had time to expose those mistakes systematically, then we say, 'Let's go on. Let's get moving.'"

Later that evening, after dinner, we continued the conversation at the president's home. "The people who committed crimes have never been punished," Museveni said, adding that he found this regrettable. The problem, he explained, was that different groups of Ugandans saw history in opposing ways. Museveni often railed against the "killers" who had ruled the country before him, but he recognized that substantial portions of the citizenry still saw those same tyrants as heroes. As a simple matter of governance, it would be impossible to hold all the malefactors responsible—not when so many people found their crimes unobjectionable, or even laudable. "That's why we have not insisted on trying them: because there's no consensus," the president went on. "Since we defeated them, and since we were making progress, we decided not to pursue justice."

Even Museveni, who exercised absolute control over so much else, could not defy the power of memory. The compromise the country had accepted, which the president presented as reconciliation, was actually something more complex and less sturdy. It was as if, having found themselves unable to forgive, his people had concentrated on forgetting, and that when they'd failed at forgetting, they'd chosen to believe what they wanted to believe. So long as nothing disturbed their conceptions of the past or exposed them to scrutiny, the nation could continue its halting procession along Museveni's chosen path. To the president's way of thinking, therefore, justice was a threat to progress, not because it promised verdicts and punishments, but because it forced people to remember. Back in Kampala, however, an unprecedented event was about to bring memories into open conflict—the trial of the three men accused of murdering Eliphaz Laki.

PART **4**

17

THE PROSECUTION

"Do you know the meaning of the word *wrath*?" Justice Moses Mukiibi asked a quivering young lawyer. "*Wrath. W-R-A-T-H.*"

The judge possessed a hearty, mellifluous, bell-ringing voice, one a couple of sizes too big for his concrete-floored courtroom. It was, in fact, a very effective instrument for conveying wrath, an emotion that came regularly to him, in slow-gathering bursts. On this particular morning, November 20, 2002, the object of Mukiibi's displeasure was a junior prosecutor who had mishandled a procedural matter relating to a routine murder case before the High Court. The judge, a thickset man with a gray beard, glowered over the oval reading glasses that were perched at the end of his broad nose. A former prosecutor himself, he had a reputation for being a stickler and a curmudgeon. He ran his courtroom like a strict headmaster.

The unfortunate prosecutor lowered his head and stammered abject apologies. Justice Mukiibi gaveled the hearing closed, and the murder defendant, wearing a holey silkscreened T-shirt bearing the slogan VOTE YOWERI KAGUTA MUSEVENI, was led out of the courtroom by a guard. The judge scribbled away with a ballpoint pen. He took the court's official record that way, by hand on white loose-leaf pages.

The court clerk called out the name of the next case on the judge's docket for that day: "Uganda versus Major General Yusuf Gowon and two others."

Gowon and his codefendants, Sergeant Nasur Gille and Private Mohammed Anyule, shuffled into the wooden dock. It was a blustery rainy-season day in Kampala, and a stiff breeze blew through the court-room's open windows. The judge peered down at the accused men and solemnly recited the charges: kidnapping and murder.

Anyule, wearing a white robe and red-checked *keffiyeh*, cast his eyes downward. Gille stared dispassionately straight ahead, his hands folded atop the edge of the dock. Gowon, clad in a windbreaker and blithe as always, smiled and gave a thumbs-up to his supporters in the gallery.

"How do you plead to this charge, murder?" the judge asked the defendants. They replied through interpreters.

"I'm innocent," Gowon said.

"I do not know the offense," Gille said.

"I deny the charges," Anyule said.

The judge entered pleas of "not guilty" for all three men.

It was thirty years since the disappearance of Eliphaz Laki. At long last, it seemed, his nation was prepared to do him justice. But what did that mean in a country like this? Lawyers were preparing to battle, tribes were agitating to clash and three accused killers were fighting for their lives—all of them invoking this single shared word, *justice*, in support of

The accused (from left): *Mohammed Anyule, Nasur Gille, Yusuf Gowon* ANDREW RICE

their opposing arguments. Justice entered the courtroom as a pristine ideal; it would leave scuffed, muddled and altogether Ugandan.

Uganda's legal system, like so much else about the country, was a hybrid of the familiar and the exotic. The judges of the High Court sat in an impressive cream-colored colonial building, with a four-faced clock tower and columned arcades. They wore British-style scarlet robes and white ponytailed wigs, and their decisions were guided by the principles of English common law. Yet beneath the veneer of imported traditions and precedents, the system was deeply, idiosyncratically Ugandan, a creation of modern Africa and all its many adversities. If you looked through the arched windows of the High Court clock tower, you could see that its belfry concealed several plastic reserve water tanks, a necessity in a city where the public pumping system often broke down. There were regular blackouts too, though these caused minimal inconvenience to the proceedings, because the most complex electronic device in Justice Mukiibi's courtroom was a ceiling fan. When there was a dispute about a point of procedure, the judge would settle it the old-fashioned way, by consulting a heavy hardbound law book that was cracked along its spine. Perched atop the courthouse's red tile roof were flocks of gigantic marabou storks, which fed on scraps scavenged from Kampala's garbage piles. The marabou possesses one of the animal kingdom's widest wingspans, and every so often, one of the birds would launch itself past the gallery's open windows, its wings beating the air with a jolting *whup, whup, whup.*

Take away the strange birds, though, and the dry taps and power cuts—take away Africa, in other words—and the scene inside Justice Mukiibi's courtroom the day of opening arguments would not have seemed foreign to anyone who had ever watched a BBC legal drama. There were attorneys in black robes and high collars, addressing the wigged judge as "my lord," and reporters from the local papers filling the gallery's press section. The relatives of the victim were arrayed behind the prosecution's table. The defendants' supporters—taut-faced men who introduced themselves by their military ranks and women wrapped in colorful *kitenge* cloth—were seated across several rows of hard benches in the back.

There was, however, one element that was obviously missing: a jury. The British never introduced the jury system to Uganda. Historically, it was reserved for those parts of the empire with significant populations of European settlers, and even in those places it was a privilege restricted to whites. Instead of twelve peers, Ugandan trials had two "assessors," a vestige of the colonial system. In earlier times, the judge had been white and the assessors respected Africans, usually elders of the defendant's tribe, who were there, in the words of one colonial-era jurist, "as a guarantee to the native population that their own customs and habits of life are not misunderstood." The judiciary had been Africanized after independence, but the system had otherwise remained the same. The assessors' role was still purely advisory, and the judge retained absolute power.

In the gallery, all eyes were always focused on Justice Mukiibi, and the courtroom speculation was entirely about how he might be inclined to rule. Ugandans were skeptical about the concept of judicial impartiality, and throughout the trial, there was a running argument among observers about which side had Mukiibi's natural sympathies. Yoweri Museveni had appointed the judge to the bench in 1997, and he had a record as a reliable, even slavish, supporter of the president. But he was also the only Muslim among the more than twenty judges on the High Court, and for that reason the courthouse chatterers predicted that he would be inclined to side with the Muslim defendants.

But if there was one thing that really made Justice Mukiibi wrathful, it was these casual assumptions about his prejudices. One day, the judge invited me into his chambers to assure me that he was no apologist for Idi Amin, regardless of what others might assume based on his religion. Mukiibi was a member of the southern Baganda tribe, not a Nubian from the north, and although he'd worked for the Amin government as a civil servant in the prosecutor's office, he said he had suffered as much as any other Ugandan. On the day Kampala fell in 1979, his brother had been killed by one of Amin's snipers as he had tried to cross town on foot. Mukiibi had buried him almost alone, without ceremony, and then he'd gone into hiding to avoid the lynch mobs that were hunting down Muslims. If anything, Mukiibi explained, the experience had confirmed his belief in the sanctity of due process. "I judge cases," he said, "according to the evidence."

It was an admirable precept, very much in the spirit of the latest thinking in human rights law, those sweeping theories that were transforming jurisprudence around the world. There was, however, a certain circumstantial iniquity at work. If Idi Amin's regime had fallen in 1999 instead of 1979, Yusuf Gowon might have faced some form of international justice, like soldiers who had committed more recent atrocities in Bosnia or Congo. Amin might have been extradited to The Hague like Charles Taylor or Slobodan Milošević. But instead, the exiled dictator was living well in Saudi Arabia, forgotten by the world, and Uganda was feeling its own tentative way through the process of recovery. Justice Mukiibi's court was the best his country had to offer, but it was no well-funded international tribunal. It was part of a system that had a way of trying even the most enlightened aspirations.

Like most every other institution in the country, the Ugandan courts were overburdened, underfunded and mired in bureaucratic malaise. Justice Mukiibi had thirty criminal cases to dispose of during his fall court term, which was scheduled to last only a month. There was a case of armed robbery, and another in which a young woman was accused of killing her baby by throwing it into a pit latrine. More than half of the trials on the judge's calendar involved "defilement," or statutory rape. The age of consent was treated as a rough guideline in Uganda, and affairs between young girls and older men were usually resolved with weddings and dowries or discreet compensation payments, but when an offender didn't pay, the criminal cases proceeded to court, clogging the docket. Many of the defendants coming before Justice Mukiibi had already endured long stays in prison. Because the system was so overloaded, it was not uncommon for a person accused of a crime to wait five years or more before seeing a judge.

Gowon's trial, by contrast, had moved at a relatively speedy pace. Just a year and a half had passed since his arrest. The general was an important defendant, and this was a high-profile case. "It's like our Nuremberg Trial," said Simon Byabakama Mugenyi, the second-ranking official in the national prosecutor's office, who had decided to try the case personally. He felt it was of vital interest because, with so many major figures now entering old age, it would likely represent his nation's final opportunity to render a judgment on the Amin era.

Stout and bald, in a capacious black barrister's robe, Mugenyi rose to give the prosecution's opening argument. He kept it short and to the point.

"The brief facts are that Eliphaz Laki, the deceased, was the county chief of the then Ibanda County," he began. "On a certain day in September 1972, while the deceased and others were at the county [head-quarters] on duty, some three men came in a vehicle asking for the deceased. . . . They told him that he was wanted by their boss, so they had come for him. The deceased opted to travel in his vehicle, a Volkswagen with the registration number UYO-010. The men allowed him to do so. However, one of them sat with the deceased in his vehicle, which the deceased drove himself.

"The deceased was not seen again thereafter."

At first glance, the prosecution's case looked formidable. At its center were two matching confessions, which painted a convincing picture of the crime. They explained who killed Laki: Anyule and Gille, on the orders of the Simba Battalion's deputy commander, Gowon. They explained the motive: Someone had reported that Laki was a rebel sympathizer. They explained how one of the defendants, Anyule, had ended up with Laki's Volkswagen: It was a gift from his superior officer, Gowon—a sort of bonus. The confessions, in turn, had led to a body. After Duncan Laki had unearthed the decayed remains, he'd sent them to the United States for DNA testing, which had confirmed they belonged to his father.

"They killed this man—there is no doubt," Simon Mugenyi said in an interview. "The task is proving it."

But proving it would require clearing a number of formidable obstacles, as Mugenyi, a twenty-year veteran of the prosecutor's office, fully recognized. The most serious problems involved the very evidence that appeared most incriminating: the confessions obtained from Anyule and Gille. Plea bargains, an essential component of the American legal system, tended to happen fairly rarely in Uganda, in part because judges generally cast a skeptical eye when one defendant testified against another. (Precedent held that such testimony was to be regarded as "evidence of the weakest kind.") The prosecution originally hoped to get around this difficulty by exonerating Anyule, the driver, so they could call him as a cooperative witness against Gowon and Gille, the triggerman. Duncan Laki had even considered offering Anyule a job as a security guard at one of the family properties to keep him in Kampala until the trial was over.

Both Duncan and the prosecutors eventually thought better of the arrangement, however. In June 2002, a year after the initial arrests, a junior attorney in the prosecutor's office wrote a memorandum to his bosses. "I have serious reservations as regards the decision to drop charges against Private Anyule," the memo said. "This accused puts himself at the scene of the murder. His defense notwithstanding, his having transferred the victim's vehicle into his name, coupled with his admission of being present at the scene of the crime and his graphic and detailed narration of how the deceased met his death, clearly put him in the shoes of one of the murderers." The same day, the chief prosecutor reversed his prior course, reinstating the initial charges of kidnapping and murder against Anyule and ordering his arraignment alongside the other two defendants. All three were sent to Luzira Prison pending trial, and Anyule promptly recanted his confession.

Of course, this did not invalidate the earlier incriminating statements made by Anyule, as well as by Gille. It just increased the pressure on the prosecution to prove that these admissions were made voluntarily, without coercion or inducement. The two soldiers had confessed on at least three separate occasions: once, on tape, to the private investigator Alfred Orijabo; a second time, in writing, to police officers; and a third time, in sworn testimony before a magistrate at a preliminary court hearing held at a time when Anyule and Gille were still cooperating with the prosecution. Prosecutors could still try to introduce any one of these confessions at trial. When they did, and the defense contested the statements' admissibility—as it certainly would—the judge would convene a special evidentiary proceeding, called a "trial-within-the-trial" in the local legal parlance. Here, the judge would have wide latitude to scrutinize the conduct of the investigation. Internally, the prosecutor's office worried that none of the confessions would stand up. There was even discussion of dropping the charges against Gowon because his case was so heavily based on the disputable words of his co-accused.

Mugenyi had insisted on pushing the case forward, nonetheless. He, too, had to work with incredibly limited resources: His staff of just sixty full-fledged attorneys had to handle a nationwide caseload. But Mugenyi thought the Gowon prosecution was worthy and winnable. He recalled what Uganda had been like at the height of Amin's regime, when he had been a student at Makerere University. Professors and students were routinely whisked away by the secret police. Mugenyi thought that putting the retired general on trial sent a principled message. "The signal has gone out," he said. "It will never be too late for anyone to be brought to account for his actions while in power . . . however impossible it may seem at the time when he's holding the reins."

Only the passage of time had made this prosecution possible. But time was also an enemy to Mugenyi's case. Memories were clouded. Eyewitnesses were dead. Crucial evidence was long-lost. The soldiers' military service records, for instance, seemed to have gone missing during the turmoil of Uganda's civil wars, when the Simba Battalion barracks in Mbarara was leveled by artillery and the Defense Ministry in Kampala was ransacked. Laki's Volkswagen—the original object of Duncan's search—had never turned up, either. Anyule said he had last seen it sometime before Amin's overthrow, when he'd left the car at an Mbarara mechanic's garage. The lack of corroborating evidence further heightened the prosecution's reliance on the disputed confessions. "If the judge doesn't admit them into evidence," Mugenyi said, "the case is over."

Then there was a political issue: amnesty. All three of the accused soldiers had spent time in exile, and all three had returned under the repatriation programs of the 1990s. Legally, the language of the presidential amnesty only covered offenses committed against the government after Museveni's 1986 takeover, so the defendants were not immune from prosecution for crimes they had committed beforehand. But the former soldiers had certainly been given the impression that Museveni had granted a blanket pardon, and their lawyers were sure to argue that the trial violated the spirit, if not the letter, of the amnesty. After some debate, however, the prosecutor's office had decided to adhere to a narrow construction of the amnesty law. "There is generally good will in the country to let the bad past go, because there's so much of it in our history," said Richard Buteera, Uganda's chief prosecutor and Mugenyi's immediate superior. "I think the Ugandan people would rather go forward than look back. But this should not compromise the issue of justice."

Sometimes it seemed, though, that Uganda itself was conspiring against the prosecution. Tribalism, corruption, bureaucratic incompetence, war, disease—all of the country's societal ills added to the prosecution's burden. Uganda was a splintered country where citizens spoke more than fifty tribal languages. The official language of the court was English, but Anyule and Gille spoke Lugbara, an obscure tongue unknown in Kampala, while Gowon preferred to converse in Swahili, the language of the army, and some of the prosecution's eyewitnesses only understood the tribal language of Ankole, Runyankole. The deliberate pace of translation turned even a routine hearing into a stultifying slog.

The linguistic tangle, which had shaped the investigation of Laki's murder, was just one facet of the fundamental challenge: Uganda's persistent disunity. For a variety of reasons, the version of the confessions

Mugenyi wanted to use were the written statements Anyule and Gille had made to police officers while in custody. They had dictated these to a junior-ranking police officer who also happened to come from West Nile and thus spoke Lugbara. But the transcriber had since been transferred from Kampala to northern Uganda, where the army was fighting a war against the rebels of the Lord's Resistance Army, a force of several thousand child abductees led by a tribal "prophet" named Joseph Kony. Traveling from the north to Kampala was hazardous. Mugenyi, who wanted to use the policeman's testimony to introduce the confessions, finally managed to get him to court after a roundabout journey by bus and ferry that circumvented the war zone. But Justice Mukiibi threw out the officer's testimony, ruling that he wasn't qualified to translate the documents into English, the court's language. While Mugenyi looked for a translator who met the judge's standards, the trial was adjourned for several weeks.

In theory, Mugenyi had recourse to a second set of confessions, the sworn statements both defendants had made before a magistrate in April 2001, shortly after their initial arrests. In fact, such statements were generally considered more reliable evidence, and prosecutors had taken Anyule and Gille to the magistrate as a precaution against the very possibility that the two might eventually recant. But soon after the preliminary hearing, the magistrate who had recorded the confessions had been arrested himself, for allegedly taking a bribe in connection with another case. His disgrace made the sworn statements vulnerable to attack by the defense. Mugenyi didn't even try to introduce them.

The third set of confessions, the ones made to Alfred Orijabo, were even more problematic. Many affluent crime victims had taken to hiring private detectives, but such investigators operated in legally ambiguous territory. If necessary, the prosecution could call Orijabo, but it would be preferable to act as if the police were the ones who had first elicited the confessions, and that they had discovered the other corroborating evidence, such as the title documents for Laki's Volkswagen, which Duncan had actually done himself. However, relying heavily on the testimony of police officers carried its own risks. Amid stiff competition, the police force was regularly ranked the most corrupt public institution in Uganda by the national ethics czar. Officers were miserably paid, and many made a substantial portion of their income by demanding petty sums—or as they put it, "lunch"—from the unlucky people who came asking for their help. That was why Duncan had turned to private detectives in the first place. At trial, the police witnesses proved to be incapable of even pretending to be competent.

One of them, a squat, squeaky-voiced corporal, managed to turn the introduction of a sheaf of Anyule's handwriting samples into an hours-long tour de force of embarrassing lapses and stubborn evasions. As Justice Mukiibi listened, he leaned back in his swivel chair, took off his glasses and began to chew on one earpiece, a sign that he was really annoyed. He lowered his scornful gaze to meet the corporal. "It is bad to *lie!*" he thundered down from the bench.

"Our biggest problem is the quality of investigations," Mugenyi said during a break in the proceedings. "You can see this policeman is not so brilliant."

Typically, murder trials in Uganda were wrapped up in a week or less. Gowon's dragged on for a year. The stress of the trial started to wear down Mugenyi. The prosecutor's mood would swing wildly and without warning between crusading zeal and sour fatalism. In court, he wore an expression that, depending on the day's events, hovered somewhere on a continuum between bemusement and despair. When the judge gaveled the day's proceedings to a close, the prosecutor would hang his head and shake it. "This case!" he'd say as he shuffled away his papers, looking like he was ready to crumble beneath the weight of a whole country's frustration.

Private detective Alfred Orijabo, gaunt and glassy-eyed, bore his own unspoken burdens as he shuffled to a table at an outdoor café. The private detective, looking frazzled, sat down and ordered a soda, confiding that he hadn't slept in days. He kept furtively glancing over his shoulder. Leaning across the table conspiratorially, he whispered that assassins were after him. Orijabo confided that powerful people wanted him dead because he'd solved the Gowon case. "It was me particularly who did the whole thing," the detective said.

The paranoia was grandiose, but his pride in the successful investigation was merited. Orijabo was the one who had led the police to Anyule and Gille. He was the one who had worked up a rapport with the suspects. He had coaxed them to confess, and then he had convinced them to repeat their stories to the police. Now that the admissibility of those confessions had come into dispute, the private investigator's potential testimony had taken on great importance. Prosecutors were starting to worry, however, about Orijabo's reliability as a witness. For some reason, the detective appeared to be cracking up, acting erratically and expressing groundless fears.

The day before our meeting, I'd appeared on a Kampala radio talk show alongside Orijabo, where he'd discussed his role in the Laki murder case. The detective had filled the hour with a meandering account of his days fighting in a rebel army, his skill at karate and his investigative practices, which had sounded eccentric, to say the least. "Somebody told Duncan, my friend, if you are looking for the bones of your father, there is a man, dark in color, he is a Lugbara, go and talk to him," the detective told the host. "At times he is very arrogant and he is furious. But talk slowly, and he will assist you."

At the café, Orijabo leaned his head on his open palm and wearily recounted his life of flight and struggle. As a boy, he told me, he lived at a barracks in Kampala with his uncle, an officer in Amin's army. When the government fell, he and his family ran to Congo. He drifted in and out of a guerrilla group. "I am a very good target man, and I don't misuse bullets," he said, pantomiming his shooting technique and knocking his bottle of Coke all over the table. "You see, I was born wild," Orijabo went on. "It is only now that I am cooling down. You do any small thing, I give you the knife, there and then. I am hot-tempered naturally. The entire clan fears me, up to today. Even in the armed forces, the police and the army, they know you better serve this man, or else you get into a fistfight with him. I have that background."

Like many natives of West Nile, Orijabo still admired Idi Amin. "In principle, Amin was a good man—you get me? Very hardworking," he said. "But he had bad informers. His advisers were bad." In spite of his political views, the detective had decided to take the case, which had presented both a professional challenge and an opportunity to expand his business into a lucrative new niche. There were many thousands of families like Laki's.

Orijabo had his own methods of investigation; he looked for clues from the spirit world. "You have to be very observant," he explained. "The scene of the crime leaves for you an answer." For instance, when he and Duncan took the suspects to look for Laki's grave in an Ankole pasture, he believed a harbinger had showed him the way.

"A black bird," the detective said. "When I saw the movement of the bird, I took three steps behind and climbed an anthill. I studied the terrain, and I studied the movement of this bird. Then I concluded that this bird was showing us where the body was. People said I was mad. But when we were digging around there the bird was excited. It was even diving in a very nice way." Later, he said, when the grave was finally found, "it was under the tree where the bird was making noise. The bird was exact."

As our conversation went on, Orijabo started to ramble, losing coherence. He said he was feeling faint, and then nodded off in the middle of a sentence. When he jerked awake, he said he had to leave to consult his Congolese witch doctor. "I am quite accomplished in murder, actually," he shouted across the startled café as we parted ways. "I have never missed!"

Over the next few weeks, Orijabo woke me up several times in the dead of night with phone calls, complaining of harassment by invisible enemies. Then someone reported that he'd been committed to a Kampala mental institution. A little after that, I heard he had escaped by jumping over the asylum's wall, breaking his leg in the process. One day, I ran into Brian Tibo, the private detective's junior partner. "He's very sick," Tibo said, shaking his head sadly. He was employing a common Ugandan euphemism. Alfred Orijabo had AIDS. Dementia is a common end-stage symptom.

The first large-scale outbreak of AIDS in Africa occurred shortly after the war of 1979, in the Ugandan and Tanzanian fishing villages that ringed the western edge of Lake Victoria. The people of the region, who had just suffered the worst battles of the war, initially theorized that the mysterious disease was the result of "fallout" from the Tanzanians' *saba-saba* rockets, or that it was a curse brought upon them by the misdeeds of Amin. They gave this strange wasting ailment a morbid nickname: "Slim." From its point of emergence, the epidemic crept northward, a few dozen miles a year, roughly along the route of the Tanzanian advance and the Ugandan retreat. Truckers carried the disease east to the capital, and then on to Nairobi, Mombasa and beyond. Within a decade, an estimated one-third of adults in Kampala were infected with the HIV virus.

Uganda was not where AIDS originated, but it was the first country where the disease was identified in Africa, and the first to feel the full force of the plague. When epidemiologists later looked back and asked why AIDS emerged in this place, of all places, they kept coming back to Idi Amin's invasion of the Kagera region of Tanzania. All those women raped in the Ugandan rampage. All those soldiers who picked up bar girls and prostitutes. War was the perfect vector for a catastrophic epidemic.

Alfred Orijabo was a dying man, one more victim of Idi Amin's ineradicable legacy.

Simon Mugenyi called the next witness for the prosecution, one John Hitler.

"Hitler?" Justice Mukiibi said.

"That's my name, my lord," the witness replied, in a practiced deadpan. "It was given to me."

Ugandans usually don't have family surnames; their parents choose both their first and last names. There's a long tradition of calling boys after world leaders, regardless of political orientation. When I lived in Uganda, I met many Muslim boys called Saddam, as well as a youthful member of parliament named Ronald Reagan Okumu. It was John Hitler's lifelong misfortune to have been born in 1942, when it looked like the Germans might win the Second World War. Now sixty, he had a talkative manner and leathery skin. He'd been a police officer before he'd retired, and on the day of Eliphaz Laki's disappearance, he'd been stationed at the Ibanda county headquarters, where he'd watched powerlessly as Mohammed Anyule marched the chief out of his office.

"He gave me an identity card," Hitler testified. "The card said he was an intelligence officer. . . . The man told me he had his instructions to go with the late Laki to the Simba barracks in Mbarara."

"Did you know him?" the prosecutor asked.

"No, I had never seen him before," the witness replied.

Hitler testified that, looking out the window of the county headquarters, he had seen a second soldier carrying a machine gun.

"Did you know this man?" the prosecutor asked.

"I had never seen him before."

"Would you recognize any of these people?"

"Those two," Hitler said, pointing a pair of fingers at Anyule and Gille.

The retired policeman happened to possess another key piece of information. He was sure he remembered seeing Laki's car sometime shortly after his disappearance—only this time, with Yusuf Gowon behind the wheel. This conformed to testimony that a soldier had given in an unrelated legal proceeding several years before, in which he'd mentioned that Gowon was driving "in a Volkswagen" right after the invasion. Mugenyi was unaware that Hitler could testify about seeing Gowon in the car, however. He was so overworked that he rarely had time to prepare his witnesses adequately. So Hitler didn't mention the incident when he was on the stand, and the trial went on without a suggestive bit of corroborating evidence. "In High Court, you only answer what is asked," the retired policeman explained with a shrug in a later interview.

Yusuf Gowon's defense attorney, Caleb Alaka, rose to cross-examine the witness, and began to lay the groundwork for an audacious defense.

"Prior to the time when the late Laki was arrested, were you aware when he had visitors?" the lawyer asked.

"No," the witness replied.

"Did you know one gentleman named Yoweri Kaguta Museveni?"

"I knew him."

"Had he ever visited the county headquarters?"

"Yes, he used to visit."

"Are you aware whether he was a close friend to Laki?"

"I'm not aware."

"Are you aware that in 1972 he was a rebel?" the defense attorney asked.

"He was a freedom fighter," the policeman replied, with the hint of a smirk.

Alaka had elicited a useful answer—one he planned to deploy later. With the cross-examination completed, the retired policeman climbed down from the witness box, and Justice Mukiibi adjourned the trial for the day. The onlookers in the courtroom stood up on creaky legs. The intense interest that had accompanied the opening of the trial had slackened, and the gallery was no longer so crowded. Only one or two local journalists were still regularly covering the case. As far as their editors were concerned, the news was elsewhere: It was in Congo, where Uganda had foolishly intervened in a disastrous civil war; it was in the army, where the rivalries, romances and occasional fisticuffs of Museveni's generals provided constant tabloid fodder; it was in the government bureaucracies, a bountiful source of outrageous scandals—timber smuggling by the environment minister, embezzlement of AIDS funds. Updates on the trial's deliberate progress were relegated to the inside pages. That did not mean that the Laki case had disappeared from everyone's minds, though. For a few Ugandans, some of them supporters of the prosecution and some of the defense, the past remained ever-present.

As the courtroom audience milled around, discussing the afternoon's inconclusive events, a lanky, droopy-eyed man in a gray suit ambled over. I recognized him as one of the regulars from the gallery. He introduced himself as Charles Kabagambe. He was an attorney, but he told me he was attending the trial for personal reasons. His own father had disappeared in 1972. Gesturing toward Yusuf Gowon and his codefendants, who were being led out of the dock, Kabagambe said, "I think these are the ones who did it."

Peter Kabagambe had also been chief of a county in western Uganda. He too had been arrested by soldiers after the rebel invasion. His body had never been found. Charles Kabagambe talked about the immense toll of his father's disappearance, the son's own long ordeal of fear and ostracism in Uganda, his dislocation after he himself went into exile, his years of destructive drinking after he returned back home. He had only recently managed to pull his life together, and in at least a small way, the story of Eliphaz Laki had helped, giving him hope that resolution was somehow attainable. "This trial has had a very therapeutic effect," Kabagambe said. "I know that's how my father died."

18

TAKING THE STAND

The first time Duncan Laki met ~~Yusuf Gowon~~, it was by chance, at Kampala's decaying train station, years before the general was arrested for murder. Duncan was visiting a friend who worked for the Uganda Railways Corporation. Gowon was also there, on business, and they were introduced by a mutual acquaintance. The general had just recently been welcomed home from exile. Duncan had heard rumors that Gowon might have had a role in the disappearances of 1972, but he didn't feel confident enough to confront the general, so he concealed his suspicion behind polite conversation. That was life in Uganda. You could go out one morning on a routine errand and run into your father's killer.

The second time Duncan came face to face with Gowon, it was at the Kampala police station, when the general was under interrogation. Gowon swore that he'd never heard of a chief named Eliphaz Laki, with a sincere-sounding vehemence. Duncan could only assume that the general had forgotten, that the name Laki held no place in his memory, that the murder was only a trifling event in his life. Somehow, that hurt even more.

Duncan encountered Yusuf Gowon once more outside Justice Moses Mukiibi's courtroom. Duncan was about to testify as the prosecution's star witness. Inside, the trial's audience had returned, drawn by the promise of a dramatic confrontation, and the gallery's wooden benches were jammed with spectators. As he waited to be called, Duncan was passing the time on the columned breezeway that adjoined the court, pacing and making nervous conversation with his sister Joyce and a few other relatives. All of a sudden, there was some bustle as guards ushered the three defendants down the passageway—right past Duncan and his family. Eyes met and Gowon stopped.

The general smiled widely at his accuser. "I am so happy to see you!" he said, extending a plump, cheerful hand. Duncan shook it and greeted Anyule and Gille too. There was a strange feeling of reunion. Then the guards moved the defendants along.

For Duncan, the meeting triggered none of the predictable emotions. He really didn't want to see anyone hanged. He had a new life in faraway New Jersey, and his wife was about to have a child, their fourth. He'd flown many hours to get back for his testimony, taking off from Newark just ahead of a snowstorm, but his efforts were accompanied by deep reservations. Duncan recognized that he would be stuck in Uganda—mentally if not physically—so long as he remained enmeshed in the lingering case. He hadn't given in to the prosecutor's pleas that he return home to take the stand until the very last minute. But his sense of responsibility had ultimately won out. Duncan was the one who held the whole case together. He'd been a witness to every step of the investigation. He'd discovered his father's body. He was a physical reminder of the victim, the man who couldn't be present in the courtroom. So he stood there, jet-lagged and bleary-eyed, and waited to testify, because that was what justice demanded.

Justice Mukiibi swept into the courtroom and gaveled the proceedings to order. Duncan took his place in the witness box, leaning back against a wall to steady his weary legs, and sipped from a plastic bottle of mineral water. In his methodical, sober way, he recounted his story. "I was always interested in my father's car," he explained. "My father had been my hero." He described the joy he felt the day he found the car registration file with Mohammed Anyule's name in it, saying, "It was as if I had found a long-lost gem."

Without Duncan's determination, the case would never have been solved. On the witness stand, however, his testimony carried risks for the prosecution's case. Because the police never would have acted if they'd had to pay for the investigation themselves, Duncan had spent a considerable sum to underwrite hotels, meals, bus and plane fares—for the police, for his private detectives, for witnesses and even for the alleged perpetrators. The private detectives had coordinated much of the investigation, and Duncan himself had been allowed to play an informal but active role, sitting in on portions of the interrogations of the suspects, posing a few questions as well. This was unusual even by the Ugandan police force's laid-back standards, and the defense questioned the irregularities.

The issue particularly affected one very important piece of evidence: the murder victim's body. During the long period that Duncan was searching for his father's remains, the police couldn't always provide the necessary manpower, and when he finally found the exact spot of the grave he had exhumed it without official assistance, forgoing the usual step of obtaining a court order. He didn't take the remains to a Ugandan medical examiner, either, which created a gap in the chain of evidence. The prosecution was going to have a very difficult time proving that there was a grave, that it was in the pasture the defendants had pinpointed in their confessions and that the bones unearthed from it were indeed Laki's. Privately, Simon Mugenyi couldn't believe that Duncan, a lawyer, had handed the defense an argument.

On the stand, Duncan's emotions overcame him as he spoke of finding the grave.

"The bones were . . ." he began, and then his voice broke into muffled sobs.

"Do you need a seat?" Justice Mukiibi asked.

"Yes, my lord," Duncan replied.

Duncan continued with his testimony, and Justice Mukiibi took it all down by hand, picking and choosing what he considered admissible as he went along. When a witness strayed into an area he considered irrelevant, he often simply stopped writing. As Duncan went on, the judge's pen moved less and less. Finally, after several defense objections, Mukiibi leaned back in his chair and considered Duncan's testimony about the body. Ugandan law was strict on the issue of custody of evidence. "If there is a break in the chain," said one law book, "the exhibit in question will not be admitted." Because of the evident lapses in legal procedure, Justice Mukiibi ruled out Duncan's testimony about unearthing the grave. For the purposes of the court, there would be no body, no DNA test.

"We stick by the books," the judge said sternly.

This was not the vindication Duncan had expected. One of the assumptions that underlay all the recent experiments in humanitarian justice—the truth and reconciliation commissions, the United Nations tribunals, the International Criminal Court—was that the truth possessed cathartic power. The proponents of these new legal mechanisms spoke of "traumas" and "burdens," "ghosts" and "demons," language that evoked the European tradition of the psychiatrist's couch and religious rituals like penance and exorcism. Duncan wouldn't have described his motivations quite that histrionically, but he did believe it was important to speak the truth aloud. More valuable to him than any conviction or punishment was the prospect of making a record, official and indelible, of the circumstances of his father's death.

Justice Mukiibi was having none of it. To him, a courtroom wasn't supposed to function like a therapist's office or a confessional booth. His job was to impose the law. And he wasn't about to let anyone forget that, even the victim's son.

Duncan tried to testify about the toll Amin's purges took on his family. "About three days prior to my father's kidnapping, my three cousins were shot dead near the county headquarters," he said. "My uncle had also been taken."

The judge cut him off. Not pertinent, he said.

As the prosecutor tried to push on, Mukiibi ruled out Duncan's testimony time and again, finding it to be hearsay or otherwise inadmissible. When it came to the issue of the interrogations, the judge peppered Duncan with skeptical questions.

"What was the role of Orijabo?" the judge asked.

"He was translating a little bit," Duncan said. "Asking some questions."

The judge scrawled the answer into the record. He went on to press Duncan for details about Anyule's trip to Ankole during the search for Laki's grave, inquiring about sleeping and eating arrangements.

"Who bought?"

"I was doing most of the buying, my lord," Duncan replied.

The judge frowned and scribbled some more.

Duncan was infuriated. He'd done his best in the face of Ugandan realities, but now his actions were being judged according to English law. ("Unfortunately, we have a judge who lives in the ivory tower, so he can't even use his rational mind," he wrote in an e-mail several weeks after he testified.) Duncan was a lawyer, and he comprehended the legal reasoning behind the judge's rulings, but his anger was simply emotional. He wanted the truth to be revealed. Now he felt like the law itself was denying him.

"I just want to tell you the story as it happened!" he snapped at the judge in frustration.

The next evening, after a second exhausting day of testimony, Duncan joined me for a drink on my porch in Kampala. It was a warm evening, and the wind crackled through the wide torn leaves of my backyard banana tree as we gazed out over the lights of the city. "I'm doing this out of duty," Duncan said. If the judge did come down with a guilty verdict, he said he would be the first to petition President Museveni for the soldiers' pardon. "I really feel we should have a truth and reconciliation commission," he explained. "If Gowon was killed two hundred times over, if Gille was convicted and they chopped off one of his fingers every day until he is dead . . . nothing. But we need the truth to come out. That's why when I am testifying I wish I could have the opportunity to go on and on and on."

Duncan was quiet for a moment. "I mean, if you convict Anyule . . ." he went on, with a sympathetic chuckle. "The poor guy. I mean, these were just button pushers. They were just being told: 'Go here and do that. Go there and do the other thing.' For this thing to be settled, ever, we need to have a truth and reconciliation kind of arrangement."

As much as Duncan tried to distance himself from the case emotionally, however, he couldn't fully extricate himself from it. The next afternoon, he went looking for Alfred Orijabo, who had dropped out of sight since escaping from a mental hospital. The prosecutors didn't think there was any possibility that they could put him on the stand, but Duncan couldn't believe the private detective was so far gone, and still hoped he could testify. Duncan's search led to a tumbledown home in a Kampala suburb, Orijabo's wife's place. She told Duncan he had missed her husband by just a few minutes. He'd gotten wind that someone was on his trail, and paranoid as ever, he'd hopped onto the back of a motorbike taxi to make a hasty escape.

Orijabo's wife looked disconsolate. She realized her husband had lost his mind, but she was convinced it had only happened because his younger girlfriend, her rival for his affections, had cast a magic spell on him. The girlfriend's place turned out to be a shack in a hillside shantytown, where the streets ran with rivulets of sewage. No one was home.

Caleb Alaka, the brash young defense attorney, intended to make the private detective's breakdown an issue in the trial. He believed that in handing the investigation over to private investigators, Duncan had made a crucial miscalculation, one that had seriously weakened the prosecution's case. During cross-examination, the defense lawyer zeroed in on Orijabo's recent behavior.

"Do you know his whereabouts?" he asked Duncan.

"No, I don't," the witness replied.

"Duncan, I want you to be truthful with the court. Are you not aware that Alfred is now in Butabika Mental Hospital?"

"I am not aware of his whereabouts."

"Are you also not aware that this Alfred Orijabo also has problems where he always runs mad?"

"I am not aware of that," the witness said.

Alaka's voice rose. "I want to put it to you that you are telling a lot of lies to this court," he shouted. "And I am going to unveil them!"

"I want to put it to you," Duncan replied, in sober monotone, "that I swore to tell the truth."

Of the two lawyers facing each other in the courtroom that day, one a witness and the other his cross-examiner, Duncan Laki was the one with more experience. Alaka was twenty-six, and he looked even more youthful. His black barrister's robe, which had turned purple in spots from wear, looked to have more years on it than its occupant. But Alaka

Caleb Alaka, defense attorney
ANDREW RICE

was no one to underestimate. In the few years since he'd graduated law school, he had made himself a reputation as one of Uganda's top criminal defenders. He attributed his precocious success in the law to wit, charm and a "loud voice." In hierarchical Uganda, speaking softly was considered a sign of respect, and many lawyers turned into incomprehensible mumblers when facing a judge. But not Alaka. He watched American courtroom dramas such as *The Practice* and *Law and Order* to pick up techniques. Like a TV lawyer, he was prone to rhetorical hotdogging, and he relished the cinematic moment.

"I want to tackle Duncan," Alaka had bragged in an interview some weeks before. Facing down his client's accuser, he bounded around the courtroom with pugnacious glee.

"You told this honorable court that you were idolizing your father," Alaka said. "Is that right?"

"Yes, my lord," Duncan Laki replied.

"You also told this court that you followed your father's developments with keen interest."

"Yes, my lord."

"Did you also have interest into visitors of your father?"

"Visitors generally, my lord."

"Did you know of one visitor at that time . . . called Yoweri Museveni?"

"No, my lord. . . ."

"As a grown-up, have you ever known His Excellency Yoweri Museveni was close to your father?"

"Yes, my lord."

With a bit of flourish, Alaka produced a paperback copy of Museveni's autobiography, which bore the pudgy, bald visage of Uganda's president on its cover. He waved the book in the air for all to see.

"Have you ever read *Sowing the Mustard Seed*, written by Yoweri Museveni?" the defense lawyer asked.

"Yes, my lord," Duncan replied.

"Do you recall whether he ever made mention of your late father in that book?"

Duncan knew the passages by heart. "I believe it is on page forty-one and page forty-seven," he said.

Alaka handed him the book.

"Can you read it out?" the defense attorney asked.

Duncan turned to the page where Museveni described the events on the day of Amin's coup, and how he was smuggled to safety in Tanzania by Eliphaz Laki.

Alaka, his voice coiled, prepared to spring.

"Are you also aware that around this time, 1971 . . . Yoweri Kaguta Museveni, they called him a guerrilla?"

"I am not aware, my lord," Duncan replied.

Alaka flashed Duncan an incredulous look.

"Are you aware that Yoweri Museveni . . . and your late father were trying to overthrow the government of that time, of Idi Amin?"

"I sure am now," Duncan replied. "As day follows night, I am aware."

"Are you aware as of now what could happen at that time . . . to someone caught trying to overthrow the government?"

"I sure am," the witness replied. "He would have been arrested, charged and prosecuted. If he was found guilty the consequences would be from there."

"Duncan," Alaka said, in feigned exasperation. "Is that what was happening to the best of your knowledge?"

"No, it wasn't. Otherwise we wouldn't be here having this dialogue," Duncan replied. Despite Alaka's baiting, his voice was even and unruffled. "People would disappear," Duncan continued. "Some would go into exile if they were lucky enough."

"Then what would happen to the others?"

"Others were beheaded," Duncan said. "Others dismembered, my uncle being one of them. Others were shot at the stake, like my three cousins."

"Duncan, I don't know what to say!" Alaka shouted, ferocious now. "Are you aware that when such people were arrested by the government at that time of Idi Amin, they were always buried in mass graves? Are you aware of that?"

"I am aware of that," the witness replied.

Alaka had revealed the essence of his strategy. It would not be sufficient, he assumed, simply to reveal the holes in the prosecution's case. Like any good defense attorney, he remained officially agnostic on the question of his clients' guilt, but he could recognize the convincing power of the confessions. He believed he had to go beyond evidentiary issues, to recast the events of September 1972 in a way that was less devastating, maybe even understandable. To do so, Alaka had devised a daring and politically charged line of defense. He was going to put history itself on trial.

At the time Eliphaz Laki was killed, he argued, there was a war on. The victim may not have been a combatant, but there was ample evidence that he was collaborating with Museveni. The rebel of 1972 was Uganda's president in 2002, but that did not change the fact that Laki, under the laws of the day, had committed treason. And everyone knew the punishment for plotting against Idi Amin.

Outside of the courtroom, Alaka put his argument in stark terms. "These soldiers," he said, "were doing what they were supposed to do."

19

THE DEFENSE

There was something irrepressible about Caleb Alaka. The defense attorney was skinny and mercurial, with prominent cheekbones and a wide toothy grin. His suits appeared a size too big for him. He had a reputation as a carouser and a ladies' man, and he embodied the freewheeling, globalized ethos of Kampala in the Museveni era. On the weekends, like a lot of successful professionals in their twenties, he hung around bars with friends from varying tribes, eating roasted goat and watching English soccer on satellite television. His favorite club was Manchester United. He was perpetually late for appointments, and unapologetic about it, and his attention span was so short that you were liable to lose him if you blinked. Once, during an interview, Alaka stepped out of his office for a moment, saying he would be gone for just a second. A half hour later, I found him standing on the street outside his law firm, having his brown loafers shined.

"We are going to win this case!" he was boasting to the shoeshine man.

I met Alaka a month or so before the trial began, at his place of business, a down-at-the-heels two-story office building along Kampala Road. As usual, he was doing four things at once. People barged in pushing papers in front of him to sign. His several cell phones chirped incessantly. There was a meeting he was setting up with President Museveni's office. There was a reception area crammed with clients, waiting with worried expressions on black vinyl chairs, like patients in an overcrowded emergency room. As we talked, Alaka fielded a string of desperate phone calls from the family of a man who was languishing in jail. Each time, he smoothly assured his caller that he was on his way to the police station, then hung up and returned to decrying the injustices being inflicted on Yusuf Gowon. Alaka hadn't achieved his early renown by being reticent with the press.

When it came to the Laki murder case, Alaka was juggling conflicting loyalties. He had originally been retained to represent Gowon, though it was unclear whether the general was capable of paying his legal bills. The attorney's only certain reward was going to come in the form of newsprint. "The man is weak and old, so I may look upon it as a pro-bono service," Alaka said. Very much secondarily, Alaka was also representing Mohammed Anyule and Nasur Gille, for reasons that were arguably less charitable.

As Alaka knew, his three clients' legal interests were not completely aligned. From the beginning, Gowon had tried to deflect blame down the chain of command. During his police interrogation, he had referred to the two lower-ranking soldiers by a Swahili word that meant "trash," and wrote in an official statement that if they had in fact killed Laki, "they did it on their own, and they should stand [trial] for it, unless they prove I instructed them to kill the deceased." Anyule and Gille, for their parts, had continued to threaten to testify against Gowon in return for a lighter sentence, until Alaka had convinced them to instead cooperate in a united defense. The two were likely to be convicted anyway, Alaka believed, but the defense of his primary client, Gowon, had been greatly bolstered.

"Isn't that a bit of a conflict of interest?" I asked.

"No," Alaka replied, with a winning smile. "It's strategic."

Under Ugandan law, Anyule and Gille were entitled to court-appointed attorneys. But the two had decided to go along with Alaka because he was from their home province, West Nile, and a member of their tribe. They assumed that his ethnic identity would make him a strong advocate, and they weren't entirely wrong. Alaka did genuinely feel his people had paid enough for Amin's crimes. When he was a baby, his family had lived in Kampala, where his father was a banker. But in 1979, the family had been forced to abandon its home and hide out in a swamp to escape the vigilante mobs that were going door-to-door, hunting northerners. Eventually, they'd made it safely back to West Nile, but Alaka's father had been financially ruined. It was a testament to Alaka's intelligence and moxie that he'd managed to pass the entrance exams for Makerere University, where he'd earned his law degree.

The experience of retribution had shaped Alaka's view of justice. This was true for all Ugandans, he explained: The way you viewed this trial depended on where you were born. Eliphaz Laki's western tribe—now Uganda's most influential—saw the murder victim as a martyr, the savior of the president, and the prosecution as a simple matter of morality and law. People in the region of West Nile perceived things differently. Alaka was planning to argue that Gowon, not Eliphaz Laki, was the victim now, this time of a government plot to punish an out-of-favor tribe. Why had the police arrested Gowon now, so many years later? Why had they picked him while leaving so many notorious killers alone? If he had in fact ordered the chief's murder, had he really done any worse than so many others? Wasn't he just playing by the accepted rules of his time?

This line of argument—"he was only following orders"—was, of course, a time-honored defense in war crimes trials. At Nuremberg and elsewhere, courts had rejected it, finding that soldiers possessed a higher duty to disobey immoral commands. In Uganda, though, many people thought it sounded like a reasonable defense. From personal experience, they knew dictatorships often presented individuals with impossible moral choices.

Alaka had a talent for political provocation. Besides Gowon, his client roster included an opposition party leader who had been arrested on a flimsy gun charge, a court-martialed general and a politician who was appealing his death sentence for killing a tribal prince. Another regime might have had someone like Alaka shot, but Museveni's was tolerant, up to a point. But this Gowon defense was a risky ploy even by Alaka's standards, one freighted with possible dangers for his clients—and maybe even the country. By putting history on trial, by shifting the focus in the courtroom from a specific crime to the larger legacy of the Amin era, Alaka was trying to call the people of West Nile to arms. Figuratively, for the time being, but that could change. Back home, he knew, some of Amin's former soldiers were trying to revive old rebellions. The defense was deliberately stirring up resentments the government could not afford to ignore.

"I don't think it's in Museveni's interest," Alaka said, "to have Gowon face the music."

Through the year that the trial went on, Yoweri Museveni never physically appeared in the courtroom, but his presence loomed over it every day. As Alaka well knew, the president had a personal stake in the case and a political one, and the two were working in opposition. Eliphaz Laki had died because he'd helped Museveni, and the president felt a debt as a result. It was not widely known, but he had given Duncan Laki more than a thousand dollars, an immense sum by Ugandan standards, to assist in locating and exhuming his father's body. Yet an acquittal would clearly be the politically preferable result. To many Ugandans—not just people in West Nile—it looked like the president was settling a personal score with Gowon on behalf of a tribesman. Few seemed to seriously consider the notion that the defendants' guilt or innocence would be determined by a detached assessment of the evidence. If the rule of law really did exist, Ugandans imagined, it did so only at the pleasure of the president.

The government was not monolithic, though. There were many competing factions and interests within its upper echelons, and from the very outset the prosecution had run into significant resistance. Shortly after Yusuf Gowon's arrest, for instance, a memorandum arrived at the office of Museveni's principal private secretary. Written on the letterhead of the president's office and stamped "URGENT," the memo was signed by a Museveni political adviser.

"As it may have come to your knowledge, Major General Gowon was arrested on a murder case," the memo began. "I have no doubt that the government will never, and should never, interfere with a case in court. On the other hand, I am concerned about misinformation and hence misinterpretation of the case by negative political forces." The aide gently suggested that the president's secretary review the terms of Gowon's 1994 amnesty agreement with the government, which had enabled him to return from exile along with thousands of refugees. "From what I have gathered, many former Army Officers and civilians who came back are threatened," the memo explained. The political adviser recommended that His Excellency be briefed about the security threat.

The president's secretary forwarded the memorandum to the director of the police force's Criminal Investigations Division. "Your prompt response would be highly appreciated," he wrote in a cover letter, "in view of the delicacy of the matter." In the veiled language of bureaucratese, a message was being sent to those who had arrested Gowon: Were they sure it was worth it?

The adviser who wrote the questioning memorandum was a woman named Anuna Omari. Universally known as "Hajat Anuna," she served as Museveni's liaison to Uganda's Muslim community. She had been a figure of some prominence in Idi Amin's regime, as the manager of a government corporation that distributed imported food and beverages. It was a key instrument of patronage in a time of severe shortages and a well-known front for the secret police. A contemporary observer, writing in his diary, had described Anuna as "a large, fat, overbearing woman with no business knowledge or experience" and a beneficiary of "the usual nepotism." She'd been the mistress of a highly placed army officer, Major General Yusuf Gowon.

One stormy day, I went to visit Hajat Anuna at her office on the grounds of the presidential compound. She was, as advertised, quite porcine, so heavy that she struggled to raise herself from her chair to greet me. While she considered Gowon a friend, "a humble man," her interest in the case was a matter of policy, she insisted. "I can't interfere with the court process," she said. "It would look very bad for the president to support someone who committed a crime against an individual." She said that she had merely been trying to raise an alarm about the wider implications of Gowon's arrest, which had "caused some fear among the people." She had convinced refugees from West Nile that they could return to Uganda without the threat of reprisal.

Hajat Anuna was not the only important official who took actions that might be construed as meddling on Gowon's behalf. In Museveni's Uganda, where national unity—or at least its appearance—was the paramount value, any number of people from West Nile held positions of prominence in the government. Attorney General Francis Ayume, the nation's top legal official, represented Gowon's home village in parliament and was a personal friend of the general's. The attorney general was the first person to visit Gowon when he was thrown in jail. "He went to the president," Gowon said later, "but the president told him it was only the law that would release me."

"I was under pressure to find a way to help him," Ayume admitted. He was a formidable presence in the legal community—he had literally written the book on trying criminals; it was called *Criminal Procedure and Law in Uganda*—and it would have been possible for him to have intervened in quiet ways on his friend's behalf. Choosing his words very carefully, however, the attorney general maintained that his assistance to Gowon only amounted to moral support: visiting him, bringing him small sums of money and foodstuffs to supplement his meager prison diet. "I had advised him that it was unlikely that the matter would be settled politically, since this was a case of murder," Ayume said. "This government, of which I am a member, upholds the rule of law."

Some supporters of the prosecution suspected that the attorney general might have exerted informal influence over which judge was assigned the case. He would have been acquainted with Justice Mukiibi. Back in the 1970s, when the future judge was a young prosecutor and just starting his career, Ayume had been the Director of Public Prosecutions, and thus his boss. Yet there was no clear evidence of a deeper connection. Even if one existed, it was only objectionable in the context of the prevailing assumptions about the judge's pro-Muslim bias. Though Mukiibi had infuriated the prosecution with some adverse rulings, none of them had been legally indefensible.

If there was an effort to influence justice, its authors would have taken care to assure it was not publicly known. There was an overt form of political pressure brought upon the trial, however, and it was visible every day in the gallery. Though the overall attendance at the trial dwindled over time—Laki's western tribesmen had more important things to think about, like running the country—each day, month after month, Gowon's northern people, in their knitted prayer caps and Muslim headscarves, dutifully took their places in the airy courtroom gallery. During recesses, as his nonchalant prison guards looked on, Gowon would work the crowd, shaking hands and accepting comforting words.

Their sense of victimization had been building for years. In 1995, a year after Gowon's return from exile, a group of leaders from West Nile prepared a report on the roots of the district's instability, which they submitted to President Museveni. Ever since Idi Amin, the report said, "the history and image of West Nile have been read upside down by everybody, Ugandan and non-Ugandan alike." According to West Nile's own upside-down history, the atrocities that came to define Amin in the world's eyes never happened. Or if they did happen, they were rationalized as self-defense, a sad but necessary fact of life when it came to the hard business of governing in Africa. Or the crimes were blamed on a handful of mercenaries that Amin recruited from Sudan and Congo—foreigners, not Ugandans.

"Amin phobia," the report said, "has driven most if not all West Nilers into remaining apologetic all their lives."

Some weren't inclined to apologize, though. Mohammed Anyule and Nasur Gille still saw nothing shameful in their actions, and couldn't understand why they were on trial. But they could certainly recognize that their situation was even more dire than Gowon's. Not only were they facing murder charges, far from home and totally destitute—they were also unimportant.

To everyone except Caleb Alaka, that is. One day, the defense attorney went to Luzira Prison to see the two soldiers. The time had come to ask them some hard questions about their confessions. Justice Mukiibi was about to consider the crucial issue of their admissibility at an evidentiary hearing. During this proceeding, the trial-within-a-trial, the prosecution would be able to call Anyule and Gille as witnesses. Prosecutors had not yet handed over copies of their written statements to the defense, though. Alaka needed to know exactly what Anyule and Gille had confessed, and more importantly, he needed to gauge whether, given their stubborn refusal to believe that they had done anything wrong, they were likely to defiantly repeat those stories when they were questioned on the stand.

Outside of the courtroom, Alaka didn't even bother to argue that Anyule and Gille were innocent. "I think they must have killed the man," he acknowledged. "But the way I look at it, Gowon must have been a little bit, slightly, innocent." As he waited to see Anyule and Gille at the prison, Alaka said that however well he prepared his clients to testify, he wasn't optimistic about the chances of an acquittal. "There isn't much I can do," he said. "These guys shot themselves in the leg with that confession."

Two stooped men trudged into the prison's visiting room. The guards led them to a long wooden bench, where they sat facing Alaka. A year and a half had elapsed since the defendants had first been arrested. The hardships of incarceration showed in their appearances. Anyule, who was seventy, looked hungry; his skin was stretched tight over his angular face. Gille was a dozen years younger than his codefendant, but he looked like the older of the two. The yellow *kufi* on his head was dirty and crumpled, and his white shirt was torn along its sleeves. He held a scrap of paper in his hands, which were coarsened from years of manual labor. On it, he had jotted out a few elements of his defense in broken English:

"The car was not found with."

"I am not educated."

Anyule, despondent, kept his eyes fastened to the ground.

The two men had never expected to face judgment. They'd been coaxed into confessing by a tribesman, Alfred Orijabo, who had implied that they'd be granted immunity from prosecution if they implicated Gowon. The private investigator had possessed no authority

Sergeant Nasur Gille
ANDREW RICE

to make such assurances, but the defendants didn't have a sophisticated understanding of the law. Orijabo had told them that the chief they'd killed was one of Yoweri Museveni's tribesmen, and that the president had contributed money toward the investigation of the crime. Convinced that powerful forces were conspiring against them, the soldiers had taken the deal. Except, it had turned out, there was no deal. They'd been tricked.

Alaka asked the accused men in their tribal language, Lugbara, why it was they had confessed. Anyule let out a guttural groan. He'd been promised amnesty, he said. Why had the government decided to punish him? Him—a loyal supporter of the ruling party! He claimed Orijabo had elicited his confession through threats and false promises. The police had written out a statement for him, he said, which he couldn't read because he was functionally illiterate, and had forced him to sign it.

Gille, gesticulating furiously, told the lawyer that he had confessed only after police threatened him and refused him food for several days. "Alfred told him the person who they killed was from Museveni's family," the lawyer translated aloud. "Alfred said that if he, Nasur Gille, did not accept the statement given by Anyule, he would be killed."

It was important, Alaka told his new clients, that he properly understand the context of the killings of September 1972. "It is just always similar," Gille explained. "When bad people come, rebels, a man can take that kind of action."

Private Mohammed Anyule
ANDREW RICE

Anyule piped up. "If you want the real reason how that war started, why civilians were killed, I'll tell you the reason," he said. "Amin started fighting Obote. Obote fled to Tanzania. Obote started organizing guerrillas. They started recruiting people in the villages. They took them to Tanzania. Obote used Museveni." Then the guerrillas invaded, and the army knew they had collaborators in Ankole. "Because Amin was the president, he gave that order, 'let these people be eliminated.' It's not that me as a driver would be the one making directives. I was just following orders," he said—an order that he said he had received "from Gowon."

"We didn't know the man we killed was a chief," Anyule added. "We knew him as a guerrilla."

The self-justifying words kept tumbling out of the defendants' mouths—just as Alaka had feared they would. He patiently explained to his clients that when they took the witness stand, they needed to deny that they had killed Eliphaz Laki, and to emphasize their claims that the confessions had been coerced. Even if the killings were justifiable, he told them, they didn't want to concede anything to the prosecution. The defendants nodded in agreement: They understood. They just wanted Alaka to know they were not to blame.

No one in Uganda took responsibility for Amin's crimes. Southerners blamed the northerners. The northerners blamed the Nubians. The Nubians blamed "those Sudanese," Amin's foreign mercenaries. Each individual deflected the burden of guilt away from himself, his friends, and his tribe, shifting blame forever outward in radiating circles of denial. Gowon was prepared to blame Anyule and Gille. Who, then, did they blame?

"Museveni," Sergeant Gille said. Anyule concurred, citing a proverb that, in the tradition of West Nile's folklore, equated bees with mischief and dissension. "If you have got bees, and you came and dropped them at another man's home, and the bees started stinging kids, and the kids die, who would you accuse: the bees, or the person who brought them?" the private asked. "Why is it that the person who brought the problems where the civilians were killed, that that person has not been brought to Luzira?"

"That's a good defense!" Alaka interjected.

The prosecution called another eyewitness, a retired county government cashier. Blasio Buhwairoha, a seventy-six-year-old man with a deeply lined face, wore an oversized blue blazer, was missing a front tooth and spoke no English, only the tribal language of Ankole. He testified that he was present in Eliphaz Laki's office the day Idi Amin's men came for him. But his memory, he confessed, was not what it once was.

"Those three men who took away Laki in 1972," lead prosecutor Simon Mugenyi asked. "If you saw them would you recognize them now?"

"I cannot," the cashier said through a translator. "It is many years ago."

On cross-examination, Alaka went after the doddering witness.

"Mr. Buhwairoha, I am putting it to you that you are lying to this court," he said, pointing an accusing finger. "This is a serious case in which some people's lives are at stake. I want you to answer the questions as I put them to you."

Alaka poked at the cashier's fuzzy recollection. What language were Laki and the soldiers using to speak to one another?

"I do not remember," the witness replied. "It is many years ago."

Did he remember what the soldiers were wearing?

"It's been a long time," the cashier said.

Did he even remember that rebels invaded Uganda in September 1972, attacking the Simba Battalion barracks?

"I don't recall."

The cashier was forty-six years old at the time, Alaka pointed out. "You don't recall an invasion or a war in Mbarara, which is fifty-six miles from Ibanda?"

Buhwairoha looked confused. "It was a long time ago," he apologized.

To a disinterested observer, the witness's shaky performance on the stand said more about the preparation of the prosecution than the quality of the defense. But afterward, Alaka was jubilant about the way he'd humiliated the forgetful cashier. He felt the trial was starting to turn in his favor. That night, the defense attorney went to dinner with some friends of Gowon's, fellow northerners who'd watched the court session that day. Sitting at a thatch-roofed, candlelit restaurant, downing cold bottles of beer, Alaka giddily predicted that he might not even have to worry about the confessions. "After this kind of devastating cross-examination, there is also fear," he told his dinner companions. "They may just decide to withdraw the case against Gowon."

One of the men at the table, a former opposition party candidate for parliament, explained why he felt an acquittal was of vital national interest. He was acting as negotiator for the Uganda National Rescue Front II, a northern rebel group that had recently entered into peace negotiations with the government. Alaka was the rebels' legal counsel. The UNRF II was a weak force of around two thousand aging soldiers, a splinter of a splinter of a splinter of Idi Amin's defunct army. But the rebels were a nuisance up in West Nile, where they engaged in brigandry, and they wouldn't give up their arms unless they could trust the government's promise of amnesty. A guilty verdict in the Laki murder case had the potential to undermine the peace talks. "This case has taken most Ugandans by surprise," the negotiator said.

"The elite know Gowon is accused of a crime that directly relates to him," he added. But the rank and file "believe that anyone who was associated with Idi Amin is victimized by this government."

Alaka assured his dinner companions that he wasn't going to let a conviction happen. "My tactic is just to portray a war situation," the defense attorney said. "The good thing is that the killing coincided with the attack. You see, Gowon was doing the duty of the state as then established." Alaka was talking fast, getting excited. "It was not a democratic government," he shouted. "It was a dictatorial government! Even if he was the one who gave the order, as long as it was official policy, he was an implementer."

It wasn't just history that had been turned upside-down. Morality had been inverted too. One side's hero was the other side's traitor; one side's freedom fighter was the other side's insurgent; one side's murder was the other side's military necessity. Duncan Laki and Caleb Alaka had been born within the same borders, had attended the same university, had practiced the same law, but they lived in different countries.

"It was treason," Alaka concluded. "These people were supposed to be killed. That's what happens everywhere."

The lawyer's confidence proved to be short-lived, however. One day soon after the cashier's testimony, the prosecution finally handed over copies of the confessions to the defense, giving Alaka a long-delayed glimpse of the crucial evidence against his clients. The words of Anyule and Gille were far more damning than he'd ever imagined. He flipped through the photocopied pages, reading the most damaging passages aloud.

"You see, this is Gowon, Gowon, Gowon," he said.

Alaka's bravado had suddenly evaporated. In a panicked voice, he began to think aloud about changing his tactics. "If this somehow makes it into court, then we are in trouble, because this court does not understand military things," Alaka said. "If it is not retracted, then I am finished, because it is so powerful."

As luck would have it, events were about to present Alaka with a backup plan. The same day that he got a look at the confessions, the private detective Alfred Orijabo died. He had been a key figure in the prosecution's case, but now he couldn't testify—and he couldn't sue for libel, either. Soon after he learned of Orijabo's passing, Alaka was seen chatting amiably with one of the courthouse beat reporters. Then an article appeared under her byline in the *Monitor*. Headlined KEY WITNESS IN GOWON TRIAL DIES, the story reported that the private investigator had succumbed to a "mental disorder" in a Kampala asylum. "Orijabo," it continued, "worked with the Amin's [*sic*] State Research Bureau, which carried out extrajudicial killings of suspected enemies of the state."

It was a smear, and Alaka knew it. The detective had died at home in West Nile, of AIDS, as most people involved with the case knew, and he'd been younger than forty at the time of his death, meaning he'd been a child when Amin ruled and thus far too young to be involved with the secret police. But Uganda's lax record-keeping made it difficult to disprove even the most ludicrous accusations.

Maligning the dead man served a purpose for the defense. During the battle over the confessions the burden would fall on the prosecution to prove that the police had acted properly in securing the defendants' admissions of guilt. More than just lodging the suggestion that Orijabo had crafted the confessions, Alaka was setting him up as an alternate villain, in the style of those TV defense lawyers he emulated. Why did the confessions contain all those details that only the killer would know? Orijabo had put them there. How had Anyule and Gille known where Laki's body was buried? Orijabo had told them. How did the private detective know? Because he was the real killer.

The stage was set for a climactic showdown. Then, abruptly, the trial screeched to a halt. Alaka disappeared. For several days, everyone assembled at court and waited for him. He failed to materialize in court but surfaced on the national television news, sitting amid a delegation of grizzled men in military fatigues at a peacemaking ceremony up north. It turned out that the UNRF II, the rebel group he was representing, had decided to make a deal with the government. The force's original list of demands had been rather exorbitant: for West Nile, new roads, two universities, a rural electrification project and an international airport; for themselves, army commissions and four cabinet posts; for Idi Amin, the opportunity to return from exile under a grant of amnesty; for Gowon, a call for an end to "witch-hunting." In the end, the rebel commander had settled for a government payment of around two million dollars. Alaka had rushed off to West Nile to negotiate the details, and to make sure he got his cut of the settlement money.

Justice Mukiibi was furious. Back in court, the judge scowled at the empty defense table.

"Where is your lawyer?" he asked Gowon.

The general shook his head.

"It is unfortunate. He abandons court without a word," the judge said. "Maybe I will read a newspaper and find out what is happening."

Meanwhile, Justice Mukiibi had been reading Gowon's statement to police. He'd fixed on the passage where the general tried to pass the blame on to the lower-ranking soldiers. The judge advised Anyule and Gille that it was in their best interests to get another lawyer. Through their translators, the two soldiers resisted: Alaka was their tribesman. Surely, they said, such a talented young man wouldn't do his elders harm.

"My lord, the lawyer accepted to help us and I am begging this court to wait," Anyule said.

"My lord, it is like a farmer who plows his field and plants his crops," said Gille. "Now, if he leaves it to another to pick the crops, he will not harvest them properly."

Justice Mukiibi held up a copy of the general's police statement. "Gowon says, 'If Mohammed Anyule and Nasur Gille killed Eliphaz

Laki, they did it on their own and they should stand trial for it.' How can you have the same lawyer?" the judge asked. "I think if you farm in Arua, you cannot stand in three gardens at the same time."

In late February 2003, over the defendants' lonely objections, Justice Mukiibi adjourned the trial indefinitely, until administrators could enlist suitable court-appointed attorneys for Anyule and Gille. The delay lasted five months.

During this period, Gowon was in anguish. He was penniless. The government had long since cut off the stipend that had been his main source of income. His friend the attorney general had given him a little money, as had an American who worked with a Quaker organization called the Alternatives to Violence Project, with which Gowon had been associated in the years before he was arrested. But it wasn't nearly enough. Well-wishers in Kampala contributed to a defense fund. But one of Gowon's sons absconded with the money. The general had pledged a home he owned as collateral to Caleb Alaka. But the current occupant of the house, one of his several wives, had asked for a divorce, and now that Gowon was in prison she'd filed a civil suit claiming ownership of the property.

Alone and frightened, the general saw enemies everywhere. He was convinced that his arrest was the result of an ornate plot. Ironically, considering his lawyer's appeal to ethnic solidarity, Gowon believed that the prime conspirator was one of his tribesmen, an old rival from Amin's high command, Brigadier Moses Ali. During the 1980s, Ali had set himself up as a warlord in southern Sudan, putting him in a position to negotiate favorable terms for his homecoming. Museveni had agreed to integrate Ali's forces into the new Ugandan army and had made the rebel leader a general. Ali had since positioned himself as an influential political boss and held the title of deputy prime minister. The brigadier had villas and wives and mistresses all over Kampala.

To Gowon, it seemed perverse: Museveni's government offered the greatest rewards to those who had most violently opposed it. "We didn't come home like those who came with the gun," he complained. "We came without any condition. Yet we who came in peace, we are the sufferers, while those who came as rebels, they are enjoying."

Gowon and Ali had hated each other for decades. People said they'd originally fallen out over a woman, but their feud had since expanded to Shakespearean dimensions. Ali believed Gowon had been behind his purge from Amin's inner circle back in 1978, as well as a subsequent attempt to assassinate him. Once back in Kampala after their exile, they had resumed their feud as if nothing had happened in the meantime. Gowon believed that Ali had diverted some government funds that Museveni had earmarked for his charity, Good Hope, and had then arranged for his arrest in order to keep him quiet about the embezzlement. At the time, Ali was serving as Uganda's minister of internal affairs, which oversaw the police force. Gowon recounted how the night he was arrested, Ali had made a trip down to the jail just to enjoy the pleasure of seeing him behind bars.

(Ali denied that the visit occurred. "I didn't even know he was arrested," Gowon's rival maintained, until he had read it in the newspaper.)

"I have no problems with the government," Gowon swore, even as he sat in prison. "The only problems for me are with the former Amin workers inside Museveni's government." He seemed genuinely to be unable to imagine, even for a moment, that perhaps he'd been brought to trial on the basis of evidence and testimony—that he might be judged for what he'd actually done. When you looked at it from the general's perspective, it made perfect sense. In Amin's day, there had been no such thing as justice, only conspiracy. Uganda now had courts and laws and judges, but the rule of law remained a remote abstraction. For such a thing to exist, power must occasionally yield to justice. And if experience had taught Yusuf Gowon anything, it was that power could never submit.

20

JUDGMENT

Of course, the supreme injustice was that the man who was truly responsible for Eliphaz Laki's murder would never appear in any courtroom. Idi Amin lived in a villa in the Saudi Arabian city of Jeddah, fat and unmolested, under the protection of the Islamic kingdom's monarchy. In 1989, he'd made a desultory attempt to fight his way back to Uganda from Congo, never making it out of the capital, Kinshasa, where he was identified and deported by the immigration authorities, but since then he seemed to have contented himself with living out a leisurely retirement. He studied the Koran and watched satellite television. He visited a masseur at the Intercontinental Hotel. He was sometimes glimpsed driving a white Chevrolet Caprice.

"Do you feel any remorse?" the Italian journalist Riccardo Orizio asked Amin, in a rare postouster interview published in 2002.

"No," he replied. "Only nostalgia."

Amin's lavish impunity provoked remarkably little outrage in Uganda. The majority of the country's population hadn't even been born in 1979. This generation, the Museveni generation, wasn't fully aware of the country's past. "Young people now don't know Amin," said one top government minister, a former resistance fighter. "And some of them can't believe that we could have a government of that deplorable quality. They don't believe."

During the summer of 2003, as the trial of Yusuf Gowon languished in limbo, Ugandans were captivated by another kind of spectacle. Each evening, in bars and living rooms around the country, they gathered around television sets to watch a reality show called *Big Brother Africa*. The program, which was broadcast via satellite on one of the South African TV networks that had penetrated every corner of the continent, followed the arguments and flirtations of a dozen twentysomethings locked in a house full of cameras. The twist on the familiar formula was that each contestant came from a different African nation. The series' undisputed star was the Ugandan entry, Gaetano Kaggwa, a lanky, lascivious law student. His exploits included a tryst with one of the show's female housemates, an event Uganda's state-owned newspaper, the *New Vision*, played on its front page with photos. "Ugandans seized on him as the new national icon," a political columnist wrote, approvingly noting that this celebrity had garnered "more coverage in the British tabloid press than any other Ugandan in nearly 25 years"—since Amin, in other words. When *Big Brother Africa* ended its run, tens of thousands of Kampalans spilled into the streets to welcome Gaetano Kaggwa home from the airport, in the capital's largest spontaneous celebration since the day of Amin's coup.

Moving past Amin, however, was not the same as forgetting him. One Sunday morning in August, Ugandans awoke to the newspaper headline: AMIN IN COMA. Far away, in a Saudi hospital, the exiled dictator was dying of kidney failure.

The news was an abrupt reminder of the past—and a disruptive intrusion on the unsettled present. With Amin on his deathbed, his supporters felt emboldened to voice long-stifled feelings of affection. Muslim politicians called on the government to allow the dictator to return from exile so he could die at home, or at the very least, to bring his body back for a state funeral once he expired. Many ordinary Ugandans seemed ready to forgive the dying man or even to deny he had done anything requiring forgiveness. Newspapers canvassed Kampala's bars and street corners. "Every African leader makes mistakes," a salesman told the *Monitor*. "I would give him my vote if he recovers and wants to run for president," said a taxi driver. "People say he killed so many people, but I think there is no leader who has not killed," said a shop owner. Such sentiments were not universal, or even in the majority opinion, but Amin's defenders spoke at a volume that tended to drown out more reasoned views.

The sympathetic response was not simply confined to the dictator's tribesmen or coreligionists. A great many Ugandans still thought of Amin as the nationalist who had kicked out Asian merchants, proclaiming that he would redistribute economic power to black Africans. He symbolized a vanished era, one that, for all its horrors, still represented the one time in Uganda's history when the country had dared to challenge the world's great powers. President Museveni, who often derided his predecessor's "stupidity," was initially dismissive of valedictory sentiments. "I would not bury Amin," he told the newspapers. "I will never touch him. Never. Not even with a very long spoon." But such remarks sparked an extraordinary public outcry. Some Ugandans felt their current president was being callous and vindictive toward his predecessor. Reports went around that Museveni had threatened to "arrest the dead body" of Amin if it arrived at the airport. A *Monitor* editorial cartoon caricatured the president as an overzealous judge, pounding his gavel and declaring, "Amin must be tried now," as the uniformed general lay on a hospital stretcher. The outrage was such that Museveni, who seldom conceded any point to his critics, was forced to retreat, calling a defensive press conference to announce that the dictator could be buried in Uganda.

As Amin remained in his coma for several weeks, the national newspapers devoted front-page headlines to the slightest updates on his health condition. He was on life support. His vital organs were failing. Fattened by years of easy living and frequent deliveries of his favorite Ugandan foods, he was said to weigh more than four hundred pounds. His wives and children, dispersed around the world, rushed to Saudi Arabia to be by his bedside. Up in West Nile, the *New Vision* reported, some of the dictator's more distant relatives gathered at the family farm on the outskirts of the provincial capital of Arua. They marked out a burial plot and started to make preparations for an anticipated state funeral.

Despite the dire news reports, many people up in West Nile still held out hope for the return of a living, breathing, mighty Amin. For several years before he fell ill, the exiled dictator had sent money to his extended family to build him a retirement home outside Arua, in the hope that Uganda's government would allow him to return from Saudi Arabia to spend his last years at home. The invitation had never come, much to the Amin family's disgruntlement, but the house was complete: a modestly scaled structure roofed with blue-tinted sheet metal and surrounded by a barbed-wire fence.

One sunny West Nile morning, I paid a visit to the dictator's retirement home. Out in the farmhouse's front yard, dozens of women in colorful finery were sitting vigil, while a steady stream of well-wishers—the president's former chief of protocol, an ex-bodyguard—came ambling up the dirt path, seeking the latest news from the family spokesman, Captain Amule Amin, one of the dictator's brothers. "He is improving," Amule assured the visitors. "He is a fit and strong man."

When Amin ruled, Ugandans had called his people the *mafuta mingi*, a Swahili term that translates as "the very fat." The people of West Nile, always desperately poor and treated dismissively by the comparatively wealthy southern tribes, had gorged themselves on all they could acquire, confiscating homes and businesses, forming syndicates to smuggle coffee, cotton and other cash crops, enriching themselves even as the rest of the economy collapsed. Now it was all gone. Amule, who bore a certain resemblance to his brother—same squarish face, same robust voice—had once been a helicopter pilot. "Now we survive by digging," he said. By *digging*, he meant farming. When I met him, Amule had just come in from the fields, where he had been erecting fence posts, and his hands and clothes were caked with mud. He offered a tour of the farm, proceeding past fields of corn, sweet potatoes, peanuts and cassava, to a collection of jagged brick pillars assembled around a patch of broken concrete and some skeletal walls flecked with turquoise paint. These were the ruins of President Amin's country estate, which had been looted and leveled long ago by the returned exiles of the liberation army. A single scrawny cow was grazing on the grass sprouting through its cracked foundation.

"We understand those who talk bad about Amin, especially the authorities," Amule said. "They fear him because he is popular. If he comes back, he may change things upside-down here."

Over the course of my extensive journeys through West Nile, I was to repeat the same macabre home tour many times. Amin's aged henchmen all wanted me to see the remnants of the fine residences they built during their time in power, not the new, more modest homes they had built close by. The former vice president, General Mustafa Adrisi—a man who had once siphoned so much money from state coffers that he earned the nickname "Mr. Foreign Exchange"—sorrowfully recounted how his three-house complex near the Sudanese border had been dynamited by the liberators, and then asked for a donation to help rebuild it. Another general, living in a thatched hut next to a wrecked, weed-covered mansion, said, "This is what life is. Up to down."

The upended sentiment extended far beyond the small circle that had benefited most from the dictatorship. Throughout West Nile, people felt that while Amin may have been a tyrant, at least he was *their* tyrant: a son of the soil, a kinsman. When he ruled they were fat; now they were thin. When he ruled they had jobs; now they had none.

When he ruled they were strong; now they were weak. When he ruled they mattered; now, they hardly counted at all. Tribe trumped truth, grievance obviated guilt. Nostalgia was all they had.

In the remote village of Ladonga, there stood the shell of yet another ransacked mansion—Yusuf Gowon's. Ladonga, the imprisoned general's birthplace, was still home to many of his relatives, who had erected huts around the remains of their favorite son's estate. On the floor of what had once been Gowon's spacious living room, the villagers had set out white chunks of cassava to dry in the sun. When I visited, a dozen or so villagers gathered, squatting on papyrus mats, to tell their story of treacherous reversal.

In the old days, the villagers said, Gowon had been an inspiration to all his kinsmen. When he'd become a ranking military officer, every able-bodied man in Ladonga had rushed to join the army. He'd paid school tuition for many local children. He'd built a primary school and a medical clinic in the village—both of which had been destroyed in 1979. When Gowon returned from exile fifteen years later, the village had thrown a joyous feast. "It was the government that called him home, and it was the same government that arrested him," said Sheik Noah Safi, the imam of the local mosque, who acted as a spokesman for the group. "We feel like he was betrayed."

The trial of Gowon and his two codefendants had sparked a huge outcry in West Nile—one that had foreshadowed, in many ways, the national argument over the proper way to commemorate Amin's death. After Gowon's arrest, there had been vituperative attacks on the government in public meetings and on the radio, and even threats of rebellion. People saw the prosecution as the product of ethnic retribution, or personal animus, or even simple greed.

Many condemned not the three tribesmen who'd been accused of the murder, but the two who had been instrumental in solving it: the private detectives Alfred Orijabo and Brian Tibo. Gowon's defense had accused Orijabo of misconduct—and even of committing the crime himself. His junior partner, Tibo, had suffered ostracism. He came from the same town as one of the defendants, Mohammed Anyule, and shortly after the arrests, the elders of their common tribal clan called a meeting to inveigh against the actions of the locally born investigators. "They said, there are some sons of the soil, some young men, who have decided to make a living by causing problems to the elders in the area, arresting them and handing them over to the government to be hanged," said Tibo, who was apprised of the clan meeting by his father, who was present. As a result, the detective was no longer welcome to visit his ancestral region, and his family members had been shunned. In the view of his own people, Tibo was the worst kind of traitor.

His hometown, and Anyule's, was a place called Yumbe. Anyule's small house was located on the outskirts; it too stood in front of a gutted Amin-era residence. When I paid a visit, Anyule's family members said they had no idea what had become of their beloved *hajji*. He'd just disappeared. So Ibrahim Duke, a relative of Gowon's who was my guide through West Nile, gave a speech beneath a gnarled mango tree, summarizing the events of the trial so far. Anyule's wife Naima, who looked sickly and morose, told him she was unable to afford schooling for her ragged little children. (Anyule claimed to have fathered thirty-five offspring in numerous marriages.) The chairman of the local council railed against Brian Tibo. "He is originally from here," the politician said angrily. "His parents are here."

No one could fathom why the *hajji*, a local activist in the president's ruling party, had been so mistreated. "He campaigned for Museveni," the chairman said. "He was supporting the government. What happened? These very people came to arrest him."

People in West Nile weren't truly shocked that the arrests had occurred—it was only natural, in their view, for the powerful to persecute the meek—but what they couldn't believe was the government's justification, this notion that the prosecution was the product of some unseen force called justice. Standing before his own half-destroyed mansion, which he'd partially re-roofed and reoccupied, a retired lieutenant colonel named Musa Eyaga—one of the key organizers of the 1971 coup—told me that no one in West Nile accepted all this official talk about the rule of law. "The president always says that he has excused these people who have done something wrong. So why was Gowon arrested?" he asked. "If something happened, it was an invasion, war. Why did they throw Gowon inside? Why? If something happens to this present government and they hear it is me who is doing it, will they leave it alone? No, they will kill me!"

"We have become worried," Amin's man hissed. "We are looking at our footsteps."

As Amin lingered between life and death, Gowon's trial finally reconvened at the High Court in Kampala. After five months of delays, the general's codefendants had been assigned new lawyers: Patrick Nyakana representing Nasur Gille, and Arthur Katongole for Mohammed Anyule. The two defendants had only accepted their court-appointed defenders after a long period of strenuous objections. Both lawyers were non-tribesmen and neither spoke their clients' native tongue, Lugbara. The accused men felt they couldn't trust such strangers to their tribe.

Their fears weren't entirely unwarranted. "My loyalties are divided on this case," Arthur Katongole admitted. A genteel sixty-year-old who spoke smooth mission school English and favored corduroy jackets even in the African heat, he had been educated in Mbarara at the same Protestant high school that Eliphaz Laki had attended, and one of his former teachers had been murdered by Amin. Nonetheless, he said he believed that every accused criminal deserved a committed defense. The government didn't make it easy for him, though. There was no formal public defender system in Uganda. Katongole and Nyakana had been drafted into service by the courthouse administrators because they were experienced, available and willing to work for the paltry government retainer, around two hundred dollars. (Long after the trial ended, they were still waiting for their checks.)

Katongole had only been afforded a weekend to prepare for the trial, and he couldn't communicate directly with his suspicious client. But he was still optimistic about an acquittal, primarily because Justice Moses Mukiibi was a Muslim. "You see," the lawyer explained, "most of these people still think of Amin's regime as their regime."

Caleb Alaka was no longer so sure of the outcome. Newly returned from his peacemaking mission up north, Gowon's defense attorney was worried about his new cocounsels. "Katongole is exclusively a criminal lawyer," he said, "but not a very good one." In the courtroom, Alaka tried to manage the defense team, whispering instructions in their ears, but there was only so much he could control. When the prosecution introduced Anyule's confession, Katongole neglected to raise his client's claim that he was coerced by the police, and Justice Mukiibi promptly admitted the written statement into evidence.

"He's made blatant mistakes," a fuming Alaka said later.

"I was tricked by the judge!" Katongole protested.

This was a grave setback for the defense: The prosecution had essentially made half of its case. "Anyule may be convicted," Alaka said in grim assessment. The prosecution's burden of proof now rested solely on the slumped shoulders of Nasur Gille. When the chief prosecutor introduced Gille's confession, Patrick Nyakana rose to offer a feeble objection. "It was not voluntarily made," the lawyer said in a barely audible voice. "It was obtained by force and threats." Alaka jumped up to make his own argument, but Justice Mukiibi silenced him on the grounds that Sergeant Gille was no longer his client.

"If I leave Gille to go, then my client will go!" Alaka shouted in frustration.

Once Justice Mukiibi determined that the defense had serious grounds to contest the legality of Sergeant Gille's confession, he adjourned the main proceedings and convened the trial-within-a-trial. Ugandan law called for both the defendant who made the confession and the investigators who interrogated him to testify at this evidentiary hearing. Three police officers took the stand, and they all lied—baldly, repeatedly and unconvincingly. The policemen went to great lengths to obscure the involvement of the private detectives. They also dissembled about the timeline of the investigation. Under Ugandan law, police were not supposed to hold suspects for longer than forty-eight hours without charging them. So the police corporal who had arrested the men fibbed about the dates he'd brought them in, even though anyone flipping through the police file available at court could see they'd spent more than two days in custody.

"Dates are tricky," testified Detective Superintendent Victor Aisu, the police official who oversaw the case.

Aisu spent several days on the witness stand. A hulking fifty-two-year-old with a pockmarked face, he wore dark suits affixed with a small lapel pin that said "F.B.I.," a souvenir from a course he'd once attended at the agency's training center in Quantico, Virginia. A thirty-year veteran of the police force, he gave off the confident air of someone used to wielding authority. Jocularly discussing his methods of interrogation in an interview, Aisu explained that "all these criminals will never remember anything if you don't use a bit of force." Aisu liked to say he had "a knack for telling the truth," but Justice Mukiibi appeared to be of the opposite view. By the end of the police official's testimony, the judge could no longer hide how dubious he was, referring to the witness, sarcastically, as "the omnipotent Mr. Aisu."

The judge's skepticism was likely informed by Aisu's professional reputation. In a force full of scoundrels, he'd distinguished himself. A highly publicized government corruption inquiry three years before had alleged that Aisu had bungled—perhaps deliberately—a murder investigation that seemed to implicate a politically connected Kampala hotel magnate, had pocketed cash seized in connection with the case and had improperly returned a gun and ammunition to the same businessman, evidence connected to a second shooting. The inquiry had recommended that the detective superintendent be charged with "neglect of duty." Aisu did not comment on the accusations, which were subject to an ongoing disciplinary procedure, but denied he had done anything wrong.

Two individuals involved in the defense team claimed that early in the trial, Aisu had approached Alaka outside the courthouse and had struck up a friendly conversation, suggesting that Gowon's legal troubles could "be worked out." Alaka took this as a suggestion that the policeman would alter his testimony for a price. (Aisu denied saying any such thing.) According to Alaka, the bribery discussions went nowhere. "The truth is, these guys are too poor," he said. Throughout the trial, though, the lawyer did give Aisu and all the other police witnesses small daily sums for "lunch," even as they were testifying against his client. "This is our African culture," one of Gowon's relatives explained, saying he doubted the small gifts affected the officers' testimony.

On the stand, Aisu recounted his version of Gille's interrogation. "He was quite responsive," the detective superintendent testified. "He did not complain of anything." Aisu did, however, conflict with the other prosecution witnesses on one minor point, saying that he'd ordered the suspect to sit on the floor as he was questioned, as "a sign of the authority of the police," rather than offering him a chair as the other policemen recollected. The defense attacked this bit of contradictory testimony, saying it proved the police were covering up more serious abuses of the suspect's rights.

Later that day, Gille stood in the witness box, his arms crossed and his lips pursed, as his attorney questioned him about his encounter with Victor Aisu. "He didn't talk. It was Orijabo who talked," the defendant said in raspy Lugbara, rendered into English by a translator. "It was only Orijabo who told me I should tell the truth, that it was a very serious case, that if I didn't tell the truth I would be killed."

Caleb Alaka scratched written questions on scraps of paper and handed them to Gille's attorney, who read them aloud.

"How did you feel?" the lawyer asked.

"I was only thinking about what they told me, that I would be killed, and secondly I was feeling very, very hungry."

According to Gille's version of events, he was imprisoned without food for several days while Orijabo, acting on behalf of Duncan Laki, attempted to break down his resistance. "Orijabo said that I should tell the truth, that he was a Lugbara," the defendant testified. He said his tribesman had taken advantage of his weakened state, plying him with promises of leniency. "Orijabo told me to state the truth because it was not me who was wanted," the witness testified. "It was Gowon who was wanted."

Gille claimed it was Orijabo who'd taken him into the office where he'd finally given the police his confession. Gille said that when he'd been reluctant to sign the statement, Orijabo had pulled out a pistol. "[He said] that I should not take this thing lightly," the witness testified. "The person I had killed was related to President Museveni."

Gille claimed that he was terrified, and had given in. A police officer had uncuffed one of his hands, and he'd signed each of the nine pages of the confession.

Prosecutor Simon Mugenyi knew the interrogation procedure presented a problem. Even the police department's version of events raised serious legal questions. According to the police, Gille had admitted his guilt in Swahili to Aisu, who had then ordered another policeman, who spoke Lugbara, to take down the confession in the suspect's own language. That officer, however, admitted on the stand that the "Lugbara statement" was not a word-for-word transcription. Rather, the officer testified that he had "guided" the suspects in making their admissions. When Gille had been brought in to him, the policeman recounted, they'd had a long chat, which he'd summarized on paper. He'd then asked the sergeant to read and sign the confession as he'd rendered it. Even the prosecutor conceded to the judge that these methods were "very unorthodox."

Mugenyi had been looking forward to the evidentiary hearing, however, because it offered him the opportunity to cross-examine Gille under oath. Whatever the weaknesses of the confessions, if he could bait the defendant into admitting his involvement in the murder—an action that in the past he'd been eager to defend—the case would be all but won. He figured he could best the semiliterate soldier in a battle of wits.

Mugenyi flapped the written confession in the defendant's face.

"Is that what you signed?" the prosecutor asked.

"Yes, that is what I signed," the defendant replied.

"How many times did you sign? Look at it."

Gille flipped through the pages. "Nine times," he said.

"I put it to you, Gille, that you were never forced to sign the statement," the prosecutor said. "You were never threatened at all, by anybody!"

Mugenyi went on like that, berating the witness, trying to prod him into an emotional outburst. But with each confrontational question, Gille's jaw line tightened and his resolve seemed to harden. His responses were terse, even petulant, but he never broke.

"I am putting it to you that you are telling this court lies," the prosecutor said. "Orijabo was never there."

"I am the one who was there, and I am telling it to you," the defendant replied.

Mugenyi bore in on Sergeant Gille's claim that fear had motivated him to sign the confession.

"Why were you afraid?" the prosecutor asked.

"I was afraid because Orijabo said we had killed a person," the defendant replied.

"Is it true or not that you killed a person?"

"That is not true."

"Why didn't you say, 'That is not true?'" the prosecutor asked.

"Something about death is something that is not good," Gille answered. "So that is why I got scared."

"Let me put it to you," the prosecutor said. "The reason that you got scared is because you knew that at long last the long arm of the law had caught up to you. Because you *knew* you killed a person."

"That is not true," the witness replied.

Three days after Gille's testimony, on August 16, 2003, Idi Amin Dada died. He never knew the exact date of his birth, but the best estimates say he was around eighty years old.

Even from the grave, Amin continued to divide Ugandans. The front page of the *New Vision* newspaper featured a giant, glowering picture of the dictator and, under the stark headline AMIN IS DEAD, a quotation from Isaiah:

> Now you are as weak as we are! You are one of us! You used to be honored with the music of harps, but now you are in the world of the dead. You lie on a bed of maggots and are covered with a blanket of worms.

"I am not mourning at all," President Museveni said at a public event in Soroti, an eastern town. "What did he achieve? What did he do for

Uganda? What will he be remembered for?" the president asked the crowd.

"That he killed," his audience responded.

Meanwhile, hundreds of mourners gathered at the main mosque in Kampala to say the traditional Muslim prayers for the dead. The weeks of public argument about Amin's funeral had turned out to be moot. The Saudi government had swiftly buried the exiled dictator in Mecca, Islam's holiest city, a solution the mourners found appropriate.

"This is a sad moment not only for Muslims worldwide, but for Uganda," a member of parliament from West Nile said in an address to the prayer service. "We have lost a loving brother. How the world looks on Amin fulfills the saying that leadership is a dustbin. When you are gone, everything bad is heaped on you."

Four days after Amin's death, amid all the extravagant valedictions and repudiations, Justice Moses Mukiibi delivered his decision on the legality of Sergeant Nasur Gille's confession. It was a gloomy, rain-soaked afternoon, and the courtroom gallery was full for the first time in months. Even as the audience waited for the judge to appear, an estimated two thousand people were marching through the town of Arua, en route to a memorial service at the Amin family farm. "Some people are saying Amin was bad because he killed people," one of his generals said at the ceremony. "This cannot help now. It is just bad politics." The prosecution supporters in Justice Mukiibi's courtroom were hoping that the judge would render a different judgment on Amin's legacy, a condemnation of at least one atrocity inflicted in the dictator's name.

A wooden door behind the judge's bench opened, and the gallery leaped to its feet as Justice Mukiibi entered the courtroom. He sat down and pulled out a sheaf of papers. "All right," he began. "This is the ruling."

Justice Mukiibi read his decision out loud in his booming voice, periodically pausing to wipe the corners of his mouth with a white handkerchief. "The onus is always on the prosecution to prove the admissibility of any statement by an accused person," he said. "Such onus never shifts to the accused."

The judge recapped the circumstances that led to Gille's confession. He believed the defendant's claim that he was kept in custody for a longer period than the police were admitting, which would in consequence make the arresting officer "a liar." As Mukiibi spoke, a groan emanated from the prosecution's table. Simon Mugenyi was sprawled across his bench, his arms stretched wide, his eyes closed, his head tilted toward the ceiling.

The judge picked out some additional inconsistencies in the police officers' testimony before turning to the issue of Alfred Orijabo. Punching the consonants of the detective's name in a way that conveyed profound contempt, he said he didn't believe that Orijabo had been a peripheral player, as the prosecution contended. "In my view," he said, "Alfred Orijabo was powerful during the police investigations and he played a role which the prosecution witnesses were not willing to disclose."

When it came to the validity of the confession itself, Mukiibi seized on the police officer's admission that he hadn't made a verbatim transcript of Gille's statement in Lugbara. "Learned counsel for the state referred to the manner in which it was recorded as 'unorthodox,'" the judge read, his voice rising as he came to his conclusion. "I find it difficult to say with certainty that these are the accused's words." He went on.

> In my view, the statement was rendered open to inclusion of foreign matter at the instance of [the police]. On this ground alone I should reject the statement. I also find that Alfred Orijabo played a clandestine but important role in the police investigations, and particularly in the arrest and bringing of the accused to Kampala. Since the prosecution witnesses did not on their own come out clean and disclose Orijabo's exact role, a lot is left to conjecture.
>
> A lot of doubts are left as to his role in bringing the accused to record the Lugbara statement. I cannot determine with certainty what Orijabo did not do. The prosecution witnesses have not assisted in clearing the doubts raised by the accused's evidence. I hold that the prosecution has failed to discharge the onus in proving that the Lugbara statement was voluntary.

Mukiibi ruled out Gille's confession.

The judge gaveled the hearing closed and walked briskly back out the courtroom door. Over at the prosecution table, Mugenyi disconsolately filed away his papers. "That winds up our case then," he said. "It's all academic now, really."

Over at the jubilant defense table, Alaka and his cocounsels were accepting backslaps and congratulations. I asked Arthur Katongole if he was surprised by the judge's ruling.

"Not really, for reasons other than legal," the court-appointed defender replied. He gave me a knowing look, and said, "It's terrible what's happening in Baghdad and Jerusalem." The day before, Islamic militants had driven a truck bomb into the United Nations headquarters in Iraq, killing the organization's top envoy there along with twenty-one others, while in Israel a suicide bomber had blown a bus to bits. "I think the world is coming to a point where it is divided into two sections," Katongole said.

Nasur Gille grinned as the courtroom guards led him out of the dock.

The trial petered along for a few weeks, like a stubborn cold or a bad relationship, over but not yet finished. Alaka, whose interest in Gowon's case had expired sometime in February, disappeared for good after Gille's confession was thrown out. He was last sighted boarding a helicopter with President Museveni's brother, Lieutenant General Salim Saleh, heading north to try to lure leaders of the Lord's Resistance Army, another rebel group, into peace talks. When Gowon's relatives tried reaching his cell phone, the lawyer disguised his voice and said that Mr. Alaka was too busy to answer. The court appointed another attorney to represent Gowon for the remainder of the case.

Chief prosecutor Simon Mugenyi soldiered on, examining witnesses and introducing exhibits that everyone knew would have no effect on the outcome. "We are just going through the motions," he said. Even the conviction of Anyule, whose confession had been deemed admissible, was unlikely in the absence of additional corroborating evidence. Mugenyi was bitter about the collapse of his prosecution. He blamed the judge, his witnesses and even Duncan Laki, whose understandable impatience to exhume his father's body had created unintended evidentiary obstacles. "Duncan really messed up this case," the angry prosecutor said at the end of yet another dispiriting court session.

Finally, the prosecution rested. "What do you want?" Justice Mukiibi asked Mugenyi, leaning back in his swivel chair. "This is a case where the body was not found. We had high hopes for a DNA test. . . . There is no grave, no bones, no dead body, nothing to connect where these fellows went"—meaning the murder scene—"with the crime. What connects them to Laki?"

"Well, my lord, it has been a hard case for the prosecution," Mugenyi replied.

"You go talk to the DPP," Justice Mukiibi said, referring to Mugenyi's boss, the director of public prosecutions.

The judge's message was clear: He was offering the prosecution a chance to withdraw the indictment. Otherwise, he was going to acquit the defendants for lack of evidence. Dropping the case at this juncture offered the prosecution a slight strategic advantage, because the defendants could be charged again at some later date without violating their double jeopardy protections. There was always a chance, however minuscule, that one day some new piece of evidence would come to light and the case could be revived.

As the prosecution weighed the difficult decision, Duncan returned to Uganda. He was scheduled to interview at the Foreign Ministry for a job with the Ugandan delegation to the United Nations in New York. He got in touch with Simon Mugenyi, who invited him in to the office, where the prosecutor broke the news. Duncan did not take it well. He didn't want to see the case dropped. He wanted a verdict, even if it was "not guilty."

Over dinner after his difficult meeting with the prosecutors, Duncan tried to conceal his disappointment. "I want these guys to always be looking over their shoulders," he said, echoing the prosecutors' reasoning. "That is punishment enough." But he couldn't keep up the pretense for long. As he talked, the stoic veneer dropped: He couldn't understand how the police and prosecution had managed to deflate what he saw as an airtight case. "I wanted them to be held accountable," Duncan said, plaintively. But what about those, I asked, who believed accountability was less important than peace?

"What peace?" Duncan snapped in reply.

A little after noon on September 25, 2003, the trial convened for the final time. There was a healthy crowd on hand inside the courtroom, mostly people from West Nile. Duncan, dressed in a dark blue suit, sat with a small group of family members in the third row. The defendants were waiting sullenly near the dock, apparently unaware of what was about to take place.

Justice Mukiibi entered, all rose and Simon Mugenyi announced the prosecution's decision to withdraw the indictment. Behind him, Duncan stuck out his lower lip and struggled to control his tears. For several minutes the courtroom was completely silent as the judge wrote out an order. Finally, Justice Mukiibi spoke.

"I hereby discharge the accused persons," he said, reading out the defendants' names, ranks and army serial numbers, "and direct that the accused persons . . . be released from prison immediately."

As the judge's words were translated into Swahili and Lugbara, Anyule, standing in the dock, buried his face in his hands in joy and disbelief. Gille raised his palms upward in the air and said a Muslim prayer of thanksgiving. Gowon clasped his hands together and made a little bow in the direction of the judge.

Guards led the three defendants downstairs to the court's basement holding cell, which was kept shut by a big medieval-looking padlock. After a brief wait for some paperwork, the lock was opened, and the accused men were released. They emerged into a drizzle and were immediately swallowed by a throng of cheering relatives. Yusuf Gowon's daughter danced an impromptu jig in celebration, before getting on her cell phone to share the good news with relatives in West Nile. Anyule gave an emotional speech in Swahili, giving praise to President Museveni for setting him free.

Back upstairs in the courtroom, Duncan was standing with his family, hardly able to hold himself together. It was a private moment, so I left. I walked back to my car with another relative of Laki's, his cousin Kenneth Kereere. "If they have any conscience, which I think they have because they confessed, they know they are guilty and the court has not found them innocent," he said as we trudged through the rain. "It's sad for me to look at these three murderers and they just walk away like that, but that's the rule of law. We have to accept the rule of law. It hurts but . . . what can we do?"

Yusuf Gowon, enveloped by a crowd of cheering relatives ANDREW RICE

21

REPRISE

That evening, Yusuf Gowon returned home to his ramshackle Kampala compound, where his family members had hastily organized a welcoming party. A large crowd of well-wishers gathered to celebrate. Francis Ayume, the attorney general, was there; he told his friend that the people of West Nile had been praying to Allah for his deliverance. Someone else brought a goat to slaughter in thanksgiving. Mohammed Anyule, whose confession had caused all the problems to begin with, also turned up, and Gowon made a public show of offering him forgiveness.

The general spent the next day, his first full one of freedom, receiving a steady stream of congratulatory visitors. Dressed casually in a striped T-shirt, slacks and sandals, he held court on a maroon velour couch that was worn bare in patches, looking relaxed and relieved. The newspapers had reported the prosecution's decision to withdraw the indictment against him as if it was a complete exoneration. "I like the law," the general said, with an air of wonderment. "The former government I was in was blamed for lawlessness, but if someone faces the law like this, the truth will be found out."

Gowon was thankful that Uganda had changed. And perhaps that was the final great irony of this case. Maybe the seed of something remarkable was germinating beneath Uganda's ugly thicket of tangled prejudices and recriminations. Maybe both sides could comprehend the judgment as a manifestation, however flawed, of an attainable ideal called justice. Maybe the trial that had begun as a contest over the legacy of Idi Amin had ended up delivering a verdict about the Uganda of Yoweri Museveni. Eliphaz Laki had been killed for protecting Museveni the rebel. Yet Museveni the president had instituted a legal system that had given Laki's accused killers the benefit of the doubt. In a democracy, sometimes the guilty go free. This imperfection is the price we pay for the protection of the law. That Yusuf Gowon, Mohammed Anyule and Nasur Gille could walk out of their prison cells, into the embrace of family and friends, was perhaps, in a perverse way, a measure of how far Uganda had come since the days of Amin.

"I just wish they had done the same," Duncan Laki said afterward. "I wish they had taken my father to court."

Maybe, though, the lesson of the trial was not really so high-minded. Eliphaz Laki's relatives and tribesmen, and other families of the disappeared, expressed dismay at the judgment. Some placed the blame on Museveni himself. "It is not that these guys did not commit the murder," said Charles Kabagambe, the lawyer who'd taken a close interest in the case because his own father had disappeared in 1972. "It is that the present government does not want to hold them accountable. They appointed a Muslim judge." Duncan did not subscribe to such conspiracy theories. But he took little comfort from some nebulous vindication of the rule of law. At dinner one evening, as he was preparing to fly home to the United States, we talked about all those Ugandans who said it was better to forget the past and forgive what they could.

"I don't think it's forgiveness," Duncan said. "I think it's apathy."

Not surprisingly, Yusuf Gowon saw things differently. Given a reprieve from execution, he expressed a desire to promote reconciliation among Ugandans. "People should respect the government, and people should realize that peace is what is needed in this country," he argued. "We should forgive each other. The reason is that since Amin, 1971, up to now, the governments have all come by the gun and have been removed by the gun. For how long will we be doing that, changing governments by the gun? The scars remain, revenge remains. Destruction of all the projects we built continues. These kinds of things, we should *think*, and stop them in a peaceful manner."

Gowon said he wanted to revive his charitable organization, Good Hope, and was full of ideas for promoting the economic development of West Nile. But the harsh reality was that he had no way to finance his schemes. During his time in prison, he'd run up substantial legal bills. He was about to lose his other Kampala property, the one he'd pledged as collateral to Caleb Alaka, to his estranged wife. His home in Arua, meanwhile, had lost its roof in a storm. Despite all he'd been through, though, Gowon said he was still glad he'd accepted President Museveni's invitation to return from exile. "That man brought me home with a very clean heart," he said. "Let me suffer, let me have my grass house, let me have no friends, but I cannot change and be against him."

Nonetheless, for some time after his release, Gowon was afraid to leave his house for fear that the authorities might rearrest him. But then Uganda's chief prosecutor, Simon Mugenyi's boss, invited the general to his home, served him tea and told him he shouldn't worry. "I am free, free, free," he said afterward, gleefully. Gowon went back to living his life more or less as before. He spent many days wandering around Kampala, visiting relatives, cadging pocket cash, hobnobbing with army friends. Sometimes he returned to Arua, where he eventually managed to replace the roof on his home. He even talked of rebuilding his ruined mansion back in the village of Ladonga, someday when he could afford it.

In 2005, two years after the judgment, I paid one last visit to West Nile. At the time, the intermittent civil war involving the Lord's Resistance Army had flared up again, in part because the new International Criminal Court, based in The Hague, had issued arrest warrants for the LRA's leaders, scuttling peace talks between the rebels and the government. The renewed conflict made it unsafe to drive north, so I bought a ticket for the plane to Arua, a beat-up East Bloc turboprop. It flew beneath the clouds, affording a dioramic view of Uganda. The terraced hills of the south gave way to deep freshwater lakes, which fed into the wide and coruscating Nile, which guided us into the flat, depopulated expanse of the north. The plane set down on a rocky landing strip. ARUA INTERNATIONAL AIRPORT, read the cornerstone of its tiny, shabby terminal, laid by Mobutu Sese Seko in 1976—a comic vestige of one of Amin's cockamamie public works plans.

Gowon met me out on the street that ran by the Arua compound, next to a vacant lot where mechanics were hammering on broken-down cars. He shook my hand warmly and asked for the latest news about the rebels, who were rumored to have crossed into West Nile as they attempted to retreat to their rear base, in a Congolese jungle. "Everywhere guns, everywhere guns," the general said, in a disapproving tone. "I am a military man, but I have learned how bad is that African kind of military behavior."

He looked fully recovered from his prison ordeal. His face was round and glowing, and he'd regained a lot of weight. He welcomed me into his home with an apology about its appearance. "There is no money," he said, as he sat down on a daybed in his living room and kicked off his flip-flops. The room's cracked plaster walls were decorated with signs bearing Arabic devotional messages and a picture of the Kaaba in Mecca. Gowon's daughter came into the room, knelt on the floor and silently placed a tray of warm Coca-Colas and stale donuts between us.

"We want a written history, because these children don't know how the past governments were," the general said. "They think this is the first regime, and this is the first government they know. They don't sit with us elders."

I handed Gowon a folder filled with written history, copies of Ugandan newspaper articles from the 1970s. When he'd heard that I'd found the papers on microfilm at a library in Chicago, he'd asked me to bring them to West Nile; he possessed very few mementoes of his time in power. "These papers, we are no longer seeing them here," Gowon said as he flipped through the folder's contents. He smiled at the sight of a front-page picture of his younger self, giving a toast to Idi Amin. "Yes!" he exclaimed, as he pointed to a headline that read: GOWON ADVISES GOD FEARING PEOPLE.

Time rolled backward as he continued through the stack. There was Amin's triumphant visit to Mbarara after the failed invasion of September 1972. "We were given medals," Gowon said. Then the general came to the most famous photograph of all, first published in Uganda on the day before Eliphaz Laki's disappearance. Beneath the headline THE MBARARA INVASION THAT FAILED, the picture depicted eighteen soldiers with rifles and bayonets standing over the corpses of several dozen supposed rebels. The image was too indistinct to make out any faces, but the caption read, "They were being guarded by Major Gowan [sic] . . . and other soldiers."

"Oh, is that me?" Gowon said, squinting at the picture. "That is me inspecting dead bodies?" He seemed momentarily jarred. "No, it can't be. I never saw any dead bodies."

That was Gowon's story, and he was sticking to it. In the two years since his release from prison, any trace of repentance or introspection had vanished, and he had reverted to his former victimized attitude. He no longer gave any credit to the law or the Museveni government. Fixated on his perilous financial condition, he complained endlessly about other ex-generals who received generous public stipends, and talked of pursuing compensation from the government for wrongful prosecution. He was party to a class action lawsuit against several banks, which sought to recover some fifty million dollars in assets frozen in 1979. He even said he wanted an apology from Duncan Laki. "He is not aware of what peace is," Gowon said. "It could be for me to revenge. Since the witnesses proved nothing, I could be the one to complain. But I will not do that, because it would mean that I am encouraging more problems—inviting more problems to myself."

Gowon spent the afternoon paying calls on friends around Arua, including Nasur Gille, who was back to repairing bicycles on a bolt-strewn patch of dirt near a busy crossroads. In the evening, he went out to dinner with an old army buddy, Major Ratib Mududu. A thick-necked man in his fifties, the major had once been one of Amin's body-guards and was now a prominent figure around Arua, a local elected officeholder. As we sat at an empty outdoor restaurant, eating bowls of chicken stew, the two retired soldiers reminisced about their good times—the money they made, the carousing they did, the mistresses they kept—and lamented their declining fortunes. Mududu said he was still mourning the loss of a son two years before, killed by the army in the Arua town market during a roundup of suspected smugglers. "They shot him in the back," Mududu said. He'd filed a complaint, and court-martial proceedings had been initiated against the soldier who had fired the shot, but nothing had ever happened. His son's killer still patrolled the streets of Arua. He belonged to the same tribe as Museveni. "That's why he was released," the major said. "And it is not only my son. There are many incidents."

"We have been military men since the time of the *wazungu*," Gowon said, using the Swahili term for white people. "Since 1971, there has only been killing."

"There is no African government that does not kill," Mududu added.

"Even we, we live in fear," Gowon said.

Gowon was no longer held behind high walls, but he was still a captive. He was imprisoned by poverty, by weakness and by a worldview that had been warped by dictatorship. He was bound by the memories of the power he had squandered, and of the deeds he had committed to attain it so fleetingly. Most of all, he was a prisoner of paranoia, suspicion of a government that still struck him as capricious and alien. In the end, his long trial had done little to alter his bedrock beliefs. Experience had taught him that in this country, when you were in power, you had everything. Once you were out of power, you were nothing. So when you had power, you did anything to keep it.

"Another unfortunate thing about Africa: All the members of the president's clan inform," Gowon said. "They just pick up the phone and call the president."

"Everyone in the clan becomes the royal family," Mududu said.

As if on cue, another party came into the restaurant, a group of young Africans who carried themselves with the easy confidence of the ruling class. Dressed in khaki slacks and short-sleeved plaid shirts, they wore identification cards hanging from straps around their necks, and were speaking the language of a western tribe. They took a seat at a nearby table, perhaps a bit too close, and ordered a round of beers. To me, the young men looked like they worked for some international aid organization, but Gowon and his friend assumed they were spies. Their conversation suddenly hushed.

After a few uncomfortable moments, one of the drinkers, a boisterous fellow with a clean-shaven head, spoke up. "I know who you are," he said to Major Mududu, with just a hint of condescension in his voice. It went unspoken that back when Mududu was guarding Amin, he had been involved with the intelligence service, and some years ago he'd been publicly accused of participating in the infamous 1977 killing of Janan Luwum, Uganda's Anglican archbishop. Nowadays, though, he was considered harmless, incapable even of holding his own son's killer accountable. The loudmouth westerner introduced Mududu to the rest of his table. Then he called Gowon over. "The commander of Simba Battalion," he announced, intoning the words with mock gravity. Gowon greeted the youngsters awkwardly and returned to the table. We ate the rest of our meal in silence.

At the end of the night, I walked Gowon and his friend to the head of the restaurant's driveway, where we parted ways. I offered to call a cab, but they just laughed. They didn't have that kind of money. So I thanked them for coming and gave them some shillings, enough to hire a couple of bicycle taxis. As we stood there, saying our good-byes, a big SUV roared out the driveway, its high beams blinding: the cocky guys from the restaurant. Gowon and I shook hands. And then they were gone, Idi Amin's bodyguard and his army commander, off into the night to hail bicycles.

An era was ending in Uganda. You could feel it, as if the past's grip was loosening and another hand was asserting itself. One by one, the old protagonists were passing from the scene. In October 2005, Milton

Obote died, after a long and crotchety exile in Zambia. Uganda's government paid him more respect than Idi Amin, flying his body home to be buried and declaring a national day of mourning. As the former president's funeral cortege traveled from the international airport in Entebbe to Kampala, about forty-five minutes away, villagers who still hadn't forgotten the atrocities of the 1980s civil war gathered by the roadside to jeer, waving their arms dismissively as if to say "good riddance." But at a parliamentary memorial service, Yoweri Museveni, who'd often called his predecessor a "killer," laid a wreath on the coffin, bowed his head and delivered a gracious eulogy on the subject of forgiveness. He even suggested that his government would "review the question" of exhuming Amin and bringing him home for a similar state funeral. "For the Ugandans who are still alive, there is time for everything," Museveni said. "The time for reconciliation has long been here but we have not taken advantage of it."

The nation now, unquestionably, belonged to Museveni. He had ruled it for almost as long as all Uganda's previous presidents combined. His supporters called him "The Cotter Pin," after the screw on the bicycle that holds the whole thing together. A growing number of domestic opponents, however, cast a skeptical eye on such claims: True democracy, the critics contended, does not depend on indispensable men. Long ago, Museveni had promised to step aside in 2006, at the end of his second term, in accordance with limits placed in the constitution he himself had enacted. But as the end date neared, Museveni renounced his pledge, pushing a successful referendum to repeal term limits. At the outset of what promised to be a bitter reelection campaign, the aging commander in chief conducted a press conference while working out on a weight machine, as if to signal that he was getting into vigorous fighting shape.

No one doubted the president's tenacity when it came to retaining his hold on power. In the previous campaign, held in 2001, Museveni had faced off against Colonel Kizza Besigye, a veteran of the guerrilla struggle and his former personal physician, in a race that had all the overtones of a palace feud. The election had been marred by the violence of the ruling party's supporters. Besigye had contested the validity of Museveni's victory all the way to the Supreme Court, where he'd lost a close decision, before fleeing to exile in South Africa, saying he feared for his safety. While Besigye was certainly not a passive victim— he went by the nickname The Hammer—Museveni's rough tactics had cost the president the support of many of his longest-standing allies.

When he decided to seek a third term, many of those who spoke loudest in opposition were fellow veterans of the underground resistance, who said the president had betrayed the ideals of their struggle.

"His world outlook has changed," said Augustine Ruzindana, a member of parliament and a fellow survivor of the failed attack on Mbarara in 1972. "There is no doubt that his style of life has changed. He was an ascetic person, very highly disciplined. I think if you discussed something with him and agreed on it, you could rely on that. Now all these things have changed. He likes pomp. I think he likes power for the sake of it. He likes luxury now. He likes money. He has introduced an authoritarianism that was not there. I think that now it's not that he dislikes people who disagree with him. He actually hates them."

To a troubling degree, the political infighting reprised old ethnic divisions, ones that were supposed to have been laid to rest. Museveni had once governed like a consensus-building statesman, but now he was surrounded by a tight circle of loyalists, most of them army officers, many of them members of his Bahima ethnic group. The foremost leaders of the opposition came from the west's Bairu ethnic group. They believed that, far from keeping his promise to conquer tribalism, Museveni had effectively reconstituted Ankole's old class structure on the national level. Yet such grievances were rarely stated openly. The tension between the Bairu and Bahima was one of the few subjects deemed off-limits to Uganda's relatively free press. Around the time of the 2006 presidential campaign, several journalists who published stories about the ethnic dimension of Uganda's political disputes were arrested and charged with "promoting sectarianism."

Museveni still talked of his "resistance struggle." But his underlying ideology had changed. He was now such an unabashed capitalist that he wrote opinion columns for the *Wall Street Journal* about the glories of free trade. He'd made himself an important African ally of President George W. Bush, and he had even supported the invasion of Iraq. He'd cultivated influential friends within the American evangelical movement. Around the same time as Obote's death, Museveni, who as a young revolutionary had written of the "agony of listening to hypocritical messengers of God," had read from the Bible at a teeming all-night revival staged at a Kampala soccer stadium, an event broadcast by religious television networks in both Uganda and the United States.

The passage the president had chosen, from the Gospel of Luke, was a parable Jesus told about a king who rewards his servants for multiplying the dominion's wealth. "I tell you that to everyone who has, more will be given," it concludes. No one could accuse Museveni of failing to practice what he preached. In the early years of his rule, he and his lieutenants had maintained relatively frugal lifestyles, but nowadays, the streets of Kampala were clogged with gleaming new SUVs bearing government plates. Corruption was flourishing, particularly in the army, where the president's hard-living brother, Salim Saleh—a sort of ganja-smoking, gun-toting, Billy Carter figure—held enormous sway. He and other generals mounted campaigns of plunder into neighboring Congo, took kickbacks on deals for faulty weaponry, padded the military payroll with nonexistent soldiers whose wages they pocketed and constructed mansions fit for drug lords atop Kampala's hills. Foreign aid funds that were intended to finance schools and AIDS medications were diverted into ruling party coffers or private pockets.

In the 1990s, President Bill Clinton had hailed Museveni as one of a "new breed" of African leaders, but with each egregious scandal, the future was looking more like the past. At press conferences, Museveni sat in a raised white chair, beneath a large portrait of his own face, and hectored the "rumor-mongering" media. "Stop heckling us," he said. "You don't know about the problem of corruption." A satirical play showing in Kampala dramatized the extent to which the president seemed to have fallen out of touch with public opinion. At the end of the production, the playwright, who was also the lead actor, carted out a series of three papier-mâché busts of Museveni, intended to depict how the president had changed over time. One bust had two ears; the second was missing an ear; the third had no ears at all.

As public discontent mounted, some objective observers had come to believe that Museveni might actually lose the presidential election in 2006, if the opposition fielded a strong challenger. In late October 2005, that challenger arrived. One rainy morning, Colonel Kizza Besigye emerged from the arrivals lounge of the Entebbe International Airport, wearing a white linen suit and a sash that read WELCOME. To the mob of waiting journalists, he said, "I know I am definitely taking risks, but I think the risks I am taking are justified." Then he hopped into a Toyota Land Cruiser for the twenty-five-mile trip to central Kampala, where his supporters had planned a massive rally. Thousands had gathered along the road to offer Besigye a raucous welcome. As the opposition leader waved from the sunroof of his vehicle, supporters mobbed his car. They waved branches and blew whistles as children chanted the initials of Besigye's political party from the windows of their schools. It took the candidate hours to make it to Kampala, where a vast crowd awaited him at the same parade ground where Milton Obote had celebrated independence. In a combative speech, Besigye attacked Museveni for allowing his cronies to grow rich while his country sank deeper into poverty. "We now know we have the votes," the colonel said in his distinctively low, gravelly voice. "If anyone wants to use force to steal our votes, then he will be undertaking the most serious risk of his life."

Ugandans often said that the real test of their country's democracy would come the first time Museveni ever felt a true threat to his predominance. The president, clearly rattled, rushed home from a state visit to London. For the next few weeks, as Besigye barnstormed the country, drawing huge crowds, there were rumors that he'd soon be arrested. There was some evidence that the colonel had considered launching a rebel insurgency after his 2001 defeat, and on his return from exile, he'd pointedly refused to forswear the use of violence in the future. "I'm not a lawyer," Museveni told reporters. "But he must be breaking some law."

Eighteen days after Colonel Besigye's return, as he drove back into the capital from a triumphant rally in Mbarara, security forces stopped his motorcade and arrested him. As news of the colonel's detention spread across the city by text message, Kampala descended into riots, the worst urban violence the city had seen since the end of the civil war. The next morning, in a packed, sweltering courtroom, Besigye was charged with plotting rebellion. Looking grim and disheveled, he was ushered into the dock, where he flashed a V sign toward his defense team, which included the young legal star Caleb Alaka. Outside the court, police were firing tear gas and rubber bullets at protesters gathered in a park across the street. There were bonfires burning and angry chants in the air. Periodically, the staccato sound of automatic gunfire rang out.

The night of Besigye's arrest, as soldiers patrolled the darkened streets of downtown Kampala, I visited my favorite pub, a place frequented by a crowd of well-heeled, educated young Ugandans. I'd spent many nights arguing about politics there, and I knew the regulars split roughly evenly between Museveni supporters and opponents. But that evening, everyone was busy filling out yellow cards identifying themselves as members of the ruling party. Ideals were a luxury, they said; if there was going to be trouble, they wanted to be safe on the winning side. Only my friend Joseph, a hard-core Besigye man, refused to sign up. He downed his beer and stalked away.

"Politics is getting nasty," he said, disgustedly. "We are going back to those old days."

· · ·

"Go Shelby!"

"Nice job, Madison!"

"Cover for her, Sammy!"

It was early in the second half, and the girls of Howell United Spirit led the visitors from Manalapan by a score of two goals to none. Sitting on canvas folding chairs around a patchy municipal soccer field in suburban New Jersey, bundled up against the April chill in fleece blankets and Yankees bullpen jackets, the parents of Howell Township clapped and hollered encouragement in sharp northeastern accents.

"Very nice, Adrienne!"

"Let's go, Crystal! Run through it! Strike it!"

Duncan Laki couldn't stay in his seat. He was standing right along the chalk sideline, all the way down by the visitors' goal, his eyes fixed on one skinny, coltish eleven-year-old, the only black child on the field: his daughter, Otandeka, or "Oti" for short. "Get in there now," Duncan shouted, as his daughter made a speedy run up the right side of the field. "Let's go, Oti—that's your ball!"

Oti passed off to an open teammate, a lanky ponytailed forward who had already scored both Howell goals. She put a shot past the Manalapan goalie: 3–0. On the sideline, Duncan whooped with delight. "Is that a hat trick or what?"

Years had passed since I'd first met Duncan's family. Back then, Oti had been a pixyish six-year-old with braided hair. Now she was growing into a graceful young woman. Duncan had changed, too. His transcontinental shuttling had ended. He'd made a home in the United States with his wife, Cathy, and their four children. He now worked in Manhattan, as a diplomat at the Ugandan Mission to the United Nations. Every morning, he took a bus from woodsy Monmouth County to the Port Authority Bus Terminal and trekked on foot across town to the consulate on Forty-fifth Street near First Avenue. Each weekday evening, Duncan returned to his four-bedroom house in a new housing development called Concord Manor. On Sundays, Duncan and his family attended a local Pentecostal church, which was decorated with the flags of many nations. The congregation's pastor was a white Princeton graduate, the leader of its six-piece band was East Asian, and at any given service, the person sitting in the pew in front of Duncan might be an elderly black lady wearing a straw bonnet, a tattooed biker with a ponytail, an Indian woman wrapped in a sari or a West African man wearing a boubou. Earlier that morning of the soccer match, I'd attended church with Duncan. "Friends, mark my words, you know what's going to be the salvation of America?" the pastor had preached in his sermon. "It's going to be people like you who come from other countries."

When the soccer game ended, the victorious girls of Howell United, clad in snazzy green Nike warm-ups, tromped off the field with their parents. Duncan, Cathy, Oti and I got into the family's silver Acura SUV for the drive back to their home. We passed grain silos and horse corrals, and farm fields that were being partitioned into tracts of Colonials and Tudors. Duncan followed the creeping progress of suburbanization with the appraising eye of a homeowner. He would sometimes follow FOR SALE signs down the sapling-lined streets of newly paved cul-de-sacs, just to see what was on the market.

Duncan's own house, a model the developer marketed as an "Austin," was a sort of souped-up Cape Cod, with a peaked roof, a bay window, a finished basement and a two-story family room. As he pulled up his driveway, Duncan let out an exasperated sigh about the state of his lawn, which was a shade yellower than his neighbors'. For years, he'd been battling with it, strategically placing sod and sprinklers, and deploying an array of chemical and biological agents. He got out of the car, began rummaging through a pile of plastic bottles in his garage and pulled out a big green one labeled WEED-B-GON.

"Ah, this is the stuff," he said, with an air of practiced menace.

Inside, Duncan's housekeeper, a member of the extended family, was preparing a Ugandan-style lunch, mashed plantains and beans with peanut sauce and a hearty goat stew. His children straggled into the kitchen and poured themselves tall glasses of juice. Besides Oti, there were two teenage boys, Kagi and Mbagira, and a four-year-old daughter named Asiimwe, who had been born during the trial. They were typical suburban public school kids, strong-willed and talkative. None of them had lived in Africa for an extended period of time. Over on the mantle above the family room's stone fireplace, alongside other framed pictures, there was a black-and-white photograph of Eliphaz Laki standing next to a grinning Jomo Kenyatta, the first president of Kenya. The picture had been taken during a state visit in 1962, the year of Uganda's independence and Duncan's birth. He'd told his children about their grandfather, but he wasn't sure how much they understood. "I think they think it is some fairy tale from a faraway place," Duncan said.

Uganda did seem very distant now. Duncan was a representative of his government, so naturally he had followed Uganda's presidential election, reading the Kampala newspapers on the Internet. Besigye had been released on bail, but he'd spent more time in courtrooms than on the campaign trail, and Museveni had secured a comfortable victory. But the din of the country's tumultuous politics registered only faintly here. Duncan was an expatriate now, living an American life, and he found it surprisingly easy to stand aloof from the distressing events back home.

His separation from Uganda had also softened the devastation of the trial's outcome. Duncan had been crushed at first, but when he'd gotten back to the United States, his disappointment had waned, his natural disposition had reasserted itself and something close to satisfaction had set in. As he sat at his dining room table, beneath an oil painting of sailboats bobbing on the ocean, Duncan said he believed his efforts to solve his father's murder had been worthwhile. He mentioned an article that had recently appeared in a Ugandan newspaper, about some bones that had been accidentally unearthed from the basement of the notorious Nile Hotel. "I thought, no, I don't think it would be right for my father's bones to be scattered wherever," he said. "People would think, *Oh, this was a common thief.* I really thought that there should be closure, if you will . . . even if there is no such thing."

As always, Duncan kept the key to his father's Volkswagen in his dresser drawer, but it no longer caused him puzzlement or grief. The truth did have restorative effects. He even talked of returning home one day, of building a house on a lovely piece of property he'd acquired on the shores of Lake Victoria, of perhaps embarking on a political career. Duncan's whole life experience, the trial included, had taught him that his country could only break his heart—or worse. Yet he still had hope.

Duncan had even made his peace, in a way, with Idi Amin. Each morning when he walked into work at the consulate in Manhattan, he passed the polished black granite cornerstone by its first floor elevator bank, which read:

OCTOBER FIRST 1975
LAID DOWN BY HIS EXCELLENCY
AL HADJI FIELD MARSHAL IDI AMIN DADA, V.C., D.S.O., M.C.
PRESIDENT OF THE REPUBLIC
OF UGANDA AND CHAIRMAN OF
THE ORGANIZATION OF AFRICAN UNITY 1975 AND 1976

WELCOME TO ALL WHO ENTER UGANDA HOUSE
IN THE SPIRIT OF FRIENDSHIP
FOR GOD AND OUR COUNTRY

It was Duncan who showed me, one day when we met for lunch, that the portion of the stone engraved with the words Idi Amin Dada was slightly gashed, as if someone had once gone at them with a hammer and chisel. Duncan enjoyed a laugh about that. It was a typical Ugandan political protest: belated, inept, destructive and inflicted upon a powerless object. "Someone was overzealous," Duncan said of the vandal's attempt to remove Amin's name from history. "What would be the point of erasing him?"

EPILOGUE: NDEIJA

Eliphaz Laki did come home. His funeral took place in Ndeija, the village where he grew up, outside the yellow-painted farmhouse he'd built back when he was a chief. More than a thousand people attended the ceremony. They began to arrive at midmorning: peasant women with babies strapped to their backs, their bare feet dusty from a long journey; gray-haired men dressed in their best safari suits. In an adjacent pasture, longhorn cattle grazed next to parked Mercedes and Land Rovers, vehicles belonging to government dignitaries who had come to pay their final respects. Many of those in attendance had never known Eliphaz Laki. They'd just read about the case in the newspaper. All day, gray rain clouds loomed ominously overhead, but somehow the weather held.

At the appointed hour, a man with an accordion struck up an old-time gospel hymn, "Safe in the Arms of Jesus," and led a choir dressed in scarlet robes out the door of the yellow farmhouse. As the mourners sang in the local tongue, Runyankole, pallbearers carried out a lacquered wooden casket and laid it in the center of the crowd. Some of Eliphaz Laki's children came forward to place flowers on it. Amid the bouquets, someone propped up a yellowed photograph of the chief from the 1960s.

Duncan Laki sat on a stool beneath the drooping red blooms of a bottlebrush tree, a few feet from the stone he'd laid back in 1990, when the truth seemed so irretrievable, the one inscribed, "Lord Grant Us Decent Rest/And Disappearance No More."

Ndeija, August 24, 2002 PRESIDENTIAL PRESS UNIT

There was a reading from the Book of Genesis, the story of Joseph, who, keeping a pledge, carried his father back from Egypt for burial in the Promised Land. Then there were several hours of testimonials. Stooped octogenarians shared stories of Eliphaz Laki's schoolboy soccer prowess. Women wearing brightly colored headscarves recounted how the chief had brought clean water to their villages. Survivors of the Ankole leadership of the 1960s stepped forward to testify to the clarity of their friend's political ideals. A member of parliament, a woman from a northern tribe, told the audience that Amin had murdered her own brother. "We have all lost members of the family," she said. "We are all one in this sorrow."

Over and over, friends and relatives saluted Duncan for his strength and persistence, called him a hero, said his father would have been very proud. At certain moments, he dabbed his eyes with a handkerchief. But most of the time he bounded about the crowd with uncharacteristic ebullience. It was as if, as Duncan said in his eulogy, he'd spent his life carrying a millstone on his shoulders and now suddenly it had been removed. "We forgave those people, as we have given our hearts to

Duncan Laki, Kampala
VANESSA VICK

God," Duncan told the mourners. "But what hurts me most is that the people who killed my father did not know what they were doing. They did not know the people whose lives were affected afterward. When you kill someone, you don't know how many lives are going to shatter."

At the time the funeral was held, in August 2002, the disappointments of the trial still lay in the future. As he delivered his eulogy, Duncan didn't know that he'd ultimately be denied the resolution he'd sought for so long. But if there was to be no verdict in the sad case of Eliphaz Laki, there was, on this day, some measure of redemption, achieved by a son who had defied the willful amnesia of his wounded society to discover the truth for himself. Duncan may not have won his father justice, but he had secured him the peace of a well-tended grave, reclaiming Eliphaz Laki's name from the long roll call of the disappeared. This is how Ugandans have dealt with the atrocities of Idi Amin. Not by forgiving, but by resigning themselves to the injustices of an imperfect peace. Through hard experience, they have learned that history affords few happy endings. When they can, they comfort themselves with partial victories and small consolations.

Late in the afternoon, a convoy of four-wheel-drive vehicles roared up in a cloud of dust and President Museveni appeared, wearing a business suit and a wide-brimmed, floppy hat. As a pair of military officers washed the orange grime off his white Mercedes jeep, the president delivered his own eulogy. "For a state to exist, people have to die for it," he said. "They must sacrifice their lives so that those who are lucky survive. I cannot bring him back," he continued. "I cannot do anything beyond my means, but I want to show you that the peace you have is the result of the sacrifice of people like this one."

Then the choir began singing another hymn, "O Guide Me O Great Jehovah." The pallbearers picked up the coffin and began the steep trek through Laki's banana groves. The mourners followed behind in a long, breathless procession, the elderly men's canes and the young women's heels struggling against the loose ground, sending clods of dirt cascading down the hill. Near the summit, the procession stopped next to a small mud hut. This was the spot where Laki had grown up. A family of clucking chickens was milling about. At the edge of the clearing, in the shade of a stand of parasol trees, some gravediggers had excavated a deep rectangular hole.

"Ashes to ashes, dust to dust," the minister read, as the casket was lowered on ropes.

Yoweri Museveni (center) and the Laki family at the foot of the grave PRESIDENTIAL
PRESS UNIT

Duncan Laki stood with his wife and the president at the foot of the grave. He looked down into the hole and tossed in a handful of soil. Then he turned and walked back down the hill, as the gravediggers picked up shovels and began pushing earth back over the coffin.

From the top of this hill, this ripple of the Western Rift, you could take in the whole of Ndeija. You could trace the thin reddish path of the road where a chief, riding in his Studebaker, first caught sight of a poor boy named Eliphaz Laki. You could look down on the bright red roof of the farmhouse Laki built for his family, the place where his young son imagined a homecoming. You could survey the valley, dense with lush green foliage, where Duncan's mother had taken cover during the invasion of 1979. You could just glimpse the meandering Rwizi River, where vengeance was once meted out with machetes. And you could recall that there was a time before Yoweri Museveni and Idi Amin, before the betrayals and the reprisals, before colonialism and Christianity and the collision of uncomprehending worlds, a time when the river used to flood, cutting the village in half and dividing its people. That was why it was called Ndeija—"I'll come back." And as you stood there, at the top of Eliphaz Laki's hill, next to his grave, you could imagine that perhaps this is all the justice he would have desired.

He rests there still, beneath a stone that reads:

ELIPHAZ MBWAIJANA LAKI

1920–1972

DISAPPEARED 1972

REMAINS RECOVERED 2001

BURIED 2002

NO LONGER "MISSING"

BETRAYED BUT NOT FORGOTTEN

NOTES

INTERVIEWS

Nasur Abdallah, November 18, 2002

Yoga Adhola, November 7, 2005

Mustafa Adrisi, July 24, 2003, and July 25, 2003

Caleb Alaka, multiple interviews, 2002–2005

Moses Ali, 2004

Amule Amin, July 26, 2003

Mahmoud Angoliga, December 27, 2002

Mohammed Anyule, November 1, 2002

Naima Anyule, July 25, 2003

Dennis Asiimwe, October 2, 2005

Brian Atiku, July 25, 2003

Rajab Atiriko, July 25, 2003

Solomon Ayile, July 26, 2003

Francis Ayume, 2004

Zubairi Bakari, January 15, 2003

Isaac Bakka, October 7, 2003

Fred Bananuka, multiple interviews, 2003

Sarah Bananuka, November 23, 2002

Francis Bantariza, January 23, 2003

Michael Bashaija, February 3, 2003

Bishop Amos Betungura, October 26, 2005

Samuel Bishaka, February 3, 2003

Alfred Buhugiro, January 5, 2003

Blasio Buhwairoha, February 2, 2003

Richard Buteera, September 25, 2002

Boniface Byanyima, February 4, 2003

Nuru Dralega, July 26, 2003

Ibrahim Duke, multiple interviews, 2002–2004

Musa Eyaga, July 25, 2003

Ali Fadhul, October 6, 2005

Omia Farijalia, July 26, 2003

James Ganaafa, February 3, 2003

Fasul Gille, July 24, 2003

Nasur Gille, November 1, 2002, and September 21, 2005

Afsa Gowon, July 24, 2003

Yusuf Gowon, multiple interviews, 2002–2007

John Hitler, February 1, 2003

Haruna Adam Imaga, July 24, 2003

Charles Kabagambe, December 2, 2002

James Kahigiriza, November 23, 2002, and October 29, 2005

George Kahonda, February 2, 2003

Richard Kaijuka, September 23, 2005

Ephraim Kamuntu, November 9, 2005

Ali Kangave, October 28, 2005

Yona Kanyomozi, October 8, 2002

Eliab Kapasi, January 6, 2003

Donozio Katarikawe, January 5, 2003

Eriya Kategaya, December 3, 2002, and October 18, 2005

Arthur Katongole, multiple interviews, 2003

Manasseh Katsigazi, January 7, 2003

Alice Katundu, February 3, 2003

Drakuawuzia Kazimiro, January 3, 2003

Kenneth Kereere, multiple interviews, 2002–2007

Haruna Kibuye, November 8, 2005

Joab Kiharata, January 5, 2003

George Kihuguru, November 8, 2005

Francis Kwerebera, January 7, 2003

Henry Kyemba, September 27, 2005

Grace Kyotungire, January 6, 2003

Douglas Laki, October 23, 2005

Duncan Muhumuza Laki, multiple interviews, 2002–2009

Joyce Birungi Laki, December 3, 2002

Justine Tumwine Laki, July 16, 2005

Isaac Lumago, July 26, 2003

Yoasi Makaaru, January 6, 2003

Mahmood Mamdani, interview and multiple e-mail communications, 2005–2006

Zeddy Maruru, September 26, 2005

Emilio Mondo, multiple interviews, 2003–2005

Dr. Yusuf Mpairwe, January 26, 2003

Ratib Mududu, July 24, 2003

Justus Mugaju, September 28, 2005

Simon Byabakama Mugenyi, multiple interviews, 2002–2004

Justice Moses Mukiibi, October 3, 2005

President Yoweri K. Museveni, November 4, 2005

Reverend Anaiya Mutaahi, January 5, 2003

Simon Mwesiga, October 9, 2005

Dr. Mwambustsya Ndebesa, 2002

William Nganwa, October 15, 2005

Reverend George Nkoba, February 2, 2003

Conrad Nkutu, October 8, 2005

Kesi Nyakimwe, November 30, 2002

President Milton Obote, e-mail correspondence, December 10, 2002

Justice Arthur H. Oder, October 17, 2002

Wafula Oguttu, October 24, 2005

Michael Okwalinga, November 27, 2002

Hajat Anuna Omari, November 19, 2002

Alfred Orijabo, August 28, 2002

Kahinda Otafiire, October 5, 2005

Ruhakana Rugunda, October 16, 2005

Edward Rurangaranga, January 8, 2003

Augustine Ruzindana, multiple interviews, 2004–2005

Ephraim Rwakanengyere, March 30, 2003

Bernard Rwehururu, December 31, 2002

Noah Safi, July 25, 2003

Bashir Semakula, October 28, 2005

Noor Serujunge, October 28, 2005

Seth Singleton, September 5, 2006

A. M. Tabu, 2002

Brian Tibo, multiple interviews, 2002–2004

Willie Waigo, September 17, 2002

Juma Wani, July 25, 2003

Hajji Kalifan Zabasaja, October 27, 2005

PROLOGUE: 1979

4   "that in itself is a great thing": BBC Summary of World Broadcasts, January 27, 1979.

5   "poisoned food for a month": Moses Isegawa, *The Abyssinian Chronicles* (New York: Knopf, 2000), p. 297.

5   "grey hair and female traits": *Voice of Uganda*, April 22, 1975.

5   three-quarters of the town's buildings: "A Visit to Masaka and Mbarara," *Uganda Times*, August 16, 1979.

5   between the two tallest hills: Simon Heck, "In the Presence of Neighbors: Land Property and Community in Ankole, Uganda," Boston University dissertation, 1998, p. 40. The hills are called Kiara (6,484 ft.) and Kashasha (6,331 ft.).

5   Katyusha rockets: These rockets, known as *saba-saba* in Uganda, provided the liberators a decisive military advantage. See chapter 15.

6   notes were always anonymous: The "dozens of notes" found by the liberation forces in and around Mbarara are described in Tony Avirgan and Martha Honey, *War in Uganda* (Westport, Conn.: Lawrence Hill and Company, 1982), p. 86.

1: THE WESTERN RIFT

7   Around 30 million years ago: This passage summarizes, and by necessity simplifies, complex processes that are still not fully understood. Useful works on the geology of the rift include: Nigel Pavitt, *Africa's Great Rift Valley* (New York: Harry N. Abrams, 2001); Anthony Smith, *The Great Rift: Africa's Changing Valley* (London: BBC Books, 1988); Andrew Roberts, *Uganda's Great Rift Valley* (Kampala: The New Vision, 2006).

7   the first European: The best description of John Speke's encounter with the Baganda is contained in Alan Moorehead, *The White Nile* (New York: Harper and Row, 1971). The authoritative work on the colonization of Uganda, and the rest of the continent, is Thomas Pakenham's *The Scramble for Africa* (New York: Avon Books, 1991).

8   between 100,000 and 300,000 Ugandans were killed: Martin Meredith, in his survey history *The Fate of Africa* (New York: Public Affairs, 2005), places the number of killings under Amin at

250,000, and repeats an estimate (which originated from a Red Cross report) that at least 300,000 Ugandans died during the 1981–1986 civil war. But Justice Arthur Oder, the chairman of the Uganda Commission of Inquiry into Violations of Human Rights, told me that his committee had never been able to confidently estimate the death toll. Some oft-cited numbers are based on suspect methodology. For instance, former Ugandan health minister Henry Kyemba, in his book *State of Blood* (Kampala: Fountain Publishers, 1997), estimated 150,000 deaths by extrapolating from the number of bodies a boatman reported pulling from the waters of the Nile beneath Owens Falls Dam each day.

9   creating "black millionaires": Mahmood Mamdani, *Imperialism and Fascism in Uganda* (Trenton, N.J.: Africa World Press, 1984), p. 39.

9   a relaxed, unpretentious manner: Blaine Harden, "New Ugandan Leader Vows to End Terror; Ex-Teacher Instructs Soldiers on Civil Rights," *Washington Post*, January 30, 1986; Sheila Rule, "Rebel Sworn in as Uganda President," *New York Times*, January 30, 1986.

9   "clear objectives and a good membership": Yoweri K. Museveni, *What Is Africa's Problem*? (Minneapolis: University of Minnesota Press, 2000), p. 3.

10   served as the protagonist: Schroeder's film is "Général Idi Amin Dada: Autoportrait," while the blaxploitation flick is entitled "The Rise and Fall of Idi Amin."

10   because of the Watergate affair: Adam Seftel, ed., *Uganda: The Rise and Fall of Idi Amin* (Lanseria, South Africa: Bailey's African Photo Archives, 1994), p. 155.

11   hardly discussed in schools: Of course, Amin's era was discussed occasionally, for instance in high school history classes. Even then, however, care was taken to give similar weight to Amin's failures and his "accomplishments." One textbook, meant for Advanced Level high school students, listed six pages of the latter: "Amin tried as much as possible to make Islam popular"; "he fought tooth and nail to uplift African culture"; "[crime] subsided when he ordered the army and the public to shoot or stone to death the thieves."

11   "the dungheap of history": Museveni, *What Is Africa's Problem?*, pp. 5–6.

PAGE

11   Hundreds of people testified: Priscilla B. Hayner, *Unspeakable Truths: Facing the Challenge of Truth Commissions* (New York: Routledge, 2002), pp. 56–57.

12   they would be granted amnesty: An excellent discussion of the post-Amin rebellions and the subsequent amnesty process can be found in Mark Leopold, *Inside West Nile* (Santa Fe, N. Mex.: School of American Research Press, 2005).

12   not distributed for years: Hayner, *Unspeakable Truths*, pp. 56–57.

12   thousands and thousands of pages: Republic of Uganda, *Report of the Uganda Commission of Inquiry into Violations of Human Rights* (Kampala, 1995).

13   "Nobody bothered to follow up": Michael Okwalinga, interview, 2002.

14   "been dead for a long time": Charles Kabagambe, interview, 2002.

14   led a 1971 massacre: The minister referred to is Brigadier Moses Ali. In 1993, Ali was called before the Oder Commission after civilian eyewitnesses placed him at the scene of the mass killing of soldiers loyal to the ousted president Milton Obote at an army barracks in the northeastern town of Moroto. Ali told the commission that his troops had merely "shot in the air." The general, who had led a rebel group before making peace with the government, warned Oder: "I can be arrested. I am used to arrests—and I can fight my way out again." Oder said that the case against Ali was not pursued further, for reasons of "political expediency." In a 2004 interview, Ali, by then promoted to lieutenant general, told me: "They cleared me. This was a case of mistaken identity."

14   tyrannical former military governor: Most notoriously, Lieutenant Colonel Abdallah banned wearing flip-flops within the city of Kampala; those caught wearing them were reportedly forced to eat them. See Peter Allen, *Interesting Times* (Lewes, Sussex: The Book Guild Ltd., 2000), pp. 450–51. When I asked Abdallah about the flip-flops story, he said, "This is just rumors."

15   Amin's "result-oriented management": Obol Sylvester Awach, letter, *Monitor*, October 31, 2002.

15   "less and less of a monster": Augustine Ruzindana, interview, 2004.

17   "to answer charges of murder": "Gowon Committed to the High Court," *New Vision*, July 18, 2002.

18   "abandoned, bare earthed fields": Arthur Gakwandi, *Kosiya Kifefe* (Kampala: East African Educational Publishers, 1997), p. 86.

18 people would shout: This account of the village's naming, and much additional information about Ndeija's history, economy and physical geography, can be found in Simon Heck's Boston University dissertation, "In the Presence of Neighbors: Land Property and Community in Ankole, Uganda" (1998). Heck lived in Ndeija while doing his anthropology fieldwork in the 1990s. His translation of the village's name was confirmed by several Ugandans.

20 one early anthropologist: John Roscoe, *The Banyankole* (Cambridge, U.K.: Cambridge University Press, 1923), p. 25.

2: THE KEY

22 That first night: Voluminous descriptions of the independence celebrations around Uganda can be found in contemporaneous articles from the *Uganda Argus*, including "Mbarara Marks Uhuru," October 10, 1962. Additional information was provided by Justine Tumwine Laki, Eliphaz's daughter, in a 2005 interview.

22 "fairytale" kingdom: Winston Churchill, *My African Journey* (London: New English Library, 1972), p. 52.

23 the "Ba-men": Joshua Muvumba, *The Politics of Stratification and Transformation in the Kingdom of Ankole, Uganda*, Harvard University dissertation, 1982 (Ann Arbor: UMI, 1982), p. 207.

23 "ready to serve my country": Eliphaz Laki, letter to the *Enganzi* of Ankole, May 26, 1955. Laki family papers. Translated from Runyankole by Duncan Muhumuza Laki.

24 "For God and My Country": "Independence!" *Uganda Argus*, October 9, 1962.

24 literally means "provider": Muvumba, *The Politics of Stratification*, p. 261.

25 by their license plates: Ugandans are oddly fixated on license plate numbers. In fact, the villagers of Ndeija nicknamed Laki "runanakyenda," after the Runyankole pronunciation of his first plate number. He owned three cars over the course of his life: a Beetle, a Peugeot and finally another Beetle, which he was driving at the time of his disappearance. Even many years later, elderly friends of Laki's remembered that car's plate number, UYO-010, off the top of their heads.

26 "no cause for panic at all": "No Cause for Panic," *Uganda Argus*, September 22, 1972. The bulletin was reportedly read over the radio on the evening of September 21. (Charles Mohr,

"Uganda's Capital in Agitated Mood," *New York Times*, September 22, 1972.)

27   delivered the news: Francis Kwerebera, interview, 2003.

27   the headmaster had no answers: Reverend George Nkoba, interview, 2003.

28   "Just pray": Joyce Birungi Laki, interview, 2002.

28   called Idi Amin a "killer": David Martin, *General Amin* (London: Faber and Faber, 1974), p. 53.

28   "bizarre" behavior: "African Racist," *New York Times*, September 16, 1972.

28   "prehistoric monster": Nixon Tapes, Conversation 154–57, September 24, 1972, phone call between Nixon and Henry Kissinger. Included in *Foreign Relations of the United States*, vol. E-5, part 1. Transcript available at: http://www.state.gov/r/pa/ho/frus/nixon/e5/c15649.htm.

28–29 cover picture of the saluting general: *Time*, March 7, 1977.

29   a 1974 report: International Commission of Jurists, *Violations of Human Rights and the Rule of Law in Uganda* (Geneva: ICJ, 1974), p. 61.

30   spelling out messages: The summit festivities are described in considerable detail in "Big Daddy: The Perfect Host," *Time*, August 11, 1975.

30   forty successful military coups: Martin Meredith, *The Fate of Africa* (New York: Public Affairs, 2005), p. 218.

31   sky-blue field marshal's uniform: Peter Allen, *Interesting Times* (Lewes, Sussex: The Book Guild, 2000), p. 408.

31   subsequently liquidated: George Ivan Smith, *Ghosts of Kampala: The Rise and Fall of Idi Amin* (New York: St. Martin's Press, 1980), pp. 166–67.

32   "a chapter that balances history": *Voice of Uganda*, July 19, 1975.

32   "In no way can they survive": BBC Summary of World Broadcasts, April 9, 1979. This passage was translated by the BBC's monitoring service from the original Swahili.

32   "defense of his motherland": BBC Summary of World Broadcasts, February 26, 1979.

33   "Amin is no longer in power": BBC Summary of World Broadcasts, April 12, 1979.

35   Banyankole tribe had a proverb: Mario Cisternino, *The Proverbs of Kigezi and Ankole* (Kampala: Comboni Missionaries, 1987), p. 202.

3: UYO-010

40   "be my witness": *New Vision*, December 4, 2000.

42   "what the magic was": All conversations are recounted according to the recollection of Brian Tibo, interviewed on several occasions between 2002 and 2004.

44   "my trigger scar": Alfred Orijabo, personal interview, 2002.

44   "God-made police": Alfred Orijabo, radio interview, *Patrick Kamara Live*, Monitor Radio, August 2002.

46   "I am a hajji": Unless otherwise noted, all quotations from interviews with the suspects under interrogation are taken from tapes made by the private detectives, and translated from Lugbara by Samuel Andema of Kyambogo University, Kampala.

47   facedown in the tall grass: Mohammed Anyule, statement to police, April 19, 2001.

48   Gille just laughed: Alfred Orijabo, personal interview, 2002.

48   Within the army: Nasur Gille, interviews, 2002–2005; Fasul Gille, interview, 2003.

4: THE BIG MAN

51   dust that hung in the air: I visited Gowon's house in Ntinda on several occasions. The description of the daybreak routine of the muezzin's call is derived from my own experience of living just up the hillside from Ntinda, less than a mile from Gowon, during my stay in Uganda.

52   "I hear Gowon, a whole major general": Onapito Ekomoloit, "Amin Stays Put in Jeddah," IPS-Inter Press Service, November 12, 1995.

52   "Mind if I give you a lift?": The encounter was described in interviews with both Tibo and Gowon.

54   Gowon added a capitalized postscript: Yusuf Gowon, statement to police, April 24, 2001.

5: DECENT REST

57   one of several conflicting accounts: The story that Amin was born on the grounds of the Nile Hotel, widely repeated in Uganda, was first told to me by Michael Okwalinga, an investigator who worked with the Oder Commission. Other origin stories are recounted by Mark Leopold, *Inside West Nile* (Kampala: Fountain Publishers, 2005), p. 58.

57 soldiers chanting, "Kill!": Republic of Uganda, *Report of the Uganda Commission of Inquiry into Violations of Human Rights*, Testimony of Mustafa Adrisi, p. 6199.

57 doubled as torture chambers: *Report of the Commission of Inquiry into Violations of Human Rights*, pp. 73–76.

57 While excavating the basement: "Skulls Dug Out at Nile Hotel," *The Monitor*, June 1, 2005. The Serena Hotel corporation, which was renovating the hotel, subsequently claimed that what had been unearthed were animal bones, which the police had misidentified, and the *Monitor* retracted its story. However, a former *Monitor* editor assured me the article was in fact true, and the retraction only ran because the newspaper and the Serena chain are both owned by the same corporate entity.

58 "We do not like Ugandans to forget": "Fascist Amin's Death Centre Turned into National Museum," *Uganda Times*, December 17, 1979.

64 "wasn't interested in politics in Ankole": George Kihuguru, interview, 2005.

64 "They are all murderers": Boniface Byanyima, interview, 2003.

65 "That's us. We forgive": Yoasi Makaaru, interview, 2003.

6: THE BRIGHTEST STAR

66 "a load of cloth": Frederick Lugard, *The Diaries of Lord Lugard*, vol. 2, ed. Margery Perham (Evanston, Ill.: Northwestern University Press, 1959), pp. 225–27.

66 "rejected suitors should go to Africa": Arthur Alexander Thompson and Dorothy Middleton, *Lugard in Africa* (London: R. Hale, 1959), p. 17.

67 partners in their own subjugation: Two useful studies of indirect rule and its application to Uganda are Edward Steinhart, *Conflict and Collaboration: The Kingdoms of Western Uganda, 1890–1907* (Princeton, N.J.: Princeton University Press, 1979), and Mahmood Mamdani, *Citizen and Subject: Contemporary Africa and the Legacy of Late Colonialism* (Princeton, N.J.: Princeton University Press, 1996).

67 "nose often aquiline": Frederick Lugard, *The Rise of Our East African Empire*, excerpted in *East African Explorers*, ed. Charles Richard and James Place (London: Oxford University Press, 1967), pp. 316–17.

68   "extraneous races": *The Diaries of Lord Lugard*, vol. 2, p. 222.

68   metamorphose into a cow: The fascinating story of the enchantresses of Ibanda is recounted in Sir John Milner Gray, "A History of Ibanda, Saza of Mitoma, Ankole," *Uganda Journal*, vol. 24, no. 2, 1960, pp. 166–82.

68   "build another Kampala!": *The Diaries of Lord Lugard*, vol. 2, p. 230.

68   "seeing the size of the caravan": Lugard, *East African Explorers*, pp. 320–21.

69   the "arch-collaborator": Steinhart, *Conflict and Collaboration*, p. 151.

69   "brightest star near the moon": Steinhart, ibid., p. 138.

69   had first made his reputation: S. R. Karugire, *Nuwa Mbaguta* (Nairobi: East African Literature Bureau, 1973).

70   The Bahima tell stories: K. Oberg, "The Kingdom of Ankole in Uganda," *African Political Systems*, ed. M. Fortes and E. E. Evans-Pritchard (London: Oxford University Press, 1969), pp. 122–25.

70   environmental factors, such as droughts: David Lee Schoenbrun, *A Green Place, A Good Place: Agrarian Change, Gender and Social Identity in the Great Lakes Region to the 15th Century* (Portsmouth, N.H.: Heinemann, 1998).

70   crackpot anthropology: The relationship between the Bairu and Bahima is similar, though not identical, to that between the Hutu and Tutsi people in neighboring Rwanda, where the Hamitic hypothesis was also applied, and where conceptions of Tutsi "foreignness" were a key aggravating factor in the ethnic tension that gave rise to genocide in 1994. An enlightening discussion of the Hamitic myth can be found in Mahmood Mamdani's study of the genocide, *When Victims Become Killers* (Princeton, N.J.: Princeton University Press, 2001).

70   "born gentlemen": Martin Doornbos, *Not All the King's Men* (The Hague: Mouton, 1978), p. 77.

70   "making you bury their dead": Mario Cisternino, *The Proverbs of Kigezi and Ankole* (Kampala: Comboni Missionaries, 1987), p. 152.

71   collected taxes and demonstrated beneficence: An excellent examination of the changing role of Ankole's chiefs can be found in Joshua Muvumba, *The Politics of Stratification and Transformation in the Kingdom of Ankole, Uganda* (Ann Arbor: University of Michigan, 1982).

PAGE

71   "as from a loving son": Muvumba, ibid., p. 182.

71   Eliphaz Laki ended up going to school: The account of Eliphaz Laki's early life has been assembled through interviews with his family members, contemporaries and—when possible—documentary evidence such as personal letters and published histories. The primary source for the story of Laki's encounter with the chief Ernest Katungi was Manasseh Katsigazi, a fellow resident of Katungi's home who became Laki's lifelong friend and confidant.

72   "like his own children": Manasseh Katsigazi, interview, 2003.

73   a census counted: B. W. Langlands, *Notes on the Geography of Ethnicity in Uganda* (Kampala, Makerere University Department of Geography, 1975), p. 25.

73   could afford to send their children: Martin Doornbos gives the best account of the economic and social transformation that took place in Laki's formative years in his excellent book, *Not All the King's Men*.

73   "they are smaller in number": Amos Betungura, interview, 2005. Betungura's memoir, *Beginnings of Prosperity* (Mbarara, Uganda: Archway Publications, 2003) also provides useful perspective.

74   "heroes of the rural community": Arthur Gakwandi, *Kosiya Kifefe* (Kampala: East African Educational Publishers, 1997), p. 52.

75   "look at you and see your talents": Yoasi Makaaru, interview, 2003.

76–77 had the air of a state occasion: For the account of the scene of Nganwa's funeral, as well as much of the political infighting that followed, I am indebted to Fred Bananuka, who discussed the events in several interviews, as well as in his university thesis: "Uganda People's Congress in Ankole District," Dar Es Salaam University, 1971.

78   after reading *Paradise Lost*: Ali Mazrui, *Soldiers and Kinsmen in Uganda: The Making of a Military Ethnocracy* (Beverly Hills, Calif.: Sage Publications, 1975), p. 182.

78   "a cloud of tobacco smoke": "The Cool and Determined Milton Obote," *Drum*, July 1959, reprinted in Adam Seftel, ed., *Uganda: The Rise and Fall of Idi Amin* (Lanseria, South Africa: Bailey's African Photo Archives, 1994), p. 27.

78   local DP organizer "chased away": Boniface Byanyima, interview, 2003.

79   Kahigiriza was inaugurated: "New *Enganzi* Installed," *Uganda Argus*, June 26, 1963.

80   mob chanting "UPC!" had attacked: "Opposition Leader's Home Stoned," *Uganda Argus*, July 1, 1963.

80   plead for a few shillings: A large proportion of Laki's surviving correspondence consists of pleas for such small-scale financial assistance.

82   "disgusted" with frequent elections: "One Party the Only Way, Says *Enganzi* of Ankole," *Uganda Argus*, January 20, 1964.

82   "wreck the country": "No Room Here for Communism— *Enganzi*," *Uganda Argus*, June 19, 1964.

83   one unfortunate schoolteacher: Joseph Kaguuri, letter to Eliphaz Laki, June 10, 1965. Laki family papers. Runyankole portions translated by Duncan Laki.

83   "the *enganzi* of all Banyankole": James Kahigiriza, *Bridging the Gap: Struggling Against Sectarianism and Violence in Ankole and Uganda* (Kampala: Fountain Publishers, 2001), p. 29.

84   "deep concern" about corruption: Martin Doornbos and Michael Lofchie, "Ranching and Scheming: A Case Study of the Ankole Ranching Scheme," *Institutionalizing Development Policies and Resource Strategies in Eastern Africa and India* (New York: Macmillan, 2000), p. 151.

84   "He was going to cling to it": Edward Rurangaranga, interview, 2003.

85   "that kind of radicalism": Yoasi Makaaru, interview, 2003.

86   "He was not rude": Francis Bantariza, interview, 2003.

86   "religion that had just come yesterday": Kenneth Kereere, interview, 2002.

86   two men traded allegations: Eliphaz Laki, letter to F. X. Tibayungwa, February 1, 1969. Laki family papers.

87   labour for those that divide it: James Kahigiriza, letter to all civil servants, June 3, 1966. Laki family papers.

87   "masses did not taste it at all": "President Draws Thousands to Ankole Rally," *Uganda Argus*, March 20, 1967.

88   hauled away to a government warehouse: "Last Days of a Kingdom," *Uganda Argus*, September 28, 1967.

88   an assassin stepped: "Shots at President," *Uganda Argus*, December 20, 1969; "Assassination Bid That Failed," *Drum*, June 1970, reprinted in *Uganda: The Rise and Fall of Idi Amin*, pp. 70–72.

PAGE

88 "line up behind Bananuka": Kahigiriza, *Bridging the Gap*, p. 42.

89 It has been necessary: "The Army Takes Over," *Uganda Argus*, January 26, 1971.

90 "the overthrow of that guy": Yoasi Makaaru, interview, 2003.

7: A SERIOUS YOUNG MAN

91 "ascetic life": Yoweri K. Museveni, *Fanon's Theory of Violence: Its Verification in a Sub-Saharan African Territory*, Dar es Salaam University dissertation, 1970, p. 14.

91 "some problems during the night": Yoweri K. Museveni, *Sowing the Mustard Seed: The Struggle for Freedom and Democracy in Uganda* (New York: Macmillan, 1997), p. 46. Museveni's written account of his actions after the coup has been supplemented by interviews with the president and several others who interacted with him, including Zubairi Bakari, Richard Kaijuka, Yona Kanyomozi, Ruhakana Rugunda and Eriya Kategaya.

92 Peugeot, which they drove downtown: Richard Kaijuka, interview, 2005.

92 "just like academicians debating": Kaijuka, interview.

93 "ore into iron without melting it": Museveni, *Fanon's Theory of Violence*, p. 35.

93 "if he fights, he may die": E. P. S. Kiyingi, "Who Is Museveni?" (pamphlet published circa 1986).

93 Born during the waning days: Unless otherwise noted, all biographical details are derived from Museveni's *Sowing the Mustard Seed*.

94 arrived at boarding school barefoot: Kaijuka, interview.

94 "at a very early age, as rebellious": Ephraim Kamuntu, interview, 2005.

95 emulating Patrice Lumumba: Eriya Kategaya, *Impassioned for Freedom* (Kampala: Wavah Books, 2006), p. 12.

95 "[to] Dar es Salaam—to Tanzania": Yoweri Museveni, "My Three Years in Tanzania: Glimpses of the Struggle Between Revolution and Reaction," *Cheche*, undated clipping. The author expresses his gratitude to Steven Hippo Twebaze for providing him with this and other articles from *Cheche*.

95 "Nyerere as our Bismarck": Museveni, ibid.

96 "watching decadent western films": Museveni, ibid.

96 "infected by the liberation virus": Eriya Kategaya, interview, 2005.

96 "the arch Uncle Tom": Museveni, "My Three Years in Tanzania."

96 "a Big Man in the African sense": Seth Singleton, interview, 2006.

96 the following graffito: Mahmood Mamdani, interview, 2005.

98 "while we were history-students": Museveni, *Fanon's Theory of Violence*, p. 12.

98 "Marxist of almost Maoist virility": Justus Mugaju, interview, 2005.

98 "not going to have puppets ruling us": "No Puppets Here," *Uganda Argus*, August 1970.

99 "That was the 1960s": Yoweri Museveni, interview, 2005.

99 "the General Service Unit": Kategaya, interview, 2005.

100 "people are to return to work as usual": "Fair and Free Elections Soon," *Uganda Argus*, January 26, 1971.

101 "hearing bad, bad things": Edward Rurangaranga, interview, 2003.

101 "As a student of politics, he knew": Yoasi Makaaru, interview, 2003.

101 came back to the house with Eliphaz Laki: The account of the trip to Tanzania is reconstructed from the accounts of the two surviving travelers (Museveni and Bakari), from the recollections of friends and family members who subsequently discussed the trip with Laki and from various documentary records, including Obote's voluminous published reminiscences of the period immediately after the coup.

102 a huge rally: David Martin, *General Amin* (London: Faber and Faber, 1974), p. 53.

102 lawn where peacocks roamed: William Edgett Smith, "We Can't Go to the Moon," *The New Yorker*, October 16, 1971. In addition to containing a detailed description of the Tanzanian State House during the time period Obote occupied it, Smith's three-part profile of Julius Nyerere is a masterful work.

102 He pressed the men: In an e-mail correspondence with me from his exile in Zambia, conducted before his death in 2005, Obote said he had no recollection of this encounter, claiming he did not even meet Museveni until 1972. "[He] was a very junior officer on his very first job whose status was far removed from the President," Obote wrote. This denial conflicts with Museveni's autobiography, an account given to me by Bakari, who attended the meeting, and what Laki told confidants on his return.

102 "I will contact you": Zubairi Bakari, interview, 2003.

PAGE   **8: SINGAPORE**

103   "very . . . *sensitive*": Yona Kanyomozi, interview, 2002.

104   "resumed duty accordingly": Eliphaz Laki, letter to administra-
       tive secretary of Ankole, February 6, 1971. Laki family papers.

104   "Tie your things up and go": Joshua Muvumba, *The Politics of
       Stratification and Transformation in the Kingdom of Ankole, Uganda*,
       Harvard University dissertation, 1982 (Ann Arbor: University of
       Michigan, 1982), p. 264.

104   "knew how to work underground": Kanyomozi, interview.

104   "a very, very brave guy": Yoasi Makaaru, interview, 2003.

105   "Obote's scratching paws": George Wepukhulu Zepwe, letter,
       Uganda Argus, February 13, 1971.

105   "atmosphere of normality that prevails": Anonymous, "A Per-
       sonal Letter from Uganda," *Transition*, June–July 1971, p. 12.

105   to kiss the general's feet: The story of the prostrate police chief,
       Ephraim Rwakanengyere, was recounted by many sources,
       including the retired police officer John Hitler.

106   "people spying on Uganda": "Nyerere, Obote Train Freedom
       Fighters," *Uganda Argus*, March 29, 1971.

106   dirt would bring them good luck: Peter Allen, *Interesting Times*
       (Sussex: The Book Guild, 2000), p. 313.

106   "Have you also been arrested?": Reverend George Nkoba, inter-
       view, 2003.

106   Kampala barracks called Makindye: The account of Laki's impris-
       onment has been assembled through interviews with fellow
       inmates, family members and friends who visited him, and doc-
       umentary records of the notoriously bad conditions within the
       prison.

107   "This is the last supper": Edward Rurangaranga, interview, 2003.

107   "When they had been hammered": Rurangaranga, interview.

109   "they had rehabilitated us": Rurangaranga, interview.

109   dances in the general's honor: "President Amin to Visit Ankole,"
       Uganda Argus, August 9, 1971.

110   "We were doing nothing": Fred Bananuka, interview, 2003.

110   "What many people want is a fresh beginning": Tony Avirgan
       and Martha Honey, *War in Uganda* (Westport, Conn.: Lawrence
       Hill and Company, 1982), p. 41.

110   cover the noise as they drilled: The Front for National Salvation
       training was described by two former members of the Kampala

cell, Haruna Kibuye and Kahinda Otafiire, in interviews conducted in 2005.

111   "nothing to make them panic unduly": P. K. Kitonsa (permanent secretary, Ministry of Internal Affairs), letter to district commissioner of Ankole, November 24, 1971. Laki family papers.

111   "permanently resentful": John Hitler, interview, 2003.

111   "They kept their eyes on us": Nkoba, interview.

112   "going to get us killed!": Hitler, interview.

112   all the major figures: The godfather of Laki's children was named Jonas Mutembeya. The other chief was Blasio Ntundubeire. The story of the latter's hasty circumcision was told by several sources. According to a report on disappeared persons that was prepared, but never disseminated, by Amin's government, Ntundubeire was in fact arrested at a hospital. See The Republic of Uganda, *Report of the Commission of Inquiry into Disappearances of People in Uganda Since the 25th of January 1971* (Entebbe, 1975), p. 506. (A copy of this fascinating document, apparently the sole surviving one, is available at the library of the Uganda Human Rights Commission in Kampala.) The report also provides the basis of the account of the killing of Nekemia Bananuka and his three sons (pp. 479–88). The latter story was supplemented by interviews with, among others, Bananuka's children Fred and Sarah.

113   last piece of paternal advice: Both letters have apparently been lost, but Justine Laki described their contents in a 2005 interview.

9: A SHALLOW GRAVE

115   cutting weeds by the roadside: The account of Laki's arrest and killing has been assembled from the several confessions made by Nasur Gille and Mohammed Anyule, court testimony and interviews with differently positioned eyewitnesses, including John Hitler and Blasio Buhwairoha, who were inside the county headquarters; Francis Kwerebera, who was outside it; Grace Kyotungire, Laki's housekeeper; Michael Bashaija, a chief then stationed in Nyabuhike near Ibanda; and James Ganaafa, the chief in Bwizibwera, who was the last person known to have seen Laki alive other than his killers.

115   hues of sand and ash: According to the records of the Uganda Department of Meteorology, significant amounts of rain were recorded only twice in Ibanda during the three weeks before

Laki's disappearance, and only a trace fell in the twelve days before the disappearance.

116   "like seeing a snake": John Hitler, interview, 2003.

116   Just to talk. He'd be fine: Mohammed Anyule, statement before magistrate, April 26, 2001.

118   "Lie down," the snaggletoothed man said: Mohammed Anyule, statement to police, April 19, 2001.

118   "going to Kampala I might suffer the same fate": James Kahigiriza, *Bridging the Gap: Struggling Against Sectarianism and Violence in Ankole and Uganda* (Kampala: Fountain Publishers, 2001), p. 44.

118   "Ankole was now calm and free": James Kahigiriza, interview, 2002.

118   "I am ready to serve": Kahigiriza, *Bridging the Gap*, p. 45.

119   "difficult to distinguish fact from fiction": Kahigiriza, ibid., p. 47.

10: EXHUMATION

122   like a witch doctor: This odd scene was described in detail by several eyewitnesses.

122   "wait with incomplete puzzles": "Thirty Year Search for Dad's Killers," *The Monitor*, August 11, 2002.

123   "the risk is still perceived": Yusuf Mpairwe, interview, 2003.

123   "a long list of names": Nasur Gille, taped confession made to private detectives, 2001.

123–124 "the assistance of the local people": Eriya Kategaya, interview, 2002.

124   assessment Museveni himself echoed: "This is true," the president said in our 2005 interview.

124   "what some of us think is doubtful": Kenneth Kereere, interview, 2002.

125   angrily denied the charge: In a 2003 interview, Rwakanengyere scoffed at her accusation, calling it "rubbish" and saying he was preparing a slander lawsuit against Sarah Bananuka. "That woman said, 'My father was killed,'" the former police chief said. "She said, 'Mr. Rwakanengyere, get saved as I got saved.' I was shocked!" Rwakanengyere's denials were undercut by the fact that in 1979 he had been imprisoned for killing an Anglican bishop on behalf of Amin's regime. He spent seven years in prison, but when Yoweri Museveni took power, in 1986, he was mysteriously released. Many Bairu suspected the former police chief was freed not because he was wrongly convicted, but

because he and Museveni shared a Bahima kinship bond. "Rwakanengyere is the same clan as Museveni," said Augustine Ruzindana, a resistance veteran who is now an opposition party leader. "And I think Museveni very seriously believes in clans."

125   "Naturally, you arouse some sentiments": Kesi Nyakimwe, interview, 2002.

126   "reviving the culture of Ankole": James Kahigiriza, *Bridging the Gap: Struggling Against Sectarianism and Violence in Ankole and Uganda* (Kampala: Fountain Publishers, 2001), p. 77.

126   monarchist movement remained highly controversial: In 1993, Kahigiriza and others arranged for the heir to the throne of Ankole, Prince John Barigye—who at one time served as Idi Amin's ambassador to Germany—to be crowned in a secret ceremony. When news of the coronation became public, President Museveni immediately abrogated it, despite his support for a ceremonial role for "traditional rulers" in other parts of the country, because he feared the return of Ankole's king would heighten ethnic tensions. The debate over the monarchy persists, however, and can be seen as a proxy battle between long-opposed political factions in Ankole. A detailed discussion of the issue can be found in *The Ankole Kingship Controversy*, by Martin Doornbos (Kampala: Fountain Publishers, 2001).

127   "I had to keep on my farm": Republic of Uganda, *Report of the Uganda Commission of Inquiry into Violations of Human Rights*, Testimony of James Kahigiriza (Kampala, 1995), p. 1519. Many details of Kahigiriza's 1977 imprisonment are also derived from this testimony.

127   "how the split started in UPC": Kahigiriza testimony, p. 1532.

127   "a respected citizen not only of Ankole": Kahigiriza testimony, p. 1534.

11: THE PRISONER

133   "refractory type of prisoner": Uganda Protectorate, *Statement by the Protectorate Government on the Incidents in the Upper Prison, Luzira, in July and August, 1960* (Kampala, 1960), p. 1.

133   over three times that many: According to the Ugandan prison service, the Upper Prison held 2,126 inmates in August 2008. I thank Glenna Gordon, a journalist who has done excellent work on Ugandan prison conditions, for obtaining this statistic.

134   "last one is the most important": Conrad Nkutu, interview, 2005.

135   a helping of weevil-riddled beans: Several reports contain
      detailed descriptions of conditions inside Luzira, including Inter-
      national Federation of Human Rights, *Uganda: Challenging the
      Death Penalty* (Paris, 2005); Anita Hadley, "A Community of
      Hope: The Condemned Prisoners of Luzira Prison," *Correctional
      Service of Canada*, http://www.csc-scc.gc.ca/text/prgrm/chap/faith/
      le/14-eng.shtml; and reports by Glenna Gordon for the *New York
      Sun* and other publications.

135   Gowon tried not to dwell: For the most part, descriptions of
      Gowon's life inside prison are derived from his own accounts, in
      numerous interviews between 2002 and 2005, as well as personal
      observations during my visits to Luzira.

135   comfort to the turncoats Anyule and Gille: The ex-general, Ali
      Fadhul, Gowon's former commanding officer in Mbarara, may have
      hoped that Gowon's conviction would bolster his appeal for a par-
      don in a similar case of murder, also committed in September 1972.
      By 2003, Fadhul was the only Amin regime figure of any signifi-
      cance who was still serving a prison sentence. At his trial fifteen
      years before, Fadhul had tried to claim Gowon was responsible for
      all the civilian killings in Mbarara. The two men hadn't ever cared
      for each other, but their mutual enmity deepened at Luzira. I was
      told by prison authorities that special precautions had to be
      taken to keep the two elderly prisoners separated. In January
      2009, long after the Gowon trial concluded, Fadhul was finally
      granted a presidential pardon and released. Suffering from vari-
      ous ailments, he returned to his dilapidated family home, where
      he gave interviews to the *Monitor* and *New Vision* in which he
      offered extravagant praise for Museveni and promised to cam-
      paign vigorously for his reelection in 2011.

136   250,000 to 350,000 refugees: Mark Leopold, *Inside West Nile*
      (Santa Fe, N.Mex.: School of American Research Press), p. 55.

137   "participate in the democratization and development": Colonel
      Kahinda Otafiire, Office of the President, letter to Major General
      Yusuf Gowon, November 3, 1994. Gowon personal papers.

137   announced his repatriation deal: "Gowon to Return," *New Vision*,
      March 28, 1994.

137   came as the head of a delegation: *New Vision*, December 10, 1994.
      The estimate of ten thousand civilians was provided in an interview

by Hajat Anuna Omari, the presidential adviser who negotiated Gowon's return.

137 picture of a happy, healthy Gowon: "Amin's Chief of Staff Returns," *New Vision*, December 6, 1994.

137 "home for all Ugandans": "Museveni Welcomes Returnees," *New Vision*, December 15, 1994.

138 "I sought Gowon's support": Francis Ayume, interview, 2004.

139 "old inmates aged above 60": International Federation of Human Rights, p. 40.

142 "Gowon saved a lot of lives": John Hitler, interview, 2003.

12: AMONG THE CANNIBALS

143 blamed the Turks for bringing the demons: The following passage is derived from two principal sources, each representing one side of the story of first contact. *The Opening of the Nile Basin*, ed. Elias Toniolo and Richard Hill (New York: Barnes and Noble Books, 1974), contains the invaluable journals and travelogues of the missionary priests who first traveled to what is now the Sudan-Uganda border region in the late 1840s. Of particular use were the accounts of Ignaz Knoblecher, Emanuele Pedemonte and Angelo Vinco, from which all scenes described in this passage were taken. The indigenous people did not record their own reactions to the appearance of white men on the Nile, but modern observers have described the traditional belief that white-skinned beings were demonic. John Middleton, the foremost anthropologist of West Nile, recounts in a reminiscence of his early fieldwork how the women of the area would spit at him because "they were fearful that I had come to eat their babies." See John Middleton, *The Study of the Lugbara: Expectation and Paradox in Anthropological Research* (New York: Holt, Rinehart and Winston, 1970), p. 14.

143 "Back to the boat!" *The Opening of the Nile Basin*, p. 71.

145 nicknamed "Maneater": Ibid., p. 79.

145 "European" literally meant "evil spirit": John Middleton, *The Lugbara of Uganda* (New York: Harcourt Brace Jovanovich, 1992), p. 71.

145 went by the name Mehemet Emin: In reconstructing the story of Emin Pasha and Equatoria, I relied most heavily on the explorer's

own journals and letters, collected in *Emin Pasha in Central Africa*, trans. Mrs. R. W. Felkin, ed. Georg Schweitzer (London: G. Philip and Son, 1888). A contemporary biography written by Schweitzer based on these documents, *Emin Pasha: His Life and Work*, 2 vols. (New York: Negro Universities Press, 1969), was also of immense value. Several of the handful of other Europeans who encountered Emin in Equatoria ended up writing their own memoirs, including A. J. Mounteney-Jephson, *Emin Pasha and the Rebellion at the Equator* (New York: Scribner, 1891); Gaetano Casati, *Ten Years in Equatoria and the Return with Emin Pasha* (New York: Negro Universities Press, 1969); and, most famously, Henry Morton Stanley, *In Darkest Africa: The Quest, Rescue and Retreat of Emin, Governor of Equatoria* (New York: Scribner, 1891). There have been many modern reexaminations of the history, the most extensive of which is *The Last Expedition: Stanley's Mad Journey Through the Congo*, by Daniel Liebowitz and Charles Pearson (New York: Norton, 2005). For the insight that Emin Pasha's story was in some sense a precursor to Idi Amin's, I am indebted to Mark Leopold's *Inside West Nile* (Santa Fe, N.Mex.: School of American Research Press, 2005).

145 water lilies and the blue-green snakes: *Emin Pasha in Central Africa*, p. 12.

146 demand for ivory: Leopold, *Inside West Nile*, p. 112.

147 "no better and more workable material": *Emin Pasha in Central Africa*, p. 487.

147 a comet appeared in the sky: Emin made mention of this famous astronomical occurrence in a letter (*Emin Pasha in Central Africa*, p. 453).

147 called himself the Mahdi: The Mahdist rebellion, which in some ways presaged the Islamic fundamentalist movements of the 20th century, is described in detail in Alan Moorehead's *The White Nile* (New York: Harper and Row, 1971) and Thomas Pakenham's *The Scramble for Africa* (New York: Avon Books, 1991). Both books also include lengthy sections about Emin and Equatoria.

147 "if one man dies, another will take his place": *Emin Pasha in Central Africa*, pp. 426–27.

148 "in no case abandon my people": *Emin Pasha: His Life and Work*, p. 263.

148 "degeneration into the Negro and the egoist": Ibid., p. 160.

149 inspiration for the novelist Joseph Conrad: Leopold, *Inside West Nile*, p. 13.

149 "the Dark Forest and dwarfs": Frederick Lugard, *The Diaries of Lord Lugard*, vol. II, ed. Margery Perham (Evanston, Ill.: Northwestern University Press, 1959), p. 317.

149 "Thrash them first, conciliate them afterwards": Quoted in Mahmood Mamdani, *Citizen and Subject: Contemporary Africa and the Legacy of Late Colonialism* (Princeton, N.J.: Princeton University Press, 1996), p. 77.

149 Lugard found the kingdom: Pakenham, *The Scramble for Africa*, pp. 414–19.

150 Finally, he reached Lake Albert: Lugard's search for Emin's men is described in the second volume of his diaries, pp. 297–334.

150 a series of difficult trials: The story of the army's abandonment and subsequent infighting is recounted in *Emin Pasha: His Life and Work*, vol. 2, pp. 239–45. Emin reencountered the troops on his last expedition into the African bush, in July–August 1891. Shortly afterward, Emin was killed by Arab slavers in Congo, and they described what had happened.

150 "noble remnant who were fanatical in their loyalty": *The Diaries of Lord Lugard*, vol. II, p. 332.

152 They called themselves "Nubians": For a detailed explanation of the unique dynamics of Nubian ethnicity, see Nelson Kasfir, "Explaining Ethnic Political Participation," *World Politics* (April 1979) pp. 365–88; Omari Kokole, "The Nubians of East Africa: Muslim Club or African 'Tribe'? The View from Within," *Journal of the Institute of Muslim Minority Affairs* (July 1985), pp. 420–48; J. A. Meldon, "Notes on the Sudanese in Uganda," *Journal of the Royal African Society* (January 1908), pp. 123–46.

152 "men whose names are known": Middleton, *The Lugbara of Uganda*, p. 47. Middleton's work is a key source for describing the way of life in West Nile in the middle of the 20th century. Though he concentrated specifically on the Lugbara people, much of what he described also held true for the neighboring Kakwa. See Ade Adefuye, "The Kakwa of Uganda and Sudan," *Partitioned Africans: Ethnic Relations Across Africa's International Boundaries 1884–1984*, ed. A. I. Asiwaju (London: C. Hurst and Company, 1984), pp. 51–69.

152 Churchill shot elephants and rhinos: Winston Churchill, *My African Journey* (London: New English Library, 1972), p. 103.

152 Jung visited in order to observe the primeval psyche: Leopold, *Inside West Nile*, p. 81.

152 "almost fanatically opposed to any change": Uganda Protectorate, *Annual Report of the Provincial Commissioners, Eastern and Western Provinces, On Native Administration for the Year Ended 31st December, 1939* (Entebbe, 1940), p. 25.

153 literally meant "little prison": Leopold, *Inside West Nile*, p. 31.

154 "Brave, brave soldiers": Ratib Mududu, interview, 2003.

154 idolized one soldier in particular: Several contemporaries of Gowon said that Amin used to interact with them as schoolchildren. "Amin was so friendly to the young boys," said Ratib Mududu.

154 mythology surrounds the circumstances: Middleton, in *The Lugbara of Uganda*, writes that despite their reputation as an "aggressive and quarrelsome people," the people of West Nile were not especially warlike. Their armed conflicts, though glorified in tribal lore, were actually quite tame: "Killing and even serious wounding were not all that common" (p. 56). According to *Criminal Homicide in Uganda*, a sociological study by Tibamanya Mushanga (Kampala: East African Literature Bureau, 1974), West Nile's reported murder rate between 1965 and 1968 was less than half that of the nation as a whole. Nonetheless, the stereotype of West Nile as a place of savage violence was already in place when Amin came to power. For instance, in his contemporary biography *General Amin* (London: Faber and Faber, 1974), the journalist David Martin wrote, without citing any evidence, that "long before the 1971 coup" Uganda's Nubians "enjoyed an unenviable reputation of having one of the world's highest homicide rates."

154 "a warrior tribe" that lives on the margins: George Ivan Smith, *Ghosts of Kampala: The Rise and Fall of Idi Amin* (New York: St. Martin's Press, 1980), p. 45.

154 says that he ate his enemies: Though Amin committed many well-documented atrocities, the cannibalism charge is the one with which he is indelibly associated—for good reason. The stories are incredibly lurid. George Ivan Smith, for instance, relates that a nameless Ugandan "in a position to know such things" told him that Amin sacrificed his own son and ate his heart "so that he could stay in power as long as he lived on earth." Henry Kyemba, a minister in Amin's government who fled and wrote a tell-all memoir, *State of Blood* (Kampala: Fountain Publishers,

1997), writes that on many occasions his boss "boasted . . . that he has eaten human flesh." There is some evidence that the mutilation of enemy corpses was a custom of warfare in West Nile—Middleton writes that he heard such tales—but the grotesque rituals Amin supposedly practiced appear to be the stuff of folklore. If you trace any of the cannibalism stories back to its source, you inevitably end up with a flimsy account from an aggrieved exile like Kyemba, or, one suspects, a creative Fleet Street editor. Mark Leopold, who is properly skeptical, writes that such stories turned Amin into a "fairy-tale figure."

154   "places them in a category with animals": William Arens, *The Man Eating Myth* (New York: Oxford University Press, 1979), p. 140. For his valuable insights on this subject, I thank my father, Thomas J. Rice, the author of *Cannibal Joyce* (Gainesville: The University Press of Florida, 2008).

155   discouraging the introduction of cash crops: D. P. S. Ahluwalia, *Plantation and the Politics of Sugar in Uganda* (Kampala: Fountain Publishers, 1995), pp. 100–141.

155   "embarrassing to the local district officers": *Annual Report of the Provincial Commissioners*, p. 17.

155   seventy-seven thousand Ugandans: Gardner Thompson, *Governing Uganda: British Colonial Rule and Its Legacy* (Kampala: Fountain Publishers, 2003), p. 96.

156   "recruiting safaris": Iain Grahame, *Amin and Uganda: A Personal Memoir* (New York: Granada, 1980), pp. 9–20.

156   "For he comes of a fighting race": Grahame, ibid., p. 39.

156   "soldiering as a job of failures": Zeddy Maruru, interview, 2005.

157   December 20, 1946: Amii Omara-Otunnu, *Politics and the Military in Uganda, 1890–1985* (New York: St. Martin's Press, 1987), p. 38.

157   "a Grecian sculpture": Grahame, *Amin and Uganda*, p. 34.

157   he was among friends and kinsmen: Ali Fadhul, interview, 2005.

157   "had reached his ceiling": Grahame, *Amin and Uganda*, p. 41.

158   "distrust of all the soap-box orators": Grahame, ibid., p. 44.

158   the ceremonial end to colonial rule: "Independence!" *Uganda Argus*, October 9, 1962.

13: THE LIONS

159   fifteen times more than the average Ugandan: Holger Bernt Hansen, *Ethnicity and Military Rule in Uganda* (Uppsala: The Scandinavian Institute of African Studies, 1977), p. 81.

PAGE

160   both belonged to the same minuscule tribe: If these layers of
       identity seem hard to keep straight, imagine an immigrant who
       is a Latino to his white neighbors, a Colombian to other Latin
       immigrants and a mestizo to his fellow Colombians.

160   countered by creating a new secret unit: Henry Kyemba, *State of
       Blood* (Kampala: Fountain Publishers, 1997), p. 33.

161   Colonel Bolka Bar-Lev: Moshe Brilliant, "Israeli Asserts He
       Helped Amin Achieve Rule in '71," *New York Times*, July 17, 1976.

162   the Malire Mechanized Battalion: The role of the Malire Battalion
       in Obote's overthrow is described at length by David Martin in
       General Amin (London: Faber and Faber, 1974). Amii Omara-
       Otunnu, in *Politics and the Military in Uganda, 1890–1985* (New
       York: St. Martin's Press, 1987), is an authoritative source with
       regard to the reshuffles and infighting within the army leading
       up to the coup. The narrative of the event itself has been recon-
       structed from these and other documentary sources, as well as
       the personal recollections of several soldiers who witnessed or
       participated in it, including Emilo Mondo, Musa Eyaga and
       Mustafa Adrisi.

163   "within the chaos was order": Emilio Mondo, interview, 2003.

163   "tanks surrounded the parliamentary building": Andrew Mwenda,
       "I Left Amin to Pull the Trigger," *Monitor*, April 12, 2005.

163   "might be more conservative than Obote's": Theodore L. Eliot,
       Jr., memorandum for Mr. Henry A. Kissinger, January 25, 1971.
       Included in *Foreign Relations of the United States*, vol. E-5, part 1.
       Available at: http://www.state.gov/r/pa/ho/frus/nixon/e5/c15649
       .htm. All U.S. government communications cited in this chapter
       are from this source.

164   "all potential foci of resistance": Richard Dowden, "Death of a
       Despot: The 1971 Coup—Why Israel and Britain Were Delighted
       at Amin's Rise," *The Independent*, August 17, 2003. For a detailed
       description of the British response based on declassified Foreign
       Office records, see also "Who Put Gen. Idi Amin in Power?" *Mon-
       itor*, March 31, 2002.

164–65 "a festering mass of ancient grievances": Daniel K. Kalinaki,
       "Were UK, Israel Involved in the 1971 Coup?" *Monitor*, October
       23–October 29, 2005.

164   "one of the most stable areas in Africa": U.S. Department of State,
       telegram to Ambassador C. Clyde Ferguson, January 27, 1971.

164   "capacity to govern (which Amin decidedly has not)": C. Clyde Ferguson, telegram to U.S. Department of State, January 28, 1971.

165   "a decent chap": David Martin, *General Amin*, p. 167.

165   a signed portrait of Her Majesty: "Thirty Year Secrets of Israel, UK's Role in Amin Coup Revealed," *Monitor*, March 31, 2002.

165   "a sergeant and a boxing champion": Anthony Lewis, "The Coup Had a Certain Air of Familiarity," *New York Times*, January 31, 1971.

165   wholeheartedly endorsed: The passages from the *Telegraph* and the *Spectator* are quoted in Martin, *General Amin*, pp. 61–62.

165   "none too bright, but he was available": Martin, ibid., p. 57.

166   sophisticated new Harrier fighter jets: Martin, ibid., pp. 143–44.

167   Gowon's fast rise created considerable resentment: For the description of Gowon's rise, I relied on the assessments of fellow former officers, some of whom bore grudges against the general dating back to the 1970s. Despite the inherent unreliability of such sources, a fairly uniform picture of the general emerged, which was corroborated (sometimes reluctantly) by Gowon's friends and the general himself. Those who provided useful information included Emilio Mondo, Omia Farijalia, Ratib Mududu, Isaac Lumago, A. M. Tabu, Mustafa Adrisi, Moses Ali, Nasur Abdallah, Zeddy Maruru, Bernard Rwehururu and Ibrahim Duke.

167   "he was specially favored and specially selected": Emilio Mondo, interview, 2003.

167   "Lots of blood flowed": Bernard Rwehururu, *Cross to the Gun* (Kampala: Monitor Publications, 2002), p. 31.

168   clubs, bayonets and hippo hide whips: The most detailed account of the Mbarara barracks massacres can be found in the *Report of the Commission of Inquiry into Disappearances of People in Uganda*, pp. 618–63, and in the accompanying testimony transcripts.

168   "planned and coordinated at the command level": Emilio Mondo, interview, 2003.

168   the morning of July 9: Republic of Uganda, *Report of the Commission of Inquiry into the Mission Americans Messrs. Stroh and Siedle* (Entebbe, 1972).

169   assigned to lead a special board of inquiry: "Probe into Missing Americans," *Uganda Argus*, July 30, 1971.

169   "more polite and liberal than the others": Boniface Byanyima, interview, 2003.

PAGE

170 "several thousand full-time agents": Mahmood Mamdani, *Imperi-alism and Fascism in Uganda* (Trenton, N.J.: Africa World Press, 1984), p. 43.

171 which suddenly gave him mighty influence: Sebi is discussed at length in the *Report of the Commission of Inquiry into Disap-pearances of People in Uganda*, pp. 76–80. He also testified before the commission (pp. 5869–87). Additional information was gath-ered from interviews with many people who encountered him, including Yusuf Gowon, Yoasi Makaaru, John Hitler, George Kahonda and Boniface Byanyima.

171 "He would arrest people he knew were rich": Francis Bantariza, interview, 2003.

171 mockingly praying along: Yoasi Makaaru, interview, 2003.

171 "favorite watering hole": Peter Allen, *Interesting Times* (Lewes, Sussex: The Book Guild Ltd., 2000), p. 319. The following party scene comes from the same diary passage.

172 "ideal targets": Henry Kyemba, *State of Blood* (Kampala: Fountain Publishers, 1997), p. 56.

173 "so much in the hands of non-citizens": Idi Amin, "Message to the Nation on British Citizens of Asian Origin and Citizens of India," August 12, 1972.

174 "appealed vastly to his own sense of humor": Iain Grahame, *Amin and Uganda: A Personal Memoir* (New York: Granada, 1980), p. 151.

14: SEPTEMBER 1972

175 the final of the 400-meter hurdles: The description of the race is derived from the following sources: *The Olympic Series: Golden Moments 1920–2002*, documentary film, 2004; John Rodda, "Obituary; John Akii-Bua: Triumph, Then the Terror," *The Guardian*, June 28, 1997; Frank Litsky, "John Akii-Bua, 47, Is Dead; Ugandan Won Olympic Gold," *New York Times*, June 25, 1997.

175 "Akii-Bua [. . .] is building the nation": "He's Uganda's Golden Boy!" *Uganda Argus*, September 4, 1972.

176 "that is why they burned the Israelis": "Amin Praises Hitler for Killing of Jews," *Reuters*, September 12, 1972.

176 "representative of his unhappy land": "African Racist," *New York Times*, September 16, 1972.

176   giant headline: "Uganda Put On The World Map," *Uganda Argus*,
       September 16, 1972.

176   to deliver weapons to clandestine armories: This gunrunning
       mission is described in great detail in a column Museveni wrote
       for the state newspaper: "Museveni Relives the 1972 Attack on
       Mbarara Barracks," *New Vision*, September 18, 2002.

178   "a perfect failure": S. R. Karugire, *Roots of Instability in Uganda*
       (Kampala: Fountain Publishers, 1996), p. 80. In describing
       the planning and execution of the invasion I relied heavily
       on Museveni's writings, principally *Sowing the Mustard Seed:
       The Struggle for Freedom and Democracy in Uganda* (New York:
       Macmillan, 1997), as well as the perspective of Milton Obote,
       who wrote me an extensive e-mail before his death in which
       he described the events of 1972 and their aftermath. The two
       men's perspectives are, of course, often conflicting—each blamed
       the other for the attack's failure. It was Obote's opinion that
       Museveni had connived with allies in the Tanzanian intelligence
       service to "promote Museveni from a nonentity to a grand
       seignior" and the "Tanzanian Viceroy of Uganda." A more mea-
       sured analysis can be found in David Martin's *General Amin*.

179   "two groups of fools": Museveni, *Sowing the Mustard Seed*, p. 63.

179   forced to abandon his fleet: P. M. O. Onen, *The Diary of an Obedi-
       ent Servant during Misrule* (Kampala: Janyeko Publishing Centre,
       2000) pp. 89–104.

179   in charge of the defense of Mbarara: The following passages,
       which describe the rebel attack on Mbarara and its aftermath,
       were derived from multiple sources. For events on the army's side
       of the lines, I relied on interviews with several combatants,
       including Ali Fadhul and Yusuf Gowon. Documentary sources
       include contemporary newspaper accounts and the *Report of the
       Commission of Inquiry into Disappearances of People in Uganda*,
       which contains extensive testimony from many soldiers taken at
       a time when the events were still fresh in their minds (and they
       were feeling unconcerned about prosecution). The Ugandan gov-
       ernment related a propagandistic account of the attack in
       Uganda: The Second Year of the Second Republic (Entebbe, Republic
       of Uganda, January 1973). A final and most useful source was the
       transcript of Ali Fadhul's murder trial (*Uganda v. Ali Fadhul*, High
       Court Criminal Session Case No. 35/87), his various appeals and
       his subsequent retrial (Supreme Court of Uganda, Criminal

Appeal No. 13/93). Transcripts of these proceedings are available at Uganda's Supreme Court.

179 the back of an open Bedford truck: Very few participants in the rebel attack have survived, for obvious reasons. Museveni has provided the most detailed rendering, both in his book and the newspaper column "Museveni Relives the 1972 Attack on Mbarara Barracks," cited above. His account was largely confirmed in extensive interviews with another participant in the attack, Augustine Ruzindana. David Martin's *General Amin* also contains an extensive description, told largely from the perspective of Obote's men (pp. 170–97).

180 "We are too few": Museveni, *Sowing the Mustard Seed*, p. 65.

181 "changed the course of the whole adventure": Museveni, ibid., p. 66.

181 "hottest ever experienced by the enemy": "Battle Was the Hottest," *Uganda Argus*, September 18, 1972.

182 "Obote is drinking Bell [Beer]": "President Sees Captured Guerillas," *Uganda Argus*, September 19, 1972.

182 such as taxi drivers: "Invaders' Plan Revealed," *Uganda Argus*, September 20, 1972.

182 "that was when the hunting started": Francis Bantariza, interview, 2003.

182 "anyone harboring any of these people": "Invaders' Plan Revealed," *Uganda Argus*, September 20, 1972.

182 "a full list" of rebel sympathizers: "General Amin Cheered at the Battle Area," *Uganda Argus*, October 2, 1972.

183 the leadership of a local tea-growing cooperative: The Muslim leader, Hajji Abbas Kayemba, was later appointed a chief by Amin's government. His role in the death of his rivals in the tea cooperative is detailed in the *Report of the Commission of Inquiry into Disappearances of People in Uganda*, pp. 495–506. As a postscript to this story, Gowon said the reprieve he granted proved to be temporary: All the people he saved were subsequently killed.

184 pictures of the corpses for propaganda: During Ali Fadhul's retrial, Edirisa Mutagana, a former army photographer, testified that on September 21, he took pictures "of guerrillas dead or alive" around the Simba barracks (transcript, p. 72).

184 front page of Uganda's official state newspaper: "The Mbarara Invasion That Failed," *Uganda Argus*, September 21, 1972.

184   front page of the *New York Times*: *New York Times*, September 24,
       1972.

184   Naturally, it was taped: Nixon Tapes, Conversation 30-17, Sep-
       tember 21, 1972. Included in *Foreign Relations of the United States*,
       vol. E-5, part 1. Transcript available at http://www.state.gov/r/pa/
       ho/frus/nixon/e5/c15649.htm. All U.S. government communica-
       tions cited in this chapter are from this source.

185   again trying to foil British plans: Nixon Tapes, Conversation 154-
       7, September 24, 1972.

186   Nixon scrawled his initials: Henry Kissinger, memorandum for
       the President, December 4, 1972.

186   has never been exhumed: William Bagwegirira, a police officer
       who was in charge of the prison gang who buried the corpses, tes-
       tified at the first Ali Fadhul trial that the corpses remained in the
       barracks until September 21, five days after the invasion. He also
       provided a detailed description of the location and dimensions of
       the mass grave.

186   a "pure gift": Henry Kyemba, *State of Blood* (Kampala: Fountain
       Publishers, 1997), p. 58.

187   "The net had been widened": Emilio Mondo, interview, 2003.

187   floored Amin in a boxing match: The case of the newscaster, Ben
       Ochan, is examined in the *Report of the Commission of Inquiry into
       Disappearances of People in Uganda*, pp. 476–79. The story that
       he'd once knocked out Amin is recounted by Onen, *The Diary of
       an Obedient Servant*, p. 60.

187   "the destruction of the Ugandan elite": Central Intelligence
       Agency, Intelligence Information Cable, October 19, 1972.

187   "his kith and kin to retain power": George Kahonda, interview,
       2003.

188   "he won't need keys": John Hitler, interview, 2003.

188   "we accomplished the work he assigned us": Nasur Gille, state-
       ment to police, April 24, 2001.

188   to kiss his immense hands: "General Amin Cheered at the Battle
       Area," *Uganda Argus*, October 2, 1972. All subsequent quotations
       are from this article. Witnesses at the Ali Fadhul trials also
       described this event at length, adding details such as Amin's gift
       to Gowon.

189   along with ten other commendations: Amii Omara-Otunnu, *Pol-
       itics and the Military in Uganda, 1890–1985* (New York: St. Martin's
       Press, 1987), p. 121.

PAGE

190   sole command of Simba Battalion: "Four Promoted to Lt. Col.," *Uganda Argus*, December 21, 1972; "Gowon Is Promoted," *Uganda Argus*, September 1, 1973.

190   "Do you have any meat for me?": Anyule told this story to private investigator Brian Tibo, who related it to me.

15: BAD OMEN

191   "luckier ones have simply been shot": Quoted in David Martin, *General Amin* (London: Faber and Faber, 1974), pp. 227–28.

191   firing squad in a square in Mbarara: The professor's name was James Karuhanga. His execution is described by Peter Allen, *Interesting Times* (Lewes, Sussex: The Book Guild Ltd., 2000), p. 347. See also "Stern Warning to Others," *Voice of Uganda*, February 12, 1973.

192   "spoiling the good name of Uganda": "President Warns on Danger of 'FRONASA,'" *Voice of Uganda*, June 7, 1973.

192   "subversive forces": Martin, *General Amin*, pp. 204–5.

192   sympathizers mostly dispersed: Tony Avirgan and Martha Honey, *War in Uganda* (Westport, Conn.: Lawrence Hill and Company, 1982), p. 39.

192   returning home was vanishingly remote: Details of Yoweri Museveni's life in exile are contained in *Sowing the Mustard Seed: The Struggle for Freedom and Democracy in Uganda* (New York: Macmillan, 1997), as well as Eriya Kategaya's *Impassioned for Freedom* (Kampala: Wavah Books, 2006). Supplementary information was provided in interviews by other Ugandans who lived in Dar es Salaam during this period, including Kategaya, Augustine Ruzindana, Ruhakana Rugunda, Wafula Oguttu, Fred Bananuka and Yoga Adhola.

193   three vertical slash marks: Mark Leopold, *Inside West Nile* (Santa Fe, N.Mex.: School of American Research Press, 2005), p. 15.

193   more profitable to smuggle: For a detailed examination of the military's plunder of the economy, see Mahmood Mamdani, *Imperialism and Fascism in Uganda* (Trenton, N.J.: Africa World Press, 1984).

193   "Big Men, they could say anything": Bernard Rwehururu, interview, 2002.

193   "evil-minded sadist in a moment": Allen, *Interesting Times*, p. 511.

193   "everybody in Uganda must act as a member": Mamdani, *Imperialism and Fascism in Uganda*, pp. 54–57.

193   "the Defense Council has taken such a decision": *Report of the Uganda Commission of Inquiry into Violations of Human Rights*, Testimony of Mustafa Adrisi, p. 6107.

194   noms de guerre: The adoption of self-creating surnames is not so unusual in Uganda—as described in chapter 12, Gowon's actually originated as a childhood nickname. Henry Kyemba, in a 2005 interview, said many contemporaries assumed Gowon had taken his name to emulate the then-military dictator of Nigeria, General Yakubu Gowon. However, the defendant's friends said he started going by "Gowon" long beforehand.

194   "minimal, inaccurate and misleading": Allen, *Interesting Times*, p. 496.

194   lashed him with barbed wire: Alfred Buhugiro, interview, 2003.

194   "He could have done anything": *Report of the Commission of Inquiry into Disappearances of People in Uganda*, Testimony of Francis Xavier Kawuki, p. 6213. Details of the incident are also discussed in the testimony of the arresting officer, Selestino Bbale (pp. 5394–407), who said he was "frightened," and that of Sebi himself (pp. 5869–87).

194   "I was not a friend to Sebi": Under the judge's questioning in 1974, Sebi likewise denied being well acquainted with Gowon. The judge reacted incredulously. "Can you think of a reason why a responsible army officer should leave the barracks, go all the way to the Mbarara police station and instruct the policeman there not to proceed against a man called Sebi, who is you?" he said in challenge to the witness. "Why should he tell the police to withdraw the case against a person he didn't know? Does it make sense to you?" (*Report of the Commission of Inquiry into Disappearances of People in Uganda*, pp. 5881–82).

195   "He was a very clever man": Emilio Mondo, interview, 2003.

196   powers he'd supposedly picked up from witches: Bernard Rwehururu, *Cross to the Gun* (Kampala: Monitor Publications, 2002), p. 74.

196   "they printed money and could always print more": Henry Kyemba, *State of Blood* (Kampala: Fountain Publishers, 1997) p. 51. This book describes the economic crisis in detail.

197   "They were missionaries": Amos Betungura, interview, 2005.

197   imprisoned by the Bureau of State Research: This incident is recounted in James Kahigiriza's memoir, *Bridging the Gap: Struggling Against Sectarianism and Violence in Ankole and Uganda* (Kampala: Fountain Publishers, 2001), pp. 56–63. A government

minister who attempted to clear up the dispute, Henry Kyemba, added details in a 2005 interview.

197   "driving them away for interrogation": "Oryema, Ofumbi, Luwum Dead," *Voice of Uganda*, February 17, 1977.

197   a pistol shot through his mouth: Kyemba, *State of Blood*, p. 189.

198   time off to build a house: Isaac Lumago, interview, 2003.

198   "capable of telling lies": Emilio Mondo, interview, 2005.

198   "He was a snake!": This individual requested that he not be identified.

198   charged Ali with mismanaging: "Big Headed Ministers Warned," *Voice of Uganda*, April 11, 1978. Gowon told me Amin threw the ashtray at Ali, although other versions of the story say that Ali threw it at Amin, or that the two men drew pistols on each other.

198   "no one except the president is above the law": "77m Embezzled from UMSC," *Voice of Uganda*, May 13, 1978.

198   fought them off with a machine gun: The incident, reported by Avirgan and Honey in *War in Uganda*, p. 56, was described in detail by various knowledgeable sources.

199   his stretcher loaded on the plane: "Mustafa Injured in Motor Accident," *Voice of Uganda*, April 20, 1978; Avirgan and Honey, *War in Uganda*, pp. 49–50; *Report of the Uganda Commission of Inquiry into Violations of Human Rights*, Testimony of Mustafa Adrisi.

199   chief of staff toasting Amin's long life: *Voice of Uganda*, June 12, 1978.

199   burning down two houses: Avirgan and Honey, *War in Uganda*, p. 54. This book is the definitive history of the war between Uganda and Tanzania. Along with Bernard Rwehururu's *Cross to the Gun*, it provided the basis of the following account. Additional details were gathered from contemporary news accounts and through interviews with Yusuf Gowon, Emilio Mondo, Mustafa Adrisi, Moses Ali, Nasur Abdallah, A. M. Tabu, Omia Farijalia, Ratib Mududu, Nuru Dralega, Ali Fadhul and others.

199–200   TANZANIA TROOPS ATTACK UGANDA: *Voice of Uganda*, October 13, 1978.

200   "his children" in Tanzania: "Uganda Troops Won't Cross into Tanzania," *Voice of Uganda*, October 19, 1978.

200   Tanzanian corpse, supposedly a soldier's: "Frontline News in Pictures," *Voice of Uganda*, November 2, 1978.

201   a bovine curse: Museveni, *Sowing the Mustard Seed*, p. 95.

201   "he would have kissed him": "Malire Troops Back from Frontline," *Voice of Uganda*, November 13, 1978.

201   "Except on military matters": Wafula Oguttu, interview, 2005.

201   moles inside Amin's Bureau: Museveni had in fact placed informants inside State Research. In a 2005 interview, Major General Kahinda Otafiire, now a powerful government minister, told me that he and Amama Mbabazi—Uganda's current minister of security—worked as double-agents within the secret police agency in the late 1970s. "It was extremely risky," he said.

202   "I felt so buoyant": Museveni, *Sowing the Mustard Seed*, p. 93.

202   "This is the opportunity": Milton Obote, "The UPC Role in the Removal of Amin, *Uganda People's Congress*, 2001, http://www.upcparty.net/obote/upc_role_Idi_Amin.htm.

202   a party for the army high command: "Marshal Amin Notes Dar Troops Build Up with Grave Concern," *Voice of Uganda*, November 25, 1978.

203   "weak and mindless cowards": A. M. Tabu, interview, 2002.

203   "Do you fight with maps?": Bernard Rwehururu, interview, 2002.

203   "dying and leaving their money": A. M. Tabu, interview.

203   "we'd get an outburst from Amin": Emilio Mondo, interview, 2005.

204   "prowling in other officers' affairs": Nasur Abdallah, interview, 2002.

204   disgruntled generals headed by Gowon: "Plot Reported in Uganda," *Washington Post*, January 23, 1979.

204   standing at attention behind him: "Marshal Amin Calls On Nation to Work Hard," *Voice of Uganda*, January 26, 1979.

205   nicknamed him *bisirani*: Rwehururu, *Cross to the Gun*, p. 125. The story that the troops believed Gowon was a supernatural magnet for missiles was repeated by several other veterans.

205   openly dismissive of Museveni: Avirgan and Honey, *War in Uganda*, p. 75.

205   Amin removed Gowon and appointed himself: "Marshal Idi Amin Appointed Chief of Staff of Joint Services," *Voice of Uganda*, March 8, 1979.

205   "didn't care what happened to Uganda": Emilio Mondo, interview, 2005.

PAGE

206 "Only hell knows where he is": "The End of an Era," *Drum*, April 1979, reprinted in *Uganda: The Rise and Fall of Idi Amin*, p. 231.

206 "rumor-mongering and loitering about": BBC Summary of World Broadcasts, March 31, 1979.

16: THE SCARS

208 "night of the wheelbarrows": Steven Strasser, "The Fall of Idi Amin," *Newsweek*, April 23, 1979, p. 41.

208 typewriters, couches, refrigerators: Peter Allen, *Interesting Times* (Lewes, Sussex: The Book Guild Ltd., 2000), p. 514.

208 implicated several thousand Ugandans: Tony Avirgan and Martha Honey, *War in Uganda* (Westport, Conn.: Lawrence Hill and Company, 1982), p. 148–49.

208 aggrieved and mistrustful men: Works consulted regarding the politics of the liberation period include Avirgan and Honey, *War in Uganda*; Yoweri Museveni, *Sowing the Mustard Seed: The Struggle for Freedom and Democracy in Uganda* (New York: Macmillan, 1997); George Ivan Smith, *Ghosts of Kampala: The Rise and Fall of Idi Amin* (New York: St. Martin's Press, 1980); David Lamb, *The Africans* (New York: Vintage, 1987), pp. 77–95.

209 no longer the stately British-designed city: For postwar living conditions in Kampala, see Stephen Maikowski, "Uganda: A Country Returns to Life," *Christian Science Monitor*, April 1, 1980; Robin Knight, "Uganda on the Bottom and Still Sliding," *U.S. News and World Report*, October 13, 1980; Gregory Jaynes, "African Apocalypse," *The New York Times Magazine*, November 16, 1980; "Uganda: The Horrors Come Out at Night," *The Economist*, November 21, 1981.

209 "considered tribalism as 'natural'": Uganda National Liberation Front, *Basic Documents of the UNLF* (Kampala, 1979), pp. 32-33.

209 spreading scurrilous rumors about him: Specifically, the rumor was that Museveni's men were massacring Bairu civilians. During the liberation government's unity conference in Moshi, Tanzania, Museveni complained that someone "had gone around alleging" that he "was killing people in Mbarara" (*Basic Documents of the UNLF*, p. 32). In *Sowing the Mustard Seed*, Museveni claims that Rurangaranga was the source of the false charge (p. 99).

210 "shooting, killing and whatnot": *Report of the Uganda Commission of Inquiry into Violations of Human Rights*, Testimony of Clement

Kaboggoza-Musoke, p. 4524. Much of this chapter's description of the postwar political situation in Ankole is taken from the same report, particularly the discussion on pp. 89–98. Further citations within this chapter will be abbreviated as *Commission of Inquiry*. See also Museveni, *Sowing the Mustard Seed*, and Eriya Kategaya's *Impassioned for Freedom* (Kampala: Wavah Books, 2006).

210   "to revenge on the Muslims": *Commission of Inquiry*, Testimony of Kaboggoza-Musoke, pp. 4533–34.

210   Sebi apparently died in exile: I was told of Sebi's death by multiple sources, including Nasur Gille and Mohammed Anyule, but was unable to confirm it.

211   required to register with the police: "Nubians Required," *Uganda Times*, July 19, 1979.

211   published as a daily feature: The collaborators' names were published for more than a month between November and December 1979. A quarter-century later, Charles Onyango-Obbo, the country's foremost political columnist, wrote: "One could literally hear the country hold [its] breath when the morning papers came out. Wives of husbands who had disappeared turned up on the list, as did young people from middle-class families, dozens of the most liked students at the prestigious Makerere University, professionals of all types. None of them fitted the profile of the illiterate thugs who were seen as the bedrock of Amin's vicious control machine. The whole list was never published. Today, no one talks about it. And many people on it have found respectability. Some are even [cabinet] ministers." ("Amin's Foot Soldiers: The Untold Story," *The East African*, August 18, 2003).

211   "Everything has got an end": Joseph Ssonko, letter, *Uganda Times*, November 19, 1979.

211   three thousand cattle across the border: "The Ugandan Exodus," *Sudan Now*, July 1979, p. 17.

211   killing civilians indiscriminately: "Genocide Report Shocks Ugandans," *Weekly Topic*, March 13, 1981.

211   "Amin-ism remained": Yoweri Museveni, "The 8-Year Armed Struggle Against Dictator Amin," *Weekly Topic*, April 11, 1980.

211   Bashir Semakula received a visitor: The following account of reprisals in Kiziba is taken from the *Commission of Inquiry* testimony of Bashir Semakula (pp. 4106–14), Clement Kaboggoza-Musoke (pp. 4520–50) and numerous other witnesses whose

testimony appears between pages 4093–142. Additional informa-
tion was provided in interviews by Semakula, his brother Noor
Serjunge, Augustine Ruzindana, Kahinda Otafiire and Edward
Rurangaranga.

213   Abbas Kayemba was one of the local Muslims: Kayemba was also
the leader of the group that brought a truckload of Christian prisoners to the Simba barracks in the aftermath of the September
1972 invasion, according to Yusuf Gowon (see chapter 14).

213   "up to you to cut the branches": *Commission of Inquiry*, p. 89. In
an interview, Rurangaranga denied that the rally occurred as
described in the report. What the proverb was meant to convey,
he said, was that terror was larger than any one man. "You see,
Amin ruled this country for eight years, and created a system
called Amin-ism," Rurangaranga said. "Amin-ism meant taking
people away in the boots of cars, people disappearing, people
smuggling. I said now we have a duty as liberators to make sure
those habits stop. To remove Amin personally is not enough. It
has to change. If that is what I am being accused of, of saying
that Amin-ism is a system that has been created, and it has to be
removed—if that is a crime, then I accept it."

214   "To Idi Amin": *Commission of Inquiry*, Testimony of Jaliya Nkwen-
jenje, p. 4111.

215   "Machote is killing me!": *Commission of Inquiry*, Testimony of
Dauda Serujumbe, p. 4100.

215   Bashir's father rose to question: Rumors that Museveni might
have played a role in inciting the violence in Kiziba have followed him throughout his career. The Commission of Inquiry,
which Museveni appointed upon taking power in 1986, concluded
in its final report that it had "no doubt" that the allegations
"were without any foundation." Nonetheless, the allegation that
Museveni had a hand in the atrocities committed against Muslims in Ankole remains a common refrain among Uganda's opposition politicians. In my extensive investigation of the events, I
never found a single piece of evidence to substantiate this claim.

215   "it had become political": *Commission of Inquiry*, Testimony of
Frank Guma, p. 4097.

216   "greatest occasion in the whole history": "Obote Home after
'Long Trip from Singapore,'" *Weekly Topic*, May 30, 1980.

216 "heal old wounds": "New Party Picks Up," *Weekly Topic*, June 6, 1980.

216 couldn't recall having made a single error: "UPC Made No Mistakes, Says Obote," *Weekly Topic*, July 11, 1980.

216 "meet intimidation with intimidation": Jeremy M. Weinstein, *Inside Rebellion: The Politics of Insurgent Violence* (New York: Cambridge University Press, 2007), p. 63. Weinstein's book provides an excellent analysis of Museveni's tactics during the civil war. See also Nelson Kasfir, "Guerrillas and Civilian Participation: The National Resistance Army in Uganda, 1981–86," *Journal of Modern African Studies* (June 2005); Ondonga ori Amaza, *Museveni's Long March: From Guerrilla to Statesman* (Kampala: Fountain Publishers, 1998).

217 "Mr. Fix-It": Yoweri Museveni, *What Is Africa's Problem?* (Minneapolis: University of Minnesota Press, 2000), p. 6.

217 "key architects of this tragedy": *Commission of Inquiry*, p. 97.

17: THE PROSECUTION

227 "Uganda versus Major General Yusuf Gowon": Unless otherwise noted, all descriptions of the trial come from one of two sources: my personal observations as a reporter in the courtroom, or a transcript of the proceedings recorded by hand by Justice Mukiibi and subsequently retyped by a court secretary (*Uganda v. Major General Yusuf Gowon and two others*, High Court Criminal Session Case No. 70/02). In general, for the purposes of direct quotation, I favored my own notes over the court record, because the judge was not primarily interested in recording courtroom exchanges verbatim, and often chose not to write down testimony that he considered irrelevant or inadmissible.

230 "as a guarantee": Baron James Atkin, quoted in J. H. Jearey, "Trial by Jury and Trial with the Aid of Assessors in the Superior Courts of the British African Territories: I," *Journal of African Law* (Autumn 1960), p. 91. Other works that were useful in preparing this and all subsequent discussion of Ugandan law include J. H. Jearey, "The Structure, Composition and Jurisdiction of Courts and Authorities Enforcing Criminal Law in British African Territories," *The International and Comparative Law Quarterly* (July 1960) pp. 396–414; Francis Ayume, *Criminal Procedure and Law in Uganda* (Nairobi: Longman, 1986); B. J. Odoki, *Criminal Investigations and*

Prosecutions (Kampala: LDC Publishers, 1999); Douglas Brown, *Criminal Procedure in Uganda and Kenya* (London: Sweet and Maxwell, 1970); R. W. Cannon, "Law, Bench and Bar in the Protectorate of Uganda," *The International and Comparative Law Quarterly* (October 1961), pp. 877–91; H. R. Hone, "The Native of Uganda and the Criminal Law," *Journal of Comparative Legislation and International Law* (1939), pp. 179–97; R. Knox Mawer, "Juries and Assessors in Criminal Trials in Some Commonwealth Countries: A Preliminary Survey," *The International and Comparative Law Quarterly* (October 1961), pp. 892–98, and Richard Vogler, "The International Development of the Jury: The Role of the British Empire," *International Review of Penal Law* (2001), pp. 525–50.

232   "evidence of the weakest kind": Brown, *Criminal Procedure and Law*, p. 83.

232   "I have serious reservations": Michael Wamasebu, Memorandum to the Director of Public Prosecutions, June 19, 2002.

235   roundabout journey by bus: Interview with police officer Drakuawuzia Kazimiro.

236   "It is bad to *lie!*": Testimony of police officer Willy Waigo. When I attempted to interview Waigo about the case, he arranged to meet me at a Kampala bar in the company of another officer who worked with him in the Serious Crimes division of Uganda's police force. After about a half-hour of unenlightening conversation, the corporal stopped answering questions. "You know," Waigo's friend said, "you will be making money off of this article you are writing." He suggested that I would have to share an advance on those proceeds with him and Waigo if I wanted the rest of the story. I refused to pay up. This was the only time I was directly asked for a bribe in the course of writing this book.

237   "bones of your father": Alfred Orijabo, radio interview, *Patrick Kamara Live*, Monitor Radio, August 2002.

238   the epidemic crept northward: Works consulted on the history of the spread of AIDS in Uganda include Helen Epstein, *The Invisible Cure* (New York: Farrar, Straus and Giroux, 2007); numerous articles by the same author from *The New York Review of Books*; Alex Shoumatoff, "In Search of the Source of AIDS," *African Madness* (New York, Vintage: 1986), pp. 129–202; Laurie Garrett, "Children of the Plague," *Newsday*, July 6, 2000; and Edward Hooper, *The River: A Journey to the Source of HIV and AIDS* (New York: Little,

Brown, 1999). Hooper's book has encountered controversy because of its highly debatable conclusion that the emergence of AIDS was connected to polio vaccine trials conducted in the Belgian Congo during the 1950s, but it remains the most voluminous account I have yet encountered of the early years of the epidemic in Africa.

239   "in a Volkswagen": A retired captain named Ayub Noah Ajobe mentioned this in his testimony at the first murder trial of Ali Fadhul (transcript, p. 97).

18: TAKING THE STAND

244   "break in the chain": B. J. Odoki, *Criminal Investigations and Prosecutions* (Kampala: LDC Publishers, 1999), p. 14.

19: THE DEFENSE

252   "kill the deceased": Yusuf Gowon, statement to police, April 24, 2001. According to several witnesses to his interrogation, the Swahili word he used to describe Anyule and Gille was *takataka*.

254   stamped "URGENT": Hajat Anuna Omari, letter to J. B. Okumu, principal private secretary to President Museveni, May 3, 2001.

254   "delicacy of the matter": J. B. Okumu, letter to Elizabeth Kutesa, director of the Criminal Investigative Division of the Uganda Police, May 7, 2001. After several weeks, the police department sent a four-page reply listing the evidence amassed against Gowon in great detail, and tersely promising that the president's office would be "kept informed of any developments." (Godfrey Bangirana, letter to J. B. Okumu, May 31, 2001.)

255   "the usual nepotism": Peter Allen, *Interesting Times* (Lewes, Sussex: The Book Guild Ltd., 2000), pp. 490–91.

255   She'd been the mistress: Gowon and others told me this.

256   there was no clear evidence: I interviewed Ayume once, in 2004. Shortly after we talked, he was killed in a car accident, so it was never possible to question him in any greater detail. Details of his career were gathered from various posthumous testimonials and newspaper obituaries, including (the rather cheekily headlined) "Bye Bye Ayume!" *Weekly Observer*, May 20, 2004. Justice Mukiibi, in a brief 2005 interview, adamantly denied any suggestion of prejudice toward the defendants.

256   "Ugandan and non-Ugandan": The report is quoted at length by Mark Leopold, *Inside West Nile* (Santa Fe, N.Mex.: School of American Research Press, 2005), p. 56.

258   "take that kind of action": All of the following dialogue was simultaneously translated aloud by Caleb Alaka.

260   West Nile's folklore: A. T. Dalfovo, *Lugbara Proverbs* (Rome: Comboni Missionaries, 1993).

261   a former opposition party candidate: His name was Mahmoud Angoliga.

262   Kampala asylum: Lominda Afedraru, "Key Witness in Gowon Trial Dies," *Monitor*, January 15, 2003.

263   "witch-hunting": Uganda National Rescue Front II, *Agenda for Peace Talks with the Government of the Republic of Uganda* (September 2002).

264   He was penniless: Lominda Afedraru, "Gowon Faces Fresh Charges," *Monitor*, January 27, 2002.

265   denied that the visit occurred: Ali didn't take pains to hide the fact that he enjoyed watching Gowon's trial, however. "I think this is the best system, the best method," he said. "If anyone has a grievance he should be able to take it to court." When it came to the struggle over aid funds that Gowon claimed was the origin of his prosecution, Ali didn't deny that there was a dispute, but said his rival had expected more money than he deserved from the government. The details of the saga are far too labyrinthine to summarize here; suffice it to say that there is no evidence that it had anything whatsoever to do with Gowon's arrest.

20: JUDGMENT

266   "Only nostalgia": Riccardo Orizio, *Talk of the Devil: Encounters with Seven Dictators*, trans. Avril Bardoni (New York: Walker and Company, 2002), pp. 9–32.

266   "They don't believe": Eriya Kategaya, interview, 2002.

267   "British tabloid press": Charles Onyango-Obbo, "Ear to the Ground," *Monitor*, July 2, 2003.

267   dying of kidney failure: David Kibirige, "Amin in Coma," *Monitor*, July 20, 2003.

267   canvassed Kampala's bars and street corners: Mercy Nalugo and Victor Karamagi, "Dead or Alive, Amin Should Return," *Monitor*, July 22, 2003.

268   "very long spoon": Ogen Kevin Aliro, "Museveni: No Tears for Amin," *Monitor*, August 19, 2003.

268   "arrest the dead body": Felix Osike, "Amin's Body Can Return—Museveni," *New Vision*, July 23, 2003.

268   four hundred pounds: David Kibirige, "Idi Amin Overweight," *Monitor*, July 22, 2003.

269   asked for a donation: I didn't give him one, but assured him I'd publicize his plight.

269   "Up to down": Isaac Lumago, interview, 2003.

271   "His parents are here": Brian Atiku, interview, 2003.

274   "neglect of duty": Republic of Uganda, *Report of the Judicial Commission of Inquiry into Corruption in the Uganda Police Force* (Kampala: May 2000), pp. 15–22, 156–60.

274   "our African culture": Ibrahim Duke, interview, 2004.

275   sign the confession: Testimony of police officer Drakuawuzia Kazimiro.

276   blanket of worms: Alfred Wasike, "Amin Is Dead," *New Vision*, August 17, 2003.

277   "That he killed": Ogen Kevin Aliro, "Museveni: No Tears for Amin," *Monitor*, August 19, 2003.

277   "leadership is a dustbin": Alfred Wasike, "Idi Amin Buried in Mecca," *New Vision*, August 18, 2003.

277   "just bad politics": Kefa Atibuni and Tabu Butagira, "Thousands Mourn Amin in Arua," *Monitor*, August 21, 2003.

21: REPRISE

282   goat to slaughter: This event was described to me by many people who were present, including Gowon, Anyule and Ayume.

286   fifty million dollars in assets: Halima Abdallah, "Nubians Petition for Sh90B," *Monitor*, May 12, 2004.

287   1977 killing of Janan Luwum: *Report of the Uganda Commission of Inquiry into Violations of Human Rights*, Testimony of Mustafa Adrisi, pp. 6188–264.

288   "time for reconciliation": "There Is Time for Everything, Says President Museveni," *Monitor*, October 21, 2005.

289   "promoting sectarianism": Among those arrested for publishing such reports were three writers from the *Weekly Observer*, a respected independent newspaper, and Andrew Mwenda, then of the *Monitor*, the country's best-known journalist. ("Journalists under Fire over Bairu/Bahima, Passport Stories," *Monitor*, June 7, 2006.)

PAGE

289   Kampala soccer stadium: Raphael Okello, "TBN Leads Namboole
      Worship," *New Vision*, October 17, 2005.

290   finance schools and AIDS medications: These and many other
      scandals have been exhaustively chronicled in the Ugandan
      media. An excellent analysis can be found in a confidential—
      though now well-publicized—report prepared for the World
      Bank: Joel D. Barkan et al., "The Political Economy of Uganda:
      The Art of Managing a Donor-Financed Neo-Patrimonial State,"
      unpublished, 2004. "Once touted as one of the 'new leaders of
      Africa,'" the report concludes, "the President, over the last eight
      years, has increasingly resembled the old."

290   "Stop heckling us": Yoweri Museveni, press conference, Septem-
      ber 29, 2005.

291   "I'm not a lawyer": Yoweri Museveni, interview, 2005.

ACKNOWLEDGMENTS

A journalist I greatly admire, someone who knows Africa well, passed along a piece of wisdom before I departed for Uganda: "Try to tell just one story." This book is my attempt to follow his advice. If I could tell just one tale behind its creation, however, it would be the heroic story of my wife, Jennifer Saba. When we first met, this book was just an unformed idea. Through years of research trips, rough drafts and sacrificed weekends, she has stood behind the project, offering me her love, her sound editorial judgment and her steadfast reassurances that somehow, someday, it would reach its completion. I know that she will be pleased to see herself proved right, yet again.

My family has likewise offered continual support. My parents, Thomas and Diane Rice, raised me in a house full of books and never questioned my decision to pursue a writing life, while my sisters, Jennifer, Carrie and Katie, are never afraid to affectionately reacquaint me with reality. My grandmother and grandfather, Greta and Edward, who took me on some of my first foreign travels, were the ones who taught me to get going.

It was Peter Bird Martin who taught me to stop. In 2002, Peter, then the executive director of the Institute of Current World Affairs, sent me to Uganda with few instructions other than: Slow down, look around and write to him about what I saw. This book began as a series of articles published by the institute; to its staff, its board and its generous donors, I offer my eternal gratitude. I am grateful, too, to P. J. Mark, my tireless agent, who looked at those articles and saw something, and to Riva

Hocherman, my perceptive editor, who took a raw manuscript and transformed it into a book.

Throughout this process, many friends and colleagues have taken the time to critique drafts, hash out ideas and offer consolation—so many that I could never manage to thank them all. In the United States, Anne Barnard, Josh Benson, Bucky Gardner, Andrew and Robin Goldman, Jessie Graham, Roy Gutman, Sheelah Kolhatkar, Devin Leonard, Douglas Meehan, Beth Nottingham, Lily Parshall, Sridhar Pappu, Manolis Priniotakis, Christopher Stewart and Paul Wachter cheerfully gave guidance, while Brendan Vaughan, Vera Titunik, Hilary Stout, Adam Shatz, Nick Paumgarten, John Palatella, Peter Kaplan, Robert Guest and Philip Gourevitch kept me employed and in print. Barry Link, Phillip Niemeyer, and Vanessa Vick helped to make this book look good. In Uganda, a convivial fraternity of fellow journalists offered me company while I was around and kept me abreast when I was absent. In particular, I thank Paul Busharizi, Tim Cocks, Glenna Gordon, Tristan McConnell, Andrew Mwenda, Dan Wallis and Rachel Scheier, who also provided able research assistance. Ibrahim Duke was a trusted guide through West Nile. And Allan Begira Abainenamar—my friend, travel companion and interpreter—was literally there every step of the way. This book is very much his accomplishment too.

Portions of what I've written describe events I witnessed firsthand. Other sections contain reconstructions of things that happened in the past, which in every case are the product of extensive research. Those who sat for interviews are listed in the notes, but I wish to express my special appreciation to a few who were particularly giving. First and foremost, I thank Duncan Muhumuza Laki, his wife, Cathy, and the rest of his family, who welcomed me into their homes on countless occasions to talk about events that remain painful. Kenneth Kereere, Fred Bananuka and Brian Tibo also explained a great deal. Yusuf Gowon agreed to answer my questions, and kept talking to me long after it ceased to offer him any foreseeable benefit. Emilio Mondo provided many revealing insights about the inner workings of Idi Amin's regime. Caleb Alaka and Simon Byabakama Mugenyi were accessible and helpful throughout the long trial. Robert Kabushenga and Onapito Ekomoloit helped me to secure one very big interview.

Ironically, I found that the best place to conduct archival research about Uganda was a school outside Chicago. I thank the extremely accommodating staff of the Melville J. Herskovits Library of African Studies at Northwestern University, and also Matthew and Patricia

Rich, who offered me a place to stay while I did my work there. Much of what I've written about Uganda's history and culture is indebted to the previously published work of others. I depended particularly on two outstanding academic books: *Not All the King's Men*, Martin Doornbos's analysis of Ankole's political and ethnic dynamics, and *Inside West Nile*, Mark Leopold's corrective excavation of the background of Amin's people. Nelson Kasfir of Dartmouth College and Neil Kodesh of the University of Wisconsin also provided me with much expert perspective, and their friendship.

The most important sources of information for this book were not outside observers, however, but Ugandans themselves: not only those I managed to interview, but also an immense number of people who recorded their experiences in other forums. I frequently consulted the report and collected testimony of the Commission of Inquiry headed by Justice Arthur Oder, who regrettably did not live to see this book completed. I also relied upon the 1975 *Report of the Commission of Inquiry into Disappearances of People in Uganda Since the 25th of January 1971*. (The story of this forgotten document, produced under unimaginably adverse circumstances by a Ugandan judicial commission, is remarkable in itself.) Finally, I learned a great deal from the many memoirs recently published by Ugandans who lived through Amin's regime. In the eight years since Duncan Laki set off to solve his father's murder, Ugandan publishers have produced a copious library of such reminiscences, accounts of the past that vary immensely in terms of quality and candor, but which suggest by their very existence that the story of rediscovery described in this book did not occur in a vacuum. It is often said that Africans haven't written down their history because of some intrinsic cultural resistance. I hope that this book, in some small measure, can help to dispel that myth.

INDEX

A

Abdallah, Nasur, 14–15

Adrisi, Mustafa
   after liberation, 269
   assassination attempt on,
      198–99
   background of, 193–94
   defense of Gowon, 195, 197,
      207
   picture of, 195

Africa
   AIDS epidemic in, 238
   colonization of, 143–49, 151,
      155
   tribal identity in, 151

"Africanization" policy, 81

AIDS epidemic, 238

Aisu, Victor, 273–74

Akii-Bua, John, 175, 176

Alaka, Caleb
   on Aisu's request for a bribe,
      274
   background of, 251–52, 253
   on cocounsels, 272
   cross-examination of
      witnesses, 240, 246–49,
      260–61
   defense of Besigye, 291
   defense strategy of, 248–50,
      253–54, 261–63
   on guilt of Anyule and Gille,
      257
   picture of, 247

Ali, Moses
   attack on, 198, 336
   political position of, 264
   relationship with Gowon,
      264–65, 344
   role in 1971 massacre, 308

Alternatives to Violence Project,
   264

Amin, Amule, 269

Amin, Idi
   assassination attempt on, 196
   in the British military, 155,
      157–58

Amin, Idi (*cont'd*)
in coma, 267, 268
coup by, 89–92, 99–100, 163–65
death of, 276
exile in Saudi Arabia, 11, 15, 231, 266–70
expelling of Indians, 172–73, 175–76
folklore surrounding, 154, 157, 196, 326
Great Britain and, 166, 172
international media's portrayal · of, 28–29
Israel and, 163, 164, 165, 172
Kahigiriza and, 118–19
on murders at the Munich Olympics, 176
in Obote's military, 159–62
opposing histories regarding regime of, 13–16
at Organization of African Unity, 30–32
overthrow of, 8
pictures of, 166, 200, 204
promotion of loyal tribesmen, 166–67
purges under, 26–29, 112, 166, 167–68, 186–87, 199
reactions to rebel attacks, 181, 182, 184, 189–90
rebuke of Museveni, 191–92
religion and, 196–97
telegrams of, 10, 173–74
Ugandans' initial support of, 104–6
use of Cold War rhetoric, 30
use of mercenaries, 168

visits to the Simba Battalion, 171–72, 188–89
war with Tanzania, 199–205
world leaders' underestimation of, 164–65
Amin, Moses, 188, 189
amnesty policies, 14–15, 40, 136–37, 234, 254
Ankole
British colonization of, 66
education in, 73
ethnic divisions in, 67–68, 70–74, 76, 123, 210, 313
party politics in, 77, 78, 80
resistance to revisiting history in, 123–25
social and economic development in, 81–84
Anyule, Mohammed
arrest of, 43–48
attorneys for, 252, 264, 271–72
background of, 40, 43
confession of, 233, 234, 257–59
Duncan on role of, 246
encounter with Duncan at trial, 243
Gowon's offer of forgiveness, 282
at Luzira Prison, 135
ownership of Laki's car, 38–39, 190, 232
picture of house of, 45
pictures of, 228, 259
plea at trial, 227–28
release from prison, 280–81, 283
retracing of steps in murder, 59–60, 121

support for, during trial, 271
  witness testimony against, 239
Arens, William, 154
Arua, 153
Ayume, Francis, 255–56, 282

B

Baganda, 8, 92, 165–66
Bahima
  ethnic division between Bairu
    and, 68, 70–73, 76, 123, 126,
    289, 313
  Kahigiriza's advocacy for,
    125–26, 128, 321
  view of education, 94
Bairu
  Catholic vs. Anglican, 76
  cooperative ranching societies
    of, 82
  ethnic division between
    Bahima and, 68, 70–73, 76,
    123, 126, 289, 313
Bakari, Zubairi, 98–99, 100
Bananuka, Fred, 110
Bananuka, Nekemia
  after Amin's coup, 104
  Kahigiriza and, 85–87, 88
  murder of, 112, 125
  Museveni's recruitment of,
    109–10
  picture of, 113
  reaction to Amin's coup, 100
  relationship with Eliphaz,
    101
  rise to political power, 88–89
Bananuka, Sarah, 124–25, 128
Bantariza, Francis, 128
Banyankole, 18, 67–68, 123

Banyankole Cultural Foundation,
  128
Bar-Lev, Bolka, 161–62, 164
Barigye, John, 321
Besigye, Kizza, 288, 290–91, 294
Betungura, Amos, 111
Big Brother Africa, 267
Bokassa, Jean-Bédel, 31
British East Africa Company,
  66–67
Brooke, Edward, 96
Buganda, 85, 149, 151
Buhwairoha, Blasio, 260–61
Bureau of State Research, 194,
  197, 208
Bush, George H. W., 37
Bush, George W., 289
"Butabika," Juma
Buteera, Richard, 234
Byanyima, Boniface, 187

C

cannibalism, 154, 326
Carmichael, Stokely, 96
Catholicism, 76, 170
Christians, 20, 170, 196–97,
  210–15, 217
Churchill, Winston, 152
class system, 193
Clinton, Bill, 40, 290
colonization
  of Africa, 145–49, 151, 155
  of Uganda, 7–8, 66–70,
    149–51, 155–56
Conrad, Joseph, 149
cooperative ranching societies,
  82
crackpot anthropology, 70, 313

D

Dar es Salaam, 95, 96–97
Defense Council, 193–94
Democratic Party (DP), 77, 78, 82,
    83–84
Duke, Ibrahim, 271

E

education
    in Ankole, 73
    Bahima's view of, 94
    Katungi's views on, 71, 72
Elizabeth II, 165, 174
Emin, Mehemet. *See* Pasha, Emin
Entebbe International Airport,
    179, 196
Equatoria, 144, 146, 151
ethnic divisions in Uganda, 65,
    67–74, 76, 123, 126, 289,
    313
ethnicity, fluidity of, 152
Eyaga, Musa, 271

F

Fadhul, Ali
    antipathy toward Gowon, 135,
        322
    on assistance from Ankole
        citizens, 128–29
    conviction of, 14, 128, 322
    investigation of rebel attacks,
        179, 183
    position in Amin's military, 167
FRELIMO, 97
Front for National Salvation, 110,
    177, 178, 191

G

Gadhafi, Mu'ammar al-, 172
General Service Unit, 99, 105
Gille, Nasur
    on Amin's use of local
        intelligence, 123
    arrest of, 48
    attorneys for, 252, 264, 271–72
    confession of, 50, 234, 235,
        257–58, 277–78, 279
    defense strategy of, 272–75
    encounter with Duncan at
        trial, 243
    at Luzira Prison, 135
    murder of Eliphaz, 47, 48,
        63–64
    pictures of, 49, 228, 258
    plea at trial, 227–28
    release from prison, 280–81,
        283
    retracing of steps in murder,
        60, 63, 121
    testimony at trial, 274–76
    two years after release from
        prison, 286
    witness testimony against,
        239
Good Hope charity, 265, 283, 344
Gordon, General, 147
"Gore," Christopher, 194
Gowon, Yusuf
    actions after rebel attacks,
        182–84, 332
    arrest of, 17, 52–54, 195, 197,
        206–7
    attorneys for, 263, 279
    childhood of, 152–53
    on collaborators, 194–95

defense strategy of, 248–50,
    253–54, 261–63
denial of knowledge about
    Eliphaz, 53, 54, 59, 140, 219
encounter with Duncan at
    trial, 242–43
exile in Congo, 207
at Luzira Prison, 133–35,
    138–39, 140, 264–65
military training of, 160, 162
in Obote's military, 159–60, 161
order to kill Eliphaz, 50
pictures of, 161, 195, 200, 204,
    228, 281
plea at trial, 227–28
promotion in Amin's military,
    167, 169–70, 190, 192, 197,
    198, 199
prosecution's case at trial of,
    231–36
reactions to prosecution of,
    134, 141–42, 270
on reconciliation, 283–84
relationship with Ali, 264–65,
    344
relationship with Amin, 160
release from prison, 280–83
repatriation deal with
    Museveni, 136–37, 234, 254
residence of, 51, 285
return from exile, 53, 137, 142,
    270
role in war with Tanzania, 201,
    203–6
on Salim Sebi, 194, 335
and Simba Battalion's defense,
    180–81
two years after release from
    prison, 284–87

on war with Tanzania, 199,
    203–4
witness testimony against, 239
Grahame, Iain, 157, 158
Great Britain
    Amin and, 166, 172
    colonization of Uganda, 7–8,
        66–70, 149–51, 155–56
    objections to murders in
        Uganda, 192
    power-sharing agreement with
        Uganda, 84
    reaction to Amin's coup, 164
    Uganda's independence from,
        8, 23–24, 77, 78
Great Rift Valley, 7
Guevara, Che, 96

H

Hamitic myth, 70, 313
Hemery, David, 175
High Court of Uganda, 229
Hitler, John, 239–40
Human Rights Commission, 11,
    12–13, 127, 217
hut tax, 155
Hutu people, 313

I

Ibanda, 68
Indians in Uganda, 172–73,
    175–76
indirect rule, 67
Innis, Roy, 191
Islam. *See* Muslims
Israel
    Amin and, 163, 164, 165, 172

Israel (*cont'd*)
   athletes at the Munich
      Olympics, 176
   Uganda's partnership with, 161
ivory trade, 146

J

Jinja mutiny, 159
Jung, Carl, 152

K

Kabagambe, Charles, 241, 283
Kabagambe, Peter, 241
Kaggwa, Gaetano, 267
Kahigiriza, James
   advocacy for Bahima
      monarchy, 125–26, 128, 321
   arrest of, 127, 197
   Bananuka and, 85–87, 88
   celebration of Amin's coup, 90,
      126, 169
   as chief minister, 78, 79
   Eliphaz's friendship with,
      78–79, 80, 86, 125, 129
   Obote's relationship with,
      82–83, 88
   pictures of, 79, 80
   political style of, 82–84
   on student protests, 95
   Uganda Land Commission
      and, 118–19, 126
Kahonda, George, 114
Kampala
   after overthrow of Amin, 208,
      209–11
   colonization of, 7–8

Museveni's return to, 8–9, 11,
   34, 208
Kanyesigye, Cathy, 36, 37, 292,
   293
Kanyomozi, Yonasani, 39, 40
Karuhanga, James, 191, 334
Katongole, Arthur, 272, 278
Katundu, Yuda, 110–11
Katungi, Ernest
   chief minister nomination, 74
   prejudice towards Bairu, 73, 85
   progressive views on
      education, 71, 72
   retreat to private ranch, 80
Kayemba, Hajji Abbas, 213, 332,
   340
Kenyatta, Jomo, 293
Kereere, Kenneth, 108, 281
King's African Rifles, 155–56, 160
Kissinger, Henry, 163, 184–86
Kiziba, 212–15, 217
Kony, Joseph, 235
kumanyana, 75
Kwerebera, Francis, 115, 117
Kyemba, Henry, 307, 326, 335

L

Ladonga, 270
Laki, Asiimwe, 293
Laki, Cathy. *See* Kanyesigye, Cathy
Laki, Dennis, 30, 34, 61–62
Laki, Duncan Muhumuza
   on accepting father's death,
      20–21
   on Amin's place in history, 295
   birth of, 24
   children of, 36, 292, 293

encounter with defendants at
trial, 242–43
family's reaction to
investigation of, 39–40,
60–62
at funeral for father, 296,
298–301
hope for father's return, 3–4, 5
learning of father being taken,
27
life in America, 18–19, 36–37,
292–94
at Makerere University, 34
marriage of, 36
meeting with Anyule, 46,
48
meeting with Gille, 48
meetings with Tibo, 41–42,
43–44
on morning of father's
disappearance, 24, 26
Mugenyi on, 279
Museveni's support of efforts
by, 121, 134, 254
at Organization of African
Unity, 30, 31, 32
pictures of, 25, 298
reaction to trial's outcome,
280, 281, 294
as representative of Ugandan
government, 292, 294
retracing father's murder with
Anyule and Gille, 59–60
search for father's car, 29–30,
33, 37–39
search for father's remains,
58–59, 62–64, 121–22
testimony at trial, 243–49

on Ugandans and forgiveness,
283
Laki, Eliphaz Mbwaijana
appointment as county chief,
80
arrest of, 116–17, 239
Bananuka's relationship with,
101
cattle ranch of, 82
childhood of, 71–72
covert resistance to Amin's
dictatorship, 35, 104
education of, 71, 72, 73
funeral for, 296–301
as health inspector for colonial
government, 77–78
imprisonment at Makindye,
106–7, 318
Kahigiriza's friendship with,
78–79, 80, 86, 125, 129
letters to family before
disappearance, 113–14
loyalty to Nganwa, 76
memorial service for, 35
on morning of disappearance,
24, 26
murder of, 21, 47, 103, 118,
119–20, 188
pictures of, 21, 80, 81, 108
political activity after release
from Makindye, 109
political position of, 22–23
position after Obote's exile,
25–26
reaction to Amin's coup,
100
reaction to British exit, 24
reaction to rebel attack, 112

Laki, Eliphaz Mbwaijana (*cont'd*)
    refusal to go into exile, 108,
      113–14
    release from Makindye, 107–8
    role as chief, 23, 24–25, 80–81
    role in kumanyana, 75
    views on religion, 86
    visit to Colorado, 82
    visit to Obote after Amin's
      coup, 101, 102
Laki, Jane, 33, 41, 108
Laki, Joyce
    on father's refusal to flee, 113
    glimpsing of father's car, 30
    grief after father's
      disappearance, 61
    inquiry into father's
      disappearance, 28
    picture of, 63
    support of Duncan's
      investigation, 62
    treatment for scoliosis, 81
    at the trial, 243
    visit to father at Makindye,
      107
Laki, Justine
    at celebration of Uganda's
      independence, 22
    Eliphaz's letter to, 113
    on father's reaction to British
      exit, 24
    grief after father's
      disappearance, 61
    opposition to Duncan's
      investigation, 60, 61, 62
Laki, Kagi, 293
Laki, Mbangira, 293
Laki, Otandeka, 292, 293
\and ownership, 19, 94, 119

Last King of Scotland, The, 10
legal system in Uganda, 229–30,
    231
license plate numbers, 25, 309
Lord's Resistance Army, 235, 279,
    284
Lugard, Frederick, 66–67, 68–69,
    149–51, 155
Luwum, Janan, 57, 127, 197, 287
Luzira Prison
    description of, 133, 135, 321
    executions at, 138–39

M

Machote, 212, 214, 215, 217
Mahdi rebellion, 147
Makaaru, Yoasi, 109, 183–84
Makerere University, 34, 193
Makindye, 106–7, 318
Malire Mechanized Battalion, 162
Malyamungu, Isaac, 194
Maruru, Zeddy, 142
Mbabazi, Amama, 337
Mbaguta, Nuwa, 69–70, 71
Mbarara
    ethnic division in, 73
    massacres by Amin's soldiers
      in, 168–69
    picture of, 72
    rebels' invasion of, 178–82,
      185, 322
mercenaries, Amin's use of, 168
Milošević, Slobodan, 41
Mobutu Sese Seko, 31
Mududu, Ratib, 286, 287
Mugenyi, Simon Byabakama
    cross-examination of Gille,
      275–76

decision to withdraw
indictment, 279–80
on importance of trial, 231
opening argument at trial,
231–32
prosecution burden of,
233–36, 275
questioning of Buhwairoha,
260
reaction to ruling on Gille's
confession, 277, 278
stress of trial on, 236
Muhumuza, Duncan L. *See* Laki,
Duncan Muhumuza
Mukiibi, Moses
advising of Gille and Anyule
on defense, 263–64
annoyance during trial, 236
description of, 227
indefinite adjournment of
trial, 264
offer for prosecution to
withdraw indictment,
279–80
on police witnesses, 273
religion of, 272
ruling on Duncan's testimony,
244–45
ruling on Gille's confession,
277–78
ruling on officer's testimony,
235
speculation about sympathies
of, 230
Munich Olympics, 175, 176
Museveni, Yoweri Kaguta
Amin's rebuke of, 191–92
amnesty policies of, 14–15, 40,
136–37, 234, 254

background of, 93–96, 103,
219
changes in ideology of, 289–90
creation of investigatory
commission, 11
on day after Amin's coup,
91–92
early political activity of,
95–99
at Eliphaz's funeral, 299, 300,
301
at Eliphaz's memorial service,
35
exile in Tanzania, 191, 192,
201
as a gentleman-rancher,
219–21
meeting with Nyerere, 177–78
Obote and, 102, 110, 178,
208–9, 317, 330–31
at Obote's memorial service,
288
pictures of, 94, 220
political pressure of trial on,
254–55
position on Amin's burial,
268
preparation for rebellion
against Amin, 93, 102, 104,
176–77
presidential campaign in 1980,
33–34, 216
presidential campaign in 2006,
288, 290–91, 294
presidential style of, 220–23
reaction to Amin's death,
276–77
reaction to massacres after
Amin's overthrow, 211

Museveni, Yoweri Kaguta (*cont'd*)
  on reconciliation, 223, 288
  recruitment of Nekemia
    Bananuka, 109–10
  return to Kampala, 8–9, 11, 34,
    208
  role in rebels' invasion of
    Mbarara, 178–81
  support of Duncan's efforts,
    121, 134, 254
  support of Tanzania during
    war with Amin, 201–2, 205
  visit to Obote after Amin's
    coup, 101, 102, 317
Muslims
  interactions with Christians,
    20, 170, 196–97, 210–15, 217
  rebellion in Uganda in the
    1990s, 222
Mutembeya, Jonas, 319

N

Namanve, 58
National Rescue Front II, 261
National Resistance Movement,
  9, 34
New York Times, 165, 176, 184
Nganwa, Kesi, 74–77
Nigeria, 100
Nile Hotel, 57–58, 294, 312
Nixon, Richard, 28, 174, 184–86
Nkoba, George, 106–7, 318
Nkrumah, Kwame, 186
Nkutu, Conrad, 123
noms de guerre, 194, 334–35
Ntare V, 66, 67
Ntinda, 51
Ntundubeire, Blasio, 319

Nubians
  ethnic fluidity of, 152
  history/origins of, 146–48,
    150–51
Nyakana, Patrick, 271–75
Nyakimwe, Kesi, 128
Nyerere, Julius
  on Amin, 28
  attempt at "African socialism,"
    95
  Museveni's meeting with,
    177–78
  peace agreement with Uganda,
    192
  role in rebels' invasion of
    Mbarara, 102
  support of Obote, 101–2
  support of Ugandan rebels,
    102
  war with Amin, 5, 202
Nyigilò, 144

O

Obote, Milton
  Amin's ousting of, 24, 163–64
  assassination attempt against,
    88, 161
  ban on opposition parties, 88
  death of, 287–88
  declaration of Uganda as a
    republic, 87–88
  exile of, 177, 192, 288
  Israel's partnership with, 161
  Kahigiriza's relationship with,
    82–83, 88
  memorial service for, 288
  Museveni and, 102, 110, 178,
    208–9, 317, 330–31

Nyerere's support of, 101–2
ordering of Amin's arrest, 89
as prime minister, 23–24,
    77–78, 84–85
return from exile, 33–34, 216
role in rebels' invasion of
    Mbarara, 178–79, 330–31
undermining of potential
    electoral competitors, 82
Obura, Kassim, 14
Ochan, Ben, 187, 333
Oder, Arthur H.
    appointment as chair of
        investigatory commission,
        11
    on death toll under Amin, 307
    escape from secret police, 13
    on the Oder Commission, 12,
        13
    on revisionism in Uganda, 15
Oder Commission. *See* Uganda
    Commission of Inquiry into
    Violations of Human Rights
Omari, Anuna, 254–55
Onyango-Obbo, Charles, 339
Organization of African Unity,
    30–32
Orijabo, Alfred
    accusations of misconduct by,
        270
    arrest and questioning of
        Anyule, 43–48, 257–58
    background of, 237
    death of, 262
    description of, 44
    erratic behavior of, 236–38
    on Gille's arrest, 48
    interrogation of Gille, 49–50,
        257–58, 274–75

Mukiibi on role of, 278
    on search for Eliphaz's grave,
        237–38
Orizio, Riccardo, 266
Otafirire, Kahinda, 337
Ottoman Empire, 144, 146

P

Pasha, Emin, 145–48, 150, 151, 325
polygamy, 42

R

reconciliation
    Gowon on, 283–84
    Museveni on, 223, 288
    Ugandans' attitudes about,
        10–11, 13–14, 16–17,
        123–25
religion
    Christian and Muslim
        interactions, 20, 170,
        196–97, 210–15, 217
    in Uganda, 8, 36, 76, 170,
        196–97
retributive sentencing laws, 135
Rodney, Walter, 96
Rurangaranga, Edward
    arrest of, 217
    encounter with Amin soldiers,
        209–10, 212–13, 219
    on Gowon's role in murders,
        219
    on Obote's return from exile,
        216
    picture of, 213
    political activity after release
        from prison, 218–19

Rurangaranga, Edward (*cont'd*)
  position in Obote's
    government, 216–17
  role in violent incidents
    against Muslims, 210, 213,
    215, 219, 340
  on role of Kahigiriza, 128
Ruzindana, Augustine, 289, 321
Rwakanengyere, Ephraim, 111,
    125, 320–21
Rwakanuma, Yonasani, 60, 63,
    119–20, 124
Rwanda, 14, 41, 313
Rwehururu, Bernard, 203
Rwizi River Massacre, 214–15,
    217, 218

S

Saleh, Salim, 279, 290
Saudi Arabia, 11, 15, 231, 266–70
Schnitzer, Eduard. *See* Pasha, Emin
Sebi, Salim
  death of, 210
  extortion attempts by, 170–71,
    187
  on Museveni, 335
  role in Eliphaz's murder, 60,
    117, 118, 187–88
  role in the Bureau of State
    Research, 194
Semakula, Bashir, 211, 212, 215,
    217–18
Simba Battalion
  Amin's visits to, 171–72,
    188–89
  attempted attack on, 178–81,
    184, 185, 186
  massacres by, 168–69

Singapore cell, 107, 108
slave trade, 144, 146
Smith, George Ivan, 326
Speke, John Hanning, 7–8
Stanley, Henry Morton, 148
Stroh, Nicholas, 168–69
Sudan, 23, 168
surnames, self-created, 194, 334–35

T

Tanzania
  peace agreement with Uganda,
    192
  resistance to Amin's incursion
    into, 5–6
  role in overthrow of Amin, 8
  role in rebels' invasion of
    Mbarara, 110, 178, 330–31
  war with Amin, 199–205
Tibo, Brian
  capture and questioning of
    Anyule, 43–48
  capture of Gowon, 52–53
  description of, 41
  meetings with Duncan, 41–42,
    43–44
  on Orijabo's illness, 238
  ostracism of, 270–71
  search for Anyule, 42–43
tribal identity in Africa, 151
Tutsi people, 313

U

Uganda
  AIDS in, 238
  Amin's coup in, 89–92,
    99–100, 163–65

class system in, 193
colonization of, 7–8, 66–70,
149–51, 155–56
economy in the mid-1970s in,
196
ethnic divisions in, 65, 67–74,
76, 123, 126, 289, 313
independence from Britain, 8,
23–24, 77, 78
Indians in, 172–73, 175–76
Israel's partnership with, 161
legal system in, 229–30, 231
liberation governments of,
208–9
power and patronage in, 83
religion in, 8, 36, 76, 170,
196–97
as a republic, 87–88
retributive sentencing laws in,
135
Tanzania's peace agreement
with, 192
Uganda Commission of Inquiry
into Violations of Human
Rights, 11, 12–13, 127,
217
Uganda Land Commission, 119,
126
Uganda National Rescue Front II,
261

Uganda People's Congress (UPC),
77–78, 82, 85, 112, 319
United States
objections to Amin's regime,
28, 174, 184–86, 192
reaction to Amin's coup, 163–65
University Students' African
Revolutionary Front, 96

V

Vinco, Angelo, 144

W

Waigo, Willy, 236, 342
West Nile
British authorities in, 155
history of, 151
massacres after Amin's
overthrow in, 211
people of, 152–53
stereotypes about, 154, 326
treatment by southern tribes, 193
Whitaker, Forest, 10

Y

Yumbe, 43, 270–71